GLOBAL INTERESTS

in the

ARAB GULF

GLOBAL INTERESTS

IN THE ARAB GULF

edited by

Charles E. Davies
Centre for Arab Gulf Studies
University of Exeter

St. Martin's Press
New York

First published in the United States of America in 1992

Printed in Great Britain

ISBN 0–312–08574–5

Library of Congress Cataloging-in-Publication Data

Global interests in the Arab Gulf / edited by Charles E. Davies.
    p. cm.
    Papers originally presented at a conference entitled "External
Interests in the Arab Gulf," held at Exeter University, Centre for
Arab Gulf Studies, July 12–13, 1990.
    Includes index.
    ISBN 0–312–08574–5
    1. Persian Gulf Region—Foreign economic relations—Congresses.
    2. Persian Gulf Region—Strategic aspects—Congresses.
    3. Natural resources—Persian Gulf Region—Congresses.
I. Davies, Charles (Charles E.)
HF1584,5.G55 1992   92–18276
337.536—dc20   CIP

CONTENTS

Part Six: Internal Change

TABLES AND FIGURES

Figures

PREFACE

The chapters in this book were all originally delivered, substantially in their present form, at a conference entitled 'External Interests in the Arab Gulf', which was held at Exeter University's Centre for Arab Gulf Studies on 12-13 July 1990. The symposium was well attended, as ever, and made up the eleventh of the Centre's nearly annual meetings concerned with the internal and external affairs of the contemporary Arab Gulf.

The last day of the conference fell on Friday 13 July. The following Tuesday, the Iraqi President made a speech openly critical of Kuwait in respect of OPEC-quotas, war loans and certain border-issues. In the early hours of Thursday 2 August Iraqi paratroopers descended on Kuwait city, and by evening of the same day the military occupation of the state of Kuwait was, by and large, complete. Subsequent events, and the manner in which Kuwait eventually regained her freedom, are too well known. The profound repercussions flowing from that invasion, both in the region and for the world at large, have yet to run their full course.

Two things were made especially apparent by the crisis in Kuwait: in the first place, the region once again showed itself to be politically volatile; and it is widely felt that, as yet, there is no compelling reason to suppose that this will not potentially remain the case. In the second place, it was forcefully demonstrated that the world cannot, and will not, ignore the Gulf: the area is at the heart of a sensitive global web of intertwined economic and strategic interests. Underlying both these points is oil, consideration of the prospects for which is a theme that runs through many of the chapters in this book: Richard Murphy, for example, takes note of one view that, Soviet production aside, by the year 2000 supplies of oil for export sufficient to meet world demand may, to all intents and purposes, have become restricted to only a handful of Gulf producers.

Events have, therefore, sad to say, made the organisers' choice of theme for the July 1990 conference seem particularly apt. This is, to take one example, evinced in the inclusion in this collection of a chapter detailing the role of the Western European Union and its activities during the 'tanker war': the recent events in the Gulf have likewise again involved the Union, a body for which the recent fortunes of NATO and the Warsaw Pact, and developments within the European Community, seem to many to presage an enhanced future. Equally noticeable is the appropriateness of the contributions themselves: Anthony Cordesman's consideration of the American military response to an Iraqi invasion of Kuwait was, in fact, written a few months before the event. His essay therefore presents a remarkable snapshot of American military resources and planning almost on the eve of the Iraqi invasion.

Had the papers delivered at July's colloquium been later proved very wide of the mark, there would have arisen a stark choice between extensive rewriting and the submission for publication of an 'honest', but markedly imperfect product. Happily, this was not at all the case. The majority of authors, upon consideration, chose to leave their pieces unaltered, precisely as submitted in early July 1990. A number of others*, the last of whom in point of time were Peter Davies and Paul Stevens, their postscript dating to mid-December 1990, chose to make slight additions to their texts to take due account of subsequent developments.

The coincidence of the conference's timing, so close before the invasion, might suggest to the casual observer that the relevance of certain parts of this volume to the situation that has subsequently begun to emerge, has somehow been attenuated. But this is really to miss the point: this book was never intended to be an essay on the problems between Iraq and Kuwait, or the like. It has to do with something quite different and more fundamental - the interests enjoyed by the rest of the world in the small Gulf region. These concerns have not changed. Far from it, what has happened has served only to underline their validity and their importance, and an understanding of these issues alone can explain the rationale for the events of 1990-1.

The subject examined in this book is, then, accurately described by the conference title: it is a book about why the world regards the Gulf as important. Chapters either treat of the way in which individual countries, such as Japan, view their vital interests in the Gulf, or they deal with specific themes, such as the question of militarisation and the international arms-trade. This work makes the point that different countries and continents are conscious of possessing a variety of practical interests in the region: for some the Gulf represents a market for manufactured goods, for some a field for expatriate labour, for some a source of oil, while, for the Superpowers, it has also been an area of conspicuous political and strategic importance. This last topic, closely linked as it now is with changes in Eastern Europe and the former Soviet Union, is analysed at greater length in this collection. Finally, and almost as a converse to this, one author argues that the crucial politics of the Gulf itself cannot so easily be divorced from wider trends, and that, in consequence, patterns from history and contemporary experience might seem to suggest the course of political development in the Gulf states over the next decade.

To many, the inclusion of two purely historical chapters at the start of this volume might appear incongruous. This merely follows an earlier tradition at these conferences of seeking to recall once again that the Gulf has a long history, and that not all that appears to be, is new.

The aim of the Exeter symposia is to invite the expression of individual and sometimes divergent views: the opinions aired in this book, therefore, are their authors' and should not be confused with those of the Centre itself. The 1990 colloquium was well received, and the credit for this success and its organisation at all stages should go to the Director of the Centre for Arab Gulf Studies, Brian Pridham. A further debt of gratitude is owed Jennifer Davies for her patience and skill in the production of the published work.

---

* Those who have made some additions to their chapters following the events of early August 1990 include: Davies and Stevens, Ehteshami, Ishida and Vassiliev (Chapters 3, 6, 8 and 10). Birks and Sinclair's chapter is dated 27 January 1990, forming as it does part of a sequence of projections by them. Cordesman's essay is dated 12 July 1990, and, like all the remaining chapters in this book, represents the views of its author at that particular time.

NOTE ON TRANSLITERATION

The system of transliteration employed in this book is highly simplified and, it is hoped, consistent. Diacritical marks are omitted, although the *hamza* is represented by ' and the ᶜ*ain* by ᶜ, unless either of these letters occurs before an initial capital, in which case it is omitted entirely; the *ta' marbuta* appears where it would generally be pronounced. Certain proper names which have familiar English spellings are left in that form. The few Persian words that occur in the text follow the same principles as the Arabic, while the Persian *idafa* is indicated by *-e/ye*.

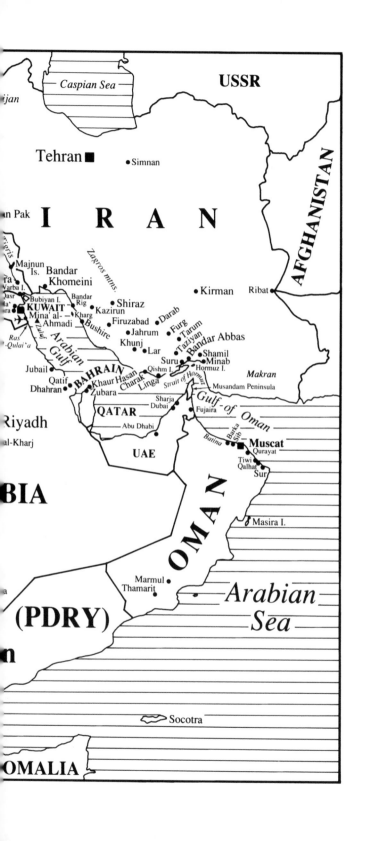

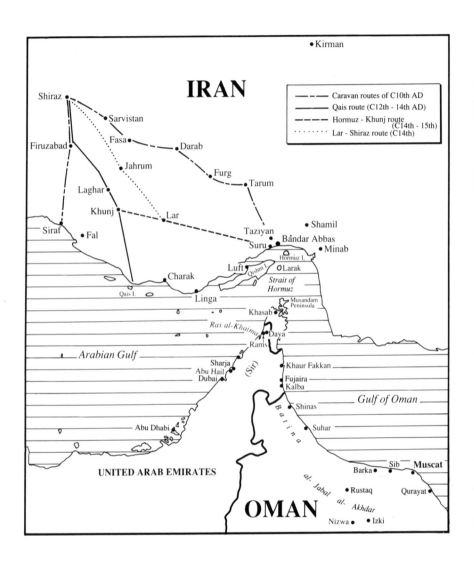

1. SIRAF AND HORMUZ BETWEEN EAST AND WEST: MERCHANTS AND MERCHANDISE IN THE GULF

V. Fiorani Piacentini

The aim of this chapter is as follows: (a) to stress once again the importance of the Gulf as one of the main maritime trade-routes between the Indian Ocean, together with those regions which either border on or gravitate towards it, and the Mediterranean basin; (b) to underline this 'mercantile attraction' through an analysis of the history of two of the most important trading-centres of the Gulf from the 9th to the 16th centuries AD; (c) to focus upon the role played in this world-wide international trade by local merchant families; (d) finally, to point out the political and cultural homogeneity of the Gulf area during these centuries, occasioned as it was by the *leading role* of its merchant-families, by the *mobility* of these prominent individuals, who were able to move from one political centre to another in spite of dynastic upheavals, and by the *flexibility* of their policy. This mercantile, political and cultural supremacy was to survive the collapse of individual ruling dynasties and the consequent urban decline of the political and/or trading centre concerned. Indeed, in the hands of these talented personalities, the real protagonists of life in the Gulf, this mercantile supremacy became at the same time a political and cultural pre-eminence, a positive *local* power, one which was to last until the arrival on the scene of the 'European West'.

Part One

Siraf was a maritime city and a very rich emporium (termed *bulaid* and *bandar* by Yaqut), one that arose artificially on the parched Iranian coast of the Gulf around 200 kms south of

Bushire, a coast which is scorched by the sun and unimaginably inhospitable but made inhabitable and even fertile thanks to a number of delicate and complex operations and innovations brought about by man, such as the building of dams, canals, aqueducts, wells and cisterns. As was the case with all ports of this kind, the life of Siraf was closely linked to broader mercantile interests. An account of its history will not therefore be complete without an examination of the history of that city (or cities) for which it served as the chief port, and also of the history of the region of which that same city was the political and economic capital. Finally, given its maritime position, no full account can exclude the history of the other maritime centres with which its interests became ever more closely intertwined over the course of the centuries. This indeed was the cause both of its rise, in the 9th and 10th centuries AD, and later also of its slow decline, which resulted in its becoming once again a small fishing- and coasting- centre in the 13th century AD and thereafter, one whose pearl-fishing industry and shipyards continued nevertheless to attract a specialised workforce.[1] In other words, the history of Siraf is also the history of the Gulf and of its mercantile activity as a whole.

Islamic Siraf was recently brought to light again in the course of excavations carried out between 1969 and 1975 by the British Institute of Persian Studies, supported by the British Museum, the Calouste Gulbenkian Foundation of Lisbon, the British Academy, the Ashmolean Museum and Edinburgh's Royal Scottish Museum under the direction of Dr D. Whitehouse. These excavations gave life to and provided material evidence for the literary image of one of the most important outlets of the intercontinental maritime trade-routes hitherto provided by the written sources.

Concerning Islamic Siraf - the trading city, the international emporium and 'threshold of East and West' - there is an extensive literature at our disposal which starts from the 9th century AD and contains precise references to it. The oldest evidence for Islamic Siraf is to be found in the *Akhbar al-Sin wa-al-Hind*, written in 237 AH/851 AD by an anonymous writer, with additions by a certain Abu Zaid Hasan al-Sirafi (d. 916 AD).[2] This chronicle was subsequently largely drawn upon by Ibn Khurdadhbih, Ibn al-Faqih, Ibn Rusta,[3] al-Mas'udi,[4] al-Marwazi[5] and Yaqut.[6] Probably al-Idrisi, too, must at least have known of its existence,[7] as must other later authors,[8] including Abu al-Fida', Hamdullah Mustaufi Qazwini (d. 628 AH/1238 AD), Ibn al-Wardi (d. 861 AH/1457 AD) etc.

This rich material, complemented by and combined with other historical sources (oriental as well as occidental) and with the archaeological evidence, today allows us to outline a vivid image and portrait of this important Gulf centre and of the central role that it played for several centuries through the tireless activity of its merchants.

In the 9th and 10th centuries AD, Siraf was undoubtedly one of the busiest and most important ports on the commercial sea-routes which linked China, South-East Asia, India, the eastern coasts of Africa and the Arabian Peninsula with the Levant and the Mediterranean Sea through the Gulf. Medieval writers have left us a vivid image of this city, 'which equalled Shiraz in size and splendour' (to quote al-Istakhri[9]), and which rivalled even Basra on the mouth of the Tigris and Euphrates (to quote al-Muqaddasi[10]). These same writers give richly detailed descriptions of the opulence of its bazaar and storehouses, full of very valuable merchandise - natural products and artefacts of rare beauty coming not only from Fars, but from all parts of the world - and of the vigorous life of its artisans.[11] They speak of how impressive was the gorgeous Friday Mosque, 'the Great Mosque', with its elegant teak (*saj*)[12] columns, of how grand were its houses and palaces, being 'of several storeys and built of teak (saj) and of another wood imported from the country of the Zanj (*bilad al-Zanj*)'[13] - the luxurious residences of those merchants who financed the immense volume of international trade for which Siraf then acted as one of the main intermediaries.[14]

These same writers devote many pages also to the Sirafi merchants, who were the real protagonists of the life of Siraf, and they record pithy anecdotes which make them positively legendary figures. Abu Bakr Ahmad ibn Umar al-Sirafi, for instance, whose stores were bursting with precious stones and perfumes at the beginning of the 10th century AD, or the 'millionaires' like Ramisht of Siraf, whose income amounted to millions of *dirham*, and whose warehouses - to be found at all ports of call along the monsoon routes - were among the richest thus far known.[15] These merchants 'used their capital to equip every convoy which traded with India, China and Zanjabar', as

Ibn Hauqal says. These families, or rather positive dynasties, were to survive the decline of the local port of Siraf, and give to the Gulf and neighbouring seas a real sense of cultural unity and homogeneity. With the decline of the local port of Siraf - a decline in turn strictly linked to the dynastic upheavals that took place in Fars at the end of the 11th century - they rebuilt their economic (and political) empire elsewhere, nevertheless still continuing to add the *nisba* 'al-Sirafi' after their names. These families had immense riches and property in the form of 'goods and estates' in Siraf. They had seasonal residences there and - as we are told - they used to visit the place so as to be present at the arrival and departure of convoys of ships, and to administer the landed possessions which they owned there.

And here we see a new dimension emerging: these merchants with their legendary riches - which concentrated capital, trade and landed property in their hands - also possessed learning and constituted respected and reputed *qadis*, a situation which was new and gave them immense *de facto* political power, a power which ruled the life of the Gulf and of the geographical area dependent upon it. They retained the nisba 'Sirafi', but lived elsewhere in the region (in Fal and Khunj or, later on, in Qais and Hormuz) and gravitated towards the dynastic power that ruled in Shiraz. And Shiraz - the capital town of Fars - was the *de facto* centre of their true power. Ibn al-Balkhi, Wassaf and the historians of the Salghurid and Mongol periods talk at length about these outstanding families, as is the case in later periods, proving the vitality of the trading tradition of Fars, which - passing over the period of 'economic stagnation' under Seljuq governorship in this region - was to ensure that a considerable degree of activity returned during the Salghurid and Mongol Ilkhanate. The merchant families were the same and they still retained the nisba 'Sirafi', but now they had moved: they had emigrated to other centres which, in the changed circumstances of the age, had gained new political and economic importance.

Among the best-known members of this traditional Persian class were: that powerful man of politics, Majd al-Din Ismaᶜil al-Sirafi (d. 666 AH/1268 AD), whose fortune derived from landed property owned by the family at Siraf, land which remained in their hands in the 13th century AD; those celebrated jurists of the 12th and 13th centuries AD, Qutb al-Din Muhammad Sirafi Fali and his better known father Safi al-Din Masᶜud al-Sirafi, the source of whose fortune lay in the generosity of a Sirafi merchant who took it upon himself to pay for their studies; the millionaire merchant, Ramisht of Siraf, the very richest merchant of his generation, who lived in the 12th century AD, and whose warehouses in Aden overflowed with incalculable riches, his interests extending to all the main harbours of the time. Though a millionaire, this last was also a pious and devout Moslem, his donations being recorded in epigraphs as far afield as Mecca.[16]

These merchants therefore usually lived in Shiraz during that glorious period of Sirafi supremacy, which spanned the 9th and 10th centuries AD: from here it was that they ran their immense businesses, sending orders to their bankers (*sarrafs*) and representatives (*wakils*), who were present and active in all parts of the world. From here it was that they administered the fabulous riches accumulated in warehouses situated along the monsoon routes. From here also they controlled new and ever more distant markets, doing so sometimes even by means of a shrewd choice of wife. Moreover, they were not above occupying important positions such as that of qadi, *wali* etc. in the public administration at Shiraz and in the provinces. Thus, by combining economic and political prestige, they were able to exercise ever tighter control over their mercantile empire.

Convoys moved from east to west and back along the monsoon routes, while carriers reaped fortunes by importing and exporting raw materials (such as teak and timber), manufactured goods (such as silk), and other precious items (such as precious and semi-precious stones including lapis lazuli, turquoise, carnelian, ivory, pearls, porcelain, pottery and spices etc.) from Africa, India and the Far East to the Mediterranean world via the Gulf.

The 9th and 10th centuries undoubtedly represented a period of great economic prosperity for Fars and its coastal region, the Garmsirat, stimulating all other activities that related to trade and urban life. Shiraz attained unprecedented power and so too did its commercial seaport of Siraf. This is not to say that there were not other trade routes quite apart from the Gulf. During certain periods these other routes were actually highly competitive with the Gulf itself. I refer, in particular, to the 'Samanid' routes of the north, between the end of the 9th and the first half of the 10th centuries, and to the Red Sea route during the high Fatimid period, the latter contributing greatly to the decline and ruin of the harbour at Siraf.

But let us return to what, after all, is the central issue in this chapter, namely, the mercantile attraction of the region. In this precise connection, it is most reasonable to assert that the real protagonists of the life of the Gulf were then none other than those families mentioned above, as indeed many others whom we have omitted to mention, such as the Tibis. Their power survived the decline of Shiraz and Fars which, in turn, paved the way for a new set of political and dynastic balances and to a new political and military order in Iran. They then 'emigrated' to other centres along the main trade-routes, places such as Fal, at the very beginning of the 12th century, and Khunj, Qais, Lar and Hormuz, etc. in mainland Iran and along its shoreline. Or else they followed the sea routes, either to the coasts of the Arabian Peninsula and eastern Africa, or to Makran, India and South-East Asia, eastward as far as China, or, finally, moving westwards, they travelled to the Mediterranean basin. Once there, these same families reorganised their finances, built new political links and relationships, and, through the prosecution of an immense volume of trade, they confirmed the Gulf in its cultural centrality, almost without any break in continuity and despite the disorders, unrest and decay that occurred in neighbouring lands.

Part Two

From the 11th to the 13th centuries AD, overseas trade developed once again and was to flourish alongside the now revitalised urban life and urban activities. This network of commercial links extended from the Tigris and Euphrates to the eastern coast of Africa (the *Zanjabar* of the Arab geographers), from the Arabian Peninsula to Sri Lanka, India and South-East Asia, *and* from the East to the Western world, the Mediterranean basin and the civilisations there. The participants in this network of intercontinental trade were many, rich and powerful, and spread worldwide along the main sea and monsoon routes.

But a well documented period of economic decline afflicted the Gulf in the 11th and 12th centuries AD. This was due to different factors: (a) the vitality of activity along alternative trade-routes consequent upon new dynastic, political and military balances; (b) the political instability of the Gulf coastal regions; (c) the revival of piracy, a chronic local malady and one which made seafaring unsafe, not to say highly perilous.

With specific regard to Fars and Kirman - two former great intermediaries in the overseas trade - the situation was far from being settled. Tribal disturbances and continuous raiding against the main urban centres made life very insecure. The Jats fought to get control of the southern districts of Fars and its coastal area which included Siraf. They attacked and plundered all caravans, and struggled with the Salghurids, later on faithful vassals of the Mongol Ilkhans, who aimed at political supremacy both in the region and at sea. Archaeological evidence, when combined with the existing literature on the subject,[17]allows us to assert that the decay of Siraf (along with that also of mercantile activity in Fars) had already started at the beginning of the 11th century; but it was very gradual and mainly linked to the local circumstances of military disorder, political instability and economic insecurity. People began to migrate towards other regions and other 'markets'. The great wave of migrations from Siraf - especially towards Qais - can be dated to around the beginning of the 12th century. Slowly, these same families gave rise to a new order in the region - including the Gulf area - an order which was cultural, political and economic at one and the same time. And with the establishment of order and security, sea trade flourished once again.

Fal became the capital town of the surrounding area, while the Salghurids succeeded in defeating the Jats, thereby gaining full control of the southern regions of Fars including the Garmsirat. By the beginning of the 13th century the Falis had grown in power and influence. They were organised as a 'cultural group' linked to Arab (*Sunni*) culture and adhered strictly to the principles of the *Shariᶜa*. Having reorganised their economic fortunes, these families then built new political links and relationships with the ruling class in Shiraz (the Salghurids and the Mongols). As qadis, walis and bureaucrats, they extended their influence, which was backed up by their sheer economic and financial power, all over Fars, both to the region's maritime outlets and to the seaborne trade-routes. We have already mentioned Ramisht of Siraf, Majd al-Din Ismaᶜil al-Sirafi, Qutb al-Din Muhammad Sirafi Fali, Safi al-Din Masᶜud al-Sirafi. To these we can add *Shaikh* Rukn al-Din Danyal, founder of a dervish *khanaqah* in Khunj at the beginning of the 13th century (the Kazirunis), which, being strictly linked to the local mercantile class, was to gain great influence in Laristan and Kirman.[18]

It was in this precise framework that a new leading-force emerged, that of Qais, on the present island of Qais off the southern coast of Iran.[19] The supremacy of Qais as a new centre of mercantile attraction in the Gulf was to last for about a century. Its leadership is associated with the ever increasing power of another family of merchants - the Tibis - whose members were the typical champions of the local mercantile class. Their immense wealth and their political influence at Shiraz under the Ilkhanid rule in Fars during the 13th century also gave them the role of protagonists of life in the Gulf, a role contested only by Hormuz. The ruins of Qais will be associated with the ruin of this same family, an outcome at the beginning of the 14th century largely brought about by the Kazirunis of Khunj and Fal.[20]

Finally, Hormuz stood alone, its position as the leading power in the East-West seaborne trade-routes now uncontested.

Part Three

Until about the 11th century, the city-emporium of Hormuz stood on the mainland somewhere near the present-day oasis of Minab. Istakhri provides us with a vivid description of its mercantile life. The city was linked to the sea by means of a very deep artificial channel, which opened up on the inside into a large harbour which was well sheltered from the seasonal typhoons, while behind it, steep mountains and thousands of miles of desert acted as natural defences. Istakhri, Ibn Hauqal and al-Muqaddasi also describe its beautiful mosque, its rich storehouses, the flourishing surrounding villages with their green orchards, gardens, palmgroves and fertile fields of indigo, millet, cumin and sorghum etc. One important caravan route linked this Hormuz - conventionally termed 'Old Hormuz' or 'Hurmuz-e Kuhna' in the later literature - first with the hinterland and the most important markets of Kirman, then with the other important bandars of Shahru/Suru, and finally, via the Tarum - Furg - Darabjird - Fasa - Sarvistan route, with Shiraz (see Map of the Lower Gulf).[21] Its particularly favourable position on the monsoon routes, together with its outlying location in relation to the Iranian mainland, always gave this port a special advantage over others. Furthermore, whenever invasions, wars or tribal and family rivalries upset the political and economic order on the mainland, Hormuz would yet find itself only marginally affected by such upheavals: thriving commercial traffic was carried on in its harbour untouched, and it remained one of the safest and most sought after harbours for the convoys coming from India and the Far East, or from East Africa and the Arabian Peninsula, laden with merchandise for the Near East and European markets.

After the arrival of the Seljuqs around the second half of the 11th century, Hormuz managed to strengthen its position and its commercial influence within the new order established in the Iranian world by these new lords and masters: strong in her autonomy and backed by the Seljuqs of Kirman, she gained the political and military control of the nearby coast of Oman, with which region she had had commercial relations and dealings and cultural links for centuries. While Fars was being raided by nomadic tribes under Seljuq leadership, and its commercial routes were becoming more and more insecure, thereby contributing to the decay of Siraf, Hormuz took advantage of the situation. It was a key moment in the history of this bandar: the fact that it controlled vital access to the Gulf made it possible for its rulers to impose a sort of monopoly on all the sea traffic passing through. And this monopoly, rather than taking the form of regular acts of piracy, developed into a system of commercial control and mercantile activity and incentives.

With the decay of Siraf and the beginning of migration on the part of its families, we find more than one Sirafi merchant settled in Hormuz, contributing in large measure to the growth of that harbour both with their riches and with their experience and political links. And with the increase of their wealth and influence, the families of the merchants and bankers of Hormuz became increasingly enterprising. The possibility of recruiting good soldiers from the nearby Omani coast, in addition to the availability of a fleet of its own, allowed Hormuz to develop a trading policy that was independent in practice, even if *de jure* it was still dependent on the Iranian mainland to which this bandar paid tribute until the end.

When in the first half of the 13th century the Iranian plateau was ravaged by the arrival of fresh nomadic hordes, the

Mongols or Tartars of Genghiz Khan, Hormuz did not suffer directly, because the terrible Mongol armies never thrust right to the sea.

Following the disintegration of the Seljuq empire, and after the collapse of the Khwarazm Shahs, an independent kingdom grew up on the Iranian shore and in Kirman in particular, one which then became a vassal of the Mongol Khans, namely that of the Qutlugh Khans (1224 - 1303 AD). This dynasty guaranteed these regions a period of relative calm, defending them from the continual attacks of their turbulent neighbours, the Shabankara'is and the Salghurids, whom we saw fighting and establishing power in Fars. Hormuz profited enormously from this particular situation. Favoured by the resumption of trade with the East via the Gulf sea-routes during the Ilkhanid period, she retained a *de facto* independence and managed to keep control of her own markets by paying tribute to the various local petty kings.

At this very moment, the only redoubtable rival to Hormuz that remained in the Gulf region was Qais, situated on the island of the same name to the north along the Iranian coast, and which - as we have said - had gradually established itself as the new commercial port of the city of Shiraz. The Ilkhanid governor of Fars, resident in Qais, provided further incentives, in that the proceeds from trade and craftsmanship provided most of the revenues needed to supply its own and the empire's treasure. Moreover, the local Ilkhanid bureaucracy was drawn from the local Iranian families, one of the most important being that of Jamal al-Din Ibrahim Muhammad al-Tibi, known as al-Sawamili, who received the *laqab* of *Shaikh al-Islam* and *Malik al-Islam* from the Ilkhan Jaikhatu. Apart from occupying prominent political offices in the administration, this family also had warehouses at Qais and an immense economic and commercial turnover extending as far as China. According to the historian Wassaf, almost all the merchants from India and the Far Eastern regions 'whence derived the prosperity of the islands of the Persian Gulf in particular, and of other countries in general, including Iraq and Khurasan as far as the country of the Rumis and the country of the Franks', were effectively controlled by the merchants of Qais. At this point a clash between the two bandars, Qais and Hormuz, was inevitable, the difference between them being that the power of Qais depended on the strength of the Mongol armies, whilst that of Hormuz was based on its own fleet and army.

Towards the end of the 13th century, a very important figure in the history of Hormuz emerges, namely that of Mahmud Qalhati. An enterprising trader, and a leader as tyrannical as he was the centraliser, he probably came from the Omani coast to the south-east of Muscat - as his nisba seems to indicate - and he may reasonably be considered the true founder of the power of Hormuz. His work of organisation was completed by a Turk, the temporary regent on behalf of the infant prince, a certain Baha' al-Din Ayaz (d. 711 AH/1311-1312 AD). Once his position on the throne had been ensured, he played on the rivalry between the princes of Fars and the *sultans* of Kirman. Alternately using cunning and force, and not averse to convenient compromises, he effectively managed to resist the despotism of the merchants of Fars and to free Hormuz completely from all external control. In practice he created a real power base, for he strengthened the fleet, fortified the city and actively recruited an army from the Arabian coast. At the same time, he sought a safer site for the commercial heart of his small kingdom, a matter which was assuming increasing urgency as its survival became threatened by the burgeoning rivalry of Qais. In this respect, he found a good ally in the dervishes of Khunj, the Kazirunis, who gave all their support to Hormuz against the strangling policy of the Tibis.

Old Hormuz was no longer so safe and well protected from behind by mountains and desert. In fact, groups of 'Tartars' - probably the Nikudri or Nigudari, also called the Qarauna, Central Asian Turco-Mongol nomadic tribes who came from the Chaghatai *ulus* - were lured by the city's reputation and the wealth lying piled up in its storehouses and, taking advantage of the increasing weakness of the Ilkhanate along its eastern borders, they pushed south several times between the end of the 13th and the beginning of the 14th centuries AD. These nomads had come down along the desert caravan-routes, attacking towns, laying waste, raiding and plundering, and had reached Hormuz, which they took and sacked repeatedly, seriously unsettling the prosperous activities carried on from there.

Ayaz is credited with having located the new centre on the island of Jirun, 'acquired' according to legend by that same Malik al-Islam thanks to the mediation of a pious shaikh, Shaikh

Danyal - whom we have already mentioned - and of having begun its fortification about the year 1300 AD, thus encouraging the gradual migration of the rich merchant-families from the mainland towards the new capital city.[22] Beyond the veil of this legend we can discern a historical reality, namely the existence of rivalry between Hormuz and Qais, a rivalry which had as its aim the political control of the two key-regions of the Iranian plateau (Fars and Kirman), aiming thereby also at supremacy on the seas. We also read that in this contest the merchant families of Khunj and Fal, or the old Sirafi mercantile and cultural class, played an important role in supporting Hormuz and its policy against Qais, the latter having cut these two centres off from the main trade-routes.

At this point, it was inevitable that the rivalry between Hormuz and Qais should have entered a key phase. The Ilkhan ordered the Mongol governor of Fars, Sughunjaq, to reassert his lost influence and to break the growing and increasingly worrying power of Hormuz. This operation was entrusted to the lord of Qais. A large fleet was equipped, leather decks installed and the terrible Mongol archers boarded. At this very moment one cannot but return to a legend that the inhabitants of the island of Hormuz still recount:

and then Iblis, jealous of the power of the king of Hormuz, unleashed the forces of the infernal Tartar against him. Demons, horrid in appearance, came right down to the sea from the north, terrible and invincible with the strength of their bows. And then Allah, touched by the faith and devotion of the sovereign of Hormuz, sent his messenger to earth, and he stretched his broad rainbow-hued wings out over the city shielding it from the sight of the aggressors, and he stirred up the waters of the sea, raising up a storm so violent as to shipwreck and completely destroy the 'Tartar' fleet.

In this way Hormuz was saved, and the island on which it stands was called 'the island of the four colours'. However it was, Wassaf mentions that the island of Jirun, when besieged, was freed by its own ships. The enemy's fleet, once lured on to the low surrounding coral reef where it ran aground, was attacked by the small Hormuzi fleet, then annihilated once and for all by a terrible storm. Other attempts by the Mongols followed, with varying degrees of success, but the Mongols were never able to break the back of the enemy fleet. The Tibis' power came to an end about 1320 AD. And about the year 1330 AD, the army of Hormuz landed on Qais and the island, core of the Malik al-Islam's power, was definitively conquered and annexed to the kingdom of Hormuz. Finally, about 1350 AD, the collapse of Ilkhanid power in Iran, along with the decline of the great merchant-families of Fars, left Hormuz 'mistress of the sea'.

Part Four

The new capital city of the kingdom of Hormuz was renamed 'New Hormuz' or 'Hurmuz-e Jadid'. It stood on the island of Jirun (the present-day island of Hormuz at 27° 03' N, 56° 27' E), a place described by all as 'arid' and 'sterile', being 'scorched' by the torrid climate in the summer months and scoured by strong winds from May to October. Almost completely devoid of all vegetation, its soil was covered by a salt crust, it was visited with very rare but torrential rainfall and, in addition, it lacked a supply of freshwater (with the exception of rainwater which was collected in numerous cisterns). All in all, then, it seemed about as inhospitable a place as nature could offer. Yet, Hurmuz-e Jadid became the site of one of the loveliest and best known cities of the time.

The island, with a diameter of about 18 kms, had two natural harbours, situated one to the east and one to the west, yet both so close as to constitute a single very large bay protected from the winds and from the very strong offshore currents. Along this bay runs a flat sandy strip on which the actual city was built, protected at the rear by bleak, bare, sharply rising hills, which constituted the best of natural defences against possible enemy attack.

This was the island of 'the four colours' in the local legend which attributed that particular feature to the archangel Gabriel, or the 'mountain of the four colours', in the vivid description of the place by the Chinese traveller Ma Huan who went there at the beginning of the 15th century. It was, in his words, 'a great mountain of colours different on each of the four sides...: green as rock salt, white as gypsum, red as blood and yellow as clay.'[23] It is, therefore, no surprise that everyone who visited Hormuz was deeply impressed by the singular quirk of nature that made of it a veritable concentration of colours and minerals (minerals such as haematite, iron oxide, sulphur, rock salt, gypsum and aluminium ore - some of which, even then, were used and exported, such as rock salt and iron oxide which were taken to China).

Yet, despite the inhospitable nature of the site chosen, its particularly advantageous position at the mouth of the Persian Gulf made Hurmuz-e Jadid a positively impregnable stronghold, not being taken until 1622. For about three centuries, therefore, it acted as the capital city of a kingdom which controlled much of the trade between Europe and Asia.

Travellers, chroniclers and Western merchants, amongst whom features the Arab traveller Ibn Battuta, have left us lively and admiring accounts, which describe it as a real commercial city, quite unrivalled in the world at that time and which, possessing a magnificent bazaar, acted as a port for India and China. Here, goods coming from the Far East were negotiated over and re-exported to the two Iraqs, and thence to the Near East and the Mediterranean world, to Fars, to Khurasan and to the rich markets of Central Asia, or towards the bandars on the eastern coasts of Africa. Dealings between merchants of all manner of colour, race and religion took place here, between men who came from all over the world to replenish their stocks of spices, musk, aloes, indigo, raw silk, pearls, precious stones (such as rubies, lapis lazuli, turquoise and carnelian), horses, elephants, cloth of gold, rare porcelain imported from China, ivory and other precious commodities in demand on the markets of East and West.

With the aridity of the soil, the few springs of brackish water that existed were used to irrigate the gardens of the notables; whilst, for everyday use, supplies of water and provisions had to be brought from the two adjacent islands of Qishm and Larak, or else from the Batina coast of Oman. It was a city noted less for its size than for its beauty, a city of solid walls and many castles, with a rich and extensive bazaar, situated in the shadow of the palace-fortress of the *Malik*. Its houses, arranged in rows along broad streets, were solidly built of local materials; and the 'light stone' quarried from the hills on the island and the 'coloured stone taken from the sea' (madrepore), both of which were used in construction, being joined together with mortar (or 'gesso branco', to quote João de Barro, the Portuguese who visited Hormuz in 1553), produced an altogether polychrome effect which was often extremely elegant and evocative.[24]

With time, the position of this capital city was further consolidated by the building of a defensive system that hinged on two circles of fortresses, one island-based and the other upon the mainland, a system which proved effective in the time of Tamerlane. Suitably fortified, the two islands of Qishm and Larak became the main guardians and sentinels of Hormuz. On the Arabian and Iranian coasts, the defensive system was based on a series of fortresses: Shami, author of the *Zafar-nama* (15th century AD), lists six fortresses on the Iranian mainland, that is, Kushkak, Shamil, Minab, Namuqan, Shurnik and Taziyan.[25] To these, one might add Old Hormuz which we know to have remained in existence after the arrival of the Portuguese, as a fortress and favourite hunting-residence of the king of Hormuz during the hot summer months. On the Arabian coast, Ibn Battuta states that the power of the lord of Hormuz in Oman comprised Qalhat and Sur (the extreme south-western points of his domain) and Tiwi (another village near Qalhat), and from here - inland from the Batina, at the foot of the western slope of the Jabal al-Akhdar - it extended to Nizwa; then, following the coast northwards from the south, it stretched as far as Izki, Qurayat, al-Shaba, Kalba, Khaur Fakkan and Suhar. In the Gulf, the islands of Qais and Bahrain, and the port of Qatif, were part of the direct possessions of the Malik of Hormuz, and it seems that even the bandar of Basra paid tribute to Hormuz at certain times. We know that Siraf still existed during this period, for it was a small village, mainly inhabited by fishermen, which was nevertheless renowned for its shipyard and its skilled craftsmen.[26]

The fabulous kingdom (*mulk*) of Hormuz, then, was at the very height of its splendour when, in 1498 AD, the vessels of Vasco da Gama rounded the Cape of Good Hope and appeared in the Indian Ocean.

What we have is a Moslem kingdom, a cosmopolitan trading-state, one whose nucleus was a barren island in a key strategic position at the mouth of the Gulf, but whose influence extended far beyond its immediate domain in the Gulf, stretching as far as the eastern coasts of Africa, Makran, Sind and the numerous ports of call on the monsoon route to South-East Asia. Governed by a rich family of merchant-princes who were apparently Omani in origin, supported by a local aristocracy which also had an economic base in trade (in which class the Iranian element predominated, especially those from the areas of Siraf, Khunj and Fal, even though it is also possible to discern certain Omani elements therein), it was equipped, as has already been emphasised, with a fleet and army of its own. These two last elements - the fleet and the army - are particularly striking, since they distinguish Hormuz from all the other emporia in the Gulf, which constituted but 'commercial centres' for the political capital of the moment.

We are, therefore, dealing with a genuine kingdom, which possessed internal structures strong enough to guarantee it not only commercial and financial independence, but also political and territorial integrity, and, on top of all this, these structures gave it a high degree of cultural influence. Agents of Hormuz merchants were present throughout the 16th century in the main ports of call along the routes to the Indies, whilst a skilled matrimonial policy on the part of the royal family of Hormuz was to reinforce more than one link with other emporia and ports along the main international maritime trade-routes.

The sources available, both literary and archaeological, underline the relationship between the Arabian coast and the Arabian cities on the one hand, and the Iranian coast and the Iranian cities and markets on the other. We know that there were rivalries, sometimes very bloody ones, between families living on one or the other shore or island, especially between the Tibis and the merchant families of Hormuz, and, later on, when succession to the throne of Hormuz became involved. We learn, for instance, of a Buyid expedition against Suhar, which set off from Siraf and purposed to reassert influence, control and order on the Arabian coast. We know that when the kings of Hormuz were in serious danger, they would take refuge in Oman, reorganise their army, and thence seek to effect their own deliverance and revenge. The literature, however, especially that for the period when Hormuz was dominant, never actually reports episodes of open disagreement or dramatic 'breaks' between the two coasts and their respective hinterlands. We know, too, that the small islands around Ras al-Khaima were not only well suited by nature to becoming a base for that chronic scourge of the Gulf, pirates, but also, in fact, did so become. Nevertheless, piracy never seriously affected the regular passage of convoys with their precious cargoes. Furthermore, it is possible to distinguish close cultural links between the Arabian and Iranian littorals: in the 12th and 13th centuries Suhar was the centre of a renowned school of Islamic law, and we have seen also how Sirafis would travel to Suhar to attend this important school, thus highlighting the strong Sunni/Arab legal tradition in Fars and Kirman, one which was to last until the onset of Safavid rule. These cultural links were undoubtedly strengthened by the economic interdependence of the two Gulf littorals, for centuries a major factor in trading and mercantile activity there.

To sum up, therefore, it is far from clear whether one can, with strict accuracy, speak in terms of a 'foreign presence in the Gulf' from the 9th to the 16th centuries AD. This short historical outline offers a striking image of real cultural homogeneity, characterised by a strong mercantile dimension. In this context, the so-called 'foreign' presence becomes the mere 'dynastic' foreign presence of the Turks, the Mongols and the Atabegs etc.; while the true protagonists of life and history in the Gulf were its great families of merchants, who used their immense fortunes and economic influence to control the particular dynastic (foreign) power of the moment. Alternately by means of cunning and force, and not averse to pragmatic compromises, these families were always ready to emigrate to new political centres and more convenient markets, and, all in all, they effectively managed to secure for the Gulf a political order and prosperity, that gave rise to a unique cosmopolitan life based on international cultural and trading activities.

Part Five

The date 1470 AD marks the death of one of the last effective sovereigns of Hormuz, Turanshah II (1436-1470), and the beginning of the decline of this dynasty. The petty kings who were to succeed him were to be shadowy, insignificant figures. *This, then, marked the end not only of Hormuz itself, but of a whole era.*

It was also the eve of Portuguese involvement in South-East Asia and, with their appearance on the scene, 'a real foreign presence becomes apparent for the first time', the ineluctable beginning of the overthrow of the cultural, political and economic balances that were so rooted in ancient tradition.

The European West was now coming to seek out the sources of its imports at first hand; and it was a new Europe, one very different from that of the Christian civilisations and principalities that the Persian world and the Arabs had come to know during the Crusades. This new Europe now intervened decisively, upsetting the old equilibriums throughout the new and old worlds alike.

The years which followed saw the kingdom of Hormuz shaken by a great and bloody crisis which afflicted its institutions and the matter of the succession, a crisis made even more complex by the confused situation on the mainland. But this did not prevent trading convoys from carrying on their lucrative journeys to and from the East, or the merchants of Hormuz, who continued to pay tribute now to the one and now to the other contender, from carrying on their commercial traffic undisturbed.

In 1503, when the *Qizilbashes* of *Shah* Isma'il Safawi conquered Simnan and Fars with its capital at Shiraz, Hormuz hastened to pay tribute to this new political and military power on the Iranian mainland; but when the Safavid thrust southwards ceased because of new military commitments on the eastern and western borders, the regularity of this conventional act of vassalage became very dependent on the fortunes of the Safavid armies.

When in 1507, therefore, the fleet of Alfonso d'Albuquerque appeared before the island of Jirun, this was considered to be merely a new and regrettable event, most certainly not one that was exceptional.

At the time, the young Saif al-Din was Malik of Hormuz, a weak and less than warlike personality completely dominated by his all-powerful minister, Hajji Attar, an Omani by origin. This latter, still underestimating Portuguese power and its possible future implications, had the idea of playing off the Christian foreigners, who had come from so far away, against the very much more proximate and alarming Safavids. For this reason, after an initial siege that was followed by a naval encounter, though a mere skirmish, he advised the young prince to come to terms with these *Masihi*.

Negotiations were opened with d'Albuquerque through the intermediary of an Armenian, who acted as interpreter, and Saif al-Din agreed to pay tribute. The events which followed led to a local revolt against the foreigners. A mutiny broke out among d'Albuquerque's troops, already sorely tried, and in 1505 the first Portuguese siege and occupation of Hormuz ended with the withdrawal of the Christians.

But d'Albuquerque did not completely abandon his plan for the foundation of a Portuguese trading-empire in the Indies founded on military strongholds and supremacy at sea, which would enable the Portuguese to gain control not only of the Indian Ocean but also of the western seas that link it to the Near East, namely the Red Sea and the Persian Gulf. In the Red Sea the Portuguese met with firm resistance, first from the Mamluks, then, after 1517, from the Ottomans who were temporarily allied with Venice. For this reason, and on account of the strategic position of this small yet still powerful kingdom, the control of Hormuz became a key element in Portuguese strategy for the Persian Gulf.

Having learnt through prior experience, d'Albuquerque decided to play a 'waiting game'. He left two captains, Martim Coelho and Diego de Mello, at the head of a fleet in the Gulf, to carry out raids and systematically to boycott the trade of Hormuz; at the same time he ordered them to pursue concerted action against the islands of Qishm and Larak on the one hand, and against the Hormuzi Arab and Iranian strongholds on the mainland on the other, and these were several times bombarded and sacked. In 1508 Qalhat was taken and destroyed, Suhar, Rustaq and Socotra receiving similar treatment.

Despite these pressures, Saif al-Din, on the advice of Attar, agreed to pay tribute to the Portuguese in accordance with local custom, but categorically refused to allow them to disembark and occupy a fortress on the island of Jirun. At the same time, Attar managed to gather forces and bring order back to the kingdom: Hormuz still had the fleet, the strategic defence positions and the maritime and economic strength which had enabled it to survive other such instances of aggression in the past; it was therefore in a good position to try now to keep the new aggressors and their fleet at bay. Once again the Hormuz merchants made agreements, offering men, money and ships for the defence of their common interests. Once hostilities were resumed, d'Albuquerque was forced by this fierce resistance to suspend the siege of Hormuz; and the attempt to force the Gulf had failed again.

After the fall of Goa and Malacca in 1510, d'Albuquerque turned once more to the Gulf. He resumed both his commercial boycott, to the detriment of Hormuzi convoys, and his military attacks on her fortresses. But this third attempt at forcing the Gulf and overcoming the resistance of Hormuz also failed, and Hormuz remained the supreme, unopposed mistress of the region.

With the death of Attar things changed. The weak Saif al-Din found himself in the thrall of untrustworthy advisers, more concerned with pleasing Shah Ismaᶜil Safawi than with caring for the interests of the kingdom. Ultimately, Saif al-Din found himself caught between the intrigues of his new ministers and advisers on the one hand, and the threat of the Safavids and the Portuguese on the other, and he decided that the Portuguese were, at this juncture, the more dangerous of the two outside powers, particularly following their conquest of the Iranian stronghold at Gombroon, whence d'Albuquerque could now threaten the island of Jirun directly. Negotiations, therefore, began and, as a pledge of the agreement reached, a solemn banquet was held in which the Malik of Hormuz also took part. It was during this occasion that d'Albuquerque had the dangerous advisers of Saif al-Din murdered at the very feet of their young prince, apparently at the hands of one of his three nephews accompanying him on the expedition.

Agreement was reached in 1515. Trade resumed with its earlier intensity, even if the monopoly of trade in some goods, such as spices, passed from the hands of the local sovereigns into those of the effective new masters. The fortresses of Hormuz on the Iranian coast were dismantled, whilst those on the Arabian coast were converted into Portuguese strongholds, being rebuilt and reorganised by this new, military 'foreign' force. Strengthened with new, more massive walls and tall corner-bastions, these forts were fashioned along the lines of the ground-plans and defensive and strategic techniques used in India. The fortress on the island of Hormuz was decisively occupied by the Portuguese and the most rebellious princes seized and sent to India. In exchange, the life of the Malik and the legitimate succession of his descendants, were fully guaranteed, as was his sovereignty over his subjects, though under certain limitations. With the treaty of 1515, Hormuz lost its political independence, but she did not lose her strategic and commercial importance. The beautiful city on the island of Jirun was still one of the most important ports and emporia on the sea-routes for Euro-Asian trade, especially after the Turco-Venetian attempts to revive the old Red Sea route had failed.

In 1515, Hormuz had indeed lost her political and territorial integrity, and - for the first time in her history - a real foreign presence was now active in the Gulf. Nevertheless, until the last days of this kingdom, a century later, the life of the Gulf lay, in effect, still at the beck of its traditional forces. The volume of trade-dealings controlled by the Moslem merchants and their fleets was still extremely large. Documents in Lisbon, which are still largely unpublished, particularly those in the Torre do Tombo, like those in other Western archives offer clear evidence of this situation. The city built on the island of Jirun became even more illustrious and beautiful, and the volume, value and variety of goods traded there increased proportionately. Merchants of all manner of races, tongues and religions poured in from all parts of the world, leaving us new and vivid descriptions of this 'marvellous' city.[27]

Part Six

Events in Europe at this time, in particular the agreement reached between England and Holland through the skilful diplomacy of Queen Elizabeth I, led to new international relations in the eastern hemisphere as well. Europe was now breaking forth into the Indian Ocean via the sea, in pursuit of supremacy there; and it became the major aim of the nations of Europe to dismember the Portuguese empire and crush its monopoly of the spice-trade.

The bare facts of all this, the very events and their protagonists, are well known. The 16th century saw the accession to the throne of two able and energetic Safavid rulers: Shah Tahmasp I (d. 1576) and Shah Abbas 'the Great' (1587-1629). Iran had been territorially reunified under Shah Ismaᶜil and was now thoroughly established within her new borders. Shahs Tahmasp and Abbas, therefore, now resolved to restore the country to her former power and splendour, including her former economic and commercial prosperity, and so they adapted themselves to the European power-play, fully grasping how the mood of these latter had now changed. In this context, the kingdom of Hormuz with its Portuguese garrison constituted the one really serious obstacle to an independent economy.

Shah Tahmasp I acted in accordance with ancient Persian custom: he used plots and intrigue to intervene in the internal politics of the kingdom, favouring the succession of such candidate to the throne of Hormuz as was prepared to act as his loyal puppet. But these intrigues were nonetheless foiled by the shrewd Portuguese captain of the fortress of Jirun, and the various pretenders were disowned and deported.

Shah Abbas 'the Great', on the other hand, pursued a more energetic policy aimed at a radical and permanent solution to the old problem. Having determined to retake Hormuz and develop the new port of Gombroon in its place, he was equally aware that the Portuguese, whilst they still had the upper hand in the Indian Ocean, would nevertheless be unable to continue excluding other European powers from these waters indefinitely. Persia, by now, had a well trained and well equipped modern army, but it did not have a fleet. From here to an *agreement with the East India Company* was but a short step.

In December 1621, an English fleet arrived 'to safeguard the shipment of the Company's silk'. In 1622, the Portuguese castle of Qishm being taken and demolished, the joint Anglo-Persian force besieged the last *fortaleza* still remaining, that is New Hormuz, which still adamantly refused to surrender.

This siege lasted from the end of March to September; and if, in the archives of the Torre do Tombo, we can still read the reports of the captain of the island - he witnessed their dramatic and pertinacious resistance, which was made even harder by the scorching heat of summer, the lack of water and widespread plague - this means that control of the monsoon-routes and supremacy at sea were still not definitively in the hands of the English.

When the fortress fell, the conquerors' reprisals were very harsh indeed: every bastion was demolished by Shah Abbas's troops, the harbour was ravaged and dismantled, the bazaar plundered, every house sacked and the city literally razed to the ground, and even today common graves testify to the massacres carried out on every survivor, whether military or civilian, who had lived through the exhausting siege. Hormuz was thus reduced to a small, arid and deserted island. Its very name disappeared from subsequent cartography.

This did not mark the end of the mercantile attraction of the Gulf. But it did mark the end of an era, for it constituted the decisive overthrow of a local cultural, political and economic supremacy which, as we have seen, had its roots in the very ancient traditions which characterised the nature of power and the political balance in and of the region. The European powers, who were now a positively foreign presence in the Gulf, had become ever stronger and more competitive since the Portuguese had first appeared in the Indian Ocean at the end of the 15th century.

Indeed, the close network of commercial interests, which the great families of merchants had over the centuries built up and maintained control of, partly by means of kinship-links, did not simply crumble away either wholly or abruptly. In fact, with the renewed impetus given by Shah Abbas to the port of Gombroon on the mainland, the vast range of commercial and financial transactions, those which still depended on these families and on the well stocked warehouses still owned by them along the great international maritime trade-routes, fell into motion once again. The families, thus, soon re-emerged. Some of them moved to the Safavid capital, others to other Persian trading-centres, and still others migrated to Arab, Makrani, Sindi and even more distant commercial ports. Reorganising their affairs, and taking advantage of their financial and commercial capital and experience, they soon became a newly emerging socio-political class, one whose influence let itself be felt at large upon the sea. The effects of this economic system were soon sensed in the extraordinary development of craft production and in the increasing impetus of trade during subsequent years. But this was at heart a new system: the old monopoly once enjoyed by traditional local forces was at an end, and things were now heavily conditioned by and balanced against the increasingly weighty European interests and involvement.

Notes

1   Ibn al-Balkhi, *Fars-nama*, G. Le Strange and R.A. Nicholson (eds.), (Cambridge University Press, E.J.W. Gibb Memorial Series, London, 1921), p. 136.

2   Anon, *Akhbar al-Sin wa-al-Hind*, J. Sauvaget (text, tr. and ed.), (Les Belles Lettres, Paris, 1948), pp. 2 *et infra*.

3   Ibn Khurdadhbih, *Kitab al-Masalik wa-al-Mamalik*, C. Barbier de Meynard (tr. and ed.), in *Journal Asiatique*, VI ser., vol. V (1865), p. 60; Abu Bakr Ibn al-Faqih al-Hamadhani, *Mukhtasar Kitab al-Buldan*, M.J. De Goeje (ed.), (Brill, Leiden, 1885), pp. 9, 11; Ahmad b. Umar Ibn Rustah, *Kitab al-Aʿlaq al-Nafisa*, M.J. De Goeje (ed.), (Brill, Leiden, 1892), p. 154.

4   Ali al-Masʿudi, *Muruj al-Dhahab*, C. Barbier de Meynard and Pavet de Courteille (text and tr.), 9 vols. (Imprimerie Imperiale, Paris, 1861-77).

5   Sharaf al-Zaman Tahir al-Marwazi, *Sharaf al-Zaman Tahir Marwazi on China, the Turks and India* (Royal Asiatic Society, London, 1942).

6   Yaqut, *Muʿjam al-Buldan*, F. Wüstenfeld (ed.), 6 vols. (Brockhaus, Leipzig, 1866-73), vol. III; C. Barbier de Meynard (ed.), (repr. Amsterdam, 1970), pp. 331-3.

7   Muhammad al-Idrisi, *Opus Geographicum*, E. Cerulli, G. Levi Della Vida, L. Petech, G. Tucci, A. Bombaci, U. Rizzitano, R. Rubinacci, L. Veccia Vaglieri (eds.), 9 vols. (Istituto Universitario Orientale, Naples-Rome, 1970-84), vol. IV, pp. 379, 403, 405, 410-11.

8   Ismaʿil Abu al-Fida', *Kitab Taqwim al-Buldan/Géographie d'Aboulféda*, M. Reinaud (ed.), 3 vols. (Paris, 1840), esp. vol. II/1, pp. 27-8 and vol. II/2, pp. 91-5 and esp. 96: (reprinted Maktabat al-Muthanna, Baghdad, c. 1963). Hamdullah Mustaufi Qazwini, *Nuzhat al-Qulub*, G. Le Strange (ed.), 2 vols. (Brill, Leiden, 1915-19).

9   Ibrahim b. Mhd. al-Istakhri, *Kitab al-Masalik wa-al-Mamalik*, M.J. De Goeje (ed.), (Brill, Leiden, 1870), pp. 97, 127; Abu al-Qasim Ibn Hauqal, *Kitab Surat al-Ard*, M.J. De Goeje (ed.), (Brill, Leiden, 1873), p. 198.

10   al-Muqaddasi, *Ahsan al-Taqasim fi Maʿrifat al-Aqalim*, M.J. De Goeje (ed.), (Brill, Leiden, 1877), p. 426.

11   al-Istakhri, *Kitab al-Masalik*, pp. 138 ff; Ibn Hauqal, *Kitab Surat al-ʿArd*, pp. 198-200; al-Muqaddasi, *Ahsan al-Taqasim*, pp. 442 *et infra*.

12   When Yaqut visited Siraf at the beginning of the 13th century AD (the first half of the 7th century AH), he observed the state of desolation of the city, but nonetheless records: 'I saw remains of notable buildings and of a beautiful mosque adorned with teakwood columns'. Yaqut, *Muʿjam al-Buldan*, C. Barbier de Meynard (ed.), p. 332. Cf. al-Istakhri, *Kitab al-Masalik*, p. 106: this author actually mentions three mosques.

13   al-Istakhri, *Kitab al-Masalik*, p. 127; Ibn Hauqal, *Kitab Surat al-Ard*, pp. 39-40, 198-9; al-Muqaddasi, *Ahsan al-Taqasim*, p. 426; cf. also Abu al-Fida', *Géographie*, p. 96. al-Istakhri, while describing the opulence of the city of Siraf during his own time, says that one merchant had spent as much as 30,000 *dinar* on the building of a certain palace.

14   al-Muqaddasi, *Ahsan al-Taqasim*, pp. 426-7 and 442 *et infra*: this author gives a minute description of the goods traded at Siraf, goods which came from

all parts of the then known world. Cf. also Ibn al-Balkhi, *Fars-nama*, pp. 136-7.

15   The history of Abu Ahmad ibn Umar al-Sirafi is interpolated into the work of Ibn Hauqal (*Kitab Surat al-Ard*) and dates from the 12th century AD. Ramisht of Siraf was a well known figure in his time, and he is mentioned in a great variety of sources, both literary and otherwise. Abu al-Qasim Ramisht b. al-Husain b. Shirawaghi b. al-Husain b. Jaʿfar of the province of Fars (as he is described upon his tombstone, which is lost but was transcribed by al-Shaibi: cf. Carl Brockelmann, *Geschichte der Arabischen Litteratur*, 5 vols. (Brill, Leiden, 1937-49), vol. II, p. 222) died about 1140 AD. A merchant of incalculable wealth and legendary fame, he was also especially pious and a well known benefactor, while he is mentioned by several authors in connection with the gift of a hospice at Mecca. He is also mentioned by Mhd. b. Ahmad al-Fasi, *Shifa' al-Gharam bi-Akhbar al-Balad al-Haram*, 2 vols. (Maktabat al-Nahda al-Haditha, Cairo, 1956), vol. I, p. 103; Jamal al-Din Ibn Zuhaira, *al-Jamiʿ al-Latif fi Fadl Makka wa-Ahliha wa-Bina' al-Bait al-Sharif* (Isa al-Babi al-Halabi, Cairo, 1922), p. 107. He is also mentioned by Ibn al-Athir, Ibn Jubair and others. See the very short but documented note on the subject by S.M. Stern, entitled 'Ramisht of Siraf, a Merchant Millionaire of the Twelfth Century', in the *Journal of the Royal Asiatic Society* (1967), pp. 10-14.

16   Yusuf b. Yaʿqub Ibn al-Mujawir, *Ta'rikh al-Mustabsir*, O. Löfgren (ed.), 2 vols. (Brill, Leiden, 1951-2), vol. I, p. 43; Muʿin al-Din Junaid al-Shirazi, *Shadd al-Izar*, Muhammad Qazvini and Abbas Eqbal (eds.), (Chapkhana-ye Majlis, Tehran, 1949-50), pp. 61, 421, 522 *et infra*; Abi al-Khair Shirazi, *Shiraz-nama*, B. Karimi (ed.), (Roushana'i, Tehran, 1932), p. 145. Wassaf, *Kitab-e Wassaf*, M.M. Esfahani (ed.), (Bombay, 1269 AH/1852-3 AD), pp. 170 *et infra*; see also, *supra*, note 15 and S.D. Goitein, 'Two Eye-Witness Reports on an Expedition of the King of Kish(Qays) against Aden', in *Bulletin of the School of Oriental and African Studies*, XVI (1954), p. 253.

17   At the beginning of the 12th century, Siraf and its district fell into the hands of a tribal chief, Abu al-Qasim of the Jat tribe. See Ibn al-Balkhi, *Fars-nama*, p. 136; cf. also Wassaf, *Ta'rikh*, pp. 174-5. Wassaf mentions also the name of Abu Dulaf, *Amir* of the Jat tribe, with reference to a later period, and praises his generosity and bravery.
   During the excavations carried out at Siraf in 1968, a very interesting inscription was brought to light, in which the name of one of the Jat tribal chiefs of the latter half of the 12th century occurs. See D. Whitehouse, 'Excavations in Siraf - Second Interim Report', in *Iran*, VII (1969), p. 44; cf. N. Lowick, 'The Coins and Monumental Inscriptions', in *Siraf XV* (The British Institute of Persian Studies, 1985), pp. 88-9.

18   In Shirazi historiography of the Salghurid and Mongol periods, the nisba 'Fali' occurs regularly and is usually associated with the complementary nisba 'Sirafi'. The most prominent 'Fali' family is also called 'Sirafi'; the first member of this family to have had access to public office is the already mentioned Majd al-Din Ismaʿil (d. 666 AH/1268 AD) (on this family see also note 20). Another family also originally 'Sirafi' is that of the famous jurists Qutb al-Din Muhammad Sirafi Fali and Safi al-Din Masʿud Sirafi

commonly called Fali. Another reputed citizen of this district was Amid al-Din Asᶜad Abzari (from the Garmsirat), who became wazir of the Salghurids and was among the best known scholars of the epoch. Reference to these people can be found in Shirazi, *Shadd al-Izar*, pp. 421 *et infra*; Wassaf, *Ta'rikh*, pp. 170 *et infra*. With regard to Amid al-Din Asᶜad, see specifically Shirazi, *Shadd al-Izar*, p. 215 note. 1, pp. 517-27 (with notes); Ali M. Sabeti, *Asnad wa Namaha-ye Ta'rikhi* (Kitabkhana-ye Tahuri, Tehran, 1346 AHs/1967-8 AD), pp. 161 ff.

With reference to Shaikh Danyal, his *tariqa* and the Kazirunis, see Mahmud b. Uthman, *Firdaus al-Murshidiya*, F. Meier (ed.), (Brockhaus, Leipzig, 1948), pp. 466-70, 475-7; Muhammad Ghauthi, *Gulzar-e Abrar*, ms in John Rylands Library, fol. 45b *et infra*; Hamdullah Mustaufi Qazwini, *Ta'rikh-e Guzida*. Literature provides us with very rich material concerning the life and death of this pious 'holy-man' of Khunj; but there is more than one discrepancy in the information which the written texts give us. Mention of the Kazirunis and of Shaikh Danyal also occurs in Ibn Battuta, *Rihlat Ibn Battuta*, C. Defrémery and B.R. Sanguinetti (eds.), 4 vols. (Paris, 1853-8), II, p. 242. In Khunj, as in Laristan, the fame and memory of the (legendary) life and miracles of Shaikh Danyal are still very strong; in a local shrine - which is known as 'the tomb of Shaikh Danyal', or 'Masjid-e Shaikh Danyal', and was personally visited in 1984 - there is still a dedicatory inscription in the name of Shaikh Danyal dated 849 AH. On the role of this khanaqah in the dispute between Qais and Hormuz, see also João de Barros, *Da Asia*, II, 2 and Pedro Teixeira, *Relaciones de P. Teixeira d'el origen, descendencia y succession de los Reyes de Persia, y de Harmuz, y de un viage hecho por el mismo autor dende la India oriental hasta Italia por tierra* (H. Verdussen, Antwerp, 1610), II, p. 12. On this topic in general, see Ahmad Eqtedari, *Laristan-e Kuhna* (no publ., Tehran, 1334 AHs/1955-6 AD), pp. 170 *et infra*; and the documented studies by J. Aubin in *Journal Asiatique*, 1953, 1954 and 1956, and notes 19, 20 and 21 here below.

19   During the Mongol period, Qais achieved a *de facto* autonomy that was to last until the final clash with Hormuz around 1330 AD. During that period, the great merchant-family of the Tibis controlled the whole province and, along with it, the volume of trade to and from Shiraz via the Gulf. In the second half of the 13th century, they were challenged only by that other influential family from the 'Fali' milieu, whom we have already had cause to mention, namely that of Amid al-Din Asᶜad Abzari (see *supra* note 18) in the person of his great son Izz al-Din Muzaffar Shirazi. At the beginning of the 14th century, the relations between Qais and Hormuz deteriorated sharply. At this very moment the dervishes of Khunj entered the dispute and gave all their support to the Hormuzi Malik; this support was to be decisive in the final clash between the two islands, their respective 'ruling' merchant-families and the political and economic interests which they represented (see also above).
See Wassaf, *Ta'rikh*, p. 338 and note 18.

20   In this specific occurrence, that is in association with the ruin of Qais and the Tibis, it is possible to discern the re-emergence of the *Fali* family of Majd al-Din Ismaᶜil. The great influence which the members of this family

had attained, both in Shiraz and in Hormuz during the late Salghurid period and that of the last Mongol Khans (i.e. the first half of the 14th century), is well documented in the available literature. Within this framework, there emerge the twin-personalities of Majd al-Din Isma'il II and his brother, the qadi Ruh al-Din Ishaq; Ibn Battuta and Shirazi (Ibn Battuta, *Rihlat*, II, pp. 61, 240; Shirazi, *Shadd al-Izar*, pp. 427-8) also record their great activity as builders of *qanats*, mosques, *madrasas*, bridges and *ribats* - which is a response only to be expected from the great quantity of trade passing along the caravan route linking Hormuz with Shiraz via Lar and Khunj, a route which was very active after Siraf began to decay and its population to migrate elsewhere. See also J. Aubin, 'La Survie de Shilau et la Route du Khunj-o-Fal', in *Iran*, VII (1969), pp. 21-37; and note 21 below.

21   al-Istakhri, *Kitab al-Masalik*, pp. 163-4, 166. With regard to the caravan route which linked 'Hurmuz-e Kuhna' and its harbour with the hinterland, see al-Istakhri, *Kitab al-Masalik*, pp. 131, 132, 170. Cf. also Ibn Hauqal, *Kitab Surat al-Ard*, pp. 52, 53; and al-Muqaddasi, *Ahsan al-Taqasim*, pp. 154, 155. Ibn al-Balkhi mentions this same route, which means that in his time it was still active: Ibn al-Balkhi, *Fars-nama*, p. 85. Mention of 'Hurmuz-e Kuhna' occurs also in Mustaufi with specific regard to the building of the new city on the island of Jirun, and the emigration of the population from the city and harbour on the mainland: Hamdullah Mustaufi Qazwini, *Nuzhat*, pp. 138, 141.

The history of Hormuz (the old and new cities) and its kingdom has been studied by many scholars. Among them, see: V. Fiorani Piacentini, 'L'Emporio et il Regno di Hormoz (VIII - fine XV secolo d. Cr.) - Vicende Storiche, Problemi e Aspetti di una Civiltà Costiera del Golfo Persico', in *'Memoria' dell'Istituto Lombardo - Accademia di Scienze e Lettere*, XXXV, 1 (Milan, 1975); P. Schwarz, *Iran im Mittelalter nach den Arabischen Geographen*, 8 vols. (Harrassowitz, Leipzig, 1896-1933), vol. III, pp. 244 ff. The Persian Literature on this topic is rich and well documented. See: Ahmad Eqtedari, *Athar-e Shahrha-ye Bastani: Sawahil wa Jazayir-e Khalij-e Fars wa Darya-ye Oman* (no publ., Tehran, 1348 AHs/1969-70 AD), esp. pp. 537-70 (Suru and Gombroon), pp. 573-97 (Jirun and Minab) and pp. 683-743 (Hormuz and Larak); Ahmad Eqtedari, *Khalij-e Fars* (Ibn Sina, Tehran, 1345 AHs/1966 AD); Abbas Eqbal, *Mutala'ati dar bab-e Bahrain wa Jazayir wa Sawahil-e Khalij-e Fars* (Chapkhana-ye Majlis, Tehran, 1328 AHs/1949 AD); Abbas Faroughy, *L'histoire du Royaume d'Hormuz jusqu'à son Incorporation dans l'Empire Persan des Séfevis en 1622* (no publ., Brussels, 1949); etc. The literature concerning the ethno-anthropological legacy of the Persian Gulf is also very rich, but largely deals with the contemporary situation.

Fundamental to the accurate and precise reconstruction of the chronologies and the dynastic history of Hormuz are the studies by Aubin: see J. Aubin, 'Les Princes d'Ormuz du XIIIe au XVe Siècle', in *Journal Asiatique* (1953), pp. 77-137; J. Aubin, 'Le Royaume d'Ormuz au debut du XVe Siècle', in *Mare Luso Indicum*, vol. II (Geneva, 1973), pp. 77-237.

22   See, for instance, V. Fiorani Piacentini, 'L'Emporio e il Regno di Hormoz', pp. 69 ff., 106; and J. Aubin, 'Les Princes d'Ormuz'. See also *supra* text, and

notes 18, 19 and 20.

23   Ma Huan, *Ying-yai Sheng-lan (The Overall Survey of the Ocean's Shores, 1453,* J.Y. Mill (ed.), (The Hakluyt Society Publications, XLII, Cambridge, 1970), p. 166.

24   One of the most vivid images and descriptions of the new city of Hormuz on the island of Jirun is that given by Ibn Battuta, *The Travels of Ibn Battuta, AD 1325-1354,* H.A.R. Gibb (ed.), 3 vols. (The Hakluyt Society Publications, Cambridge, 1958-71), vol. II, pp. 400-3. Marco Polo also visited Hormuz, but this was the city on the mainland, that is 'Hurmuz-e Kuhna'. Later on, another traveller coming from Europe (Odorico da Pordenone) spent some time on the island of Jirun, and he gave us a description of the new city, its people and its inhabitants, but his account is far from being accurate or reliable: Odorico da Pordenone, *Cathay and the Way Thither,* H. Yule and H. Cordier (eds.), 4 vols. (Kraus, Nendeln, 1967), vol. II, p. 112.

25   Nizam al-Din Shami, *Ta'rikh-e Futuhat-e Amir Taimur: Zafar-nama,* Tauer (ed.), (Czechoslovak Oriental Academy, Prague, 1937-56), p. 168. Cf. also Aubin, 'Les princes d'Ormuz' and Schwarz, *Iran im Mittelalter,* p. 532. Cf. also the 'other' *Zafar-nama,* that of Sharaf al-Din Yazdi, *Zafar-nama,* 2 vols. (no publ., Tehran, 1336 AHs/1957 AD), vol. I, p. 562. Also interesting on this subject is Duarte Barbosa: Duarte Barbosa, *The Book of Duarte Barbosa* (The Hakluyt Society Publications, no. 44, London, 1918), vol. I, pp. 97 ff.

26   Ibn Battuta, *The Travels,* vol. II, p. 399; see also Duarte Barbosa, *The Book of Duarte Barbosa,* vol. I, pp. 68-74. Pedro Teixeira, *The Travels of Pedro Teixeira,* W. Sinclair and D. Ferguson (eds.), (The Hakluyt Society Publications, 2nd series, no. 9, London, 1902), pp. 168-9.

27   See 'Bibliographic Note' on the existing literature and archives in: V. Fiorani Piacentini, 'La Rinascita dell'Economia di Mercato in Iran: l'Emporio e il Regno di Hormoz dal 1300 al 1622', in *Rivista Storica Italiana,* XCIV (1982), pp. 490-507.

2. BRITAIN, TRADE AND PIRACY:
THE BRITISH EXPEDITIONS AGAINST RAS AL-KHAIMA
OF 1809-10 AND 1819-20

C.E. Davies

Introduction

By the evening of 20 December 1819, Major Warren of H.M. 65th Regt. of Foot, veteran of the first such expedition against Ras al-Khaima a decade before, and quite possibly also of campaigns against the Marathas, the Pindaris and Mauritius[1], had encircled Hasan bin Ali (Chief of Rams) with his 400 or so men in the fortress of Daya. With six smaller guns and two mortars already in place, it took until the morning of the 21st to send to HMS *Liverpool* for two great twenty-four pounders, which then had to be manhandled across three miles or more of swamp and rocky ground into their position beneath the walls.[2]

At this point, responding, as he put it, to the dictates of humanity, Major Warren despatched a courier to the young Shaikh offering safe conduct for the women and children. The messenger either did not return, or, in another version, did so, but with a message of defiance and resolve: 'We are enduring all this, taking our stand on nothing but our religion, and preferring the death of the faithful to the life of the reverse'.[3]

The two hours of precision bombardment that ensued was such, however, that when, at 10.30 a.m., Major Warren was on the point of ordering the final assault, he observed a white flag appear above the fort. Hasan bin Ali had surrendered. In this engagement, as before, two elements seem to have been particularly decisive. The first of these was expressed ten years earlier at Ras al-Khaima, when it was stated of the defenders that although 'brave and skilful in single combat, they were unable to withstand the shock of adversaries acting in a body'.[4] The second was, of course, the superior British artillery.[5] Major Warren summed up his capture of Daya in the following epigram: 'The service was short but arduous. The enemy defended themselves with an obstinacy and ability worthy of a better cause.'[6]

The fall of Daya marked the end of hostilities during the second British expedition against Ras al-Khaima and associated states. In January and February 1820 the Shaikhs first of Sir, then too of Bahrain, acceded to the terms of the General Treaty. By the time the main force was withdrawn all the fortifications between Rams and Abu Hail, excepting Ras al-Khaima, had been razed, whilst about 200 of the larger vessels from these ports had been seized and in some cases burnt.[7] It was decided at first to maintain a small British garrison at Ras al-Khaima. But it soon proved potentially troublesome, of too little advantage and too precarious. By July, many of the garrison had been brought low by fever.[8] The decision was therefore taken to destroy what remained of the fortifications and retire to Qishm:

Houses, walls and towers have all been levelled with the dust; and the scattered fragments of buildings lie in all directions, exhibiting a most perfect scene of destruction, and the ruins are left these people as a lesson of retributive justice, as a memorial of our expedition, and a lasting testimony against them for their misdeeds.[9]

In many respects the second British expedition followed the pattern of the first, each of them ostensibly a response on the part of the East India Company to the piracy which it believed was committed by the Qawasim on the trade of the Gulf, the Red Sea and the north-west coast of India. Both expeditions were planned in Bombay and involved varying degrees of Omani military and naval assistance.[10] The second was, however, militarily rather more successful than the first and employed roughly twice its 753 European troops, 527 Indian fighting-men and 256 Indian followers.[11] The first had commenced in November 1809 with a land attack on Ras al-Khaima, followed over the next month and a half by others on Linga (apparently unopposed), Luft and Shinas. The second only involved hostilities at Ras al-Khaima and Daya, both in December 1819. Each was in addition accompanied, and, in the case of the second, to some extent preceded, by the seizure or burning of 'Qasimi' vessels.

Nor was this by any means the first time in recent history an outside power had intervened in Gulf affairs either in or by force. The Dutch ruled a large colony on Kharg in 1754-66 and one occasion, at least, makes it clear that they could pride themselves on maintaining maritime security.[12] The British themselves became embroiled through their agency at Basra in tussles of a different kind with the Ka'b and Bandar Rig during the 1760's and early 1770's, even to the extent of despatching a small expedition to the Gulf, all of which effectively resulted, however, in their eventual discomfiture.[13] The British were not alone in accusing the Qawasim of piracy in some form, nor indeed was it the first time Ras al-Khaima itself had in recent years been subject to attack. Regardless of the repeated but inconclusive sallies from Oman during these years, the port had earlier, for a decade or more after 1737, been occupied by the Persians under Nadir Shah.[14] Somewhat earlier still, in 1719, the Portuguese are reported to have fallen upon Ras al-Khaima and enslaved the captives they took, in response to alleged attacks on their shipping.[15] Iran's operations against the Qawasim in the early nineteenth century were in essence confined to its own ports such as Linga, and, besides, were complicated by the somewhat ambivalent position of Bushire *vis-à-vis* the Qawasim. Nevertheless, it is worth noting that in 1809 Iran fell in with the Qawasim at sea when an expedition of allegedly 4000 men against Khaur Hasan met, and was defeated by, Ras al-Khaima.[16]

What thoroughly distinguished the British treatment of Ras al-Khaima and associated states in the first two decades of the nineteenth century, and in particular the second expedition, was, however, its lasting political outcome. The events of these years and the policies and attitudes they generated combined with Britain's henceforward unrivalled ascendancy in India to shape her whole relationship with the Gulf. It was a relationship based throughout the century upon Britain's self-imposed role as the guarantor of maritime security, a function not merely precipitated, but, in the British view, necessitated by the saga of Ras al-Khaima. Furthermore, these events, and especially their 'resolution' in the General Treaty, later subject to amendment and eventual substitution by the Perpetual Treaty of May 1853, had an immeasurable effect upon the internal and external structures of the states ruled by the signatories: the very survival of the United Arab Emirates quite in their present form probably owes much, in other words, to the events here under discussion.

The legacy of 1820, then, was to be much more far-reaching and permanent than the ruins left behind by Britain in Ras al-Khaima that July. Similarly, the causes of all this will not so usefully be confined to the stark, material facts of the Qawasim's alleged piracy, undoubted *sine qua non* for the expeditions though they were: the way an issue or event is perceived can often be of greater consequence than the event itself. What follows is an attempt to sketch in some of the elements, both tangible and less concrete, which helped to shape the important, and often emotionally-charged, events of these years.   In accordance with the general theme running through this book, the emphasis will be almost wholly upon the British side to the equation.

The Economic Background

The crime of which the 'Qawasim' stood accused in British eyes, namely the unlawful and forceable seizure at sea of vessels and/or their contents, including, at times, the enslavement of those on board, was, despite the intermittent loss of life and other circumstances, essentially an economic crime. It was directed not simply at property, but, more specifically, at the very heart of international trade within the region, the seaborne carriers and their merchandise. It has been argued that the underlying cause of the two expeditions against Ras al-Khaima was the East India Company's covert desire to destroy the power of the Qawasim as rival carriers for the Gulf trade.[17] It is obviously essential seriously to consider some of the economic factors that had a bearing on the events of these years.

(a) The East India Company's Trade

In the late seventeenth century the Company showed some concern for promoting its shipping activities in the region: in 1682 it experimented with a 'round voyage' direct from England to Surat via the Gulf, and soon thereafter considered means of winning over some of the Persian carrying trade, said to be so lucrative to the Dutch.[18] Such enthusiasm, however, is not to be found in the period c.1790-1820. It is true that a trade report for 1790[19] tentatively alludes to possible advantage in the Company's participating in the India-Gulf freight trade. But the only serious, though still somewhat underemphatic, recommendation in this and another report of 1800[20] concerns the better use of the Company cruisers which visited Basra but annually in 1790, though more frequently thereafter: the suggestion was that the Company could save on freight by shipping its remittances in treasure back to Bombay on these vessels, and, according to the report of 1800, perhaps even a part or all of its woollens to the Gulf.

By the end of the eighteenth century any vestigial desire on the part of the Company to participate in the Gulf's carrying trade had probably vanished.   It therefore requires no explanation that the dozen or so Company vessels allegedly exposed to Qasimi aggression were all members of the Bombay Marine, the Company's naval arm.[21] These cruisers frequented the region either to convey the packet or to protect others from French privateers, or local 'pirates', by means of cruising or convoy.   It might seem reasonable to suppose that Company merchandise itself, especially the bulk variety, was now for the most part conveyed on 'country' vessels under British colours, whether they belonged to Europeans or to others, as was the case with the *Ahmad Shah*, wrecked in 1814.[22] Nevertheless, in relation to the question of general attitudes, it is interesting to note that a committee report for 1797 recommended, in case of need, the use of Arab vessels over European country shipping for the transmission of the packet between Bombay and Basra, a decision based on questions of economy.[23]

The Company's only real, though tangential, interest in Gulf shipping during these years has been alluded to above: a few years before the second expedition the traveller Buckingham observed that the merchants of Muscat had recently been in the habit of shipping their treasure to India in Company and naval vessels, a practice that tended to reconcile their commanders 'to all the other inconveniences of being stationed in the Persian Gulf'.[24] This procedure, occasioned, it is said, by fear of Qasimi aggression, can hardly have been very regular, although it may have been repeated off the Kathiawar coast, for similar reasons, in 1818-19.[25]   Similarly, the collection of consulage and Company's duties at Bushire, credited to the Company and part-retained by its local representatives, cannot be considered an interest in shipping *per se*: the report from 1790 once again makes it clear these charges formed a levy not on British shipping but on British-subject merchants.[26]

The Company still traded to the Gulf during the period c.1790-1820, and the general fortunes of this commerce, based as it was on the export of English woollens such as broad cloth and perpets, together with iron, steel, lead and tin,[27] seem well established. The Company's average annual export of woollens to the Gulf in 1753-62 was 868 bales and this rose as high as 1,407 bales *per annum* in 1763-7 when it formed a significant proportion of its sales in the East.[28] During the period 1780/1-1789/90, however, the yearly average had sunk to a mere 229 bales[29] and in the 1790's there even appear to have been years when the Company exported no cloth at all to the Gulf.[30] There are perhaps suggestions of a slight upturn in trade with Persia, at least, at the turn of the century,[31] but the overall trend persisted. In 1816-17 small quantities of the Company's staples were still being sent to Bushire and Basra,[32] but within a short time, possibly c.1819, the Company had ceased altogether to trade in the Gulf.[33]

The commercial reports of 1788-90 and 1799-1800,[34] the instructions issued to Mahdi Ali Khan as Resident at Bushire in 1798,[35] and Malcolm's commercial treaty of 1801,[36] are evidence of the Company's desire to reverse this decline. But by the turn of the century it had probably been accepted by most that the Company could not hope to compete with the private merchant or seriously attempt to diversify.[37] Underlying this was the virtually unbroken unprofitability of Company trade in the Gulf in these decades, combined, perhaps, with a certain failure in the requisite commercial and political will. It is quite probable that there was no serious attempt or even, perhaps, concern to boost the Company's Gulf trade in the first two decades of the nineteenth century, and Buckingham remarked that this trade was only continued at all in order to satisfy the Company's charter requiring the proportionate export of English goods.[38]

One particular factor in the unprofitability of the Company's Gulf trade has a certain bearing on the subject of piracy. The whole structure of British trade in the Gulf was founded upon an abiding conception of the region: it was believed that foreign traders could not hope to do business in the area without protection from insecurity, be it piracy at sea or extortion on land, together with assistance in coping with the delicate and involved politics of local society.[39] In consequence, the Company, which provided these services increasingly for those under its protection rather than simply itself, assuming thereby a rather more paternal role, was burdened with huge costs. A report for c.1790 records that the average sale of woollens at Bushire and Basra equalled £7,655, but this had to be offset against a total average annual expenditure and loss of -£9,555: this latter sum comprised sheer commercial loss (13 per cent), factory expenses (59 per cent) and the cost on the two factories of the Company's cruisers (28 per cent). This figure apparently ignores the basic cost of building, manning and maintaining the cruisers, which was borne by Bombay.[40]

(b) The 'Country' Trade and Related Themes

But now, Sir, a Country Captain is not to be known from an ordinary man, or a Christian, by any certain mark whatever.[41]

To accept that the Company had no significant corporate interest or ambition regarding the commerce or freight-trade of the Gulf is, of course, very far from saying that it had no interest of any kind in the matter. As ruler of parts of India it had an obvious interest in fostering the trade between its territories and the Gulf in the hope of greater internal prosperity and increased revenues, while at the same time, though the subject is less straightforward, it could not wholly ignore the interests of the private merchant[42] subject to its government or in receipt of its protection. The following brief examination of Gulf trade in these years naturally reflects what contemporary British observers felt to be the case and it would be wrong to place absolute reliance on their information, particularly since accurate statistics were almost wholly lacking at the time.[43]

Of the three principal ports of the Gulf in 1790, only the entrepot port of Muscat, whose merchants were able to deal in ready cash and derived great wealth from the coffee and sugar trades, seemed to Manesty and Jones to be flourishing.[44] Basra's international trade had received a heavy blow in the plague of 1773 and this had subsequently been compounded by other economic and political factors.   Bushire, whose prosperity likewise principally depended on the internal condition of the country despite its large measure of effective political independence, was also languishing, most of all, it was felt, on account of the disturbances in Iran in 1779-95. Local merchants almost certainly had a very firm grip on trade at each of the three ports and it may well be that their commerce had weathered the recent storms rather better than that of others such as the British.

The fortunes of private British and Indian trade in the then recent decades are less easy to establish and the picture is perhaps most complete with regard to the trade between India and Basra. In 1763-73 it is asserted that an average of 3,000-3,500 bales of Indian piece-goods were annually brought to Basra in 10-12 vessels belonging to British subjects and to the Moslem merchants of Surat.[45]   The cloth belonged to merchants of Masulipatam, Madras and Surat. It is also implied that in general, though the Company's trade flagged, that of private British traders was relatively sizable and profitable in the northern Gulf during much, though not all, of the 1760's and 1770's.[46] During the next decade, 1780-90, however, it is stated that 'British individuals resident in India' almost completely abandoned the Gulf trade, this commerce consequently largely falling into the hands of Armenian and Moslem merchants resident in British India.[47] These two latter were apparently for the most part also owners of the vessels in which they shipped their goods, although these had British captains and officers, and naturally went under British colours. In 1787 it is estimated that imports on vessels under British colours at Bushire and Basra amounted to nearly 2 million rupees, a very large sum if at all accurate.[48] The situation for Britain in the Red Sea had been somewhat less gratifying.[49]

The question of competition is not one that can be answered with any precision, but the information given on the Indian trade of Muscat and Mocha in 1790 might suggest the following:[50] European ships tended to import different categories of goods and from further afield, and the English not unnaturally dominated the Masulipatam and Bengal trade.

Surat shared with European vessels and those of Muscat the bulk of the trade, and, like Malabar shipping, tended to carry out the goods of its own area. Muscat, however, competed directly with the Moslem merchants of India in the trade to the west coast of the sub-continent, and had even latterly opened up the route to Calcutta. Muscat shared with other Arab shipping the carrying trade of the Gulf, but it was beginning to sense competition from the Utub, who took Bahrain in 1783 and who had even begun sending vessels direct to India. An English merchant in Basra in 1790, conscious of the future potential for trade in the area, might well have sensed strong competition from Basra merchants, but his keenest and most direct rivals would have been the above-mentioned Armenian and Moslem merchants resident in British India.[51]

This depiction of Gulf trade in 1790 finds general confirmation and some elucidation in another by Malcolm in 1800.[52] The commerce of Bushire and Basra had continued to recover and these ports did an extensive trade with India, roughly 60 per cent of which, or more, may have come via Muscat and been freighted in Muscat boats. Indian imports to Basra are very roughly estimated at 30 lacs of rupees, to Bushire at over 17.5 lacs rps., and to Bahrain and the southern shore of the Gulf at 10 lacs rps. Only goods from Masulipatam and Bengal came direct to Bushire and this freight trade was, one presumes, that dominated by British vessels;[53] some corroboration of this appears in the statement that Gulf shipping charged only one-third of the freight of European vessels which were consequently reserved for long voyages.[54] The efforts of the Utub to bypass Muscat by sailing direct to India were about this time followed in part by the merchants of Bushire who began to establish agencies in Bombay.[55] Another writer also makes the rather perplexing comment that the merchants of Bushire preferred to invest in shipping rather than straight commerce due to the latter's low profitability at this time.[56]

Such figures and estimates as exist for British India and Bushire convey the impression that India-Gulf trade achieved a significant, though not always a steady, overall increase in the period c.1800-20.[57] The trade of the three Presidencies, the Red Sea and the Gulf, like that between Bombay and the Gulf, seems to have approximately doubled between 1802-3 and 1817-18.[58] It may be that the commerce and carrying trade of Muscat, whose ships still visited Bengal, had somewhat declined over the same period from its earlier peak, though Buckingham's observation on the matter should possibly be qualified by another report for 1823.[59]   In contrast, the prosperity of Bahrain was, by now, assured and the importance and 'advantage' of its trade with India well recognised by Britain: the principal reason why Britain conceived of the trade of the Gulf with British India being so much in her favour, for example in 1805 to the tune of £500,000 with Basra alone,[60] was on account of the bulk of remittances being made in treasure, 'we only supplying the produce of our soil and labour'.[61] Given the peculiar nature of the pearl and the pearl industry, however, and the importance of pearls in the Indian trade, it would, perhaps, be wrong to overestimate the converse 'disadvantage' of this trade to the Gulf itself. Despite this, it was still undoubtedly true that the Britain-India-China trade had required huge injections of specie and this made the Gulf trade all the more attractive.

A good proportion of India-Gulf trade must by 1817 have been carried in British shipping, although it should perhaps be observed that some part of this, particularly that sailing from Bombay, was Arab-built, -owned and -stocked, though commanded by European officers.[62]   Whereas in 1816 Buckingham put the number of Muscat ships engaged in the trade to and from India and Africa at 20, he noted that in the previous year 15 ships, most or all quite possibly under British colours, visited Basra from Bombay and Bengal.[63] This picture of the recent health of British shipping on the Gulf-Bombay, as well as the less competitive -Bengal, route is confirmed at this time, though probably with less accuracy, by the traveller Heude: using an average of 300 tons per vessel he arrives at an annual average of 7,000 tons of outward shipping which he then roughly translates into a figure of c. 600,000 rps. or £70,000 employed in bottomry.[64]   More reliable figures exist for British shipping at Bushire: direct imports from India on British bottoms totalled 3,003,947 NPR (= c. £225,296) in 1817 and roughly doubled over the next five years. It may be that the quantity of Indian goods that entered Iran through Bushire was equalled by the amount that was brought in by Gulf shipping via Muscat at other Persian ports. Nevertheless, of total imports at Bushire in 1817, it is estimated that three-quarters came in on British vessels, one-quarter on non-British or Arab ships. The picture may well have been similar at Basra.[65]

The foregoing account, selective and open-ended though it is, yet serves to show that India-Gulf trade, already very sizable in 1790, may have increased substantially over the next three decades. The proportional share of British shipping over the same period may also have increased, more especially, perhaps, due to the apparent expansion of the direct route from Bombay to Bushire and Basra at the expense of Muscat. The presence of European merchants in the Gulf in these years was quite possibly hardly felt, except perhaps at Basra,[66] and the experiences of Bushire and Bahrain demonstrated that rapid commercial expansion was possible, even with Bombay, particularly once Muscat could be bypassed.

Important as the trade of the Gulf seemed to the Company in these years, its importance was still further magnified by changes in India: in 1787 the Company had had very little territory at all outside Bengal, Bihar and Madras (Chingleput), but by 1818 it found itself governing virtually all the coastline from Gujerat in the north-west to Bengal in the north-east,[67] together with Ceylon and large tracts in southern and north-eastern India. With the exception of certain areas such as Sind, India-Gulf trade had therefore now become British India-Gulf trade. And, at a level slightly removed, this transformation, which naturally entailed the extension of the Company's pass, as is recorded of Surat in 1800,[68] must have helped account for the increased share of British shipping in the Gulf region at this time. It was an increase, however, that should still be set against the general background of the primacy of British shipping in the Indian Ocean region, one that is believed to have been achieved after the American Wars largely at the hands of the British country captain.[69]

The above narrative should furthermore be adequate to show that the two attacks on Ras al-Khaima could not have been caused by commercial rivalry between the East India Company and the Qawasim. It is also, on the whole, unlikely that commercial rivalry between the Qawasim and private British traders or shipowners was a significant factor in the attacks: nowhere in the British sources consulted are such feelings apparently expressed, nor do the Qawasim appear as anything but small carriers and traders in these years except, perhaps, in the past tense.[70] The real competitors were others such as Muscat, the Utub, and the merchants of Bushire and Basra who were not, of course, perceived as pirates like the Qawasim and received very different treatment.[71] Furthermore, the inability of the Qawasim to use Muscat and the intermittent bans on their visiting British ports, and even Basra and perhaps Bushire,[72] must have made it difficult, if not impossible, for them to compete on the major routes plied by the British. It is, in fact, more likely that the Qawasim, for their part, would now have encountered the stiffest rivalry from other Arab shipping and, in the coastal and Gulf trades of north-west India, from the Indian ports of Sind, Cutch and Kathiawar: noticeable and direct competition between the Qawasim and British-Indian shipping, if it existed, would have lain in this latter area.

Reason alone dictates that the several-hundred reported incidents at sea in these years, ranging from threatening behaviour to the bloody seizure of ships, the majority of which were attributed to the Qawasim, constituted a most material influence upon trade. Some, however, commencing from the premise that piracy depresses trade, express surprise that an overall increase in Gulf trade should have occurred despite the alleged piracy, and are tempted to conclude that either the premise or the piracy is a falsity.[73] The cynic might, of course, simply reply that the point at issue is not the real increase in trade, or its decrease, but the hypothetical increase or decrease had that 'piracy' not existed. Amongst the many reasons why the trade figures might not so obviously register the impact of piracy are the fact that this 'piracy' was not indiscriminate, while the figures overly reflect the health or otherwise of British trade; and more important still, the great majority of reported incidents occurred not in the Gulf at all, but off the coasts of Sind, Cutch and Kathiawar.

The true effects of this piracy are almost impossible to gauge, but two consequences are self-evident: fear by others of Qasimi piracy eventually helped cause the Qawasim themselves to lose their grip on trade and, more significantly, led other shipping for a number of years prior to each expedition to depend upon Company cruisers for protection. The resultant convoys in the Gulf region and off north-west India, though apparently free, were, if used, irksome to the merchant, restrictive of his commercial freedom and may have had the net effect of reducing profitability.[74] It is similarly quite possible that the actual loss of vessels would cause insurance rates to rise, the effect of the alleged piracy on insurance being attested at Porbandar in June 1818.[75]   Buckingham makes the intriguing assertion in 1817 that English shipping from Bombay had for a time profited from Muscat's loss while the latter was at war with the Qawasim, in the same way that Muscat shipping had earlier performed the neutral role when Britain fought France.[76] It is, in fact, quite often stated both now and later, more especially at Bushire, that the continued existence of the alleged Qasimi piracy was actually beneficial to British shipping in Gulf. Very soon after the second expedition of 1819-20 it is, indeed, observed that Gulf shipping had expanded at the comparative expense of British shipping.[77] One of a number of implications from this, if true, would be that freight costs must have decreased noticeably after 1819-20.

Political Factors

(a) Some Undercurrents

The pirate Jasmy has this year caused such depredation in sea to the vessels belonging to your petitioners and others, as has rendered your petitioners in active to have any trade to the ports of Muscat, Cutch, Veraval, Mangrol, Porbandar, Karachi etc. (sic).

So begins a petition of 4 November 1817 addressed by c. 36 Indian merchants of Bombay to the Governor, Sir Evan Nepean.[78]   One of a number of such requests for relief or protection, these documents are indicative of a certain pressure which the British-Indian merchant interest sought to apply to the Bombay Council.[79] The government's perception must also have been affected, though in a wholly different fashion, by the indirect transmission of the relevant views of local merchants in Kathiawar (and Cutch) via its agents there.[80]   Whilst the Council's deliberations leading up to the second expedition give distinct primacy to the Company's narrower interests, when it comes to the *'casus belli'* the Council is in no doubt at all as to who had and did suffer most by the Qawasim's alleged piracy.[81]

The character of the government of Bombay had undergone profound and rapid change since the late eighteenth century, when this poor cousin had seemed almost ripe for closure.[82]

Reprieved by the development of the cotton trade to China, the arguments of the private trader and the temporary acquisition of Malabar, its existence was assured by territorial gain in the first two decades of the nineteenth century. Events at Malabar in 1792-1800 showed the extent to which the interests of the European private merchant, whose influence was still particularly strong at Bombay, might combine with and countermine the often unwieldy efforts of the Company with its classic monopolistic tendencies.[83] But the underlying trend was by now for a separation of these interests, as exemplified in the edict of 31 August 1804 forbidding private commerce by Company servants at Bombay.[84] This divorce, however, masked a more subtle and gradual transformation: the Company was becoming the soldier and administrator financed by revenue and with crescent reciprocal duties, while the independent private merchant, buoyed up by ideas such as those of Adam Smith and the freetraders, now openly began to attack the Company's monopolies.   As early as 2 July 1811, in fact, Bombay had decided in advance of the rest of India to throw open the Gulf to private trade.[85] What the freetraders wanted, however, was not just the freedom to trade, but the right conditions in which to do so. Given the circumstances of time and place, this appeared to imply the need for greater governmental intervention than the old Company's monopolies had seemed to warrant.

The Gulf was, in one respect, something of an anachronism at this time in that Company officials at Bushire and Basra were still allowed to trade on their own private account.[86] The Basra Resident, Colquhoun, was still profitably exporting horses in 1816,[87] but it was his long-serving predecessor Samuel Manesty, appointed for over a quarter of a century in 1784, who must be accounted the principal of these officials-cum-merchants at this time. Manesty, in fact, suffered most particularly at the hands of the Qawasim, to whom he lost no less than three vessels in the years 1804 and 1809.[88] It is noticeable, however, that neither men were early or very great advocates of the military, as opposed to the political, solution to the Qasimi problem.[89]

Those who did so, by contrast, were the new breed of political officer, some with a military background, men like Seton and Malcolm who came to the fore in the decade before the first expedition. For Malcolm, political and strategic advantage outweighed the commercial, his imperial views in

1800 wholly new to the Gulf and, in their way, an anticipation of the future.   Indeed, one of the lesser arguments which he also employed to urge upon Bombay his plan for a 'British establishment' in the Gulf was that it was for Government actively to protect private commerce and to leave the trade in Indian goods entirely in its hands; the Company, as he put it, should strive 'to excite a liberal spirit of commercial enterprise and address' amongst its 'numerous Indian subjects' as the means for increasing the prestige, and revenues, of 'that great empire of which they are sovereigns'.[90]

(b) More Immediate Causes

Englishman man very good man, drinkee de punch, fire de gun, beatee de French, very good fun.[91]

Between 1798, when Napoleon invaded Egypt, and the fall of Mauritius in 1810, British policy toward the Gulf region was no longer conditioned simply by its importance for trade and as a channel of communication.[92]   French maritime activity in the Indian Ocean during these years occasionally touched South Arabia, Muscat and the Gulf, enough to stimulate increased British concern for its naval strength in the region and, more specifically, for the protection of India-Gulf trade.[93]   Of greater import, however, was the French diplomatic activity in Turkish Arabia, Muscat and Iran that raised for the first time the haunting spectre of a European invasion of India from the northwest, a potential scenario in which Russia was soon to assume the leading role.[94]

Muscat's abiding strategic importance was grasped earlier on in the 1790's, situated as it was at the mouth of the Gulf, holding the key to India-Gulf trade and possessing the most powerful fleet in the region.   The Company's first diplomatic efforts were therefore concentrated here, activity which seemed all the more important when for a short time a French seaborne invasion via Suez seemed feasible: these approaches soon resulted in the *Qaulnama* of 1798, ratified in 1800.[95]   During the next ten years, punctuated by absence and the frequent death of incumbents,[96] British interests at Muscat were represented by a series of Residents who strove, often with less than overwhelming success, to influence the ruler in their distinct favour and to the detriment of France.

The longest-serving and most influential of these men was, until his death a few months before the first expedition, the conscientious and untiring Captain Seton, an officer who during these years also undertook political work in connection with local powers, piracy and the French in Cutch, Sind and South Arabia.[97]   Under the circumstances of his appointment, and given the proximity of Sir, it was not unnatural that Seton's ample intelligence reports from Muscat should come to constitute Britain's prime source on Qasimi affairs up to the time of the first expedition.   Indeed their influence upon British perception[98] of the Qawasim was more lasting still in consequence of their priority and their detail, an outcome which served to magnify the effect of such special traits as they possess: Seton was assiduous in his cultivation of friendly relations with rulers of Muscat and was, moreover, under the necessary constraint of relying upon sources there accessible. One needs no reminding of the deep mistrust and animosity that then existed between Muscat and her neighbours, the Qawasim.[99]   It is understandable, therefore, that this milieu should have been reflected at certain points in Seton's writings.[100]

Seton first became personally involved in the issue of alleged piracy by the Qawasim in 1805-6, when he successfully negotiated an agreement with them on behalf of the Company.[101]   A noticeable feature of this particular episode was his ready inclination to identify East India Company with Muscat interests, a tendency which on this occasion incurred the censure of Iran[102] and, if pressed, would have precluded any form of dialogue with the Qawasim. This regard for Muscat was also reflected in his historical sketches, implying, as they do at times, that Qasimi piracy rose and fell essentially in accordance with converse fluctuations in Omani strength.[103]   By 1808-9 the focus of Anglo-French rivalry had shifted to Iran, but Muscat had by then come to be regarded as a valuable friend.   When Seton returned to Muscat in February 1809 he was forcefully struck with the changes that had occurred, in particular the increase in *Wahhabi* activity both within the country and across its borders.[104]   These, his last reports, betray an infectious anxiety, predicting as they do the imminent loss of Muscat to the Wahhabis and, with it, the extinction of British interests.   It is this tone, pressing the timely need to prop up Muscat, or, as he put it, to assist in the struggles she had already begun,[105] added to the strong identification drawn between Wahhabi and Qasimi, and furthermore assuming a too literal community of interest with Muscat in suppressing 'piracy',[106] which constitutes the second of Seton's peculiar contributions to British perceptions before the first expedition: the conclusions were there to be drawn by India.[107]

In May 1807 Napoleon wrote, 'La Perse est considérée par la France sous deux points de vue: comme ennemie naturelle de la Russie et comme moyen de passage pour une expédition aux Indes'.[108]   The Treaty of Finkenstein, the Peace of Tilsit and General Gardane's mission to Iran, all in 1807, caused Britain grave concern, for they seemed to imply the possibility of a fatal combination between France, Russia and Persia against her Indian possessions.[109]   These fears were further fuelled by news of French naval forces being despatched eastwards from France in June 1807, and seemed perilously close to fruition when in early/mid-1808 the Shah was said to have reached a draft agreement with the French, in which, amongst other things, he agreed to cede Kharg and Hormuz.

The worried British response was energetic to the point of confusion:[110] the Foreign Office in London had Harford Jones, formerly the Resident in Baghdad, knighted and despatched him post-haste en route to Iran.   Whilst India, for its own part, sensing greater urgency, sent a small naval force to the Gulf in February 1807, had Seton reopen the Muscat Residency and, following his grandiose efforts of a decade before, recruited Malcolm for a second mission to Iran. Malcolm was at the same time given overall control of Gulf affairs, and it was via him that Seton's reports now reached Bombay.

Before Jones arrived from England, Malcolm had already landed at Bushire, received a bruising rebuff from the Persian government and sailed back to India to arrange a suitably demonstrative response. Malcolm's already ambitious ideas of eight years before had by now grown more robust. His honour was also at stake in the matter, and he keenly sensed the competition between the East India Company as represented by himself and the Home government as embodied in Harford Jones.[111]   In the face of the European threat Malcolm lost patience with local regimes and recommended that 'the English government should instantly possess itself of means to throw those states that favoured the approach of its enemies into complete confusion and destruction'.[112]   With the constant support of Minto, therefore, he immediately set about preparing an expeditionary force to seize Kharg.

What Malcolm wanted was a 'fine mess' in the Gulf.[113] But, as it turned out, the peaceable diplomatic overtures of Harford Jones, with other factors, all helped to ameliorate the British position in Iran during 1808, and therefore made such a demonstration of might both unnecessary and unjustifiable.[114] Yet passions were running high in 1808-9, and Malcolm's experiences combined with Seton's reports from Muscat to offer an outlet for these pent-up emotions: rather than abandon the expedition altogether, Ras al-Khaima now presented itself as a more politically, even 'morally', sound alternative destination. Both psychologically and in terms of planning and preparation,[115] then, the expedition of 1809-10 against the Qawasim was in essence Malcolm's Kharg expedition tempered somewhat, and with its object displaced, by circumstance.

Some Questions of Perception

There being no crime held in such general detestation as that of piracy on the high seas, such as by the laws of all countries is punished capitally ...[116]

The first expedition had set a clear pattern for the later enterprise. The latter's aims, however, namely the attainment of the semi-fulfilled literal objectives of the first, or the lasting eradication of piracy, were, by comparison, far more emphatic and explicit.   In point of timing, the circumstances seemed particularly apt: Ibrahim Pasha's seemingly propitious advance against the Wahhabi power in Arabia initially suggested the possibility of some kind of military alliance with Britain.[117] At the same time, following the triumph over Napoleon in 1815, the defeat of the Marathas and the Pindaris in 1818 now afforded British India the time, confidence and resources to concentrate upon matters rather less pressing and close to home.[118]

Despite what was said above of the confluence of circumstances by which the earlier operation was eventually conditioned, there is no doubt that the theme of piracy was still its *leitmotiv* and a belief in Qasimi culpability its *sine qua non*. It is important to bear in mind throughout that the principal object and duty of the Bombay Marine, the Company's naval arm, was in normal times none other than the protection of trading vessels from attack.[119] It is, indeed, instructive to see the first expedition in the light of earlier moves against pirates in India. This, in fact, is how it is described in an official account of the time which begins by specifically referring to recent operations against 'freebooters' in Malabar and Sind.[120] A further connection was, as referred to above, provided by Captain Seton, who in 1802-4 was involved with plans to combat piracy in Cutch and Kathiawar said to be an obstacle to the trade of Bombay with the north, particularly the growing cotton trade: the fact that Qasimi piracy only seems to be reported in this area after Major Walker's successes of 1807, could, if not mere coincidence, be quite suggestive.[121]

However that may be, it is at this stage of some importance to attempt to consider certain aspects of the British attitude towards piracy and the Qawasim, a range of views which helped mould the character of the two expeditions. The central point at issue is naturally the relationship between pre- or otherwise-formed ideas and feelings on the part of Britain, and the real experiences she encountered in the Gulf region.

There are strong elements of morality and emotion in many of the contemporary British reports of and reactions to alleged Qasimi piracy. In an empire founded on trade and which increasingly saw its role as the protection of, rather than participation in, commerce, it is not surprising to find British observers praising 'the innocent and industrious trader',[122] attaching a moral value to trade[123] and displaying faith in its improving qualities.[124] Piracy, then, was in some sense its antithesis and its practitioners morally deficient.[125] The results of this may be seen in Taylor's historical views on past European involvement in the Gulf as, too, in Britain's generally higher regard for and better treatment of the Utub by contrast with that afforded to the Qawasim.[126]

A second accompaniment of the growth of the administration in India, as well as of its trade, one which also perhaps owes a little more than the first to trends in British society and sentiment, was a somewhat heightened attachment to certain categories of order and authority. The Qawasim are thus at times described as 'lawless'[127] and their 'piratical' activities clearly distinguished from those who act 'with any authorised state in regular warfare according to the principles of civilised war'.[128] Concepts such as these were, of course, no absolute and they tended to presuppose some position of strength for their application, but they do possibly suggest certain parallels between British treatment of the Qawasim, on the one hand, and of other groups such as the Pindaris and Thugs, on the other.

The most powerful emotional element in the events of these years was undoubtedly the violence attributed to the Qawasim.[129] Often colouring British thinking, this theme was felt to provide Britain's strongest moral justification for its action;[130] while, in some hands, it could also, at times, give rise to certain elements of sensationalism. It was characteristic of such matters that British perception before each of the two expeditions should have focused above all upon a small number of particular, identifiable and vividly-evoked maritime incidents which, as it were, stood for the whole.[131] It also seems probable that there were at the time a variety of parallel visions of the Qawasim: certain Indian mariners, for example, would tend to emphasise different maritime incidents and represented a lurid picture of wanton cruelty.[132] There is, however, no doubting the palpable reality of the fears inspired by the bloodthirsty reputation of the Qawasim, a trait felt by Colquhoun to mark them out from their counterparts in the Gulf.[133] In response to this fear, Indian sailors off Kathiawar sometimes abandoned ship at the approach of reputed Qasimi vessels.[134] In a voyage up the Gulf in 1817 Heude records the following incident involving the English captain of his (Arab) ship:[135]

Early on the morning of the 28th we were suddenly disturbed by a loud call from our commander, to rise and defend ourselves, or we should all be murdered instantly ... We had always slept with loaded arms since the first alarm: ... on rushing forth, I found myself attacked and grazed ... by a sabre thrust. On closing and disarming my adversary, ... he was discovered to be our unfortunate commander who, his wits having entirely forsaken him, had imagined himself beset ... Renewed attempts of the same nature obliged us to confine him.

In varying degrees the two expeditions were, in one light, missions to retrieve a slighted British 'honour',[136] the goal being the Governor's 'atonement',[137] or the 'handsome chastisement' of the military commander.[138] The use of opprobrious epithets in relation to the Qawasim by some such as the Bushire Resident Bruce, his background the Bombay Marine,[139] is evidence of a gall which seems to imply that personalisation sometimes took a discernible part in this dispute. At a space of 20 years Bruce recalls with indignation the manner of his treatment at the hands of the Sudan: 'The packet taken from me, the boat's crew with myself stripped ..., [they gave] me in particular a severe bastinadoing with skates' tails and cut me in the most cruel and severe manner'.[140] The state of communications and the structure of Company authority was such that individuals could still exert a significant influence upon events, even though this effect may have lessened somewhat since the later eighteenth-century heyday of Moore and even the early years of Manesty.[141] The practical conduct of Anglo-Qasimi relations in the second decade of the century was often for the most part in the hands of Bruce, and it would perhaps be wrong to underestimate the importance of the forthright and irascible stance he adopted, as at Ras al-Khaima in 1816.[142] Alongside the issue of personality was that other, symbolic, repository of pride and prestige, felt at the time to be so much at stake in the issue of piracy, namely the British flag. Gone were the days when the Company's pass could, albeit temporarily, be auctioned off by a Basra Resident such as Moore.[143] Qasimi attacks were thus conceived as insults to the British flag,[144] an emblem whose 'honour and dignity'[145] was 'so sacred to every English subject'.[146] Language apart, this was a sentiment of some practical import given the nature of Britain's position in the East at this time.

During the first two decades of the century, emotion was such as to leave little room for any great display of sympathy for the Qawasim, even though it was quite common for military and naval officers to show respect for their prowess and skill.[147] Indeed the only partly 'ameliorating' factor which the British were at all regularly wont to acknowledge had some bearing on the cause of the alleged Qasimi piracy, if not their culpability, was the poverty and aridity of the region they inhabited.[148] By the time of the second expedition, however, hints, at least, of a slight retraction from this hitherto overly uncompromising stance were in some quarters already partly in evidence. The main proponent of these rather more qualified views was Francis Warden, Secretary to Government and temporary member of the Bombay Council just prior to the second expedition. The gist of his arguments and testimonials, which nevertheless encountered the unyielding opposition of the Governor, Nepean, was that no fair appraisal of the acts of the Qawasim could ignore the duress under which they laboured from the Wahhabis.[149] His historical researches, in fact, had led him to the conclusion that in the less recent past Muscat, and not the Qawasim, had been the true 'villains of the peace', whilst his natural sympathies seemed to lie with the smaller states in the Gulf. Warden's understanding, it might be noted, was one laboriously, if swiftly, constructed from the old Company's records. Nepean's, on the other hand, less tolerant and more sweeping as it seemed, was one based by preference upon contemporary reports from the area, particularly those submitted by naval and military officers.[150]

It would, of course, be quite mistaken to seek to imply that British opinion in these matters was either unchanging or monolithic. There had been noticeable developments since the later eighteenth century. The reports of Henry Moore, for example, who was involved whilst Resident at Basra in 1767-75 in a series of events that bear some comparison with those under discussion, seldom employ the term 'pirate': when they do so of Husain Khan in 1771, it is not a descriptive term so much as a term of abuse.[151] For Moore, like others soon thereafter, the Gulf's seemingly chronic maritime-insecurity often appeared to be but a product of the complexities of Gulf politics; and where Moore felt himself a part of this, others such as John Beaumont, the Resident at Bushire, stood back a little, more perplexed.[152] Some, such as Manesty, managed to preserve elements of this degree of immersal in the local environment into the early nineteenth century.[153] But the guiding forces behind policy in the Gulf in the first two decades of the nineteenth century were often now those such as the specially commissioned political officer, the military and naval officer on tour of duty, and the Company official in Bombay. These individuals were prima facie less likely to adjust so much to the circumstances of the Gulf and, moreover, entertained a sense of strength and distance that men such as Manesty, proud though they were, had lacked.

The outcome of these changes was apparent on a number of levels, whether in a greater readiness to remould the *status quo*,[154] or in a mere increased propensity towards a form of 'moralising': there are even suggestions that Captain Thompson, framer of the General Treaty, had hopes in 1820 of converting some amongst the Qawasim to Christianity.[155]

Final Word

So here we are, with hareems, and the lattices, and Shiraz wine, and banks of pearl, and groves of palm, and all the rest of it - and altogether, if you will know the truth, it is but a dry and dusty view, and moreover hath an ancient and fish-like smell owing to the heaps of oyster-shells which ... can hardly be dispensed with in reality, however they may in poetry:[156]

thus reflected Mrs. Thompson as she sat in the erstwhile harem of Hasan bin Rahma at Ras al-Khaima in April 1820. In other senses, too, the sometimes heavy coloration of the British perception in recent years now subsided somewhat and, like the waters of the Gulf in which these anxieties had been reflected, grew hereafter less tempestuous and a little more secure.

The events of these years had provided British India with a role in the Gulf which she was to preserve throughout the century. From being treated more in the light of pure self-interest and a desire to avoid deeper involvement in the area, the issue of piracy came to take on heavier moral overtones: the General Treaty of 1820,[157] unlike previous engagements, attempted to outlaw inter-state piracy, not simply attacks on British shipping, and this seemed to require some policing. Another effect of these years was the lasting impression they left upon British perception of the Qawasim, the Gulf and themselves. This impact was explicable by these events having inaugurated a century and a half of serious British involvement in the Gulf, but also, moreover, by their having delivered such a strong psychological impact, replete, as they were, with elements of sensation, horror, virtue, vice and romance: the General Treaty specified that the blood-red flag of the Arabs should henceforth be neatly enclosed in Britain's white border of peace.

This chapter has almost wholly omitted many of the principal actors and events, the Qawasim, the acts of piracy of which they stood accused and the numerous other mariners who played a part in these occurrences. Nevertheless, it is hoped that as it stands it may still have helped to suggest certain factors that might variously have lain behind Britain's two expeditions of 1809-10 and 1819-20, resting as they both yet did upon a distinct belief in Qasimi responsibility for piracy. For all the grand considerations and ambitions rehearsed in the political discussions of the Bombay Council prior to the second expedition, when it came to it, the eventual political settlement was in many ways the extempore production of Keir and Thompson conceived in the field. It would be difficult to argue that there was any effective, overall and conscious stratagem, or concerted policy, behind Britain's experiences in the Gulf during these years: the evidence considered by and large seems to point rather to piecemeal, even *ad hoc*, development. Nor should it be forgotten that in 1800 the region of Sir had, for the British, been largely *terra incognita*. Even at the time of the first expedition the commanders still had few reliable charts of the area and scant political information except for Seton's earlier intelligence: a hasty sketch-map of the country, drawn up by a Persian merchant, arrived too late for use. There was, then, a wider truth in Hasan bin Rahma's statement in a letter to Bruce that, 'neither of us is correctly informed [of] the state of the other arising from the distance of times and places' (sic).[158]

The period c. 1790-1820 had been a hectic one in which profound changes had occurred in the make-up of the larger powers in India, Arabia and Iran. The smaller states of the Gulf were likewise struggling to emerge from the turmoil of the eighteenth century. The Qawasim were, in one sense, caught in the midst of these changes, and perhaps found themselves a little out of step with the new political expectations and alignments. There is a moment of some poignancy when, only weeks before the second and decisive attack on Ras al-Khaima, Bruce described how he dealt a heavy, impatient, even contemptuous rebuff to a final emissary from Ras al-Khaima, who now seemed to him only to be in quest of intelligence, perhaps playing for time: the envoy, he said,

looked hard at me for a long time without replying, when at last he broke silence and said he recommended me to think well before I ventured to treat the friendly overtures of his chief with such neglect, they may not be made a second time.[159]

But the rules were changing and after 1819, upon the waters of the Gulf at least, these increasingly tended to be those devised and elaborated by Britain.

Notes

1   This, at least, was the case with his regiment: H. Moyse-Bartlett, *The Pirates of Trucial Oman* (Macdonald, London, 1966), pp. 87-8.

2   D. Lighton, Adjutant-General of the army, to Bombay Council, Bombay 20 Jan. 1820, BA S&P 477/544-66: enclosing Major General Keir, 3 Jan. 1820; Major Warren, 23 Dec. 1819; Keir, 25 Dec. 1819; Return of killed and wounded, 23 Dec. 1819; Captain Collier, 5 Jan. 1820. (BA = Bombay Archives, copies at Exeter: *S&P* = Secret and Political: *P* = Political)

3   Moyse-Bartlett, *The Pirates*, pp. 95-6. Warren's despatch of 23 Dec. (note 1), however, specifically states that no reply was received. Unfortunately Moyse-Bartlett does not state his source.

4   Wainwright, cited in Sultan Muhammad Al-Qasimi, *The Myth of Arab Piracy in the Gulf* (Croom Helm, London, 1986), p.137. Organisation was the key. At Ras al-Khaima in 1809 and, probably to a much lesser extent in 1819, the British may have been strictly speaking outnumbered though figures for the defenders are only estimates. These estimates run at about 5000 for 1809 and 4000-7000 for 1819 (see text for British numbers): Moyse-Bartlett, *The Pirates*, p. 50; J.B. Kelly, *Britain and the Persian Gulf 1795-1880* (Oxford University Press, Oxford, 1968), p. 153.

5   A brace of naval twenty-four pounders were also used to great effect in breaching the walls of Shinas in Jan. 1810 and of Ras al-Khaima in Dec. 1819: Al-Qasimi, *The Myth*, pp. 143, 224. Nevertheless, although the Qawasim still also employed spears at this time, it would be wrong to assume they were deficient in gunnery. When Daya was captured in 1819 it yielded 100 matchlocks, 40 swords, 300-350 lbs of gunpowder (damaged) and 11 guns of which, however, only three are described by the British as serviceable. At Ras al-Khaima in 1819, when 84 guns were discovered, all but three were described as unserviceable though of these 49 were termed 'available' during the five-day siege. These guns were between 2 and 12 pounders, very many of them 6 or 9 pounders. All but 22 were mounted on ships' gun-carriages, while the remainder were dismounted: BA S&P 479/1276-8. The effectiveness of the British artillery and tactics is reflected in the generally far higher casualties suffered by the defenders during the two expeditions. At Daya the British suffered 5 killed and 15 wounded: Lighton, 20 Jan. 1820, with enclosures (above note 2). At Ras al-Khaima in 1819, Britain lost 5 killed with 51-2 wounded. Keir estimated Qawasim killed at Ras al-Khaima at 300, with 700 wounded, 100 the result of a single shell burst: Moyse-Bartlett, *The Pirates*, pp. 93-4, 248-50; Kelly, *Britain*, p. 153. (note: in this chapter the term Qawasim is not used in its narrow, more correct, sense but in a broad manner approaching its then

contemporary usage by Britain)

6   Warren, 23 Dec. 1819 (see note 2).

7   Major General Keir to Adjutant-General, 5 Feb. 1820, with enclosures, BA S&P 479/1257-78.

8   Captain Thompson to Warden, Muscat 9 Aug. 1820, BA S&P 491/6132-51; Moyse-Bartlett, *The Pirates*, pp. 129-30.

9   Moyse-Bartlett, *The Pirates*, pp. 129-30, citing the *Bombay Courier*.

10   During the first expedition the ruler of Muscat had at first been in practice reluctant to join the British. His assistance was therefore limited to the loan of 20 trankeys, seven of which soon parted company. Later, however, the ruler relented and he co-operated in the attack on Shinas with troops and vessels: Ruler of Muscat, Wainwright and Smith in Al-Qasimi, *The Pirates*, pp.135-6, 142-4.

11   'Return of a detachment...', Bombay 7 Sept. 1807, Appendix 2 in Sultan Muhammad Al-Qasimi, 'Arab "Piracy" and the East India Company Encroachment in the Gulf 1797-1820', PhD thesis, Exeter, 1985.

12   J.R. Perry, 'Mir Muhanna and the Dutch: Patterns of Piracy in the Persian Gulf', *Studia Iranica*, vol. 2 (1973), p.89: the Dutch records claim that mariners declared them the mainstay of safe navigation after one of their gallivats beat off two of Mir Muhanna's which were engaged in an attack on a Basran trankey off Kharg.

13   J.A. Saldanha, *The Persian Gulf Précis* (Calcutta, 1908), vol. 1, pp.169-298, *passim*.

14   G. Rentz, 'al-Kawasim', article in *Encyclopaedia of Islam*, new edition, vol. 4, E. van Donzel, C.E. Bosworth *et. al.* (eds.), (E.J. Brill, Leiden, 1978), pp.777-8.

15   Ibid.

16   Seton, Muscat 30 March 1809, BA P 327/3745-6; Seton, Muscat 7 May 1809, enclosing Seton to Malcolm, 6 March 1809, BA P 329/4607-16; *Arabian Gulf Intelligence, Selections from the Records of the Bombay Government, New Series, no.XXIV, 1856* (Oleander Press, Cambridge, 1985), p. 305. The expedition, under Muhammad Nabi, was apparently defeated by 22 Qasimi vessels. The ruler of Muscat originally planned to join in the attack and, according to Seton, some had been pressing for the expedition to take in Ras al-Khaima also. The relationship between the ruling family at Bushire, the Al Mazkur, and the Qawasim was generally friendly in the first decades of the nineteenth century. In 1815, for example, the Qawasim sent a force to Bushire to help maintain the ruler's position, the most important of a number of instances of their acting as allies: see S.R. Grummon, 'The Rise and Fall of the Arab Shaykhdom of Bushire: 1750-1850', PhD thesis, John Hopkins University, Baltimore, 1985 (UMI, Ann Arbor, 1985), pp. 144-5. The official Persian position was, however, quite possibly at variance with that of Bushire. This is reflected in Fasa'i's later account of these years, which records land operations on the southern littoral as well as support for the British attack on Ras al-Khaima, and its justification, the elimination of piracy: H. Busse (translation of H. Fasa'i, *Fars-nama-ye Nasiri*), *History of Persia under Qajar Rule* (Columbia University Press, Columbia, 1972), pp. 145, 153-5.

17 See especially Al-Qasimi, *The Myth*, as, pp. xv, 28, 31-2, 82.

18 J.G. Lorimer, *Gazetteer of the Persian Gulf, Oman, and Central Arabia* (Calcutta, 1915), vol. 1 Historical, part 1A, pp. 73-4.

19 Saldanha, *The Persian Gulf*, vol. 1, pp. 404-34, 431-2.

20 Saldanha, *The Persian Gulf*, pp. 442-55, 453. In this connection it is in fact positively reported in 1790 that Company cruisers regularly took glass and china from Bombay to Bushire: Saldanha, *The Persian Gulf*, vol. 1, p. 423.

21 These included the brig *Viper* (1797), an unnamed vessel (1799), the ship *Mornington* and the ketch *Queen* (1805), the *Fury*, the brig *Nautilus* and the schooners *Lively* and *Sylph* (1808), the ketch *Princess Augusta* (1809), the *Turrarow* and the ship *Aurora* (1816), the pattamar *Darya Doulut* (1817) and possibly another (1818): BA and *Arabian Gulf Intelligence*, p. 311. Strictly speaking the *Aurora* and the *Nautilus* were held on the Bengal establishment: Moyse-Bartlett, *The Pirates*, p. 233.

22 Described as a 'native' vessel under Captain Herriman, the *Ahmad Shah* was wrecked on Qais Island and its cargo seized by Charak and possibly other states. It was carrying Company mares, brimstone and guns: Bruce to Warden, with enclosures, Bushire 24 July 1814, BA 415/3795-3824. Some of the less bulky items were certainly at times transported on Company cruisers.

23 The Company's vessels were understandably preferred in times of peace. Arab shipping was, according to the committee's calculations, very slightly cheaper than that of European merchants. It should be added that a dissenting voice is represented in a report annexed to that of the 'Committee for improving the channels of intercourse to Europe by the two Gulfs': Nathaniel Crowe is very much against the use of Arab shipping between Bombay and Muscat, though not in the Gulf itself; Bombay Castle 22 Aug. 1797, BA S&P 57/1618-44.

24 J.S. Buckingham, *Travels in Assyria, Media and Persia* (Henry Colburn, London, 1829 - facsimile edition, Gregg International, Farnborough, 1971), p. 511, cf. 384; cf. Kelly, *Britain*, p. 56. The usual rates from Basra were 1 per cent to Bushire, 2 per cent to Muscat, 3 per cent to Bombay and 4 per cent to Bengal. In the few years following the first expedition, English private shipping was wont to receive this lucrative cargo at Muscat as a result, Buckingham says, of the Qasimi threat.

25 The merchants of Porbandar, in Dec. 1818, offered 1 per cent for the possibility of entrusting treasure consigned to the coasts to the *Prince of Wales*: Elwood (Porbandar Agent) to Nepean, Porbandar 23 Dec. 1818, BA Sel. vol. 73. (*Sel.* = Selections on Pirates).

26 Saldanha, *The Persian Gulf*, vol. 1, pp. 411, 432-3. The report specifies 3 per cent duties and 2 per cent consulage payable at Basra and laments the decline in their total. Cf. Kelly, *Britain*, p.57 records customs of 5 per cent and consulage of 2 per cent at Bushire.

27 Malcolm (1800) in C. Issawi, *The Economic History of Iran 1800-1914* (University of Chicago Press, Chicago, 1971), p.264.

28 J.R. Perry, *Karim Khan Zand, a History of Iran, 1747-1779* (University of Chicago Press, Chicago, 1979), p. 260: Perry suggests the figure of roughly one-fifth of such sales.

29   Issawi, *The Economic*, pp. 82-3: Two bales appear to have weighed approximately one ton.

30   Grummon, 'The Rise and Fall', p. 291 note 51.

31   Lorimer, *Gazetteer*, vol. 1, part 1A, p.185; part 2, pp. 1955-8.

32   Buckingham, *Travels*, pp. 352, 382.

33   Lorimer, *Gazetteer*, vol. 1, part 1A, pp. 212-3; part 2, pp. 1955-8.

34   Saldanha, *The Persian Gulf*, vol. 1, pp. 404-55; Grummon, 'The rise and Fall', p. 174: viz. special reports commissioned by government and drawn up by Watkins at Bushire (1788-9), Manesty and Jones at Basra and Baghdad (1790), Maister and Fawcett at Bombay (1799) and Malcolm on his visit to the Gulf (1800).

35   Saldanha, *The Persian Gulf*, vol. 1, pp. 340-2: 'The great object of your appointment is the extension of the Company's European imports into Persia, and the improvement to the highest possible degree of their selling prices since those of late years have ... proved a loss to them'. It seems that Mahdi Ali Khan achieved some success: Lorimer, *Gazetteer*, vol. 1, part 2, pp. 1955-6.

36   See Kelly, *Britain*, pp. 72-3; Lorimer, *Gazetteer*, vol. 1, part 2, p. 1956; esp. Saldanha, *The Persian Gulf*, vol. 1, pp. 386-90. The treaty renewed the Company's privileges with Iran and reduced duties payable on its staples.

37   This is clear from a comparison of the two afore-mentioned commercial reports: Manesty and Jones in 1790 still entertained some hopes of boosting the Company's trade, but Malcolm's report of 1800 in essence promotes the interests of the private merchant. In another report of 1800 Malcolm refers to the Company's trade as having a natural ceiling and being confined to its staples: Issawi, *The Economic*, pp. 263-4 (262-7). After Malcolm, resignation may almost have become the rule.

38   Buckingham, *Travels*, pp. 352, 382.

39   A report for c.1790 maintains that 'no trade can be carried on with those places from the sea without a regular establishment of persons constantly residing there, to cultivate the protection of those fluctuating arbitrary governments, by making presents, at times, to a considerable amount'; 'the Bombay cruisers are a great expense to the Company, but absolutely necessary ... from the vexations of pirates': Issawi, *The Economic*, p.87; cf. Saldanha, *The Persian Gulf*, vol. 1, pp. 433-4.

40   Issawi, *The Economic*, pp. 85-9. It may be that these figures do not take account of consulage, but the basic lesson still holds. The number of cruisers visiting the Gulf naturally increased rapidly in the early nineteenth century in response to the perceived Qasimi threat, and also, more particularly in the first decade, as a result of the French wars. The cost of the Basra factory alone, put here at £4,276, was estimated by Buckingham at £5,000 *per annum* c.1816-17: Buckingham, *Travels*, p. 382.

41   *Madras Courier*, 26 April 1792, in H. Yule and A.C. Burnell, *Hobson-Jobson* (John Murray, 1903 - Routledge and Kegan Paul, London, 1985), p.267.

42   Cf. It has been guessed that in the later Safavid period Gulf and Indian merchants held 75 per cent of Gulf trade, the Company 15 per cent and other companies and private Europeans 10 per cent: Perry, *Karim Khan*, p. 256.

43 Saldanha, *The Persian Gulf*, p. 431. Manesty and Jones refer to 'the difficulty of procuring information relative to the commerce of the Red Sea, the incorrectness of the custom-house accounts at most of the ports of the Persian Gulf, the practice of smuggling prevailing at those ports, and the inability of some of the governors of those ports to afford the required communications'.

44 Viz. the report of 1790, Saldanha, *The Persian Gulf*, vol.1, pp. 404-34, upon which the following account of the situation as it appeared in, and from, that year is based. See also Perry, *Karim Khan*, pp. 246-71.

45 Saldanha, *The Persian Gulf*, vol. 1, p. 412. A somewhat difficult point in this era, and indeed, even later, is the exact nature of what was termed a British vessel. For a short period, before being cautioned, the Company's Agent in Basra apparently simply auctioned the Company's pass: Lorimer, *Gazetteer*, vol. 1, part 1A, pp. 160-1.

46 E.g. Saldanha, *The Persian Gulf*, vol.1, p. 406.

47 Saldanha, *The Persian Gulf*, vol. 1, p. 432.

48 Ibid.

49 It is stated that a brief period of often lucrative British trade between Suez, Calcutta, Bombay and Surat came to an abrupt end in 1779. By 1790 British shipping had also ceased visiting Jeddah whose trade with India was now in the hands of Surat, Hudaida and Mocha vessels: Saldanha, *The Persian Gulf*, vol. 1, pp. 416-19.

50 Esp. Saldanha, *The Persian Gulf*, vol. 1, pp. 416-19, 408, 406-7, 423. Other Europeans sailing to Muscat (and Bushire) included the Dutch and the French.

51 This hypothetical English merchant is based on the assumption that the private views of Manesty (and perhaps also Jones), himself a merchant, shine through the report of 1790.

52 Saldanha, *The Persian Gulf*, vol. 1, pp. 442-55; and, Issawi, *The Economic*, pp. 262-7; cf. also, Maister and Fawcett in Saldanha, *The Persian Gulf*, vol. 1, 435-40. Nb. Malcolm's figures (see text) are only estimates and he himself soon revised them. They do not, it seems, include the, albeit small, Company imports. Cf. Grummon, 'The Rise and Fall', pp. 175-6.

53 Saldanha, *The Persian Gulf*, vol. 1, p. 445.

54 Saldanha, *The Persian Gulf*, vol. 1, p. 453.

55 Saldanha, *The Persian Gulf*, p. 445. This is alleged to have commenced c.1798. It is possible this contributed to a growth in Bombay-Bushire shipping over the next two decades. This practice is also confirmed by Bogle at Muscat: Surgeon Bogle to Duncan, Muscat 2 April 1800, BA S&P 92/2626-33.

56 E.S. Waring, *A Tour to Sheeraz* (London, 1807 - reprint, New York, 1973), pp. 47-9, 76-80, 85-8.

57 See esp. Grummon, 'The Rise and Fall', pp. 176-80; Kelly, *Britain*, pp. 137, 249-51; Al-Qasimi, *The Myth*, pp. 230-1.

58 The total trade of the three Presidencies with the Gulf and the Red Sea is given as just over 112 lacs rps. in 1802-3 and 242 lacs rps. in 1817-18: Kelly, *Britain*, p. 137. The value of imports to Bombay from the Persian Gulf was 1,774,469 rps. in 1802-3 and 3,699,059 in 1817-18: Al-Qasimi, *The Myth*, p.

230.

59   Buckingham, *Travels*, pp. 509-10; cf. List of Gulf Shipping in Stannus to Willock, Bushire 3 June 1824, FO 60/24. (*FO* = Foreign Office files in Public Record Office, Kew). The latter is a list of the principal ships and trading-boats in the Gulf. Of a total of 20 merchantmen, 6 belonged to Muscat, 4 to Bushire, 6 to Calcutta and 4 to Bombay. Of a total of 98 large trading-boats, all of which belonged to Gulf ports, 45 per cent belonged to Muscat. Nevertheless, in view of the fact that British vessels now went directly from Bombay to Bushire and Basra, a feature not observed by Malcolm in 1800, it seems likely that Muscat had indeed lost out proportionally over these two decades to British shipping, as well as to others such as Bushire (and the Utub) in the Indian trade.

60   Buckingham, *Travels*, p.383.

61   Bruce to Bombay, Bushire 31 July 1816, BA S&P 312/1026-35.

62   Especially if Heude's experiences were representative: Lt. W. Heude, *A Voyage up the Persian Gulf and a Journey Overland from India to England in 1817* (Longman, Hurst etc., London, 1819), pp. 19, 47.

63   Buckingham, *Travels*, pp. 509-10, 383-4.

64   Heude, *A Voyage*, pp. 47-8.

65   Report on the Foreign Trade of Bushire, Stannus to Willock, Bushire 3 June 1824, FO 60/24. Of the goods brought into Bushire on British bottoms in 1817, 95 per cent came direct from India, 97 per cent being Indian and Chinese, 3 per cent European goods: the proportion of European goods was generally much higher over the next few years.

66   Residents at Basra seem to have been active in the private trade. Manesty, Resident for roughly two and a half decades (1786 ff.), is the prime example, although others such as Harford Jones and Dr. Colquhoun are known to have traded: as, Buckingham, *Travels*, p. 385.

67   E.g. Masulipatam (Guntur 1788), Malabar (1792), Ceylon (1796), N. and S. Kanara (1799), Madurai (1790-1801), Tinnevelly, S. Arcot, Trichi, Tanjore (1799), Orissa (1803), Gujarat (1800-18).

68   Statement of Surat Trade etc., Soper to Wellesley, Surat 6 Oct. 1802, BA S&P 129/6073-5.

69   H. Furber, *John Company at Work* (Harvard, 1948 - reprint, Octagon Books, New York, 1970), pp. 160-90 and *passim*. A list of free merchants and mariners at Bombay in 1749-50 records the names of 5 merchants, 16 'seafaring men' and 12 'country' ships. A similar list for 1792 names 57 'country' ships and 9 snows officered by 189 European seamen. In 1791/2 at least 70 British 'country' ships (or 27,000 tons of shipping) visited Cochin: this was double the size of six years before: Furber, *John Company*, pp. 224, 185.

70   E.g. in the account of the Qawasim supplied to Bruce c. 1816 by an Arab source: 'A summary of the information' etc., in Bruce to Bombay, Bushire 20 Jan. 1817, BA 312/1064-71.

71   There were, it is true, some such as Nepean, who was tempted prior to the second expedition to regard the Utub as pirates, or Warden, who tried to make out a case that Muscat had also been culpable, but these views were not translated into aggressive action and did not persist.

72 As early as 1805-6 when Seton negotiated with the Qawasim they found themselves denied access to British ports and Basra: Al-Qasimi, *The Myth*, pp. 72-82. The ban at Bushire is conjectural and quite possibly would not have been for very long. The Qawasim may also have eventually been denied access to the ports of Kathiawar.

73 See Kelly, *Britain*, p. 137, note 2; Al-Qasimi, *The Myth*, p. 230.

74 E.g. Buckingham, *Travels*, p. 511. At Bushire in 1802 it was remarked that fear of the Utub confined local vessels to port; in 1814, anxiety about the Qawasim made vessels unwilling to travel to Ras al-Khaima. On the Kathiawar coast, however, in the few years before the second expedition, there are repeated statements that fear of the Qawasim temporarily confined local vessels to port, as at Porbandar in January 1817 and November 1819: Grummon, 'The Rise and Fall', p. 203; Bruce to Warden, Bushire 22 March 1815, BA P 421/1059-60; Elwood to Warden, Porbandar 12 (18?) Nov. 1818, BA S&P 456/6147-9; Elwood to Warden, Porbandar 1 Feb. 1817, BA Sel. 72/235-6.

75 The seizure of Arab vessels on the Mocha route not under the Company's pass was, according to Elwood, nevertheless a blow for the whole merchant community of Porbandar on account of insurance: Elwood to Warden, Porbandar 3 July 1818, BA Sel. 72/554-5. Cf. Grummon claims that a Bombay report of 1802-3 maintains that Arabs and Persians did not then in fact pay insurance premiums: Grummon, 'the Rise and Fall', p. 204.

76 Buckingham, *Travels*, pp. 509-11. The Bombay vessels had allegedly received the small coasting trade of Muscat for a time.

77 Some had even argued against the second expedition for fear of this eventuality. There has to be a very large element of impressionism, however, in the statements from Bushire that British shipping declined after 1819-20 since until 1823 there was no serious record of non-British shipping. In that year British shipping brought in only 35 per cent of imports at Bushire: in 1817 Bruce had estimated imports on British vessels at roughly 75 per cent. In the years following 1819-20 local shipping prospered since it was cheaper and the Muscat route revived: Issawi, *The Economic*, pp. 89-91; Grummon, 'The Rise and Fall', pp. 178-80, 202-5; Bruce to Willock, Bushire 22 Sept. 1819, FO 248/38; Robertson to Sheil, Bushire 23 July 1842, FO 248/108; Hennell to McNeill, Bushire 15 Dec. 1836, FO 248/85.

78 BA Sel. 72/448-50. Nepean succeeded Duncan as Governor of Bombay in 1811.

79 Cf. C.A. Bayly, *The New Cambridge History of India, II- 1, Indian Society and the Making of the British Empire* (Cambridge University Press, Cambridge, 1988), pp. 63-4. Other petitions, complaining of Qasimi activities, all by Indian merchants of Bombay except for one of Patna, have been preserved in the records for the years 1809 and 1816-19. The petition here quoted is by far the most lengthy of these: Sunderjee Sewjee, Bombay merchant, Bombay 23 Feb. 1809, BA P 323/1820-1; Jewraz Balloo Bhatia, Bombay Merchant, Bombay 9 Feb. 1809, BA P 324/2213-8; Nawab Alee Qoolee Khan of Patna, 5 May 1816, BA P 430/1375-6; Dyal Multany, Bombay 31 Oct., (Konsoordass Ransoordass and other Bombay merchants, 4 Nov.

1817) BA S&P 438/2143-4; Dyal Multany, Bombay 16 Dec. 1817, BA Sel. 72/515; Sunderjee Sewjee, Bombay 12 July (x2) 1819, BA Sel. 73. It is also of interest that the most detailed, indeed confidential, intelligence regarding the Qawasim just prior to the first expedition was derived by Government from a certain Sayyid Taqi, Persian merchant of Bombay.

80 The depiction of Qasimi activities in this area in the second decade of the century is in the main the work of Elwood, Agent at Porbandar.

81 'In a pecuniary point of view some of the native merchants have suffered considerably': Nepean to Hastings, Bombay 22 Sept. 1818, BA Sel. 74.

82 Governor Duncan wrote in 1797 that he 'would never have gone there had he known the state it was in'. Idiosyncratic in a number of ways, Bombay was noticeable for its important Parsi shipbuilding-community with whom, it is said, the English maintained good relations and drank 'great quantities of wine and particularly Madeira': Duncan to Ross, 2 June 1797 and Mrs. Graham, *Journal of a Residence in India* (1809), both cited in Percival Spear, *The Nabobs, a Study of the Social Life of the English in 18th century India* (Oxford University Press, London, 1963), chapter 4, pp. 71, 76, notes 46, 72.

83 P. Nightingale, *Trade and Empire in Western India 1784-1806* (Cambridge University Press, Cambridge, 1970), chapter 4, pp. 73-127 and *passim*; A.D. Gupta, *Malabar in Asian Trade 1740-1800* (Cambridge University Press, Cambridge, 1967). Duncan, Governor of Bombay at the time of the first expedition, had, in fact, earlier been Commissioner in Malabar: Nightingale, *Trade*, pp. 94 ff.

84 Nightingale, *Trade*, p. 230.

85 Lorimer, *Gazetteer*, vol. 1, part 1A, pp. 212-3.

86 But, according to Lorimer, at least, this was not the case at Muscat. In 1822 Bushire and Basra had at length to conform: Lorimer, *Gazetteer*, vol. 1, part 1A, pp. 212-3. Dying only a few years after his spell as Bushire Resident 1780-5, before which he had served at Basra, John Beaumont, active in the country trade, left a will which received probate on 6 February 1788 and comprised an estate worth at least £10,000: Furber, *John Company*, pp. 210-4.

87 'The horses sent to Bengal are always of a finer kind and higher price. The greatest number of these are sent from here by the British Resident on his own private account': Buckingham, *Travels*, p. 385.

88 Viz. the *Shannon* and *Trimmer*, plundered in 1804, and the *Minerva*, taken in 1809.

89 In slight contradiction, however, Manesty had earlier, in 1798, proposed a small naval force under his command to guarantee Gulf security. Nevertheless, in the next decade he himself assisted in the 1805-6 negotiations with the Qawasim and only lost confidence in the political solution in 1809. At certain times Manesty was also an advocate of closing Indian ports to the Qawasim: Manesty to Bombay, Basra 12 April 1798, BA S&P 63/1612-20. In 1819 Colquhoun felt that the then prevailing situation would almost become acceptable if the Qawasim only spared their captives and learnt to 'content themselves with the plunder which their success might award them': Colquhoun, Bombay 21 May 1819, BA S&P 312/973-81.

90   Malcolm expected that the commercial success of such an establishment would equip Britain with a powerful political lever on neighbouring states, particularly Iran. The only merchants who he felt might lose out thereby would be those of Muscat: Saldanha, *The Persian Gulf*, vol. 1, p. 446 (442-55). Malcolm's views contrast with the more customary concerns expressed in the Company's instructions to Mahdi Ali Khan only two years before. In two decades time Warden was actively arguing in the Bombay Council that the protection of its Indian subjects was to be a major purpose of the second expedition and constituted the duty of government: Saldanha, *The Persian Gulf*, vol. 1, pp.340-2; Warden, Bombay 3 April 1819, BA Sel. 74.

91   Claimed by William Hickey to have been oft-heard repeated by Anjouan islanders, just north of Madagascar, in 1769: William Hickey, *Memoirs of William Hickey* (Century Publishing, London, 1984), pp. 97-8.

92   For the background and events of these years see Kelly, *Britain*, chapter 2, pp. 62-98.

93   In practice, such responsibilities usually devolved upon the Bombay Marine, rather than the Royal Navy, during these years.

94   Malcolm had noted Russian activity in northern Iran with alarm in 1800: Saldanha, *The Persian Gulf*, vol. 1, p. 448. Cf. Saldanha, *The Persian Gulf*, vol.2, p. 16; and Kelly, *Britain*, pp. 96-7.

95   Lt. Skinner visited Muscat two years before Mahdi Ali Khan negotiated the Qaulnama which was in turn confirmed by Malcolm in 1800. Before this, as indeed during the second decade of the century, the Company was represented at Muscat solely by an Indian broker.

96   Bogle, Watts, Seton and Bunce all died at Muscat between 1800 and 1809. Smith left the station for health reasons in 1810 and his position was left vacant.

97   Seton died on 2 August 1809: Eatwell to Bombay, Barka 3 Aug. 1809, BA P 338/8079-80. He had arrived in February after an almost unbroken absence of over two years. Seton was on duty in connection with Cutch in 1802-3, ordered to South Arabia in 1806 and to Sind in 1808: Nightingale, *Trade*, pp. 200-1, 206, 213; Kelly, *Britain*, pp. 77, 110.

98   The orders to the commanders of the first expedition are founded on local information supplied by Seton, and make a special point of mentioning 'the unfortunate loss by death of Captain Seton at a period so critical as the present': Al-Qasimi, *The Myth*, p. 132. In the second decade of the century Francis Warden relied upon Seton as his prime source for an account, since published, of Muscat and Qawasim history: see *Arabian Gulf Intelligence*.

99   Matar bin Rahma wrote to Seton in January 1806 that, 'At present it is three generations we have been at war with Muscat, and ... [have] quarrels to settle with extent to boats, blood and property': Al-Qasimi, *The Myth*, p. 74.

100   See especially his historical, geographical and political sketches: Seton to Bombay, Surat 9 July 1802, BA S&P 126/4595-4612; Seton to Bombay, Baroda 2 July 1807, BA S&P 208/4937-4950; Seton, cited in Minutes for 10 Dec. 1808, BA S&P 255/14150-9; Seton, Muscat 19 Feb. 1809, BA P 325/2640-50.

101   See Al-Qasimi, *The Myth*, pp. 72-81.

102 Seton had accompanied Badr in his expedition to recover Minab and Bandar Abbas from the Banu Ma'in. Bruce was hard put to explain the situation to the Persian authorities: Al-Qasimi, *The Myth*, pp.56-60; Seton to Bombay, Muscat, entry for 6 Aug. 1805, BA S&P 170/4067-73; Bruce, Acting Resident at Bushire, to Bombay, 30 June 1805, with other letters, BA S&P 170/4090-9. As to the more general point, note Seton's statement to the Qawasim that, 'I have entered into an agreement with Sayyid Badr that our peace and war should be one': Al-Qasimi, *The Myth*, p. 68.

103 When Oman was strong the Qawasim would 'sink into nothing and durst not show themselves': Seton to Bombay, Baroda 2 July 1807, BA S&P 208/4937-50.

104 He noted the presence of 'six Wahhabi teachers ... compelling the people by blows to pray in their manner': Al-Qasimi, *The Myth*, pp.109-10. Wahhabi success in 1807-8 had also been accompanied by the installation of Hasan bin Ali in Sir and by Qasimi military successes in the north. In early 1808 Seton had described the condition of Muscat as one of 'degrading submission' to the Wahhabis: Kelly, *Britain*, pp. 109-10.

105 A somewhat liberal interpretation of affairs: Seton to Brigadier-General Malcolm, Muscat 19 and 20 Feb. 1809, BA P 325/2633-50.

106 Wainwright and Smith to Bombay, including substance of discussion with ruler, Muscat Dec.1809, BA P 350/29-36. The ruler of Muscat complained in April 1810 that the British expedition had 'involved him in a perpetual and implacable war with the Wahhabis with whom he was before at peace': Smith to Warden, with enclosure, Muscat 14 April 1810, BA P 355/2212-26.

107 The Supreme Government (Lord Minto and others) wrote in April 1809, 'the interest of the British government in the suppression of the pirates is not exclusively of a commercial nature' ... 'the independence of the state of Muscat is of material importance to our interests and the preservation of that independence appears at the moment to turn upon the co-operation of the British power against the Joasmee pirates': Al-Qasimi, *The Myth*, p. 121. This was, of course, essentially Seton's reasoning, transmitted via Malcolm.

108 Kelly, *Britain*, p. 82.

109 The secret Treaty of Finkenstein, signed on 4 May 1807, offered Iran French support over Persian claims to Georgia in return for a number of anti-British concessions. The Peace of Tilsit soon after represented an accommodation between France and Russia. Gardane reached Tehran in December 1807.

110 See Kelly, *Britain*, pp. 78-96; Saldanha, *The Persian Gulf*, vol. 2, pp. 9-21. It was later even stated, though the charge was not apparently pressed and did not, it seems, figure largely in British planning, that Shaikh Sultan of Ras al-Khaima had been 'promised assistance by the French': Al-Qasimi, 'Arab 'Piracy'', Appendix 1, ' A Sketch of the Proceedings ...' (an official account of the first expedition, ?c. 1810).

111 Malcolm referred to 'the fools at home ... [and] their mischievous propensity to interfere with the local government': Kelly, *Britain*, p. 93. The East India Company's sphere of influence was destined to be limited

to the Gulf, centring on Bushire, while Tehran fell to the Foreign Office.

112   Saldanha, *The Persian Gulf*, vol. 2, p. 16.

113   Kelly, *Britain*, pp. 92-3.

114   One account of the first expedition nevertheless includes amongst its supposed results the furtherment of the 'fame of the English power so as to be favourable to the political connection between Great Britain and Persia': Al- Qasimi, 'Arab 'Piracy'', Appendix 1.

115   Troops put on standby at Surat for the Kharg expedition were thus simply transferred to that against Ras al-Khaima: Moyse-Bartlett, *The Pirates*, p. 44.

116   Duncan to ruler of Muscat, Bombay 30 March 1809, in Al-Qasimi, *The Myth*, p. 107. Cf. Coke's 'A pirate is the enemy of the human race', cited in C. Belgrave, *The Pirate Coast* (Librairie du Liban, Beirut, 1960), p. 121.

117   In consequence Sadleir was sent on his well-known mission to seek the goodwill and assistance of Ibrahim Pasha. The mission was, however, a miscalculation indicative of the measure of understanding Bombay then possessed of the politics of the peninsula. See A.M. Abu Hakima, *Ta'rikh al-Kuwait*, vol. 2, part 1 (Kuwait Government Press, Kuwait, 1393/1973), p. 45; also G.F. Sadleir, *Diary of a Journey Across Arabia (1819)* (Falcon-Oleander, Naples, 1977).

118   Nepean to Hastings, Bombay 22 Sept. 1818, (Minutes 20/11 Jan. 1819), BA Sel. 74.

119   See Kelly, *Britain*, pp. 57-61. Kelly argues that the assumption of the position of Mogul Admiral by the Commodore in 1759 could have brought with it a legal duty to protect Indian shipping.

120   Al-Qasimi, 'Arab 'Piracy'', Appendix 1.

121   In essence this could reflect either changes in the Gulf and Cutch/Kathiawar, or else it might simply reflect the reporting, or, indeed, some combination of the two.

122   As opposed to the 'misconduct and atrocious acts' of the pirate: Duncan to ruler of Muscat, Bombay 30 March 1809, in Al-Qasimi, *The Myth*, p. 107.

123   The official instructions to the two commanders of the first expedition expressed the hope that success in the enterprise would be conducive to 'the general good and to the relief of the commercial world against these irreclaimable pests to the general prosperity': Warden to Wainwright and Smith, Bombay 7 Sept. 1809, Al-Qasimi, *The Myth*, p. 133.

124   In Taylor's history of Bahrain, following Nepean to Hastings, Bombay 22 Sept. 1818, BA Sel.74; Bruce to Nepean, Bushire 20 Aug. 1819, BA Sel. 75.

125   Cf. one particularly stern, authoritative-sounding, almost apocalyptic account of the first expedition which makes claim, in relation to the alleged Qasimi piracy, that, 'It must be deemed an act of the soundest policy, as well as the most enlightened philanthropy, to crush in its bud an evil of such alarming magnitude': Al-Qasimi, 'Arab 'Piracy'', Appendix 1, 'A sketch of the proceedings of the British armament which sailed from Bombay in September 1809 for the purpose of destroying the vessels of the Joasmee pirates in the Gulf of Persia'.

126   E.g. the circumstances of Bahrain's admission to the General Treaty in 1820, and note, for example, Warden's comments in 1819: Minute by Warden, Bombay Council 16 July 1819, BA S&P 312/1102-3.

127 'It is vain to expect any restitution or redress from these lawless banditti who show such little regard or respect to the laws established by all civilised communities': Bruce to Warden, Angar Sound 28 Nov. 1816, in Minutes for 20 Dec. 1816, BA P 432/2435-40. Bruce frequently uses the term 'lawless' in respect of the Qawasim.

128 Bruce, reporting a conversation with Rahma bin Jabir, 'Piracy was what we meant and would not admit him or any other chieftain in the Gulf to commit [it]': Bruce to Bombay, Bushire 2 Feb. 1820, BA S&P 480/1701-3.

129 Adjectives such as 'ferocious and bloodthirsty' are not uncommon: Lt. Davidson to Money, HCC *Fury*, Bushire Roads 22 Jan. 1809, BA P 323/1956-8.

130 Nepean to Hastings, Bombay 22 Sept. 1818, in Minutes for 20/11 Jan. 1819, BA Sel. 74. The legal justification for each of the two expeditions was the infraction of agreements by the Qawasim to respect the British flag: this placed them 'unequivocally in the condition of public enemies' and might also have been referable to the 'admitted principle of self-defence': Adam to Warden, Fort William 22 Feb. 1817, BA S&P 312/1018-22, (BA Sel. 74).

131 The instructions to the commanders of the first expedition refer to the *Sylph*, the *Darya Doulut* and the *Minerva*. Those of 1819 refer to the *Darya Doulut* and another vessel carrying Company troops. Fort William stressed the importance of the *Ahmadi* in the breakdown of relations in 1817. Al-Qasimi, *The Myth*, p. 130. Adam to Bombay, Fort William 22 Feb. 1817, BA S&P 312/1018-22, (BA Sel. 74). Orders to Major-General Keir, Bombay 27 Oct. 1819, Minutes 27 Oct., BA Sel. 76.

132 An escaped tindal in 1815 reported at Porbandar that the 'Qawasim put their Muhammadan prisoners to death by knocking out their brains with a hatchet or with a hammer. They cut the flesh off the bones into small pieces...': Elwood to Carnac (Baroda Resident), Porbandar 31 Jan. 1815, BA P 420/440-1.

133 Colquhoun, Bombay 21 May 1819, in Minutes for 21 July, BA S&P 312/973-81.

134 E.g. Sunderjee Sewjee to Nepean, Bombay 17 Nov.1818, BA Sel. 72/578-9.

135 Heude, *A Voyage*, p. 39.

136 Malcolm: 'the late insulting and atrocious conduct of these freebooters'. Manesty: 'a very considerable degree of national dishonour attaches itself to the circumstances of Arabs having dared to retard the progress of an English vessel'. Bruce: 'atrocities which it would be impossible to overlook consistent with what is due to our national character and situation'. Cf. Wainwright of Shaikh Sultan's having had 'the audacity to demand a tribute ... to allow British ships to navigate the Persian Gulf in safety'. Brigadier General Malcolm to Warden, Bombay 15 Dec. 1808, BA S&P 255/14393-7. Manesty to Bombay, Basra 8 July 1797, BA S&P 57/1539-46. Bruce to Newnham, Bushire 25 May 1819, BA Sel. 73. Captain Wainwright to Bombay, *La Chiffone*, off Muscat Khyma 14 Nov. 1809, BA P 347/11164-5.

137 President's Minute, 26 Sept. 1819, Minutes for 29 Sept. 1819, BA Sel. 75.

138 General orders by Lt.Col. Smith, *La Chiffone*, Ras al-Khaima 14 Nov. 1809, BA P 347/11174-5.

139 Bruce uses phrases such as 'lawless freebooters, lawless plunderers,

lawless vagabonds, lawless Asiatic Algerines, inhuman barbarians and the bloody avaricious merchants of Ras al-Khaima', and claims they display 'perfidy and vice' and a 'contempt for moral principles'. Some of this bluster has an obvious nautical feel to it: Bruce to Hasan bin Rahma, November 1816, BA Sel. 72/99-104, and BA *passim*.

140   Bruce to Bombay, Bushire 16 Nov. 1816, BA Sel. 73.

141   Both were Residents at Basra.

142   Bruce to Warden, with enclosures, 29 Nov. and 2 Dec. 1816, BA P 432/2435-58.   Fort William, whilst admitting the inevitability of the outcome of this mission, still regretted the extreme nature of Bruce's rupture, fearing it might make matters still worse: Adam to Bombay, Fort William 22 Feb. 1817, 312/1018-22.   Bruce had also been offended by the seizure at Ras al-Khaima of his vessel in 1814, a vessel sent in the hope of reaching an agreement with the Qawasim.

143   For this he was censured by the Court of Directors, Saldanha, *Gazetteer*, vol. 1, part 1A, pp. 160-1.

144   General orders by Lt.Col. Smith, *La Chiffone*, Ras al-Khaima 14 Nov. 1809, BA P 347/11175-6.

145   Manesty to Bombay, near Basra 4 Aug. 1802, BA S&P 127/5133-51 (5144).

146   Smith, Bushire Resident, to Bombay, Bushire 1 Nov. 1798, Saldanha, *The Persian Gulf*, vol. 1, pp. 350-1.

147   E.g. Al-Qasimi, *The Myth*, p. 136. Elwood, Porbandar Agent, remarks, 'The coolness of the pirates when within the range and fire of cannon, the excellence in engagement of their vessels, system and resolution, has surprised and called forth the admiration of the naval commanders': Elwood to Warden, Porbandar 12 Jan. 1819, in Minutes for 21 January, BA Sel. 73.

148   Referred to, for example, by Bruce, Smith (commander of the first expedition) and Taylor: as, Taylor's account of these ports in BA Sel. 74. Cf. bin Croosh in Al-Qasimi, *The Myth*, pp.78-9.

149   Warden wrote that the prevalence of piracy in the Gulf 'may be attributed wholly and exclusively to the instigation of the Wahhabi tribe. Under that impression I feel disposed in some degree to advocate the cause even of the Joasmee tribe and to palliate their enormities': paragraph 20 of Warden's Minute of 12 Aug. 1819, Bombay, BA Sel. 77. The contrary argument, of course, tended to imply that there was something in their disposition that led them to piracy.   Wahhabi influence had also been acknowledged by Bruce in 1814, Al-Qasimi, *The Myth*, pp. 178-9.

150   Warden: 'The result of my researches has established the important fact that piracy is not indigenous to the soil or the shores of the Persian Gulf, but of recent growth; on the contrary, every tribe is rather disposed to engage in commercial pursuits.' Cf. Nepean: [contemporary naval and military officers] 'so far from thinking they are disposed to quit their present predatory habits ... consider their present habits so deeply rooted that nothing but the strong hand of power will keep them down.' : paragraph 3 of Warden's Minute of 12 Aug. 1819, BA Sel. 77; Nepean's Minute of 6 Sept. 1819, BA Sel. 75.

151   Saldanha, *The Persian Gulf*, vol. 1, pp. 268-73. Moore had previously, it

seems, entertained a personal animosity towards Husain Khan's overlord, Karim Khan-e Zand. The specific cause of his anger was Husain Khan's seizure of British ships. From labelling him 'pirate', he proceeds to impugn his humanity and his morals, and claims that 'Hosain Khan is most commonly intoxicated with liquor; ... his people are very poor and mutinous ...they constantly go armed and it is with great difficulty that he can keep them in order'.

152   'From these troubles partly this Gulf is in great confusion. The Imam continues at war with Shaikh Rashid. Shaikh Abdullah of Hormuz is at war with the people of Charak, as is also Shaikh Saqr of al-Haram with the Tamia people [?], which latter place the former has burnt. The Zubara and Grain people are at war with the Kaʿb, and Bandar Rig was a few days ago accidentally consumed by fire': Saldanha, *The Persian Gulf*, vol. 1, pp 315-6.

153   Cf. also the lessons of Manesty's earlier personal quarrel with the Jews of Basra which led to the brief withdrawal of the Residency to Kuwait in 1793: Saldanha, *The Persian Gulf*, vol. 1, pp. 328, 330-2.

154   Cf. the (unrealised) plans discussed by Nepean, Warden and the Bombay Council before the second expedition.

155   Thompson had apparently secured a stock of Arabic bibles. He also successfully secured the use of a mosque as a church whilst in charge of the temporary British garrison at Ras al-Khaima in 1820. Thompson was later especially proud of his having inserted the slaving clause in the General Treaty, 'the earliest declaration to that effect in point of time': Moyse-Bartlett, *The Pirates*, pp. 110-1, 102, 124-5.

156   Moyse-Bartlett, *The Pirates*, pp. 242-3. Mrs. Thompson had been reading Moore's 'Lalla Rookh'.

157   Cited in Al-Qasimi, *The Myth*, pp. 225-9, and other works.

158   Hasan bin Rahma to Bruce, Nov. 1816, BA P 432/2452-3.

159   Bruce to Nepean, Bushire 25 Oct. 1819, BA Sel. 76.

3. OIL IN THE GULF - INTERNAL AND EXTERNAL INTERACTION: PAST, PRESENT AND FUTURE

Peter A. Davies and Paul J. Stevens[1]

1. Introduction

The purpose of this chapter is to examine the contributions and interactions of the three players who have shaped and will continue to shape the Gulf oil industry. The three players are the Gulf producing governments representing internal influences and the consumer governments and oil companies representing external influences. In particular the extent to which the role of the internal and external influences might be characterised as proactive,[2] reactive[3] or passive[4] is examined in terms of the past, present and future of the oil industry.

2. Contributions Prior to 1970

Gulf Producers

The governments of the Gulf provided two elements - access to the geology and the operating environment in which the oil was discovered, developed and produced. The access to the geology came via the granting of the concessions which created the institutional context. There are different views of the driving forces behind the granting of access.[5] One version is that the governments were motivated by an urgent need for revenues and hence invited the oil companies in for the money associated with the granting of the concessions.[6] An alternative view is that the concessions were imposed by means of the influence of the Great Powers either through their position as the Mandate

Powers or by horse-trading between the powers seeking advantage for their oil companies.[7] The Gulf governments were also responsible for setting the oil companies' operating environment. This required (from the companies' perspective) stability and minimal interference. In general this was provided. There were occasions when the governments sought to intervene such as the Iranian nationalisation of 1951, Iraqi Law 80 of 1960 and the Saudi attempt in 1954 to secure tanker preference. However, these attempts were either contained or (in most cases) reversed. Whichever nuance of interpretation is placed upon the position of the Gulf governments in this period, there can be little doubt that their role was essentially passive and reactive. The few occasions reactive assertion was attempted by the internal forces, the external forces simply proved to be too strong.

Consumer Governments

The consumer governments contributed two elements to the international industry in the period before 1970. These were access to markets and (in some cases) protection for their oil companies. Up to the first oil shock of 1973, in the industrialised world at least, the approach of consumer governments was typified by the attitude of leaving it (i.e. the provision of oil) to the oil companies.[8] The perception was that the esoteric nature of the business meant it was best left to the experts despite the few lone voices such as Paul Frankel who saw oil as 'too important to leave to the oilmen'.[9] The consequence was that with the exception of the USA which had its own agenda,[10] most of the industrialised world placed little or no restrictions upon the movement of oil and oil products.[11] The main exceptions to this generalisation of passive acceptance were a number of Third World countries where the activities of the multinational corporations were coming under increasing scrutiny and in many cases increasing control.[12] The second contribution from the consumer governments was protection of their own oil companies. This protection was of two types. The first, predominantly in the pre-World War II period, was when the US and French governments pressured the British government to provide access for their own companies in the concessions in the region. This was a key reason for the joint control of Gulf oil production which characterised the 1950s and 1960s.[13] Equally, the British government sought to protect the interests of its own companies, although much less than their 51 per cent equity in Anglo-Persian/Anglo-Iranian might have suggested.[14] In general, with the notable exception of the Iranian problems of 1951-4, after 1945, such paternal interest appeared to decline. It was however replaced by the growing interest of other industrialised countries in promoting their own oil companies as a counter-balance to the perceived power of the Majors.[15] Thus a number of countries created and encouraged their own companies to involve themselves in the oil business.[16] In general, the contribution of the consumer governments was a mixture of a passive role (leave it to the companies) and a reactive role (support the companies).

The Oil Companies

The oil companies' contribution was the key proactive ingredient of the period and consisted of a number of elements.[17] First was the contribution of technology. This contribution was more than the provision of engineering technology to find and develop the oil.[18] Of even more importance was the whole logistical and managerial provision for the total operation in environments which had (apart from oil) absolutely nothing. Often the companies were responsible for creating whole economic infrastructures. For example, in the early days in Saudi Arabia, for every dollar spent upon the actual above ground producing equipment, two dollars had to be spent upon basic support facilities simply to keep the labour force alive and functioning.[19] The second contribution was the provision of finance. Throughout the period prior to 1970, the industry was generally self-financing.[20] Given the large foreign exchange content of much of the investment required this was important in the early stages before a cash flow was established. In other countries which attempted to develop the oil industry alone foreign exchange finance proved to be a major constraint.[21] The third contribution from the oil companies was the provision of downstream access. From the early days, the industry was vertically integrated. In 1950, the seven Majors accounted for 72 per cent of refinery throughput outside of the Communist bloc and North America and by the mid-sixties this figure was still 61 per cent.[22] Production of crude oil in a world where there was excess capacity to produce crude oil was not necessarily of itself an attractive economic activity.[23] As the Iranians found to their cost after 1951, downstream access was crucial if crude production was to generate revenue.

The final, and most important, contribution of the oil companies in this period was overall control of the market. In an industry characterised by chronic over-capacity (most of it located in the Gulf region) control of that excess capacity was crucial if the pricing structure was to be protected. Through a combination of vertical and horizontal integration the oil companies were able to orchestrate supply.[24] To be sure, this orchestration was not always welcomed by the Gulf countries. In a period when the only way to increase total revenue was to increase volume, production restraint met with inevitable hostility from the governments. However, had the governments been left to their own devices there is little doubt that the result would have been a series of ultimately damaging price wars.[25]

In this period, the companies' proactive role was the crucial contribution in the development of the international industry. For the Gulf, the external influences were the active forces while internal factors were generally passive and, where active, were so only as a reaction to outside influences.

3. Consequences of the Contributions Prior to 1970

The first consequence of the interactions of these external and internal forces was that the world's growing needs for energy were met. In 1950 the average world consumption of commercial energy was 1 tonne of coal equivalent per head. By 1973 this had almost exactly doubled. This need for ever more energy which reflected rising living standards was met increasingly by the provision of oil at declining real prices.[26] In 1950, oil accounted for 27 per cent of the world's consumption of primary energy. By 1973 this share had risen to 46 per cent.[27] By any standards this was an impressive achievement.

The second consequence of the interaction was that there emerged in the Gulf economies increasingly dominated by oil. Some indication of this domination is outlined in Table 3.1.

Table 3.1: The Role of Oil in the Gulf Economies

| | Oil revenue as a percentage of government revenue | | Oil exports as a percentage of total exports | |
	1967	1973	1967	1973
Iran	49	63	91	92
Iraq	57	74	90	92
Kuwait	87	85	97	92
Saudi Arabia	90	93	89	99

Source: D.G. Edens, *Oil and Development in the Middle East* (Praeger, New York, 1979).

The consequences of this domination by oil for the sustainable economic development of the Gulf are extremely controversial.[28] However, whatever the long-term consequences may be, there can be little doubt that in the short term at least the living standards of many ordinary people improved as a result of the development of oil. Table 3.2 illustrates some of the more conventional development indicators.

Table 3.2: Development Indicators of Selected Countries

| | Infant Mortality | | Male Life Expectancy | |
	1965	1987	1965	1987
Iran	154	65	52	62
Iraq	121	69	51	63
Saudi	150	71	47	62
Kuwait	66	19	61	71
UAE	108	26	55	69
OECD	24	9	68	73

Source: World Bank, *World Development Report 1989*.

The final consequence of these interactions was that the oil companies grew and prospered. In 1962, the net worth of the seven Majors in the eastern hemisphere had reached $9.4 billion. By 1972, this figure had risen to $19.9 billion.[29] However, the rewards were not excessive. Taking the five US Majors between 1952 and 1972, the stockholders' average rate of return was 12.5 per cent with a range of 11.4-13.7 per cent. This may be compared with the Standard and Poor's 500-stock composite index average for the same period of 15.6 per cent.[30] During the

1960s, the oil companies' prosperity began to be squeezed through a combination of increased competition forcing down crude prices coupled with the effective fixing of the governments' tax-take following the creation of OPEC in 1960.[31] In 1962, the return on net worth in the eastern hemisphere for the seven Majors averaged 13.1 per cent. By 1972, this had reduced to 10 per cent[32] giving rise to concern that in future the oil industry would be less able to pursue self-financing.

Thus the consequences of the interaction of internal and external influences were that all parties gained. There was (and still is) debate over the distribution of these gains. Nonetheless, the system delivered some degree of benefit to all.

4. The Development and Alteration of the Relationships 1970-1989

The relationships and interactions which developed in the Gulf in the 1950s and 1960s changed dramatically in the 1970s and 1980s. The history is well known and has been extensively documented.[33]

Three main features of the period after 1970 are clear. The first was the switch in control by means of participation and nationalisation which occurred between 1972 and 1976.[34] Initially, this meant the producer governments took over the decision on production levels. Despite this, the oil companies retained their crude selling role until the second oil shock of 1979-80 when this role too was taken over by the producer governments.[35]   The second feature of the period was a succession of revenue shocks. These occurred partly as a result of the price shocks of 1973, 1979-80 and 1986 but also because of fluctuations in production levels for a number of the Gulf countries, a consequence of the control which had devolved to the governments.[36] The final feature of the period was the rush to secure economic development in the Gulf with oil perceived as the leading development sector.

These features of the period signalled that the internal forces in the Gulf had become proactive and the external forces had become either passive or merely reactive. These changes were an inevitable consequence of the exertion of sovereignty by the governments.

The consequences of the changes for the three parties were significant. The oil producers gradually expanded their knowledge base in terms of both technology and general management skills.[37] They also took control of upstream operations and with it the crucial role as controller of the market when surplus capacity began to reassert itself following 1973. The oil companies on the other hand lost their traditional access to much equity crude oil. With this loss of control over production levels they also lost much of their power.[38] Finally, the consumer governments lost confidence in the ability of the oil companies to carry out their task[39] unsupervised. Part of the reason the price increase in 1973 was a shock in the OECD was that in many cases governments simply did not understand what was happening.[40] The tendency of the governments to leave oil to the oilmen prior to 1970 meant that within governments there was very limited knowledge of the international oil industry.[41] It was this ignorance which compounded the shock. The companies were treated with suspicion and in general it became apparent that the consumer governments were less than willing to leave their oil supplies entirely in the hands of the oil companies.[42] Indeed during the 1970s and 1980s, the main consumer governments transferred their traditional role as 'protectors' to the oil producing governments via various forms of military assistance. This ranged from support of the Shah in the 1970s to their involvement in the 'tanker war'.[43]

5. Forces Affecting the Gulf Oil Industry in the 1990s

The world and the oil industry in the Gulf are set to enter a new structural phase in the 1990s. New forces are likely to drive the industry and once again result in a different balance between internal and external forces in the region. Furthermore, the balance within the Gulf industry is also likely to change.

The world oil industry is in the process of entering a new cyclical phase in the 1990s. The 1980s, in particular, were a period of excess supply in almost all stages of the industry, with the notable exception of oil development and production outside OPEC. The effect of the high oil prices experienced through to the early 1980s was a decline in demand for oil and rising non-

OPEC production.   Between 1979 and 1983, oil product consumption in the non-Communist world fell from 50 million barrels per day to a trough of 43 million barrels per day by 1983; only by 1989 did consumption recover to the 1979 level.[44] As for non-OPEC supply, from a level of 16.3 million barrels per day in 1975 it rose to a peak of 25.3 million barrels per day in 1988.[45]

A number of consequences followed from these trends. Surplus production capacity within OPEC rose to an estimated 17 million barrels per day peak in 1985.[46] Of this, 85 per cent was located in the Gulf as non-Gulf OPEC members were less willing to reduce production to protect the price of oil. Within the Gulf, Iraq, Iran and Dubai all tended to produce at full capacity - or at least the maximum that they could physically export. Saudi Arabia continued to play the role of swing producer up until the mid-1980s but after summer 1985 became more concerned about market-share and revenues. Investment in crude production capacity in the Gulf virtually ceased during the 1980s[47] and, often, existing production facilities were cannibalised. The largest upstream investments were in Iraqi export pipelines through Turkey and Saudi Arabia.[48] These were needed following the closure of Iraq's Gulf seaports at the beginning of the Iraq-Iran war plus the closure of the Iraq-Syria pipeline in 1982. Oil-tanker surpluses increased as a result of the decline in demand for oil, the heavy building programme in the early 1970s and the development of some production closer to consuming markets notably in Western Europe. Refining excess capacity rose to a peak of 35 per cent in 1982 as a result of the fall in demand[49] and the capacity expansion of the late 1960s and early 1970s. Refinery investment in the 1980s tended to be in upgrading capacity (transportation demand continued to grow while fuel oil demand slumped) and in the fast-growing economies of the Third World.

By 1990 the cycle has turned in almost all sectors. Surplus capacity within OPEC has begun to decline. OPEC production in early 1990 temporarily touched 24 million barrels per day with most estimates of sustainable capacity in the 26-8 million barrels per day range. This has followed from the renewed growth of oil demand together with stagnation of oil production outside OPEC. The tanker surplus is eroding fast in the face of rising oil demand and a renewed demand for long-haul shipments from the Gulf. This capacity erosion will be reinforced by the fact that the tanker fleet is aging and much of the capacity expansion of the early 1970s may be reaching the end of its safe operating life.[50] Excess refining capacity has shrunk. Capacity is tight in the US where new product specifications are causing problems and new refineries are being commissioned in East Asia.

Thus the 1990s will be a period of investment in all sectors of the oil industry as demand for oil continues to grow and non-OPEC supply is constrained. The role of the Gulf producers will be critically affected by this and they may well be forced back into a reactive rather than a proactive role. They face the need to invest in new production capacity if they are to be able to supply the world markets with oil at prices that are not so high as to restimulate massive substitution away from oil as occurred in the early 1980s. Only the Gulf states (plus Venezuela) will be in a position to supply the oil the world seems certain to want. In addition, to the extent that the Gulf producers wish to participate in downstream activities located either within or outside the Gulf, there will also be the opportunity to invest in new capacity in global shipping and refining.

The world will also be changing in other ways which may force the Gulf producers into a more reactive role. In the late 1980s, it has become evident that concern over the environment has become a key and increasingly important force that will affect the oil sector in the 1990s. This will affect the Gulf in a number of ways. It will limit the growth in demand for oil. Responses to the desires for cleaner air, and fears about the greenhouse effect, will probably lead to the introduction of taxes and regulations that will temper the demand for oil. This will limit the growth in demand for Gulf oil but, with non-OPEC output constrained, it is unlikely to lead to an absolute decline in demand for Gulf crude unless oil prices surge. Environmental concerns will create an ever-increasing dislike for sulphurous (sour) crudes. The availability of sweet Gulf is limited. This will place Gulf oil at a continual disadvantage and force price discounts in the market. In the second quarter of 1990 Iran and Iraq have been reported to have found it problematic to sell sour crudes in a 'buyers' market'. This tendency will inevitably increase. There will be a rising demand for gas which is seen as more environmentally benign than oil. This will generate the demand for new LNG projects and possibly also for the first gas pipelines from the Gulf to consumer markets.

In addition to the environment it is probable that security of supply will become an increasingly important issue in consuming countries. US oil imports in 1990 are above 50 per cent of demand, having fallen to 34 per cent in 1983.[51] With US oil production in both the lower 48 states and in Alaska in inevitable decline, US import dependency is set to rise. Dependency on the Gulf is also set to increase in Europe and East Asia. Recently, the perception of the Middle East as an unstable region has grown and the Gulf states face the challenge of reassuring consumers that Gulf supplies are secure.

These new forces which will characterise the oil industry in the 1990s will create a very different context in which internal and external forces will interact. In addition, the internal forces in the Gulf will themselves be very different in the 1990s.

6. Contributions in the 1990s

Gulf Producers

From the 1950s through into the 1980s, the Gulf oil industry could, as a realistic approximation, be classified as a single generic group with a similar history of involvement with the international industry. This general approximation will no longer be valid for the 1990s. The Gulf industry can now be split into two, possibly three different groups. The first group is the New Rich Sisters. These are Saudi Arabia and Kuwait who have substantial oil reserves, adequate financial capacity, a national oil sector with little foreign involvement[52] and nascent downstream activities outside their borders.[53] The second group is the Financially Constrained. These are Iraq and Iran who have substantial undeveloped oil resources and an oil sector with no foreign involvement. However, they are financially constrained from effecting major investment programmes on their own. Finally, there are the Small Nation Companies which include Abu Dhabi, Qatar and Oman.[54] These have significant hydrocarbon resources but are likely to be constrained in developing them on their own, largely as a result of the need for external technical assistance.

The basic response to the 1990s' need for additional Gulf crude will be the same throughout the Gulf: invest in order to supply the demand. The reasons for this response will be similar for each player. Oil and gas reserves are available, although in many cases they will need to be developed or restored. If one producer does not invest, another will. Accordingly all Gulf producers are likely to invest to prevent declining market shares and weakening regional power. However, the New Rich Sisters are also motivated by the desire to see oil prices remaining at a reasonable level, a motivation which is less strong in some other states.

The New Rich Sisters are also likely to be more self-sufficient in the areas of management, finance and markets. They are likely to wish to continue to manage their own industry themselves.[55] There will be only a limited role for foreign assistance, through selective expatriate contract workers and oil service companies. Overall, management will remain in domestic hands. Equally, they are likely to provide their own financial funding for investment either within or outside their countries. Kuwaiti external financial resources are estimated at $75 billion[56] while Saudi Arabia's have declined.[57] This follows the current account deficits which have characterised the 1980s. However, lack of external finance is unlikely to be a constraint on Saudi Arabian investment plans.[58] As for markets, in the light of their forays into the international downstream oil business, the New Rich Sisters will, to some extent, provide their own refineries and retail markets in the 1990s. This is a significant change. As of 1989 it is estimated that 63 per cent of Kuwaiti oil was refined in its own network while 38 per cent of Saudi oil went through their own refineries.[59] Further international investments have been signalled by both countries although the share of output could however drop as production could easily rise more quickly than downstream outlets.

The New Rich Sisters are thus expected to react to the changing international situation by investing and remaining independent of the international oil companies. In this way, their role may continue to be proactive rather than become reactive and as such their actions will be the strongest determinant of the outlook for the world oil markets in the 1990s.

The other players - the Financially Constrained and the Small Nation Companies - will not be in such a powerful and independent situation. They will be passive or at best reactive.

Iran is likely to face serious financial constraints and is unlikely to be able to have the required technological capability to restore production capacity that existed pre-1979.[60]   The political uncertainty which currently typifies the Iranian situation is likely to make it difficult for the entry of foreign oil companies. Iraq is also seriously financially constrained following the burden of the Iraq-Iran war. It will be difficult to mobilise the financial resources to develop its proven reserves. In early 1990 it offered a fixed per-barrel fee to oil companies willing to develop proven oil reserves at their own expense. To date no deals have been concluded. Finally, in Abu Dhabi, it is probable that the foreign equity partners in ADMA and ADCO will continue to provide Abu Dhabi with technical and management assistance.

Consumer Governments

Consumer nations will continue to provide the markets that oil producers require to generate their oil revenues. However, demand will tend to be less concentrated in Western industrialised nations.   Oil demand forecasts point to little expected growth in oil demand in the industrialised nations with the greatest increase in demand occurring in the newly industrialising countries. This will dissipate slightly the power of consumers over producers.   Production will become more concentrated and consumption less concentrated.   This is traditionally a key shift from a buyers' to a sellers' market.

The attitudes of the major consumer governments undertook a shift in the 1980s as they sought to ensure security of supply by supporting many of the regimes in the Gulf states through military assistance. While the Cold War dimension of this link has now all but evaporated and the impetus from the Gulf War is in suspension, the support will probably continue (with consumer import-dependency growing) as long as the Gulf producer states are committed to supply the oil that the consumers want at affordable prices. Present indications are that this will continue for the foreseeable future.

Consumer governments also see that security of supply is being enhanced by producer government oil companies investing downstream in consuming countries. This financial commitment by producers is seen as likely to reduce the risk of a producer-induced supply interruption. Japan has been the exception to this trend so far.[61] Statements by Gulf producer governments indicate that such links are likely to get closer in the future and to spread into East Asian newly industrialising nations.

Finally, the rise in environmentalism will tend to put some power back into consumer government hands. Voters in consuming countries are implicitly requesting their governments to raise taxes on fossil fuels such as oil and to introduce regulations to inhibit its use. Producers will be on the defensive, fearful of yet a greater share of the consumer price of energy accruing to consumer governments. There will always be a risk that at some stage producers consider that consumers are keeping an unfair proportion of the scarcity rent of oil.

The Oil Companies

The major, and other large, oil companies continue to offer a significant contribution, although as far as the Gulf is concerned it will be essentially a passive role.[62] The contribution remains much the same as before 1970 with one crucial difference. The companies still have a great deal of technology to offer. In recent years there have been major developments in upstream technology concerning computer control of reservoirs, horizontal drilling, sub-sea completion etc. Also, many of the Majors still have a good knowledge of the Gulf fields. The companies still have access to risk capital for investment both upstream and downstream. Finally, they also can provide access to the downstream of the industry, either conventionally as refiners and marketers or by means of downstream-asset sales or alliances via joint ventures.

These offerings are valuable to each group of producer companies. The New Rich Sisters will continue to seek new downstream assets and access. The Financially Constrained will be seeking risk capital and possibly technology and management skills. The Small Nation Companies will continue to need the skills of the companies to assist them in running their industries efficiently. The crucial difference from the pre-1970 period is that the oil companies no longer provide the control of the market. They are now very much the passive players.

7. Consequences of the Contributions - Outlook for the Gulf Oil Industry

If the aims of all three parties are achieved in the 1990s, this will involve stable oil markets and oil prices, together with higher oil production throughout the Gulf.   There will be selective oil-company re-entry upstream on a risk-basis into previously   inaccessible   countries   plus   further   moves downstream especially by the New Rich Sisters.   Finally the industry might see closer producer/consumer government dialogue over supply security and environmental policies.   At the moment this appears to be the most likely path for the 1990s.

However there are risks which could produce a different outcome.   Past experience in the Gulf has shown that the expected does not always occur.   There are a number of key risks to the 'most likely outlook' cited above.   These include a political event that will interrupt the supply of Gulf oil to consumers either briefly or for a longer period.   There is also the possibility that the investment plans of the producer states will not allow sufficient oil to be supplied at steady prices.   This could occur for a   number   of   reasons   including   technical,   financial   and managerial.   Projected capacity expansion may be too little, too late.   A   consumer   commitment   to   substantially   stricter environmental policies at an earlier date than expected would cut demand and result in excess capacity re-emerging in the Gulf.   Finally, protectionism in trade and/or investment could develop, especially if the current GATT process fails to deliver a workable   agreement.   This   could   limit   producer   access   to consumer markets for oil and petrochemical products.

Any of these factors could weaken the closer and more harmonious relations that are otherwise expected.   The likely emergence   of   a   closer   and   more   co-operative   relationship between all three sets of players in the Gulf oil industry appears to imply a move to a more balanced set of interactions.   The key assumption behind this view of the future is that the key producers - essentially Saudi Arabia and Kuwait - both have long-run strategic goals which seek relatively low and stable oil prices   arising   from   fears   of   renewed   substitution   and conservation of oil if prices rise or are expected to be volatile.

However, the crucial element in the 1990s is that the New Rich Sisters have the ability to determine the future of the industry and the market by taking a proactive role.

Postscript

When this chapter was presented at the conference in July 1990, the authors put much stress on their belief in Murphy's Law - 'If it can go wrong, it will go wrong'. Subsequent events - the invasion of Kuwait by Iraq and the consequent military build-up in the region - proved this belief to be well founded. The 'political event that will interrupt the supply of Gulf oil', which this chapter identified as a 'key risk', has come to pass. At the time of writing this postscript (mid-December 1990) it is far too early to tell how much of the chapter's view of the 1990s will need to be revised. Revision will be a function of the outcome of the crisis and the route by which that outcome is achieved. The permutations are endless and the uncertainty is great.

The new cyclical phase for the 1990s which would lead to an increasing call on OPEC and the declining excess capacity foreseen in this chapter happened literally overnight as a result of the UN sanctions. So far, the remaining 'New Rich Sister' has shown itself willing and able to meet the call by increasing capacity and producing to that capacity. This however was an essentially reactive rather than a proactive role. Arguably, the other side of the crisis, or reductions in demand from higher prices and lower economic growth, plus new capacity generated by the crisis, will push the anticipated tighter market further into the future than was expected in this chapter. Prices could remain weak for some time. The only point to be made with certainty is that the proactive role anticipated in the 1990s from the two 'New Rich Sisters' was postulated upon the existence of freedom of action for their governments. That freedom has obviously been completely removed from Kuwait at present and somewhat compromised in Saudi Arabia.

Notes

1   Peter Davies is Chief Economist at British Petroleum. Paul Stevens is Senior Lecturer in Economics at the University of Surrey currently on sabbatical with the Economics Unit of British Petroleum. The views expressed in this chapter are the personal views of the authors and do not necessarily reflect the views of British Petroleum.

2   Defined as taking a strategic/tactical lead in order to shape directly the way the industry developed. A proactive role sets the rules of the game to suit the aims of the proactive player.

3   Defined as responding to a proactive policy which implies playing the game according to someone else's rules but possibly being able to bend those rules to constrain the proactive player.

4   Defined as simply being on the same playing field as the proactive and reactive players and being forced to accept rules set by others.

5   M. Kent, 'Developments in British Government Oil Policy in the Inter-War Period', in K.J. Gantzel and H. Mejcher (eds.), *Oil, the Middle East, North Africa and the Industrial State* (Ferdinand Schöningh, Paderborn, 1984); E. Monroe, *Britain's Moment in the Middle East 1914-1956* (Methuen, London, 1965); G.W. Stocking, *Middle East Oil* (Vanderbilt University Press, Nashville, 1970); J. Stork, 'Oil and the Penetration of Capitalism in Iraq', in P. Nore and T. Turner (eds.), *Oil and Class Struggle* (Zed Press, London, 1980).

6   This was certainly the basis for the concession granted in Saudi Arabia in 1933. Socal secured the agreement by paying Maria Theresa gold dollars while the IPC lost the concession through only offering paper: H.St.J.B. Philby, *Arabian Jubilee* (Hale, London, 1952); H.St.J.B. Philby, *Arabian Oil Ventures* (Middle East Institute, Washington, 1964).

7   For a long time it was widely believed that this explained the Iraqi concession of 1932. Subsequent research has cast serious doubt upon this interpretation: C. Davies, 'British Foreign Policy and the Struggle for Middle East Oil 1919-1932', unpublished PhD thesis, University of Edinburgh, 1972. There is however general agreement that the subsequent involvement of the American and French companies in the operating companies was in response to US and French government pressure on the British government.

8   J.E. Hartshorn, *Oil Companies and Governments* (Faber and Faber, London, 1962); A. Sampson, *The Seven Sisters: the Great Oil Companies and the World they Made* (Hodder and Stoughton, London, 1975).

9   I. Skeet (ed.), *Paul Frankel - Common Carrier of Common Sense* (Oxford University Press, Oxford, 1989).

10   C.D. Goodwin, *Energy Policy in Perspective* (The Brookings Institute, Washington, DC, 1981).

11   During the 1950s and 1960s, as outlined below this confidence in the oil companies did not extend to the major companies operating alone.

12   B. Das Gupta, *The Oil Industry in India* (Allen and Unwin, London, 1971); M. Tanzer, *The Political Economy of International Oil and the Underdeveloped Countries* (Temple-Smith, London, 1969).

13   The other reason was the attempts by the oil companies to absorb large oil finds into the market by linking crude short companies with crude long companies.

14   R.W. Ferrier, *The History of the British Petroleum Company: volume 1, The Developing Years 1901-1932* (Cambridge University Press, Cambridge, 1982).

15   Defined to include CFP.

16   Probably the highest profile company in this category was ENI: P. Frankel, *Mattei: Oil and Power Politics* (Faber and Faber, London, 1966).

17   Hartshorn, *Oil Companies*; E.T. Penrose, *The Large International Firm in Developing Countries: The International Petroleum Industry* (Allen and Unwin, London, 1968); L. Turner, *Oil Companies in the International System* (Allen and Unwin, London, 1978).

18   A former Iraqi oil minister once commented that a blind man could have found oil in Mosul since the erosion of the cap rock meant you could literally smell the oil.

19   D.H. Finnie, *Desert Enterprise: The Middle East Oil Industry in its Local Environment* (Harvard University Press, Cambridge, Massachusetts, 1958).

20   Penrose, *The Large International*.

21   Syria provided a classic example of this problem.

22   Department Staff Study, *Implications of Divestiture* (US Department of the Treasury, Washington, DC, 1976).

23   Before the 1960s there was virtually no international market for crude oil. The majority of crude flowed through the integrated affiliates of the oil companies.

24   J.M. Blair, *The Control of Oil* (Macmillan, London, 1977); P. Stevens, 'A Survey of Structural Change in the International Oil Industry 1945-1984', in D. Hawdon (ed.), *The Changing Structure of the World Oil Industry* (Croom Helm, London, 1985).

25   It is worth remembering that the original ideas of Zaki Yamani on participation (which included involvement downstream) were prompted in part by the damaging behaviour of the national oil companies of the producing governments in selling crude in the 1960s: Z. Yamani, 'Participation versus Nationalisation: a Better Means to Survive', in Z. Mikdashi, S. Cleland and I. Seymour (eds.), *Continuity and Change in the World Oil Industry* (Middle East Research and Publishing Centre, Beirut, 1970).

26   The price of crude in 1947 was $10.06 (1988 dollars). Apart from a slight upward trend in the mid-1950s the general trend was downwards reaching $5.48 (1988 dollars) in 1970: BP, *Statistical Review of World Energy* (British Petroleum, London, 1990).

27   C. Robinson, 'The Changing Energy Market: What Can we Learn from the Last Ten Years?', in D. Hawdon (ed.), *The Energy Crisis - Ten Years After* (Croom Helm, London, 1984).

28   H. Beblawi and G. Luciani, *The Rentier State* (Croom Helm, London, 1987); D.G. Edens, *Oil and Development in the Middle East* (Praeger, New York, 1979); A.A. Kubursi, *Oil, Industrialisation and Development in the Arab Gulf States* (Croom Helm, London, 1984); M. Rumaihi, *Beyond Oil: Unity and*

Development in the Gulf (Al Saqi Books, London, 1986); Paul Stevens, 'The Impact of Oil on the Role of the State in Economic Development: a Case Study of the Arab World' (Surrey Energy Economics Centre, University of Surrey, Surrey, 1986).

29   Department Staff Study, *Implications.*

30   E. Mitchell, *US Energy Policy: A Primer* (American Enterprise Institute, Washington, DC, 1974).

31   After 1960, existing posted prices which determined the taxable income for the oil companies became fixed. This effectively fixed the governments' per barrel revenue. The consequent decline in realised price meant that oil-company profits were squeezed.

32   Department Staff Study, *Implications.*

33   L. Drollas and J. Greenman, *Oil - the Devil's Gold* (Duckworth, London, 1989); A.M. El Mokadem, D. Hawdon, C. Robinson, P.J. Stevens, *OPEC and the World Oil Market 1973-1983* (Eastlords Publishing, London, 1984); S.M. Ghanem, *OPEC: The Rise and Fall of an Exclusive Club* (KPI, London, 1986); J.M. Griffin and D.J. Teece *et al.*, *OPEC Behaviour and World Oil Prices* (Allen and Unwin, London, 1982); Hawdon, *The Energy Crisis*; R. Mabro (ed.), *OPEC and the World Oil Market* (Oxford University Press, Oxford, 1986); A. Roncaglia, *The International Oil Market* (Macmillan, London, 1985); I. Seymour, *OPEC: Instrument of Change* (Macmillan, London, 1980).

34   P. Stevens, *Joint Ventures in Middle East Oil 1957-1975* (MEEC, Beirut, 1976).

35   J.E. Hartshorn, 'From Multinational to National Oil: The Structural Change', in the *Journal of Energy and Development*, spring 1980; J.H. Mohnfeld, 'Implications of Structural Change', *Petroleum Economist*, July 1982; Stevens, 'A Survey'.

36   Arguably, both price and volume changes were related to the switch of control.

37   This was a process which really began in the 1960s.

38   The Aramco partners continued to exercise significant power by virtue of their advice to the Saudi Arabian government who in the 1970s took over as swing producer following the demise of the companies' joint control of supply which characterised the 1950s and 1960s.

39   Defined as supplying the needs of the specific country.

40   The classic story concerns Edward Heath's attempt to force Shell and BP to ensure UK supplies and the subsequent refusal of the oil companies as multinationals to agree to such a narrow objective: Sampson, *The Seven Sisters*.

41   James Akins tells the story that when the Federal Energy Agency was first created he received a call for help on the conversion factors used in the industry. They had apparently managed to sort out most of the possible conversion factors but were unable to discover how much a Platts oil gramme weighed!

42   The creation of the International Energy Agency was the first obvious sign of this view.

43   P. Robins, *The Future of the Gulf* (Dartmouth Publishing, Aldershot, 1989). Often this support was extremly covert as for example when the US assisted the Iraqi war effort against Iran by providing satellite pictures.

44 BP, *Statistical Review.*
45 BP, *Statistical Review.*
46 BP, *Statistical Review*; CIA, *International Energy Statistical Review* (1985).
47 This was not the case in Oman and some of the emirates.
48 In the 1980s there was significant investment in downstream refining and petrochemicals both domestically (mainly Saudi Arabia) and abroad (mainly Kuwait).
49 BP, *Statistical Review.*
50 This tendency will be speeded up if the recent spate of tanker accidents leads to more stringent regulation of tankers and their operation.
51 BP, *Statistical Review.*
52 Saudi Arabia has foreign involvement only in its export refineries and petrochemicals sector.
53 Kuwait Petroleum International (KPI) has 100%-owned activities in Denmark, Netherlands, Italy, UK etc. which it acquired from Gulf, BP etc. Saudi Arabia entered into a joint venture with Texaco in December 1988 in the southern United States.
54 This group could also be seen to include Bahrain, Dubai and the northern emirates.
55 There is an important distinction here between Kuwait and Saudi Arabia when it comes to downstream investment abroad. Kuwait insists upon full ownership and control while Saudi Arabia is more interested in joint-venture arrangements.
56 Based upon data from the International Monetary Fund, *International Financial Statistics.*
57 Recent estimates place Saudi official reserves at around $50 billion, although not all of this is liquid.
58 International banks would almost certainly be willing to provide substantial financing for capacity expansion if approached.
59 For Kuwait two-thirds were refined domestically, one-third refined abroad. For Saudi Arabia, the proportions are similar.
60 Iranian reservoirs were at the point of requiring gas reinjection in 1978. This was not undertaken. Some reservoirs have been irreparably damaged; others require advanced technology.
61 In 1985 Kuwait's proposed purchase of Getty Oil's 50% share in Mitsubishi Oil Company was unsuccessful. Japanese discussions with a range of Gulf producers have so far failed to conclude any joint venture or Gulf participation in Japan.
62 Arguably, in the new Frontier Areas of the world the companies' role will be more proactive.

4. REPATRIATION, REMITTANCES AND REUNIONS; WHAT IS REALLY AT STAKE FOR ARAB COUNTRIES SUPPLYING LABOUR TO THE GULF CO-OPERATION COUNCIL STATES?[1]

J.S. Birks and C.A. Sinclair

INTRODUCTION: LABOUR-EXPORTING STATES MUST LOOK TO THE FUTURE

Rather than speculate over the present interests of labour-suppliers to the Gulf Co-operation Council states (GCC) of Bahrain, Kuwait, Oman, Qatar, Saudi Arabia and the United Arab Emirates (UAE), this chapter looks at the dimensions of likely future change. An analysis of what could happen to the labour market is largely the key to how the labour-supplying states (of whom there are about 50 of significance) should evaluate their interests.

This chapter, therefore, updates the GCC labour-market and demographic situation and then looks on into the future. The chapter scans some leading issues in labour-importing countries. The influence of these on evolving policy, with background economic projections, indicate aspects of the future scale of external supplies of labour to the GCC economies. This future labour-market picture shows dimensions of the potential open to labour-supplying countries. In the argument, the emphasis is on the Arab suppliers of labour.

MIGRANT-WORKER MOVEMENT TO THE GCC DURING THE 1980s

Over the past two decades, labour migration to the GCC states has, in reality, not been much constrained by official limits. The main concern of the Arab Gulf governments has been 'development'. Most of the labour demanded by employers in the oil economies has been allowed to enter. Reservations, expressed reticently, concerned an Asian 'invasion', but the easing of labour imports has always reflected economic realities (slowed growth), rather than effective efforts to curb imports of workers because of security or social considerations.

Despite the lessons of experience (earlier, in the Arab Gulf and elsewhere), planners in the GCC viewed migrant workers as temporary, expected to disappear after the 'development phase' was over.

In the 1980s, despite oil-price declines, reductions in development expenditures and contractions in Gross Domestic Product (GDP), migrant communities in the GCC remained. Some experienced small declines in the mid-1980s. But they stayed well established and are now growing again. Even in Oman, hardest hit by the oil-price collapse, recent work permit figures (early 1989) show a net increase in new non-national workers.

UPDATING THE GCC POPULATION PICTURE

Today, the GCC population picture has become confused, rather than elucidated, by the proliferation of secondary sources;[2] many are based on other secondary-sources, rather than drawing on primary data. Errors and myths are compounded and become accepted fact through this process. The demographic picture here is therefore derived from primary sources, not reviewed in detail here, but evaluated in another work by these authors,[3] from which the basic tables in this chapter are drawn. Source-material in receiving countries includes census series (Kuwait and Bahrain), household surveys (Saudi Arabia), establishment surveys (Oman), data-sets on work permits (UAE, Saudi Arabia), social security (Saudi Arabia), births and deaths, as well as economic data. All need both perseverance to extract and rationalisation: some governments have not placed a premium on such information; others will not disseminate it; some 'official estimates' are best thought of as guesses, others deliberate red-herrings. Often, official estimates have assumed a life of their own and have come to be seen as correct.

Sending-country information in the Arab world and Asia is less rich, less reliable, and often consists of 'recorded placements' of migrant workers, an ineffective and redundant index. Interpretation of censuses and non-specific data in sending countries is notoriously difficult.

Even so, the data available to evaluate workforces and population in the GCC is greatly improved. United Nations agencies such as the United Nations Economic Commission for West Asia (UNECWA) and the International Labour Office (ILO), country statistical officers and research by nationals of the region, have produced a series of new data-sets. Commercial interests now regard Arab development seriously, and these in turn have spawned research, for example, by banks and specialist agencies, which greatly enhances the data.

THE CHANGING FLOWS OF NON-NATIONAL WORKERS TO THE GCC

The rapid inflow of migrant workers slowed in the early 1980s; stocks of non-national workers held by employers in the GCC had built up; economic activity eased. Work-permit issues to non-nationals fell (Table 4.1).[4] In Kuwait, for example, non-national worker numbers grew by 16 per cent annually between 1975 and 1980, but by only 6 per cent *per annum* between 1980 and 1985.

Non-national worker and population numbers peaked in the early 1980s (later in Oman). During the mid-1980s, consolidation and some gentle declines in numbers, changing nationality patterns, and a tendency for workers to renew permits rather than be replaced by other workers, became leading characteristics (Table 4.2). These are symptoms of permanency.

Data from the better documented Asian sending-countries also show a decline in new worker out-migration (Table 4.3) in the 1980s. In 1985, though, non-national workers still comprised a large majority of the total GCC employment: the 5.1 million non-nationals amounted to 75 per cent of the region's 6.9 million workers.

THE SIZE OF, AND SOME CHARACTERISTICS OF, NON-NATIONAL COMMUNITIES IN THE GCC: PRESENT DIMENSIONS

Notwithstanding slower migrant-flows in the 1980s, and some associated net-declines, non-nationals in the Gulf have risen remarkably in number over the decade to 1985 (Table 4.4), when they numbered 7.2 million. Larger numbers of non-national workers (5.1 million in 1985) have been joined by more dependants. In 1985, non-nationals were over 45 per cent of the total GCC population of 15.9 million.

The economic-activity rates for Arabs have remained lower than those of the South- or East-Asian communities. Arabs are able to bring in the most dependants; Palestinians, Lebanese, Jordanians and Syrians settle most (Table 4.5). Workers comprise 96 per cent of the East Asian population in the UAE but only 23 per cent of non-national Arabs in Qatar, for example. This differing propensity of non-national ethnic groups to bring families is also evident in the share of children in non-national communities: 0.2 per cent of East Asians in Qatar are aged less than 5 years, compared to 19.8 per cent of non-national Arabs.

Arab groups have the longest duration of residence: 28 per cent of non-national Arabs in Kuwait have lived there for at least 15 years (Table 4.6). With stability, more non-national children are born in these states, namely 75,000 in Saudi Arabia and 22,000 in Kuwait (1986).

Rapid non-national growth through labour migration has transformed into steady growth, with an increased importance in natural increase and family unification (the arrival of dependants from the migrants' source-countries).

FEATURES OF THE LABOUR-IMPORTING STATES THAT AFFECT LABOUR-EXPORTERS OVER THE NEXT FIVE YEARS

A review of some key-issues in labour-importers helps shape the projection of GCC labour-markets and populations.

The Desire for Economic Growth

This desire is still strong in the GCC states. It is driven, most fundamentally, by the rapid national population increase. Increasing numbers of nationals combine with even higher consumer and service aspirations. Less individualistically, the national desire to diversify away from reliance on oil income is still interpreted as a justification for urgent manufacturing and industrial growth.

The Capacity for Rapid Economic Growth

Such capacity, in fiscal and resource terms, remains great for all but a couple of GCC states (Bahrain and Oman). Short-term revenue constraints can be (and are being) overcome by deficit-financing, with a growing confidence in a mid-term hardening oil-price.

Development Strategies

These vary from Saudi Arabia's energy-intensive drive for low-cost leadership in international petrochemicals, and regional engineering, to Dubai's 'Hong Kong replacement strategy'. The former is based on massive energy-resources and subsidies, the latter on the extension of traditional trading in a modern environment with a concentration of banking and support services. Kuwait pursues continued overseas financial and direct investment, with a domestic focus on consumer goods and services. Though the Kuwait 'Harvard strategy' examines national non-national population shares, these and other GCC strategies seek significant economic growth.

All have in common an element of domestic industrialisation and the expansion of domestic services. All rely in practice on the continued import of skilled and unskilled workers. This leads to workforce considerations.

Nationalisation or Localisation of the Workforce

This is an objective commonly held by all oil-rich states, and ideally entails the replacement of all non-nationals in the workforce by nationals. But the reliance on non-national workers is so great, economic expansion is returning to such an extent, and the absolute supply of nationals from the Education and Training System (ETS) is so limited, that, in practice, total replacement of non-nationals is out of the question for years to come.

Occupational Preferences of Nationals

These preferences have held back nationalisation. In practice, nationals only enter occupations if they are: culturally acceptable; high in social status; typically 'modern'; and, critically, have an acceptable 'white collar' physical environment. This selectivity is the result of individuals' rational economic-choices within labour-market policies that concentrated on wealth-distribution, rather than enhancing localisation. Nationalisation, in major 'undesirable' occupational areas, will only be achieved when economic pressures dictate it; there is no sign of this occurring, except in Bahrain and Oman.

Arabisation

Recruitment guidelines relating to nationality are common. Most explicitly, in the UAE, priority in appointments should be given to nationals, then to Arabs, and only then to 'foreigners' (i.e. non-national non-Arabs). This is embodied to some degree in most GCC labour-codes and was intended to mitigate the threat posed by non-Moslems to indigenous cultural values. Arabisation was also to assist nationalisation by widening the use of Arabic, for, throughout the GCC, the private sector is a non-Arab, essentially South and East Asian working-environment. This has indeed become a major constraint on widening nationals' employment-choices.

The Arabisation policy has, in fact, led to competition between national and non-national Arabs for a small group of occupations; both groups seek the same jobs (relatively few non-national Arabs work in the South and East Asian-worker dominated sub-sectors, even in Saudi Arabia). Non-national Arabs are harder for nationals to displace than Asians.

Overall, Arabisation has meant fewer nationals in productive employment and has balked nationalisation. The impetus to 'Arabise' has fallen. However, Arabisation is a frequently voiced policy-theme.

Education, Training, Qualification and Employment of Nationals

Other efforts to overcome nationals' selectivity of employment seek redirection of the ETS towards closer links with the workforce. Past interaction between planners of education and the economic and labour markets was limited, the three groups of planners working in isolation and in contradiction to each other. The need for a close relationship between these three groups of planners, located in different ministries, typically of varied status, and often physically distant from one another, has not always been accepted. When accepted, the relationship has tended to be neither close nor effective.

Past efforts aimed to provide basic education, which was seen as a right, a means of welding the national populations together, and only incidentally as a means of providing an administration for the new states. Industrialisation was not a concern. This shaped the nature of education. Awareness of the need to tailor education and training to economic objectives, to facilitate nationals' replacement of increasingly permanent non-nationals, has grown, but it is a difficult policy to implement. Education and labour-market needs continue out-of-step, fuelling continued labour imports.

The Economic Participation of Women-Nationals

The involvement of such women, who enjoy access to educational facilities unequalled in the developing world, remains limited, despite some increases. A well known recipe for future tensions, females' low effective economic-participation is rather ironically further reduced by policies ensuring generous maternity leave and benefits.

Labour-Importing Policies

These were forged when migrant flows of labour were much smaller (in the 1960s), with surprisingly little evolution. For example, the explicit policy of the priority-employment of nationals in the public sector was established at an early developmental stage, with non-nationals as a result being used to fill the deficit for the private sector. With the weak economic growth of the late 1960s, and little impetus to labour-importing, restrictions at this time (imposed because of security considerations after the 1967 War) artificially appeared effective; false confidence developed in the ability of Gulf governments to control labour immigration. Even today, this remains the case.

De facto immigration-limitation was and is still achieved by the logistical difficulties of processing visas. In fact, the labour-market effects of rapid economic growth have effectively been beyond labour-importing government control. They would be so again. Paradoxes in labour-market policy have consistently reduced effectiveness: wealth distributing policies have reduced economic incentives for nationals, exaggerating labour-imports. Yet there is not a great drive for policy-rationalisation.

Conclusion

Despite some efforts to reduce the number of migrant workers and their families in the GCC states, in practice it has grown rapidly except for short periods following acute economic recession. Indeed, occasionally, policy encouraged the settlement of non-nationals (to boost local property-markets). Such actions, and a lack of will and strategy, have undermined the longer-term efforts to reduce non-national numbers. Overall, the non-national work-forces and associated populations in the GCC will continue to grow. The extent of this growth is demonstrated by the outline projections.

PROJECTION OF NON-NATIONAL PARTICIPATION IN GCC ECONOMIES

The Methodology of Projection[5]

The methodology is straightforward for national populations and workforces, utilising demographic data, and established participation-rates. Estimation of GCC economic growth (dependent as much on the propensity of the GCC governments to borrow as on the price of oil), and consequent labour-requirements lead to conclusions about the share of labour demand that will be filled by nationals. This is difficult in these increasingly complex labour-markets, and needs different models for each GCC state.

The resulting non-national labour-force is apportioned by nationality and then linked, by nationality-specific participation rates and demographic profiles, to non-national populations. For example, the Palestinian community resembles a 'normal' population with large numbers of dependants. Sri Lankans are a composite of housemaids, labourers and medical workers, and they do not have a normal demographic distribution.

Patterns flux because different types of worker, and hence different nationalities, are required at different phases (and, indeed, at different rates) of economic growth. In construction booms, single male migrants of relatively low skill are demanded. But after booms, growth shifts towards services, requiring labour with different characteristics, and usually of different nationalities. In this, a political element of forecasting is important: often, the demands raised by economic growth can overwhelm finely-tuned political objectives; whilst as the economy declines, so political considerations sharpen.

Some Key-Assumptions in the Calculations

The resulting labour-market picture, whilst tentative, indicates likely demographic developments following from probable economic growth. The results are crude, and require further review, but serve to indicate dimensions of the potential for labour-suppliers.

Economic Growth

This is based on a short-term stable oil-price, rising in the mid-1990s (in real terms) at 2 per cent a year. The financing of budget deficits is assumed, as is a continued emphasis on diversification into services and manufacturing. The result is GDP growth to 1995 at about 5 per cent *per annum*, lower than in the late 1970s, and easily attainable with sound economic management. Mild labour-productivity gains are assumed, with some progress being made on the key issues enumerated.

Highlights of the Results

Total Employment

Such employment grows to some 7.7 million by 1995, from 6.8 million in 1985 (Table 4.7). Non-nationals are estimated to account for over 5.4 million workers in 1995. Growth from 1990 is substantial, at an extra 900,000 non-national workers. Under these assumptions, GCC nationals' share of total employment increases, but does not rise above 30 per cent.

Patently, whatever margins of error the projections might embody, a significant and increasing contribution to the economies of the GCC states will be made by non-nationals during the early 1990s. The stocks of migrant workers and non-national populations are set to increase. Interestingly, this increase in non-nationals occurs despite rising unemployment amongst nationals (2.6 per cent in 1985; 5.9 per cent in 1995). There is no sign that policies or economic pressures will remove rigidities in the labour market so as to ameliorate this national unemployment.

Non-National Populations

These fell less rapidly than workforces in the 1980s, and will grow more quickly than non-national workforces in the 1990s; even so they will comprise a decreasing share of the total GCC population in the face of rapid national population growth. In 1995, non-nationals living in the GCC will have increased to 7.6 million from the 1990 figure of 6.4 million (Table 4.8).

This result assumes continued trends in the aggregate family structure of non-nationals, with no major shifts in participation rates or the nationality blend of imported workers. Either a sharply increased use of Asians, or a major new demand for more Arabs, would change this non-national population figure; bringing it, in the case of the former, downwards, and the latter, upwards. But possible shifts of this kind, in aggregate, appear gentler over the next 5 years. Individual nationality numbers, however, will be subject to sharp variations.

Non-National Population by Ethnic Group

In 1995 the Arab and South Asian populations are roughly equal in population terms (though the South Asian workforce is rather larger than the Arab: Table 4.9). The degree to which GCC states allow in dependants varies. Oman has kept dependants out to a greater extent than any other oil-state. Kuwait was relatively relaxed in allowing dependants in, especially Arabs, until about five years ago, when the large number of non-nationals, particularly Arabs, began to concern the authorities. Residence regulations for dependants have now tightened.

Conclusion

Overall, then, in terms of what is at stake, all the labour-supplying countries have the opportunity to increase their participation in the GCC labour-market. Allied to this, for the Arab labour-suppliers, is the likelihood of exporting a larger share of their populations as more dependants gain access to residence in the GCC.

WHO ARE THE LABOUR-EXPORTERS TODAY?

Region of Origin

In 1990, less than a third of the migrant workers in the GCC are Arab (31 per cent: Table 4.10). Almost half of migrant workers are South Asian, and a further 15 per cent are from East Asia. Overall, Asian workers account for 62 per cent of migrant workers in the GCC.

By Nationality

India features as the largest labour-supplier in 1990, with nearly a million migrant-workers (who amount to 21 per cent of the stock in the GCC states). Pakistan ranks second as a labour-exporter with 691,000 (which amounts to 15 per cent of the total of migrant workers). Egypt, the most highly represented Arab state amongst the migrant workers in the GCC, supplies only 11 per cent of the 1990 stock (525,000 migrants). But this is well in excess of the numbers of Jordanians and Palestinians (231,000, or 5 per cent of migrant workers) and North Yemenis (315,000 migrants).

Some Changed Characteristics of Migrant-Flows

East Asian migrant-flows have changed markedly in character with the recession of the past few years, and the changed emphasis from construction to services. Low-paid service workers (many of them female) now feature largely. South Asian workers have increased in numbers as they have accepted lower real wages with more readiness than most other groups. Another nation that has expanded into low-wage service labour supplies is Indonesia.

The Weakening Position of the Arab Suppliers

The Arab world has, then, lost its market position as the chief labour-supplier to the Gulf states. Indeed, if Iraq is ignored as a labour-importer, Arab migrant-workers in the Gulf have increased, relative to the figures for 1975, by only about 30 per cent; by contrast, Asians have increased sixfold over this same period.

In the light of this, what does the increased demand over the next five years mean to the potential labour-exporting states, and in particular to Arab labour-suppliers? What should their stance be towards the opportunities brought about by a renewed growth that will certainly stimulate non-national labour demand? This depends, in no small way, upon what the benefits really are from the perspectives of the labour-suppliers.

HOW REAL ARE THE POTENTIAL BENEFITS OF LABOUR-EXPORTING?

The Evolving Attitude of Arab Labour-Supplying States towards Labour-Exporting

In the early (pre-GCC) period of labour-exports to the Gulf, governments of labour-exporting countries were enthusiastic. Widespread reservations in the Arab world about exporting labour postdate 1975. The deleterious effects of labour-exporting upon the economies of the Mediterranean Basin were becoming widely known only in 1974. Morocco and Algeria received an economic battering, an important part of which was the return of their migrants from Europe.

The Early Belief in the Benefits of Labour-Exporting

In the Arab states supplying the Arab Gulf with labour, however, unemployment remained a concern. Shortages of capital continued to be seen as the leading constraint on development. Remittances were perceived as a potential source of revenue to fulfil basic needs, and they were to provide foreign exchange for investment expenditure. It was postulated that outflows of labour from overpopulated areas (such as, perhaps, rural Egypt) could lead to rises in labour-productivity. Furthermore, migrant workers might have been expected to gain skills and experience in the dynamic labour-importing economies, which could later be brought back to their source countries.

Perhaps most important in perpetuating the Arab labour-suppliers' faith in the positive benefits of labour-exporting was the notion that the migration of labour within the Arab world was generically different from flows of labour out of the Arab region to, or between, other regions. The term 'circulation of labour' was used to distinguish movements of Arab workers to the Gulf states from other labour migrations. It was argued that the ill effects resulting from the movement of Arab labour within that linguistically and culturally definable region, would be mitigated or even not occur.

Both labour-supplying and -importing states subscribed to this view (at least publicly), the latter group through their Arabisation policies, and with statements supporting development plans to the effect that the development of the Arab Gulf states was for the Arab people as a whole. Arab views on the circulation of labour were a factor behind the failure of the ILO's call for consideration to be given to international compensation being paid to labour-exporters to the Arab world.

Arab Disenchantment with Labour-Supplying

By the late 1970s, however, massive increases in the scale of labour migration brought about a combination of skill shortages, inflation, import booms and balance-of-payments deficits in the Arab labour-suppliers. These features combined with an awareness that an increasing contribution to Gulf development was being made by Asian labour. All these factors, combined with a growing feeling of exposure to enforced returns by Arab migrant-workers, led to commentators expressing disquiet in Arab labour-supplying states.

It was increasingly, if belatedly, appreciated by the Arab labour-suppliers that the benefits to society as a whole and to the economy at large assumed a degree of control, regulation and moderation being applied to migration for work. It assumed an impact that was not concentrated unevenly within the economy or the country, as well as gentle changes in the rates of migrant flow. It also assumed a relatively closed flow of workers within the Arab world. None of these assumptions held in the violent economic response that came about in the wake of the oil price boom and the scaling-up of development plans in the Gulf.

The supplying states were even finding that remittances (though they were of major dimensions: Table 4.11) could not effectively be harnessed for investment. Whilst enhancing the fulfilment of basic needs, remittances, on a national basis, resulted in consumer expenditures, inflation of the price of fixed assets, and reduced local food-production, thereby increasing foreign-exchange exposure. Migrant workers to the Gulf did not gain new skills on a major scale, partly because of the tendency to utilise non-national workforces as unskilled labour.

Today's Mixed Feelings

Their role in supplying labour through international migration is now regarded by the Arab labour-suppliers as something of a mixed blessing. There is no clear rationalisation of the relative advantages and disadvantages. That migration is a net gain to the individual is not in doubt, but the overall impact on both society and the economy is not clear. Certainly it has not helped Egypt and Jordan escape major economic problems. The limited unequivocal benefits which are, even though the migrants involved are not usually the unemployed, brought by an early period of exporting a small share of the workforce - i.e. reduced unemployment and inward remittances that fulfil basic needs - are quickly outweighed as the scale of out-migration grows. Disadvantages quickly come to the fore; that is, in particular, losses of critical skills (with wage inflation and skill shortages), potential losses of output and import substitution for local production (with further hidden foreign-exchange costs, such as silos needed to import grain to Yemen).

Economic disenchantment with labour-exporting, has, with lack of clarity of view, led to the highlighting in labour-exporting states of particular social problems such as exploitation, the sexual abuse of migrants and abstract diversions such as a loss of self-sufficiency. And, of course, there have been surges of returnees to all the Arab labour-importers, either in economically bad times, or as a result of political expulsions.

The Devaluation of Labour-Supplying

Arab labour-suppliers have been obliged to compete in terms of the cheapness of labour as an export. The value of labour as a traded commodity has declined. This is one of the factors behind the depreciating currencies of the Arab labour-exporters.

The fall in the price of exported labour is really a result of competition with Asian labour-exporters whose migrants are prepared to work for less, in the face of recession in the GCC labour-importers, aggravated by their propensity to use imported labour in an unskilled mode. This is best characterised in GCC employers' making wage cuts and negotiating wages downwards as a major form of cost-reduction. It has debased many potentially high-tech manufacturing ventures (from textiles to plastics and foodstuffs) into low-quality labour-intensive processes. Service-provision has been shaped in the same way.

Indeed, the low price of imported labour has resulted in high-volume low-cost labour-intensive modes of production in non-oil industry in all the GCC states when, from many perspectives, capital-intensive production would be far more suitable. Not only private-sector employers are guilty of this; all GCC governments perpetuate, through subsidy structures and legislation, the use of high volumes of low-cost labour. For example, training is, by law in most of the GCC states, denied to non-national workers outside the oil sector.

Asian Dominance as a Consequence

Under these circumstances, the high-volume low-cost labour-exporters - the South Asian states and the less-developed East Asian states such as Indonesia - have been able to increase sharply their share of the GCC's international labour market; indeed, they have stamped their character upon the GCC labour-market, and aspects of the nature of GCC domestic development.

CAN LABOUR-EXPORTERS IMPROVE THE STATUS OF LABOUR-SUPPLYING?

Efforts to improve the status of the individuals and the states supplying labour to the Gulf were initiated in the 1970s by the ILO, and have continually been the subject of bilateral efforts initiated by the suppliers. These efforts have been constrained by the following: international legal constraints; equivocation on the part of the labour-importers; recession and market volatility in response to fluxing labour-demand; new entrants to the labour-supplying market; lack of international accountability; and the willingness of individuals to migrate on poorer terms and in poorer - even illegal - conditions.

The Regulatory Potential of Labour-Supplying Governments

Most important, however, is the structural problem that any effort on the part of labour-supplying governments to maximise national benefits from labour-exporting founders on the cut-backs (or redistributions) of the highly visible individual gains.

Besides, the controls needed are easily thwarted. As the case of Syria has shown, efforts to control (nearly always meaning efforts to restrict) the migration of workers outward are of limited success. There is little relative reduction in the numbers of workers abroad. Any potential national advantages from control are slight in view of the problems of illegal outward migrant-flows. More generally, both the momentum of migration and the exposure of labour-suppliers to international economic and political volatility undermines aspects of planning and control.

HOW, THEN, SHOULD THE ARAB LABOUR-EXPORTERS FACE THE FUTURE?

Relatively Buoyant Demand for Arab Labour in the GCC

Overall, the demand in the GCC for non-national Arabs is unlikely to fall significantly in the medium term. Demand for professional and technical groups might increase gently. Non-national Arabs employed in unskilled jobs, such as labouring, will, however, decrease further.

Two Arab groups still involved in unskilled activities in the GCC are Yemenis and Egyptians, but in large part their numbers have already suffered the consequences of Asian immigration in the late 1970s and early 1980s.   Many unskilled Egyptians returned home, and the number of unskilled Egyptians overseas is unlikely to rise again; Yemenis have settled in increasing numbers in Saudi Arabia, switching from labouring to trading. This process of settling is accelerating.

GCC-wide demand in the educational services for professional and sub-professional Arab non-nationals might be expected to decline.   Large numbers of nationals training to be teachers will ease the demand for expatriate teachers, though this will depend to some extent on how policies evolve in respect of educational enrolment and pupil/teacher ratios.

However, in sum, there will be increases in GCC demand for the better educated and qualified Arabs. These are able to work, for example, in high-quality international service-provision. Numbers are small, and this area of the labour-market is subject to GCC national, European and Asian competition, but there will be net increases of non-national Arabs. With the growing world service-economy, this could again, though, be construed as another example of the GCC drawing in critical and expensively produced scarce skills in the Arab labour-suppliers. There is no reason for Arab labour-exporters to be enthusiastic about exporting these groups of workers. Jordan may hope to see exports make some impact on unemployment amongst the educated; and Egypt to see some recovery in remittances by this means, but the evidence is not strongly positive.

Family Reunification: an Issue in the Arab Labour-Supplying States?

The settling of families in GCC states is still encouraged by major Gulf trading-families and merchant-families, who are close to political leaders. Banks are also committed to a thriving domestic housing-market.   There is therefore a politically powerful lobby in the GCC arguing for a *laissez-faire* approach to immigration. This can be seen particularly clearly in the UAE which has allowed in dependants to the extent that Asians comprise an overall majority of the population, not just the workforce.

There is also a growing perception that migrant workers, particularly those from South and East Asia, do not represent a security risk, and that they are more acceptable in family situations than as single migrant-workers. Despite the tightening in Kuwait, generally the limits on family re-unification have eased, especially for selected professional and technical occupations paying above certain salaries.

As yet, this has not become an issue in the labour-supplying states. Numbers involved are generally small relative to the supplying-states' populations. Quite often, the supplying states are relieved to see some reductions in minorities - as it is often these who are the most prone to settling. As settling becomes increasingly associated with migrant-working, a supplier-country view might develop. It will be political, not economic, in nature, and will be changing and unpredictable.

Continued Exposure to Policy Change in Labour-Importing Countries

Such exposure should engender further caution, rather than enthusiasm, on the part of labour-exporters. Near the end of the projection horizon, or later in the 1990s, three factors are likely to come into play:

(1) *The Potential for GCC Industrialisation:* this might be reassessed. GCC states are likely to see increasingly that there is little point in subsidising non-economic industries in order to employ non-nationals, if there is no future employment potential for nationals, nor any value added that will eventually accrue to the national population. A GCC-wide move might change the pattern of migrant-labour demand sharply in the late 1990s, especially if combined with more effective localisation policies.

(2) *The Wage Differential between Nationals and Non-nationals:* this might become subject to more government manipulation. Efforts to reduce it are likely to centre on taxes on non-national workers. GCC states might become prepared to carry a short-term cost, in order to gain the longer-term goal of a productive workforce within which nationals can compete. Net returns to non-nationals will be reduced.

(3) *Free Outward Flows of Remittances Cannot be Guaranteed:* this has been shown by Iraq's actions (though not GCC-based).

Controls and limitations on the outflow of remittances are not seriously considered by GCC labour-importers as yet, but as efforts to localise intensify, they become more, rather than less, likely.

CAUTION ABOUT THE FUTURE, NOT OPTIMISM, IS FITTING

Massive returns of non-national Arab workers to their source countries from the GCC are unlikely. Repatriations of non-national Arab workers on a major scale, such as have taken place, have been from non-GCC oil-states (like the recent departures from Iraq). In looking at the future of their workers in the GCC, Arab labour-supplying nations need not be too fearful of efforts to repatriate on a large scale. Having said that, the international labour-market, though looking more settled in aggregate, will continue to give individual nations supplying labour a buffeting as numbers of migrants flux sharply. The demand for individual groups or nationalities of workers will continue to be short term and volatile. Thus, whilst there is some potential for further expansions of Arab worker exports, these will not be on greatly improved terms, and will be subject to continued competition from labour-supplying states in Asia.

In response to this, there will be a continuing momentum of individual migrant-worker departures to the GCC from the non-oil Arab states, especially as their economies will remain in difficulties. Through the 1990s, individuals will still look to worker migration as a means of escaping recession and securing otherwise unobtainable consumer-goods. These migrants will increasingly be the better educated and from higher occupational levels. This will continue to be perceived as taking some of the immediate pressures off employment problems in the non-oil Arab states. This perception is important, whatever the actualities of the economic impact.

However, no longer will either individuals or Arab governments be able to construe out-migration of workers as a solution to unskilled unemployment. In this area, Arab labour-supplying states will be thrust upon their own resources. Any measured interpretation of labour migration suggests that there is not as much at stake in the GCC labour-market of the 1990s for the non-oil Arab states as the conventional wisdom has implied.

Table 4.1: GCC States: Work-Permit Issues, 1975 to 1986

Country	1975	1976	1977	1978	1979	1980	1981	1982	1983	1984	1985	1986
Bahrain	11,400	14,900	26,300	33,800	26,100	20,100	22,200	26,600	31,800	34,300	32,500	27,200
Kuwait	37,400	43,400	61,900	47,900	44,500	56,200	50,500	68,800	86,100	39,400	41,600	42,200
Oman	81,200	93,600	106,300	114,600	127,500	148,800	181,700	208,000	258,100	294,600	316,000	304,000
Qatar	n.a.	n.a.	n.a.	n.a.	n.a.	n.a.	n.a.	n.a.	n.a.	n.a.	n.a.	n.a.
Saudi Arabia	n.a.	n.a.	522,900	606,400	687,300	643,200	749,300	772,000	790,000	752,500	780,600	n.a.
UAE	46,400	51,700	88,700	149,300	134,900	124,800	146,900	178,100	140,900	n.a.	175,700	n.a.

Notes: With the exception of Oman, data is for the private sector; UAE-data is for Abu Dhabi only: cited in J.S. Birks and C.A. Sinclair, *Manpower and Population Evolution in the GCC and the Libyan Arab Jamahiriya*, World Employment Programme Research Programme Working Paper (International Labour Office, Geneva, 1989).

Sources: State of Bahrain, Central Statistical Organisation, *Statistical Abstract*; state of Bahrain, Ministry of Labour and Social Affairs, *Annual Report on Foreign Employment, 1984*; state of Kuwait, Central Statistical Office, *Annual Statistical Abstract, 1986*; state of Kuwait, Ministry of Labour and Social Affairs, *Annual Report on Expatriate Employment, 1985*; sultanate of Oman, Directorate General of National Statistics, *Statistical Yearbook, 1986*; kingdom of Saudi Arabia, Central Department of Statistics, *Statistical Yearbook, 1984*; *Saudi Economic Survey* (weekly); UAE, Central Statistics Department, *Annual Statistical Abstract, 1984*; emirate of Abu Dhabi, Department of Planning, *Statistical Yearbook, 1985*.

Table 4.2: Kuwait: Work Permit Issues (thousands), 1975 to 1987

Type of Permit	1975	1976	1977	1978	1979	1980	1981	1982	1983	1984	1985	1986	1987
New Issues	37.4	43.4	61.9	47.9	44.5	56.2	50.5	68.8	86.1	39.4	41.6	42.2	52.2
Renewals	37.3	42.8	55.4	64.0	60.0	54.9	62.3	85.9	105.3	140.7	161.7	147.2	157.1
Cancellations	n.a.	n.a.	3.3	10.5	15.6	16.9	19.9	20.9	21.8	24.6	31.4	34.1	34.4
Transfers	n.a.	n.a.	n.a.	n.a.	n.a.	11.7	11.4	10.9	10.9	21.6	42.4	35.9	51.1

Source: Ministry of Labour and Social Affairs, *Report on Employment and Expatriate Labour:*
cited in Birks and Sinclair, *Manpower and Population.*

Table 4.3: Contract Labour Placements from Selected Asian Countries Sending Labour to the Middle East, 1975 to 1986

Country	1975	1976	1977	1978	1979	1980	1981	1982	1983	1984	1985	1986
India	n.a.	4,200	22,900	69,000	171,000	236,200	276,000	239,545	220,797	198,810	160,555	109,951
Philippines	1,552	7,812	25,721	34,441	73,210	132,044	183,582	211,003	323,414	311,517	266,617	262,758
Pakistan	23,077	41,690	140,522	130,525	125,507	129,847	168,403	142,945	128,206	88,460	101,000	62,000
Rep. Korea	6,466	21,269	52,247	81,987	99,141	124,834	138,310	149,650	140,100	116,050	n.a.	n.a.
Bangladesh	n.a.	5,559	15,443	22,756	24,254	29,815	53,839	62,207	59,220	56,753	77,694	36,852
Sri Lanka	n.a.	526	633	8,082	20,980	24,053	47,800	63,522	68,905	n.a.	n.a.	n.a.
Thailand	984	1,287	3,870	14,215	8,335	20,690	23,848	105,186	63,520	67,468	61,083	72,673
Indonesia	n.a.	1,200	1,900	5,100	6,400	4,950	7,900	n.a.	n.a.	36,582	45,129	n.a.

Note: figure for Bangladesh in 1986 is estimated from first half data.

Sources: Ministry of Labour, New Delhi; Philippine Overseas Employment Administration, Manila; ARTEP, *Impact of out and return migration on domestic employment in Pakistan*; Hyunho Seok, 'Republic of Korea', in G. Gunatilleke (ed.), *Migration of Asian Workers to the Arab World* (United Nations University, Tokyo,1986); A.M.A.H. Siddiqui, 'The economic and non-economic impact of labour migration from Bangladesh', in F. Arnold and N. Shah (eds.), *Asian Labor Migration: Pipeline to the Middle East* (Westview, Boulder, 1986); Central Bank of the Philippines; Protector of Emigrants, Bombay; Ministry of Planning, Colombo; BMET, *Annual Reports*, Dhaka; Office of Labour Administration, Seoul; Department of Labour, Bangkok; National Economic and Social Development Board, Bangkok; Department of Manpower, Jakarta: cited in Birks and Sinclair, *Manpower and Population*.

Table 4.4: GCC: Non-National Populations, 1975 and 1985

Country	1975		1985	
	No.	%	No.	%
Bahrain	56,000	2.0	121,800	1.7
Kuwait	502,500	17.9	1,016,000	14.1
Oman	132,250	4.7	391,100	5.4
Qatar	97,000	3.5	129,200	1.8
Saudi Arabia	1,565,000	55.7	4,504,700	62.6
UAE	456,000	16.2	1,038,800	14.4
Total	2,808,750	100.0	7,201,600	100.0

Sources: (a) 1975: J.S. Birks and C.A. Sinclair, *International Migration and Development in the Arab Region* (ILO, Geneva, 1980).
(b) 1985: State of Bahrain, Central Statistical Organisation, *Statistical Abstract*; state of Bahrain, Directorate of Statistics, *Census of Population and Housing, 1981*; state of Kuwait, Central Statistical Office, *Annual Statistical Abstract, 1986*; state of Kuwait, Central Statistical Office, *Census of Population and Housing, 1985*; sultanate of Oman, Directorate General of National Statistics, *Statistical Yearbook, 1986*; state of Qatar, Central Statistical Organisation, *Annual Statistical Abstract, 1986*; state of Qatar, Central Statistical Organisation, *Vital Statistics Annual Bulletin, 1986*; kingdom of Saudi Arabia, Central Department of Statistics, *Statistical Yearbook, 1984*; kingdom of Saudi Arabia, Central department of Statistics, *Analysis of the 1982 Demographic Survey, 1984*; UAE, Central Statistics Department, *Census of Population, 1980*; UAE, Central Statistics Department, *Annual Statistical Abstract, 1984*; emirate of Abu Dhabi, Department of Planning, *Statistical Yearbook, 1985*; Economic Commission for Western Asia, *Demographic and Related Socio-economic data Sheets, 1985*: cited in Birks and Sinclair, *Manpower and Population*.

Table 4.5: GCC: Non-National Crude Activity Rates by Nationality Group, 1985

% Active

	Arab	South Asian	East Asian	Total
Bahrain	45	73	92	70
Kuwait	39	78	90	54
Oman	43	87	96	80
Qatar	23	91	90	55
Saudi Arabia	71	84	91	77
UAE	36	65	96	58

Sources: As in Table 4.4.

Table 4.6: Kuwait: Non-National Populations, Shares by Duration of Residence, 1985

	Residence in Years				
	0-4	5-9	10-14	15-19	20+
Arabs	27.6	26.6	17.5	14.3	14.0
South & East Asian	59.6	22.4	9.1	4.2	4.7
European & N. American	78.7	15.0	3.0	1.7	1.5
Other nationalities	67.1	25.4	5.8	0.8	1.0
Total 1985	39.7	25.0	14.3	10.6	10.4
Total 1980	45.3	22.6	16.0	9.1	7.0
Total 1975	42.2	25.0	16.4	10.6	3.8

Source: State of Kuwait, Central Statistical Ofice, *Census of Population and Housing, 1975, 1980 and 1985*: cited in Birks and Sinclair, *Manpower and Population*.

Table 4.7: GCC: Total, National and Non-National Employment, 1985 to 1995

	1985	1986	1987	1988	1989	1990	1991	1992	1993	1994	1995
Non-Nationals' Employment	5,130,254	4,856,769	4,642,492	4,441,506	4,468,153	4,539,330	4,627,523	4,808,410	5,012,757	5,209,997	5,422,289
Nationals' Employment	1,742,096	1,784,179	1,828,635	1,879,797	1,934,436	1,990,850	2,048,988	2,109,108	2,170,939	2,235,420	2,302,234
Unemployed Nationals	44,986	49,241	51,215	61,383	69,004	73,720	79,292	86,712	104,621	115,330	136,036
Nationals' Unemployment Rate	2.6	2.8	2.8	3.3	3.6	3.7	3.9	4.1	4.8	5.2	5.9
Total	6,872,350	6,640,948	6,471,127	6,321,303	6,402,590	6,530,180	6,676,511	6,917,517	7,183,969	7,445,417	7,724,524

Source: Birks and Sinclair, *Manpower and Population.*

Table 4.8: GCC: National and Non-National Population (thousands), 1985 to 1995

	1985	1986	1987	1988	1989	1990	1991	1992	1993	1994	1995
Nationals	8,690.70	8,991.50	9,299.40	9,620.80	9,955.80	10,303.90	10,657.50	11,019.60	11,396.70	11,789.10	12,194.50
Non-Nationals	7,201.54	6,831.32	6,545.16	6,279.34	6,315.70	6,414.95	6,537.07	6,779.00	7,052.48	7,317.29	7,601.61
Total	15,892.24	15,822.82	15,844.56	15,900.14	16,271.50	16,718.85	17,194.57	17,798.60	18,449.18	19,106.39	19,796.11

Note: Data are preliminary and subject to revision.

Source: Birks and Sinclair, *Manpower and Population*.

Table 4.9 GCC: Non-National Population by Ethnic Group, 1985 to 1995

Ethnic Group	1985	1986	1987	1988	1989	1990	1991	1992	1993	1994	1995
Total Arabs	2,736,828	2,597,800	2,491,460	2,390,660	2,404,220	2,442,390	2,489,420	2,581,860	2,688,390	2,791,800	2,902,520
Total South Asians	2,803,335	2,678,100	2,574,730	2,484,890	2,497,000	2,533,560	2,578,430	2,606,460	2,749,580	2,836,270	2,929,030
Total East Asians	1,158,343	1,090,620	1,035,600	981,040	988,620	1,005,940	1,027,380	1,076,060	1,132,450	1,186,490	1,245,010
Total Other	503,037	464,800	443,370	422,750	425,860	433,060	441,840	460,620	482,060	502,730	525,050
Total	7,201,543	6,831,320	6,545,160	6,279,340	6,315,700	6,414,950	6,537,070	6,779,000	7,052,480	7,317,290	7,601,610

Note: Data are preliminary and subject to revision.

Source: Birks and Sinclair, *Manpower and Population.*

Table 4.10: Major Labour-Exporters to the GCC: Estimates of Workers by Nationality, 1990

Nationality	No.	Non-National Workers % of Total	% of group
Egyptian	525,000	11.3	37.7
Sudanese	115,000	2.3	8.3
Jords & Pals	231,000	5.0	16.6
Lebanese	56,000	1.2	4.0
Syrian	42,000	0.9	3.0
Iraqi	11,000	0.2	0.8
Omani	14,000	1.0	1.0
Other GCC	7,000	0.2	0.5
North Yemeni	315,000	6.9	22.6
South Yemeni	59,000	1.3	4.2
Tunisian	10,000	0.2	0.7
Moroccan	6,000	0.1	0.4
Other Arab	2,000	0.1	0.1
Pakistani	691,000	14.8	31.7
Bangladeshi	297,000	6.1	13.6
Indian	951,000	21.0	43.6
Sri Lankan	241,000	4.8	11.1
Filipino	349,000	7.4	53.1
Indonesian	105,000	2.6	16.0
South Korean	55,000	1.0	8.4
Thai	95,000	4.8	14.5
Malaysian	11,000	0.3	1.7
Chinese	4,000	0.0	0.6
Taiwanese	15,000	0.3	2.3
Singaporean	9,000	0.2	1.4
Other	14,000	0.5	2.1
Turkish	29,000	0.4	9.5
Iranian	57,000	1.2	18.7
African	42,000	0.4	13.8
North American	23,000	0.4	7.5
European	37,000	0.8	12.1
Other	117,000	2.4	38.4
Total	4,535,000	100.0	
Arab Sub-total	1,393,000	30.7	
S. Asian Sub-total	2,180,000	48.1	
E. Asian Sub-total	657,000	14.5	
Other Sub-total	305,000	6.7	
	4,535,000	100.0	

Source: estimated by Birks and Sinclair, using sources in Tables 4.1, 4.3 and 4.4.

Table 4.11: Recorded Remittances for Selected Countries (US $million, current prices), 1967 to 1988

Year	Egypt	YAR	PDRY	Jordan	Syria	Sudan	Somalia	India	Pakistan	Sri Lanka	Bangla-desh	South Korea	Thai-land	Philip-pines	Turkey	Year
1967				19				161							93	1967
1968				12				183							107	1968
1969	32		43	19				123							140	1969
1970	29		62	16				113							273	1970
1971	27		60	14				141	142						471	1971
1972	114		48	23				145	148						740	1972
1973	117		33	45				175	178						1,183	1973
1974	189		34	75				232	258						1,426	1974
1975	366	157	42	167		151	2	430	410		15				1,312	1975
1976	755	317	42	411		172	4	645	866		18				982	1976
1977	897	795	79	455		221	13	940	1,303		78				982	1977
1978	1,761	1,157	119	520		240	28	1,022	1,578		115	585	104		983	1978
1979	2,445	1,277	155	509	136	209	36	1,424	2,116	48	167	994	187		1,696	1979
1980	2,855	1,082	182	795	547	305	57	2,786	2,224	152	379	1,102	383	305	2,071	1980
1981	2,082	974	201	1,033	418	350	64	2,338	2,887	230	424	1,359	477	328	2,490	1981
1982	3,166	1,191	255	1,085	440	415	50	2,526	2,737	289	628	1,663	617	324	2,140	1982
1983	3,930	1,244	307	1,108	304	395	51	2,587	2,446	294	552	*1,490	844	242	1,513	1983
1984	3,497	1,069	270	1,235	245	430	72	2,542	2,598	302	477	*1,663	891	428	1,807	1984
1985	2,740	809	306	1,019	183	350	20	2,674	*2,260	292	582		*900	388	1,714	1985
1986	*3,000	*600	256	1,218		*250	*25			*330	*555				1,634	1986
1987	*3,100	*525	221				*30									1987
1988	*3,300						*35									1988

* denotes provisional estimate

Source: Birks and Sinclair, *Manpower and Population*.

Sources

Al Sabah, Mohammed, *et al.*, *Study of the Kuwait Economy* (MIT, Harvard University, Cambridge, Mass., 1989).

Appleyard, R., *The Impact of Migration on Developing Countries* (OECD, Paris, 1989).

Beauge, G.A. and Bendiab, A., *Migrations Internationales au Moyen-Orient: 1975-1986* (IREMAM, Aix-en-Provence, 1987).

Birks, J.S. and Sinclair, C.A., *Manpower and Population Evolution in the GCC and the Libyan Arab Jamahiriya*, World Employment Programme Research Programme Working Paper (International Labour Office, Geneva, 1989).

Birks, J.S. and Sinclair, C.A., 'Some Practical and Theoretical Aspects of Manpower Planning in the Arab Gulf in the 1980s', *Proceedings of the Sixth Human Resources Management Conference, Towards a Productive National Workforce* (Fujaira, 1989).

Birks, J.S. and Sinclair, C.A., *Saudi Arabia into the 90s* (Durham University, Durham, 1989).

Bohning, W.R., *Towards a System of Recompense for International Labour Migration*, World Employment Programme Research Programme Working Paper (International Labour Office, Geneva, 1982).

Bohning, W.R., *International Labour Migration in the Light of ILO Instruments, with Especial Reference to the Asian Migrant-Sending Countries*, World Employment Programme Research Programme Working Paper (International Labour Office, Geneva, 1982).

Bohning, W.R., *Studies in International Migration* (Macmillan, London, 1984).

Colclough, C., *How can the Manpower Debate be Resolved?*, Labour Market Analysis and Employment Planning Working Paper, no. 33 (International Labour Office, Geneva, 1989).

Seccombe, I.J., *International Migration for Employment in the Middle East, an Introductory Bibliography* (Durham University, Durham, 1984).

Stahl, C.W., *International Labour Migration and the ASEAN Economies*, World Employment Programme Research Programme Working Paper (International Labour Office, Geneva, 1983).

Notes

1   Please note that this chapter was submitted on 27 January 1990 and forms part of a sequence of projections by its authors.

2   See the list of sources, below.

3   J.S. Birks and C.A. Sinclair, *Manpower and Population Evolution in the GCC and the Libyan Arab Jamahiriya*, World Employment Programme Research Programme Working Paper (International Labour Office, Geneva, 1989).

4   This, together with other tables, unless differently sourced, are from the analysis and projections in Birks and Sinclair, *Manpower and Population*.

5   This is discussed in detail in Birks and Sinclair, *Manpower and Population*.

5. THE INDIAN SUBCONTINENT AND THE GULF

K. Subrahmanyam

The interaction between the Indian subcontinent and the Gulf countries is multifaceted. There are close cultural and religious bonds. Urdu is understood in many Gulf countries and every year hundreds of thousands of pilgrims make their *hajj* pilgrimage to the holy places in Saudi Arabia. Hundreds of thousands of labour and middle engineering and management personnel from the subcontinent serve in the Gulf countries, and their remittances home constitute a significant source of foreign exchange for India, Pakistan and Bangladesh. The Gulf countries supply the bulk of the energy needs of Pakistan and a significant proportion of India's (around 40 per cent). For Pakistan some of the Gulf countries (Saudi Arabia and Kuwait) are major aid-donors. With the rise in oil prices, the trade between the Gulf countries and the subcontinent also increased significantly. Over and above all these commercial, cultural and labour-skills supply relationships, political and religious factors exercise a dominant influence on the interactions between the subcontinent and the Gulf countries. If there are rumours about the *Ka^cba* mosque being desecrated, the US Embassy in Islamabad gets burnt down. The Wahhabis exercise a significant influence on various Afghan *Mujahidin* groups in Peshawar. This Saudi support helped the Mujahidin in their insurgency and at the same time got in the way of unity among themselves, as well as between them and the Iran-based resistance groups.

The Pakistan-Gulf Arms Relationship

There is no doubt that Pakistani arms-purchases have been financed through lavish Arab generosity. Even the Chinese no longer provide their armaments free to Pakistan and consequently they have to be paid for. There is adequate evidence that Pakistan's nuclear programme has been financed by the Gulf states and Libya, and of late the Libyan connection has become attenuated, whilst the Gulf states constitute the mainstay of the Pakistani nuclear programme. Maulana Kausar Niazi, a member of Prime Minister Z.A. Bhutto's cabinet, in his book *Aur Line Cut Gaye*, has written extensively about Pakistan's nuclear-weapon project.

The biggest problem was the procurement of $300 million for this project. For this he (Bhutto) turned towards the Gulf states and the oil-rich nations of the Arab world. He received positive responses from them particularly from Libya, Saudi Arabia, UAE, Kuwait and Iraq who assured him of full financial co-operation... The Prime Minister knew that the programme was lengthy and would tax his patience. But he was also sure that with the help of his Arab friends he would be able to realise his dream. In this connection he sent me to the late Shah Faisal for talks at least four times. In other countries Agha Shahi, Aziz Ahmed A.G.N. Qazi, Ghulam Ishaq Khan, Munir Ahmed and innumerable other persons were acting on some of his advice.[1]

The late Prime Minister wrote in his death-cell testimony, *If I Am Assassinated*:

A country does not have to be merely wealthy to possess nuclear capability. If that were the only requirement, every OPEC country would have nuclear capability. The essential prerequisite is the infrastructure. For this reason, I gave the highest priority to train thousands of nuclear scientists in foreign countries. Now we have the brainpower, we have the nuclear power plant in Karachi. All we needed was the nuclear reprocessing plant. Arrangements for the heavy water, the uranium and the fuel-fabricating plant had been made. We were on the threshold of full nuclear capability when I left the government to come to this death cell. We know that Israel and South Africa have full nuclear capability. The Christian, Jewish and Hindu civilisations have this capability. The Communist powers also possess it. Only the Islamic civilisation was without it, but that position was about to change.[2]

This was written in 1978 and more than eleven years have passed since then. It is widely accepted that Pakistan today has a nuclear-weapon capability - a capability financed by the liberal contributions of the Gulf states.

Missile and Nuclear Proliferation

Saudi Arabia has acquired from China CSS-2 missiles with a range of 2700km.[3] It is not reputed to be a missile of any great accuracy and the price paid for the missile is in the range of tens of millions of dollars apiece. It does not make sense to acquire missiles of this range, of such a degree of inaccuracy and at this cost, unless they are to be equipped with either nuclear or chemical warheads. Pakistan has a nuclear warhead and Iraq claims to possess binary chemical-warheads.[4] What is more logical than to assume that the CSS-2 missiles in Saudi Arabia are to be equipped with either nuclear or chemical warheads?

The Gulf states have equipped themselves with missiles of various kinds. Saudi Arabia's CSS-2 missiles have already been referred to. Kuwait has FROG-7 missiles, Iraq has both FROG-7 and Scud-B missiles and claims to have developed its own indigenous Abbas and Husain missiles. Iran has acquired Silkworm missiles, from China, and Scud missiles, presumably from the USSR, China and North Korea. Pakistan claims to have developed its own Hatf-I and Hatf-II surface-to-surface missiles.[5] There are reports of some of these countries negotiating the purchase of M-9 missiles with a range of 600km from China, these having improved accuracy over the earlier missiles. The spread and development of these missiles in the Gulf region, along with the existence of such missiles in neighbouring China, USSR and the US Navy in the Indian Ocean, have compelled India to develop its own missile programme.[6] Given the close military linkages between some of the Gulf countries and the Pakistani military establishment, and the help extended by some of the West Asian countries to Pakistan when at war during 1965 and 1971, the Indian defence-planners have to take into account the possibility of such transfers of equipment at short notice to Pakistan in any possible future conflicts.

Interaction between the Gulf and the Subcontinent

Developments in the Gulf area have a significant impact upon the subcontinent. Iran appears to be in the process of cautiously readjusting its policies. The release of two hostages in Beirut has earned Iran the public thanks of President Bush. Though in public the Iranian rhetoric shows no sign of mellowing, there are three ineluctable pressures on Iran which must influence its policies towards the Western world. Firstly, Iraq shows no sign of coming to the negotiating table after such a long period of cease-fire and Iraq is holding a larger number of Iranian prisoners and Iranian territory than vice versa. Secondly, Iraq is rebuilding and modernising its armed forces faster than Iran is able to do. Iraq appears to be emerging as, relatively speaking, the more powerful military power in the region with an arsenal of missiles and chemical weapons which it has shown a will to use. Thirdly, with oil prices remaining low, Iranian earnings are not able to keep up with its requirements for funds for both post-war reconstruction and in order to re-equip its armed forces so as to balance Iraq. These reasons would explain the new policy with regard to hostages and the signals generated by Iran of its interest in improving relations with the West.

Soviet de-ideologisation of its foreign policy and permission to allow large-scale Jewish emigration to Israel have an impact on Syria which has been entirely dependent on the USSR for its weapon supplies. With the rise of the Iraqi military power, both Iran and Syria, who each have mutual strategic interests *vis-à-vis* Iraq, have to adjust their strident anti-Western rhetoric. Hence Syria, too, comes in for thanks from President Bush for the part it played in the release of two American hostages, and more is expected of both Syria and Iran in the defusing of the hostage crisis.

Though Saudi Arabia bank-rolled the Iraqi war effort against Iran when it feared Ayatullah Khomeini's attempt to export the *Shi^cite* revolution and to destabilise the Saudi regime, the Saudis do not view the build-up of Iraqi power with unmixed joy. They would prefer to be the dominant power in the Gulf area and not want the other members of the Gulf Co-operation Council to be overawed by Iraq. There are fears that under the shield of its binary chemical-weapons and missiles, the possession of both of which Iraq openly acknowledges, that country may attempt to build a nuclear arsenal as well. With the disarmament process likely to be underway in the industrialised world, both fissile materials and technological mercenaries from the Western world are likely to find their way to rich oil-exporting countries like Iraq. It is quite obvious from Iraq's acknowledged possession of binary chemical-weapons that they have already recruited a band of Western technological mercenaries.

Egypt, after its re-entry into the Arab fold after ten years of ostracism following the Camp David Accord, is playing an active role in West Asia, as demonstrated by President Mubarak's dealings with Syria, Iraq and Jordan. Egypt, too, has been modernising its armed forces. It had a joint missile-development programme with Iraq and Argentina, from which it has recently withdrawn.

All the West Asian Islamic countries, Turkey, Iraq, Iran, the Gulf emirates and Saudi Arabia, are, with caution and interest, watching the developments in the Soviet Islamic republics and the impact which *perestroika* and *glasnost* have upon them.

In this fast changing scenario, certain alignments and rivalries stand out: the Iranian-Syrian alignment *vis-à-vis* Iraq, the Saudi-Pakistani alignment, the Iran-Iraq and the Saudi-Iraq rivalries, these are some of them. It is the Pakistani-Saudi alignment which needs to be watched carefully. Pakistan's ambition, as articulated by the late Prime Minister Bhutto, was to use the best brain-power in the Islamic world to develop nuclear weaponry, to train the best army in Asia and to assert its leadership role, for which, no doubt, it stood in need of Saudi financial backing. Though Pakistan has achieved its nuclear ambition, it finds a rival in Iraq. The Iraqis have proved that they can wage a prolonged war and accept heavy casualties. They have also demonstrated their technological capabilities with their missiles and binary chemical-weapons. Unlike Pakistan, Iraq is financially independent since it exports oil.

Iraq and Pakistan have traditionally had a tense relationship. Iraq withdrew from the Baghdad Pact and always had a radical Ba'thist regime which did not view Islamic fundamentalism with favour. In 1973, the late Mr Bhutto accused Iraq of smuggling arms into Pakistan.[7] During the Iran-Iraq war, Pakistan had to adopt an expedient neutral policy since it did not want to alienate its neighbour, Iran, nor the Saudis who were bank-rolling the Iraqi war-effort against Iran.[8]

All countries now recognise that Israel has a sophisticated nuclear arsenal and long-range missile-delivery systems. Another Arab-Israeli war is inconceivable without taking into account the possibilities of its escalating to a chemical and nuclear level.   Hence Egypt has made it up with Israel. Attention should, therefore, shift from the Arab-Israeli confrontation to the explosive rivalries and tensions in West Asia among the Islamic countries themselves, and the likely involvement of Pakistan in such events. Pakistan is no longer a frontline state for the US following the Soviet withdrawal from Afghanistan. Iran is no longer the exporter of *Shi‘a* revolution, but a country which, after being bled and impoverished by a long and murderous war, is now desperately attempting to make it up with the West. Syria can no longer draw on the Soviet arsenal. Only two Islamic countries stand out as military powers, Iraq and Pakistan, and they are bound to be rivals for influence over the Gulf states and over military and technological clout in the West Asian Islamic world.

All these countries, as pointed out earlier, have acquired short- and medium-range missiles. The Saudis have obtained the long-range Chinese missiles as well. Iraq and Pakistan have their own missile development programmes. Only Iraq is in a position to threaten the use of a weapon of mass destruction, the binary chemical-warhead, and Iraq's is a credible threat since it has used chemical weapons against Iranians and its own Kurdish population. Pakistan can threaten the use of nuclear weapons. What one has to watch for is the possibility of Saudi Arabia and Pakistan attempting to counter the Iraqi military lead. That could mean the mating of Pakistani nuclear warheads with the Saudi long-range missile, or other categories of missiles either country may obtain from China.

One should not be surprised if, when the Pakistanis and Saudis decide that the time has come to counterbalance Iraq, the Pakistani nuclear weapon may also be unveiled. No doubt, it would be labelled as either anti-Indian or anti-Israeli and it would have those roles in addition to its role of countering Iraq. Pakistan was described by the late Mr Bhutto as an army with a country.[9] Both as an army and as a country it is becoming increasingly isolated. It is compelled to demonstrate its role as the foremost Islamic military power in order to continue to draw sustenance and support from the Saudis. Having messed up the Afghan adventure, being rebuffed in the Kashmir venture, slowly being distanced by the US and getting upstaged by Iraq, the pressure on Pakistan to unveil its nuclear capability is steadily increasing.

Pakistan Seeks West Asian Support

Similarly the tensions in the subcontinent have sought to be injected into the Gulf area, though one hopes this will not be a successful exercise. The Pakistani Prime Minister, Benazir Bhutto, has been to Saudi Arabia, Iran, Qatar, Iraq, Kuwait and Bahrain to enlist the support of these countries for the Pakistani stand on the Kashmir issue. She has had some limited success in obtaining verbal support from some of the countries. At the same time these regimes in the Gulf are understandably reluctant to support the cause of secessionism in Kashmir, given their own vulnerabilities in this respect. Iran has its Azari, Kurdish, Baluchi and Arab minorities and Iraq has its Kurds. With the impending merger of the two Yemens and the size of the expatriate Yemeni population in Saudi Arabia, the Saudis, too, have to be careful about extending support to secessionism elsewhere. Qatar, the UAE, Kuwait and Bahrain have large expatriate populations and Kuwait has been subjected to international terrorism of the type that Pakistan at present seeks to export into India.

Pakistan itself is in the throes of acute struggles, both sectarian and between subnationalities. Shiᶜi-Sunni sectarian violence has intensified. The passage of the Shariat (*Shariᶜa*) Bill in the Senate has created resentment among the Shiᶜis and protest against the bill is headed by Tehrik Nifar Fiqh Jafaria.[10] As the rivalry between the Shiᶜis and Sunnis intensifies, there are possibilities that the two sides will attempt to raise support from Iran and Saudi Arabia respectively. Already the two countries are locked in a power struggle over Afghanistan which has helped General Najibullah to consolidate his power there. How the rivalries in the Gulf will affect the subnationalities' struggle within Pakistan, that is among the Punjabis, the Pathans, the Baluchis, the Sindis and the Mujahirs, is difficult to say. We do not have a breakdown of the migrants, subnationality-wise, from Pakistan to the Gulf countries. It would be reasonable to assume that the bulk of labour to Saudi Arabia is Sunni Moslem, with Iran receiving the bulk of the Shiᶜis and the other Gulf countries, a mix.

The Impact of Developments in Eastern Europe

The events in Eastern Europe and the Soviet Union are bound to have an impact on the entire Islamic world. At a superficial level the orthodox Islamic countries appear to feel that the Soviet withdrawal from Afghanistan was a great victory for Islamic orthodoxy and the assertion of subnationalist identities in the Soviet Central Asian republics a blow against Communism.[11] What seems to be overlooked is that the crucial issues which the waves sweeping over the rigid, orthodox Marxist world bring up (a world where Marxism was being practised like a religion - atheism replacing God, Marx, Lenin and Mao becoming the prophets, Marxist-Leninism taking the place of the book and dissent from orthodoxy being stamped down on as much as in an orthodox Islamic country) are the issues of secularism, pluralism, liberalism, revolt against rigid orthodoxy and the assertion of individual freedom. One can see the stirrings of a similar reformist movement among the Islamic countries, in Algeria, Turkey, Egypt and Afghanistan.   It is possible that similar developments may take place in the newly united Yemen as well.   Iraq and Syria are relatively secular states. There are fierce struggles between Islamic orthodoxy and democratic pluralism in a number of states and the country of Pakistan is crucial in this struggle. Though it has regained a form of democratic government, the army and the orthodox clergy still have a powerful influence over the government. The fight over the Shariat law is to decide whether the relationships among human beings are to be regulated by laws made by the elected representatives of the people or, in place of that, by the clergy interpreting religious texts several centuries old.[12]

What happens in this struggle between religious orthodoxy and democratic liberalism in the South Asian subcontinent will influence developments in the Gulf countries and vice versa. When the Gulf countries were affluent because of high oil-prices, money came into the subcontinent to strengthen the orthodox clergy. The late Prime Minister Z.A. Bhutto, in his death-cell testimony, referred to the role of money from the Gulf states in strengthening the PNA (Pakistan National Alliance) agitation in 1976-7[13] which became the ostensible excuse for the Pakistani Army to seize power. Pakistan, under General Zia ul-Haq, was able to defy the US when President Carter imposed sanctions on

Pakistan in 1979, following the discovery of Pakistan's nuclear-weapons programme, mainly because of the financial support received from the Gulf states. The Islamic summit at Ta'if in January 1980 steered Pakistani policy over Afghanistan even as the Indian Prime Minister, Mrs Gandhi, was sending her special envoys to that country to formulate a joint political-policy on the issue *vis-à-vis* the Soviet Union.[14] The religious fundamentalism of the Gulf states, buttressed by oil money, has had impacts beyond the Islamic community. One might consider the Sikh and Hindu fundamentalisms as second and third order effects of Islamic fundamentalism.

International Terrorism

One of the offshoots of fundamentalism backed by money power is international terrorism. Iran does not deny its influence on those groups which seize and hold hostages in Beirut. Terrorism in Kuwait and the imprisonment of the terrorists led to the hijacking of an airliner.[15] What started in West Asia has moved into South Asia and today terrorism in the subcontinent is of much larger dimensions than elsewhere in the world.[16] It is not the contention here that terrorism in India and Pakistan is the direct consequence of the events in the Gulf and West Asia. But it appears rational to conclude that the latter has had a certain effect, by demonstration, upon the former.

Fundamentalism accentuates sectarian rivalries even within a religion, as witnessed in Beirut and Pakistan, quite apart from its impact on inter-religious tensions. The wave of change in Eastern Europe and the Soviet Union was occasioned partly by internal dynamics arising out of the impact of the external world through the communications revolution, and partly by prolonged economic stagnation. While the communications revolution does have an impact on the Gulf states, the future shape of their economy will very much depend on the price of oil. If the oil price does not soar again, and the population explosion in the Gulf states continues at the present rate, then most of the migrant workers - starting with non-Arabs - will be sent back home again. This development has already started, and both the demands for labour from the subcontinent and the resulting remittances home have started falling. Unless there is an upward turn in oil prices - as fondly hoped for by Arab leaders and doubtless by others - the second factor to generate a wave of change, economic stagnation, may also emerge.

There was a time when in Western strategic literature Pakistan was considered the eastern rampart of the 'wells of power'. Pakistanis themselves often proclaim that they are part of Islamic South-West Asia rather than Indocentric South Asia. It is therefore logical that future political developments in Pakistan will have a significant impact on the Gulf. In a sense, for nearly three decades out of the 43 years of its independent existence, Pakistan's political culture has been much closer to that of the Gulf countries than to India. The emergence of democracy in Pakistan, though constrained in many ways, would still constitute a divide from the Gulf's political culture. Iran is somewhere in between, with its elections and some degree of incipient pluralism. The chances of a wave of change originating in Pakistan and its effect travelling westwards appear to be much higher than in reverse.

In a sense, significant changes are taking place all around the Gulf states which will have a major impact on political and security developments in the Gulf area. The unification of Yemen, the stirrings of reform in Jordan and Kuwait, the rise of Iraqi power and its secularism, all these together should lead to Saudi Arabia focussing more on its own domestic structure and security and less on spreading aggressive Wahhabism. The possibility of Afghanistan's having a pluralistic government that is not dominated by orthodox elements, the assertion of subnational identities on the part of Soviet Central-Asian Moslem republics without their becoming rigidly orthodox, the subnationalist rivalries in Pakistan and the rise of Iraqi power, all should persuade Iran to cool her Shi'ite ardour. The fact of there being over 100 million Moslems in secular India and 160 million Moslems in secular Indonesia, together with the numbers who live in other relatively secular environments such as Soviet Central-Asia, Egypt, Algeria, etc., should also have an impact on the more orthodox Islamic communities. This could well be somewhat similar to the experience the Christian world underwent in the 17th, 18th and 19th centuries. The communications and transportation revolutions, and the increasing global focus on human rights, are likely to support the secularisation, pluralisation and liberalisation of the orthodox societies. The crucial issue is whether their transformation will be a process free of violence. Kashmir, Pakistan, Afghanistan, Lebanon, what happened in Hama in Syria,[17] the use of chemical weapons against the Kurds,[18] violence in Central Asian republics and Azarbaijan,[19] the uprising in Xinjiang[20] etc., would all tend to indicate a pessimistic rather than an optimistic future.

The Impact of Oil Prices

To a considerable extent the degree of violence in opposition to change will depend upon the financial clout of the orthodox states and, consequently, upon the oil price and the demand for oil. The recent efforts of OPEC have not succeeded in imposing discipline on the oil-producing states or in persuading them to abide by their stipulated quotas. The result is a glut in the market. Secondly, the projections the oil-producing states and some other experts make about growth in the demand for oil as an energy source may need to be reviewed in the light of increasing warnings about global warming due to the greenhouse effect.[21] There are demands from the developing nations that in order to accommodate their energy needs for development through generation using conventional technologies, the industrialised countries should cut back on their generation of greenhouse gases.[22] In some quarters a revisitation of the nuclear-energy option has also been urged.[23] Talking specifically of the subcontinent's energy needs, India already produces 60 per cent of its oil needs and further plans to tap new offshore and onshore sources are under implementation. Major programmes for coal-based thermal power, hydro-power and nuclear power are under way. Though it is not envisaged that India will become wholly self-sufficient in energy in the near future, its reliance on Gulf oil is not perhaps likely to increase significantly. India also buys its oil from different sources, both Arab and Iranian, and this has worked well, even during the Iran-Iraq war.

Pakistan's reliance on external energy-sources is higher than India's. Some new finds of oil and gas are reported. Pakistan has also planned some major hydro-power projects and is negotiating for nuclear power plants from China and France.

There is an Iranian proposal to have a 'friendship' gas-pipeline to Pakistan and India.   In India there are some reservations about the pipeline passing through Pakistani territory, and therefore being vulnerable to Pakistani interruption, but the pipeline should be beneficial to Pakistan.[24]

Mutual Impact

The energy, trade and labour-supply links between the subcontinent and the Gulf states give the two major countries of the subcontinent a stake in the stability and peace of the Gulf. Pakistan has greater involvement in the security establishments of various Gulf-states though India has a training team in Iraq. If there is any inter-sectoral violence in the Gulf states or any inter-state clashes, India is likely to keep out.   During the Iran-Iraq war, Pakistan appears to have supplied military material to both countries, while India did not do so to either.[25]   Whether in any future conflict Pakistan would be able to keep out, in view of its closer military collaboration with Gulf countries, cannot be predicted with any certainty at this stage.   There has been mention by Pakistani military figures of reviving the military links between Pakistan, Iran and Turkey that existed during the CENTO Pact.[26]   The heavy investment by Pakistan in its navy is also difficult to explain except in terms of a possible role in the Gulf area.[27]   Mention has already been made of the possibility of military rivalries in the region with the growing military capabilities of Iraq and Pakistan.

There is yet another linkage between the subcontinent and the Gulf - narcotics.   A number of banks and trading-houses in the Gulf area are reported to be playing a key role, along with similar establishments in Europe and the Far East, in the drug trade and money-laundering.   One case that came to notice was the BCCI involvement.   According to the Pakistani press a realistic estimate of drug-generated money in Pakistan would be around $8-10 billion, though higher estimates are also mentioned.[28]   This would mean that a quarter of Pakistan's GNP was accounted for by drugs.   The role of drug money and its impact on Pakistani society and politics has been dealt with by Shahid Javed Burki, Senior Economist with the World Bank, in his recent writings.[29]   Certain of the Gulf states have a vital role to play both in the onward transmission of drugs and in the inflow of laundered money into Pakistan.[30] It is reported that several large heroin-laboratories have been established in Ribat where the borders of Pakistan, Afghanistan and Iran meet.[31] While Iran has punished hundreds of drug traffickers with the death sentence, the Pakistani press talks of a heroin-Kalashnikov culture in their own country. In the light of harsh measures in Iran, the Gulf countries appear to form a more convenient route whereby drugs can reach the West. India appears to be a staging-post in this transaction. The turmoil in all the provinces of Pakistan, and in Jammu and Kashmir and the Punjab in India, perhaps make it convenient for the drugs trade to flourish since, whether in South-East Asia, Latin America or in South and South-West Asia, insurgency, civil turmoil and the drugs trade go hand-in-hand.

With the current relaxation of tension between the major powers, the Soviet Union de-ideologising its foreign policy, the increasing emphasis on subnational and sectoral identities and the demand for pluralism, the area from Pakistan to the Mediterranean (some may say from the Pacific to the Mediterranean, though I do not personally adhere to that view) is likely to become unstable and subject to both inter-state and, even more so, intra-state violence. In this part of the world the traditions of a number of civilisations interact - the Indic, the Persian and the Islamic Arab. Not far away are the Sinic, Turkic and European traditions in civilisation. All of them are undergoing profound change and these changes interact with each other. Of these traditions, the European and the Indic civilisations are secular, pluralistic and liberal democratic. Turkey is trying hard to adjust itself to gain entry into the European Economic Community. The Soviet Union, too, is transforming itself into a pluralistic society with some consequential impact on its Islamic republics. Given these pressures all around, how long can the countries of this area resist change?

Notes

1   Maulana Kausar Niazi, *Aur Line Cut Gaye*, ch. 9, 'Unknown Facts about the Reprocessing Plant', translated from Urdu and reproduced in, *Strategic Digest* (New Delhi), May 1987.
2   Zulfikar Ali Bhutto, *If I Am Assassinated* (Vikas Publishing House, New Delhi, 1979), pp. 137-8.
3   *World Military Expenditures and Arms Transfers, 1988* (United States Arms Control and Disarmament Agency, 1989), p. 17.
4   'A Survey of the Arab World', *The Economist*, 12 May 1990, p. 26.
5   *World Military Expenditures*, pp. 17-20.
6   *Jane's Defence Weekly*, 26 May 1990, pp. 1021-42.
7   *Asian Recorder*, 1973, p. 11320.
8   Rashid Ahmad Khan, 'Pakistan's Perception of peace and security in the Gulf', *Strategic Studies* (Islamabad), winter 1988, pp. 80-99.
9   Bhutto, *If I am assassinated*, p. 121.
     More recently General Aslam Beg, Pakistan's Chief of Army Staff, was compared to General Von Schlieffen, *Nation*, 17 Jan. 1990.
10   *Haider* (Pakistan), 16 May 1990.
11   *Muslim*, 24 Jan. 1990, reporting demonstrations against Soviet action against Azarbaijanis; Mushahid Husain, *Nation*, 4 Feb. 1990; *Muslim*, 12 Feb. 1990; *Frontier Post*, 12 Feb. 1990.
12   For different views on the implications of the Shariat bill if it becomes law see *Dawn* (Karachi), 16 May 1990, 21 May 1990; *Pakistan Times*, 15 May 1990; *Frontier Post*, 18 May 1990, 20 May 1990; *Jasarat*, 15 May 1990; *Nation*, 19 May 1990; *Jang*, 20 May 1990. The President of Pakistan has supported the bill. The Chairman of Pakistan's Jurists' League of Justice (Retd), Shaukat Ali, is of the view that if the bill becomes law it would supercede Pakistan's Constitution of 1973. The Ruling Pakistan People's Party, Women's Organisations, Shiʿa amd Human Rights activists have opposed the bill.
13   Bhutto, *If I am assassinated*, pp. 167-72.
14   Bhabhani Sengupta, *The Afghan Syndrome* (Vikas Publishing House, Delhi, 1982), pp. 44, 116-18, 131-2.
15   *Facts on File, 1988*, pp. 231-2, 247-8, 279-80.
16   In India and Pakistan scores of people get killed in terrorist violence every week. While even individual acts of terrorism in the West and Israel are reported in the Western media, the daily terrorism in the sub-continent does not receive the same attention. Please see pp. 36-7 on India, p. 38 on Pakistan, in *Patterns of global terrorism, 1989* (US Department of State Publication 9743, April 1990).
17   *Facts on File, 1982*, pp. 102, 134.
18   *Facts on File, 1988*, p. 215.
19   'The Soviet Union - A Survey', section on ethnic nationalities, in *Financial Times*, 12 March 1990.
20   K. Subrahmanyam, 'Muslim Separatism', *Hindustan Times* (Delhi), 31 May 1990.

21   The latest warning comes from a working-group of the UN Inter-governmental Panel on Climate Change: *International Herald Tribune*, 26-7 May 1990.

22   'The Changing Atmosphere: the Implications for Global Security', conference statement, Toronto, Canada, 27-30 June 1988; 'Recommendation of Working Group on Energy', p. 8.

23   Ibid.

24   *Business Recorder* (Pakistan), 15 May 1990.

25   This is inferred from *World Military Expenditures*, table on p. 22.

26   *Dawn*, 6 Dec. 1988, General Beg's address to the Eighth International Seminar on Defence Technology.

27   Between 1988-9 and 1989-90 Pakistan increased its major surface combatants (Destroyers and Frigates) from 8 to 17: Institute for Strategic Studies (London), *Military Balance, 1988-9, 1989-90*.

28   Karachi cover story on 'Narco Power, Pakistan's Parallel Government?', in *Newsline*, Dec. 1989, p. 17.

29   Shahid Javed Burki, *Muslim*, 12, 13, 14 and 15 Feb. 1990.

30   *Newsline*, Dec. 1989, p. 18.

31   *Newsline*, Dec. 1989, p. 19.

6. THE RISE AND CONVERGENCE OF THE 'MIDDLE' IN THE WORLD ECONOMY: THE CASE OF THE NICS AND THE GULF STATES

*Anoushiravan Ehteshami**

Stanley Hoffman wrote in the mid-1970s that the age of the bi-polar world (system) was over, claiming instead that we were moving towards a multi-polar system and identifying five major units in this system - I have termed this the 'pentagonal system'. A.W. Clausen, the ex-Chairman at the World Bank, has had some interesting things to say about the changing world-order too. He also believes that the bi-polar system is dead and buried, a process which began well before the demise of the Warsaw Pact. He has identified eight discernible poles of high 'economic significance' in the current international environment; four are the centres of high industrialisation (North America, Western Europe, Japan and Eastern Europe), and the other four are the constituent parts of the 'Third World':
- the capital-surplus oil-exporting countries of the Middle East;
- the semi-industrialised developing countries (i.e., the NICs);
- the great populous countries of Asia, and
- the absolute poor countries of sub-Saharan Africa.[1]

In different ways, Hoffman and Clausen are discussing the same process but with varying degrees of emphasis. Hoffman's pentagonal system is an account of the new *division* of power in

----

* The author wishes to note that the satisfactory completion of this chapter would not have been possible without access to the Centre for Arab Gulf Studies' extensive and varied resources, and certainly not without the assistance and generosity of the Documentation Unit's librarians, Sue, Parvine and Ruth.

the world; i.e., between China, the USSR, Japan, the EC and the US, whereas Clausen's is an account of the *distribution* of that power in economic terms. Furthermore, despite its economy, Clausen's perspective does lead the way towards facilitating an examination of the dynamism of the system and its general constituent parts.

'As a field of inquiry', wrote Raymond Platig over two decades ago, 'international relations studies the distribution of power on a global scale and the interplay between and among power centres'.[2] The two variables he identifies, namely the distribution of power on a global scale and the interplay between and among power centres, come into their own in my analysis of two of the poles in the system as identified by Mr Clausen. I intend to concentrate very much on the 'interplay between and among power centres' rather than the distributional patterns of power globally. Nonetheless, a serious study of the one will necessarily require an awareness, at the very least, of the other. So the conclusion to this chapter will in part also address the impact and implications of the interplay between the two power-centres selected for analysis for the global system as a whole and, in particular, for the distribution of power on a global scale. Therefore, far from looking at the whole picture in this study, I will primarily be concerning myself with some of the components of the global system and of the transnational system of relations.[3] Reductionism, therefore, is an unavoidable exercise here.

Top on his list of the four 'poles' from the Third World, Mr Clausen placed the following two: the capital-surplus oil-exporting countries and the NICs. While much has been written on each pole in its own right, little comparative analysis of the ways that these Third World poles interact with each other has been forthcoming. To be sure, the implications of the rise of the OPEC cartel for the position of the Third World generally has been studied at some length. So too has the impact of the rising petroleum-prices for the oil-importing countries. But too little attention, in my view, has so far been given to the nature of the interaction of the Third World poles with each other. This chapter is an attempt at exploring the bilateral relations between two such poles.

At the heart of this project is an investigation of the coming to prominence in global terms of the two above-named Third

World poles and of their interaction with each other. In an hierarchical conceptualisation of the global system I suppose these sets of countries would in general be regarded as the semi-periphery or semi-core nations (depending on one's preferences), and I have unflatteringly called them collectively the 'bit' or layer in the middle in the world economy.

The Rise of the 'Capital-Surplus' Oil-Exporting States

In historical terms the fortunes of the oil-exporting countries have been intertwined with those of OPEC's, and the latter's emergence onto the world scene has certainly proved as spectacular as the impact of the capital-surplus states. Thirteen years after its birth, this raw-material producers' cartel had managed to increase the price of crude oil from $2.59 per barrel (/b) in January 1973 to $5.04/b by December. By October 1975 the price had gone up to $11.5/b, and in November 1979 it reached $24/b. But even before the implications of these latest price hikes could be absorbed the price of crude oil crossed the $30/b barrier, reaching a new high of $32/b in November 1980 and the all-time high of $34/b almost exactly a year later.[4] The oil revenues of all the Arab oil-exporting countries and Iran experienced substantial increases during OPEC's 'Golden Decade' - the 1973-81 period (see Table 6.1). In 1980, for instance, the combined oil revenues of the Arab oil-exporters reached $213.8 billion, half of which accrued to Saudi Arabia alone, a sum nearly as great as the value of the world's total exports only 12 years earlier.[5] For the longer 1974-85 period the same group of countries' total revenues stood at the staggering sum of $1,223 billion, greater than the value of total world exports ($1,144 billion) for the 23-year period 1953-70. Thus a new layer to the world hierarchy was born; the so-called surplus-capital oil-exporters, almost all of whom (with the exception of Libya) were Gulf states. By virtue of their increased wealth this collective began to move rapidly up the 'tiers' in the global system. It is worth remembering that as recently as 1956-7 Iran, arguably the Gulf region's most industrialised country, had to rely on British credit, American aid and concessionary loans from the IMF and the World Bank in order to meet her foreign exchange requirements of only $376 million.

Some of these countries, of course, have done better than others. Generally speaking and over time, it could be said that in the Gulf as a whole, the low-capital-absorbing capital-surplus countries have done better than the two higher-capital-absorbing countries of Iran and Iraq - both of which have been ready and willing to squander much of their windfall over a bloody conflict for most of the 1980s. While Iraq steadily became a debtor nation in the 1980s, for instance, Kuwait proceeded to consolidate her international holdings and substantially increase her foreign investments. Thus, since the early 1980s her returns on these international holdings have consistently exceeded her oil revenues. Total financial reserves of the Reserve Fund for Future Generations, for example, stood at about $75 billion by 1982, over six times her cumulative oil-revenues for the 1964-73 period ($11.8 billion). Kuwait's international investment strategy was so successful that in just six years (1976-81) her exports to invisible earnings ratio had dropped from 4.3:1 to 1.5:1.[6] Since the turn of the 1970s Kuwait has been an active investor in Western markets, acquiring equity holdings in some of the major corporations of the Western industrialised countries, including a substantial share in British Petroleum, one of the founding members of the 'Seven Sisters' club. It is said that equity investments account for approximately 50 per cent of Kuwait's net foreign assets. Such investments are undertaken both in financial services institutions and in manufacturing concerns in the West. In the 1970s official Kuwaiti investors obtained equities in such well known corporations as Daimler-Benz (15 per cent), Metallgesellschaft (20 per cent) and Volkswagen do Brasil (10 per cent), reaching a total of $4 billion in West Germany and $2.5 billion in the UK by 1982.[7] Kuwaiti investments in the UK alone exceeded $6 billion by 1987. In the 1980s Kuwait continued to add to her investment portfolio in the West, acquiring the Santa Fe International Corp. of the US for $2.5 billion in 1981 and a 24 per cent stake in the West German chemical group Hoechst less than a year later.[8] Add to these investments Kuwait's 25 per cent stake in the International Energy Development Corp. and a clear investment strategy emerges which not only aims to obtain profitable outlets for the country's 'excess' capital abroad, but also attempts, according to one expert, at building up a comprehensive international oil company, and its individual acquisitions dovetail accordingly. Santa Fe has provided technical expertise and Hoechst has marketing experience which will be useful for Kuwait's petrochemical output... The overall aim of this [overseas] investment is to build a strong industrial base, not to replace the oil industry but to complement it.[9]

Many of the other capital-exporters have pursued policies similar to Kuwait's. Abu Dhabi has obtained a 12.5 per cent stake in Reuters and 33.3 per cent of Gulf Occidental Investment Co. of Geneva. Qatar has acquired a 40 per cent share in a petrochemicals refinery at Dunkirk and Saudi Arabia has continued to pour her substantial assets into government securities and other portfolio investments abroad. By the mid-1970s Saudi Arabia's foreign assets stood at about $50 billion, over 45 times her assets in 1969.[10] Indeed the rise in her foreign assets, from $2.3 billion in 1972 to $66 billion in 1977 and $75 billion only two years later, and an increase in income generated by such assets from just $125 million in 1972 to $7.5 billion, invited recognition from the international community of the importance of this capital-surplus country to the stability of the international financial system, and in part helped towards her subsequent 'promotion' to the heart of the global financial regulator - the IMF - as a governor state.[11] Furthermore, the cumulative current-account balance of $301.3 billion for the 1971-88 period for the GCC countries alone indicates the centrality of these oil-states to the world economy. The collective significance of the oil-rich Gulf states (high and low capital-absorbing alike) to the international financial system cannot be overestimated. Needless to say, the exercise of their financial muscle, collectively or individually, would have major consequences for both the developed and the developing countries. It was their huge bank deposits, for instance, which facilitated the transfer of large credits by Western European and American banks to fast-industrialising oil-importing developing countries like Brazil, Argentina, South Korea, Taiwan, India, Turkey and others. The withdrawal of their foreign bank deposits alone (37 per cent of the total in 1984), which increased from $9 billion in 1973 to $140.5 billion by 1983,[12] would naturally affect the fortunes of the great private financial institutions of the capitalist world. But any such act would adversely affect the future prospects of many of the developing countries too - particularly the resource-poor and capital-poor Third World states. Indeed it is not too unreasonable to argue that as the demand for oil continues to rise in the 1990s and the supplies outside the Gulf region and the Arabian Peninsula progressively dry up, a scenario in sharp contrast to the experience of the 1980s, these oil-rich countries are likely to consolidate their role as being influential to both the stability of the world economy and as an important variable in transnational relations for at least the next two decades. It is worth remembering in this context that in 1980 these countries' total capital exports stood at $116 billion, over twice that of the advanced capitalist countries' figure ($51.5 billion) for the same year. Hence, these capital-surplus oil-exporting countries are, in one form or another, here to stay. The rise of their current surplus may decline and revenues from oil and petroleum products fluctuate, but their huge financial and corporate assets abroad, their huge oil-reserves and economic potential combined, ensure their survival as a unique grouping in the world economy.

Most indicators would support the view that this tier in the hierarchy of states will not be a transitory one. They would seem nonetheless to have tied their own fortunes to those of the developed states in such a way that, paradoxically, they have managed to limit their own independence of action within the system. Despite their undisputed financial power, their huge foreign assets have substantial value only in the context of continuing Western economic prosperity. Partly in response to their Western-oriented pattern of investments, therefore, and partly in pursuit of other capitalist economic partners besides the OECD countries, the capital-surplus oil-exporters have been seeking closer relations with the NICs, themselves the products of the uneven development of capitalism in the post-war world economy and the increasingly vociferous competitors of the advanced capitalist countries. The oil-rich Gulf states can be seen to be reacting to their interdependent and yet evidently asymmetrical relationship with the Western countries by attempting to expand their economic ties with the leading Third World economies. The latter, on the other hand, have been compelled to explore the high-income Gulf states' markets in part as a way of balancing their substantial trade-imbalance with the oil-exporters, and also to put to the test their well nurtured economic prowess and increasingly sophisticated industrial capabilities in such rich but competitive markets as the high-income Gulf states. They have of course been able to capitalise on the expansion of the Gulf states' 'development budgets' since the oil-boom of the early 1970s. For example, Iraq allocated some ID2.4 billion to the development budget in 1977, or 60 per cent (over $12 billion) of her oil revenues and ID2.8 billion in 1978 (an increase of 19 per cent), with the industrial sector's share increasing from ID709 million in 1976 to ID966 million a year later (41 per cent of the total).[13]   Kuwait increased her development budget from KD263 million in 1976 to KD392 million in 1977; Qatar's 1978 development budget increased by 15 per cent over the previous year's, to stand at QR5.9 billion; and, Bahrain allocated some BD145 million to the country's economic development in 1978 - over half of the country's oil revenues.   To continue along the same theme, Saudi Arabia actually spent a total of SR688 billion ($206.6 billion) under the country's Second Development Plan (1975-80) instead of the projected SR498 billion ($150 billion), and as a direct consequence of the oil price rises, Iran drastically revised upwards the financial allocations devoted to her Fifth Development Plan from IR1.3 billion to IR2.9 billion - an increase of 119 per cent.[14]

The capital-exporting or high-income Gulf states (plus Libya) have thus been influencing world economic relations in complex ways since 1973. As underpinners of the post-Bretton Woods international financial system on the one hand, and as active capital lenders internationally on the other. As providers of rich markets in one sense, and as suppliers of 'excess' capital in another. As the root cause of the Third World debt problem, some would argue, and as those economies with the potential to disrupt seriously the current international system of production and exchange.   In short, despite the advent of international financial turmoil since the late 1960s they have in fact found themselves a profitable 'niche' in the world economy and a unique position in the international hierarchy of states. By virtue of the relatively high prices charged for the export of their raw material this handful of countries have formed a new pole in the international system and have, in the process, managed to turn on its head the traditional perception of Third World countries as capital-poor and economic resource-poor economies endemically and fatally dependent on the industrialised countries for investment capital as well as for the import of other goods and services. Although the recent experience of a group of high-income oil-exporting countries may not be sufficient evidence for rejecting the orthodox perception of the North and the South, it nonetheless forcefully knocks on the head the inbuilt assumptions of universality underlining the so-called asymmetrical North-South relations within the modern world economy.

It goes without saying that there still exists much debate regarding this group of countries and their role and status in the international system. Many observers have cautioned us to examine more closely this apparent 'miracle' and have urged us to ask whether real development and a tangible transfer of power have actually taken place. As Nazih Ayubi, for example, has argued, these oil-rich countries are not only quite dependent on the advanced capitalist countries for trade and investment, but are also rather 'vulnerable' as far as 'their lamentable defence capabilities are concerned'. One should remember, he cautions, 'that petrodollars notwithstanding, the OPEC countries are themselves part of the Third World and that as such they remain subject to most of the problems, contradictions and agonies from which the underdeveloped world is suffering'.[15] This said, the answer to the question of whether a real transfer of power within the international system has been taking place and whether this group of countries has developed into a pole, must in my view be a qualified yes at this juncture. Additional reasons for this conclusion will, I hope, emerge in the second half of this chapter.

But before any assessment of the new layers in the world economy can be made and the issue of a 'convergence in the middle' debated, some account must be given of the other pole in the modern-day hierarchical Third World, the NICs.

The Emergence of the NICs

The make-up of this group of countries is even more heterogeneous than the high-income/capital-surplus oil-exporters category and their role in the world economy equally controversial. Indeed, as the following will illustrate, there is little consensus among observers over the list of countries categorised as NICs. Furthermore, while at crucial junctures over the last 20 years or so a 'pax OPECica' has been in evidence, no such 'pax NICica' has as yet emerged; nor indeed, given the nature of the NICs and their position in the international system, is the emergence of a 'pax NICica' very likely in the near future. For the NICs are locked in mortal competition with each other (and with the OECD countries) as they constantly push for bigger and higher international market shares and better access to global markets, wherever they may be. In simple terms, this process could be seen as an inevitable outcome of their export-substitution industrialisation strategies and their desperate struggles, firstly, to keep ahead of the next tier of manufactured-goods exporters, the Newly Exporting Countries (NECs) of Malaysia, Thailand, Indonesia, Sri Lanka, Pakistan, Egypt, the PRC, the Philippines and Bolivia; and, secondly, and just as importantly, to continue to strive towards closing the industrial and technological gap between themselves and the advanced capitalist countries if their past success rate is to be maintained. But before the chemistry of their relations with the other poles within the world economy can be explored, the NIC phenomenon must not only be identified but also defined in the context of a rapidly changing world economy.

At about the same time as the challenge of OPEC, the OECD countries in particular became vocal about the speed of growth in the manufacturing-industries and manufactured exports of this geographically disparate group of countries. With the emergence of the NICs phenomenon, another aspect of the conventional conception of a North-South division of labour which was associated with the exchange of manufactured goods for raw materials and primary commodities was seriously called into question. This handful of countries at the top of the World Bank's middle-income list of developing countries have threatened to rewrite the traditional classification of the Third World. But what are their common characteristics and which unique features help them ride the storms of the world economy? James Caporaso is one of many authors who have attempted to formulate certain criteria for identifying the NICs: phenomenal economic growth rates, the rapid development of the manufacturing sector and the rising share of manufactures over total GDP.[16]   Add to this their increased trade in manufactures, a rising share of industrial employment and an increase in real GDP *per capita* relative to the developed capitalist countries and the qualification is complete. But inevitably, the selection of countries is dependent on the range of criteria deployed and the benchmarkers for each variable used, and as such therefore is rather arbitrary. Using his own three criteria, Caporaso puts forward a list of nine 'semi-peripheral' or newly industrialising countries; four from the Far East (Hong Kong, the Philippines, Singapore and South Korea), three from Latin America (Argentina, Brazil and Mexico) and two from Europe (Portugal and Spain). But in practice he adds Taiwan to his list and concedes that 'strong inter-regional concentration' exists whereby Asia was the leading exporter of manufactured exports from the Third World in the mid-1970s (60 per cent), followed by Latin America (17 per cent), South Asia (8 per cent) and Africa (8 per cent).[17] Within each region also one or two NICs have accounted for the bulk of this Third World pole's manufactured exports; Hong Kong and South Korea in the Far East, Brazil and Mexico in Latin America and India in the South Asian region. A concentration of economic power is in evidence even amongst the ranks of the NICs themselves.

Since the early writings on the NICs more sophisticated and rigorous models of classification have emerged. By applying a wider range of variables, one recent study concludes that only three true NICs exist (Singapore, South Korea and Taiwan), followed by half-a-dozen or so near-NIC-status countries.[18] Although a thorough discussion of the merits and demerits of these various classifications is beyond the scope of this chapter, some reference to them was deemed necessary as a way of illustrating the continuing confusion over classifying and redefining the new poles in the Third World discussed earlier. What is of considerable importance to this study, however, is the resilience of this dynamic layer in the international system, sandwiched as it is between the less developed Third World and the advanced industrial countries. In terms of global stratifications these countries occupy a similar space to that of the high-income oil-exporters (of the Gulf), having arrived here, however, through a totally different route. These two sets of countries combined would represent the narrow band of the 'middle layer' in the world economy. Together they have cornered the Third World's industrial capacity as well as its capital resources. For the purposes of this study a core of eight NICs have been identified: the Asian 'Gang of Four' (Singapore, South Korea, Hong Kong and Taiwan), India and, from Latin America, Argentina, Brazil and Mexico. Some, like Brazil and Mexico, are highly indebted countries. Some others, like South Korea, Singapore and Taiwan have come to enjoy substantial financial surpluses in recent times and are amongst the Third World's leading foreign investors. Others, like Mexico, Brazil and India, also export significant quantities of raw materials and/or agricultural products. To complete the contrast, some of the NICs are tiny city-states or pariahs, and others, like Brazil and India, are truly continental-size countries and politically regarded as leading Third World states.

To establish the arguments regarding a convergence of the middle layer in the world economy a sample of five of the 'most active' NICs have been chosen for further comment. These are: Singapore, South Korea, Taiwan, India and Brazil.   Before proceeding with an analysis of the relations between the two prominent Third World poles an empirical understanding must be obtained of the economic power of the NICs. What follows is a summary of some of the aggregate data.   It goes without saying that naturally some NICs would appear to have performed better than others if the data is disaggregated.

The average annual growth rates of the NICs have been quite impressive over the last two or three decades.[19] The six leading NICs' (Brazil, Mexico, South Korea, Hong Kong, Taiwan and Singapore) average annual growth rate for the 1964-73 period stood at 8.4 per cent and for the following decade (1973-83) at 5.3 per cent. By comparison only Japan from the ranks of the advanced industrialised capitalist countries matched these sorts of growth rates (9.2 per cent and 3.7 per cent respectively). As a consequence the NICs have increased their share of the total market-economies' GDP from 3.5 per cent in 1964 to 6.2 per cent in 1983, compared to an overall decline from 72.1 per cent to 68.7 per cent for the 'Group of Nine' highly industrialised OECD countries. If we were to add to the figures the growth rates of the countries considered as NICs by the OECD (Turkey, Portugal, Spain, Greece, Israel, Yugoslavia, Argentina and India), the share of this group in total capitalist economies' GDP (output) would easily exceed 10 per cent.   A remarkable achievement for these dozen or so countries in such a short space of time.

The trend in their manufacturing output (as measured by manufacturing value added - MVA) has been similar to that of their GDP - high and rather rapid. The MVA grew at an average of 10.9 per cent *per annum* for the six mentioned NICs during the 1964-73 period, and by 5.3 per cent *per annum* for the 1973-83 decade. Again only Japan matched these rates of growth in MVA amongst the industrialised countries. A simple conclusion emerging from the comparison of GDP and MVA growth-rates figures is that the NICs have progressively become more reliant on the manufacturing sector. The share of MVA in GDP, moreover, has increased substantially since the mid-1960s to stand, on average, at about 28 per cent in each of the six NICs mentioned above. The comparable figure for the US is 24 per cent, the UK 21 per cent, the FRG 36 per cent, France 28 per cent and Japan 39 per cent.

Furthermore, the annual growth rates figures in manufacturing of the leading NICs support the contention that a new layer in the world economy has been born from the ranks of the Third World countries who appear to have been ready and willing to industrialise and compete in world markets at any price. South Korea's average annual growth rate in manufacturing stood at 18.5 per cent for the period extending from 1960 through to 1974 (on the eve of the first oil-shock) - one of the five highest in the world - followed by Singapore (13.7 per cent), Brazil (8-9 per cent), Mexico (8.6 per cent) and Argentina (6.3 per cent).[20] The pre-1974 data is particularly interesting because it clearly illustrates the rise to prominence of the NIC pole in the world economy well before the emergence of the capital-surplus oil-exporters onto the world scene. But by 1974, when the oil-exporters pole consolidated its position as the sole source of 'excess capital' in the Third World, little sign of interdependence and mutual reinforcement was in evidence.

Concomitant with their increased share in world manufacturing-output, the NICs have also increased their share of world market-economies' manufactured exports from only 1.9 per cent in 1965 to 9 per cent by the mid-1980s. South Korea's share now in capitalist world exports of manufactures is greater than 2.5 per cent and thus exceeds that of Australia (0.5 per cent) and Sweden (2.2 per cent) for instance. Moreover, based on current projections it is likely to equal that of Canada, France, Italy and the United Kingdom by the turn of the century.

Remarkably, manufactured exports now account for over 50 per cent of the total exports of the leading six NICs; that of South Korea, Taiwan and Hong Kong exceeds 90 per cent (surpassed in the world only by Japan's 97.2 per cent). It is also this same group of countries which have accounted for the bulk of the Third World's manufactured exports since the 1960s. By 1977, the six were exporting some $32.8 billion worth of manufactured products to the OECD countries, by far the most significant Third World export category after petroleum. The combined figure for the six was greater than the manufactured exports of France ($32.2 billion), the UK ($27.9 billion) and Canada ($19.4 billion) and only marginally smaller than that of Japan ($35.7 billion) to the same group of countries. These countries' leading conglomerates and corporations have, since the mid-1970s, entered the world stage as the suppliers of technology, industrial goods and services and other expertise on par, and in conjunction, with some of the best-established Western interests in the field. More often than not in collaboration with Western corporate interests, one or more of the leading NICs have become the exporters of cars, semi-conductors, computers, light and sophisticated electronic consumer goods, steel, ships, refined petroleum products, specialist and general construction expertise, chemicals and even armaments. In short they can collectively meet the industrial and consumer needs of almost any Third World state and many of those also even of the industrial countries.

The above figures and data, I hope, have helped to arouse some interest in this group of countries, now on the fringes of the so-called sub-core states of the international hierarchy (the Nordic countries, Austria, Holland, Belgium and Switzerland) in terms of socio-economic development. Despite the controversies surrounding the nature and number of the NICs, I would tend to argue that they have found an appreciable niche in global economic relations and are continuously exploiting their advantages, thus creating new opportunities for themselves in the international market-place.

I have so far referred to these two relatively new poles in the international system in abstract form and without much cross-referencing. Their interrelationships, however, are much more direct than so far assumed. Before proceeding to discuss the links between the NIC pole and the high-income oil-exporters pole, it is of some value to establish that the NIC phenomenon is not a universal experience generally capable of emulation. It has not only been history-specific but, as many would argue, number-specific too. In other words, the NICs were born as a result of the emergence of capitalism in conjunction with a number of indigenously induced as well as exogenous factors. As Colin Bradford, has put it,

The NIC phenomenon has not arisen as a consequence of generalised forces of economic growth and industrialised spread, but rather is the result of the unusual convergence of a variety of forces and circumstances...a special phenomenon which only a few countries in any given period in history will be able to undertake and sustain.[21]

They are unique both by virtue of being what they are and for being able to capitalise on a combination of special factors and processes beyond their own control. But in essence, having been able to take advantage of a favourable international environment these two groups, the NICs and the oil-rich Gulf states, have each, for better or for worse, increased their exposure to the international system, comfortably entering realms traditionally considered the exclusive domain of the established industrialised powers. They have come to be known as the 'countries on the move' and as such tend to reflect the more dynamic aspects of transnational relations in the late twentieth century.

The Convergence of the 'Middle': the NICs and the Gulf States

As a consequence of their rapid industrialisation and more intensive use of industrial inputs, many NICs have become progressively more dependent on OPEC oil, and as the price of this energy source has increased so too have the NICs' import bills, thus potentially adversely affecting their delicate export-performance and their balance of payments situation.[22] The crude-oil imports of Brazil, for instance, more than doubled in the two decades 1969-88, from 301,900 barrels per day (b/d) to some 649,000 b/d (see Table 6.2). For South Korea and Singapore it increased by a factor of more than five, and for Taiwan it increased by over eight times over the same twenty-year period.

But, as Table 6.3 shows, the cost of their petroleum imports has been rising much faster than the rise in their total oil-liftings. So, by 1984, the highly indebted Brazil had to sacrifice about one quarter of her precious export-earnings on the import of (largely) petroleum from the Gulf; just about one fifth of South Korea's export earnings went the same way, as did one third of Singapore's. As for Taiwan, her crude-oil imports of about 350,000 b/d in 1979 cost her some $2.4 billion, equivalent to over one fifth of her total manufactured-exports to the OECD countries ($10.4 billion) in the same year. By 1985, however, Taiwan had to pay $3.3 billion for her reduced imported oil needs (from 349,700 b/d in 1979 to 324,300 b/d in 1985), but as the quantity and value of her exports had increased significantly, the increased imported-oil bill stood at only about one eighth of her total manufactured exports to the OECD countries ($23.9 billion). Some of the NICs, therefore, were more badly hit by the 'oil shocks' of the 1973-4 and 1979-81 periods (cf. Table 6.4), but almost all seem to have been prepared to turn the significantly higher imported-oil bills to their own long-term advantage.

One obvious way for the NICs to counter this huge and, in the medium term, unavoidable import-burden was to seek to increase their (largely manufactured and services) exports to the very suppliers of their energy needs - the high-income oil-exporting countries themselves (see Table 6.5).[23] They have proved flexible enough to acquire business contracts in the Gulf states through either standard commercial transactions or through the increasingly popular barter method of payments. The phenomenal rises in oil prices in the early 1980s accelerated the pace of the NICs' counterbalancing policies. To be sure, many of the NICs had managed to establish sound economic relations with the Gulf states during the course of the 1970s. The more significant amongst these were the following:

- the South Korean government's agreement with Saudi Arabia for the construction of a crude-oil terminal and storage depot on Korea's south coast through a $350 million joint-venture project.
- the South Korean government's agreement with NIOC (Iran) for the delivery of 60,000 b/d of oil over a 15-year period for a joint-venture refinery in South Korea, costing some $180 million to construct.
- Petrobras's (Brazil) discovery of oil in the Majnun region of Iraq in 1976, under its 1972 service contract with INOC.

Brazil would have lifted between 16 and 21 per cent of the total output at a preferential price.
- Brazil's negotiations with Iran over a $1 billion trade bill in 1977, whereby Brazilian imports of Iranian oil would be linked to exports of manufactured and agricultural products from Brazil.
- A joint-venture agreement to form the Hormuz Petroleum Co. for (primarily) offshore exploration activities, equally owned by NIOC and Mobil-Petrobras (Brazil).
- The Taiwan Fertiliser Company's agreement with the Saudi Arabian Basic Industries Corporation (SABIC) for the construction of a $360 million, jointly owned fertiliser complex at Jubail to produce 1000 tons/day of ammonia and 1,600 tons/day of urea.
- India being awarded a $30 million contract in Saudi Arabia for the construction of a 480km 18-inch pipeline to carry crude oil from the Marmul fields.

Political as well as economic relations in the 1980s between the two poles have undergone some qualitative changes. Partly as a response to the higher petroleum prices and partly against the protectionist measures of the OECD countries, some NICs embarked on a concerted effort to capture and hold those (high-value) markets in the Gulf hitherto monopolised by the advanced industrialised countries.

To achieve this objective political ties between the two sides were increasingly emphasised. South Korea's President Choi visited the Gulf in 1980, the first such state visit by a Korean leader, India drew closer to the Gulf Arab countries, Brazil expanded her military and political activities in Saudi Arabia and Iraq, and, amongst other activities, Taiwan re-emphasised her diplomatic ties with the kingdom (Saudi Arabia being one of the few countries which until recently recognised the anti-Communist government of Taipei at the expense of Peking).[24] If further evidence is needed, then attention should be given to the way that almost all of the NICs in question responded to the political upheavals in Iran and the war between Iran and Iraq. They all, for instance, not only resisted American pressures to apply economic sanctions against Iran, but in fact proceeded to expand their ties with the new regime. As far as the war was concerned, while some of the NICs supplied military equipment and other assistance (at times to both belligerents simultaneously) they clearly did so outside the dictates of the United States or as her proxies.

Their evident abilities to move up the global industrial ladder, of course, had enabled them to reach many of the targets set. South Korean, Brazilian, Taiwanese and Indian firms began bidding for and winning substantial industrial, construction and services contracts. On the threshold of the 1980s, talks in Saudi Arabia produced an accord in principle for South Korean partnership in some 26 industrial and development projects in the kingdom in return for a steady supply of crude oil for the expanding Korean economy.[25] Less than two years later a well established Korean transnational corporation, Hyundai Corp., landed a major contract in Saudi Arabia to supply equipment and services for Aramco's Zuluf offshore field, whose value was estimated at $600-700 million.[26] Other contracts were soon to follow. In the space of only a few months in 1982, two Korean firms won other significant contracts in Saudi Arabia. In April the Korean Shipbuilding and Engineering Co. was reported to have won a crucial contract for the management of the new ship-repair yard located in the Saudi Arabian Red Sea port of Jeddah, followed in September by Hella Construction's winning bid for the $110 million contract for construction work on the main part of the Jubail export-refinery.[27] Substantial contracts in both the petroleum sector and construction were, by the early 1980s, being regularly awarded to South Korean bidders. These conglomerates seemed to have combined their technological expertise with good management sense and cheap and skilled labour, with devastating effect so far as competition from the West or indeed the other industrialised countries was concerned. In 1983 other major contracts went Korea's way. Daewoo Corp. won a $110 million contract for the supply of a technologically advanced gas-compression platform from Saudi Arabia; SABIC awarded Lucky Oil the contract to build a multi-million dollar chemical complex at Jubail for the production of 300,000 tons per year of VCM and 200,000 tons/year of PVC; Kuwait Oil Co. placed a $26 million contract with Samsung to build eight storage-tanks at Mina' al-Ahmadi, each with a capacity of 500,000 barrels.[28] By the mid-1980s about 91.2 per cent of Korean contractors' work originated in the Middle East, taking billions of dollars of the 'petrodollars' away from the established Western concerns. Their total overseas construction contracts for the three important years before the oil price collapse were as follows: 1982 - $13.4 billion; 1983 - $10.5 billion; 1984 - $6.5 billion and 1985 - $5-6.5 billion.[29] The leading South Korean overseas construction contractor, Hyundai Corp. had struck $3.1 billion worth of construction business from the Gulf, extending its expertise to almost every aspect of construction work imaginable. The same has been true of Hyundai's seven other South Korean competitors in the Gulf markets. The range and variety of contracts won by the Korean companies is indeed impressive. They have included military constructions; the construction of infrastructural provisions for the Riyadh-based Saudi Arabian National Centre for Science and Technology complex; the building of military housing and public buildings in the Saudi Arabian Eastern Province; the drilling of water wells; the supply of pumping stations; the construction of ports, roads and bridges; the building of electricity power-stations and transmission lines; and the building of large hospitals and small health-care centres.

Taiwanese, Singaporean and Indian firms have also been active in these markets, penetrating some of the very profitable sectors of construction and infrastructural work. Sembawang Engineering of Singapore, for instance, supplied a multi-million dollar accommodation-module for a Saudi offshore oilfield; Ret-Ser Engineering of Taiwan won the contract for the construction of Dhahran's University of Petroleum and Minerals; and Bes Engineering landed two motorway construction contracts in Kuwait.[30] Though relative late-comers in the Gulf states' construction markets, by the mid-1980s Indian firms were winning important contracts too, particularly in Iran and Iraq. National Building Construction Corp. of India won a valuable order for the construction of a railway station in Iraq in 1985, for example, soon followed by contracts for other Indian firms to build bridges, roads, and street lighting in Iraq, and the assembly of steel works (by Dodsal Engineering) in Bahrain.[31] Interestingly, their business activities in Iraq did not inhibit Indian firms from penetrating the Iranian market. Primarily as subcontractors they kept a low profile during the Iran-Iraq war, but managed to win over $500 million worth of supply and consultancy contracts in the latter half of the 1980s.

Barter deals or otherwise, the leading NICs had managed to secure for themselves substantial business portfolios in the Gulf by the end of the 1980s. Furthermore, besides their investments and construction contracts, the NICs have shown themselves to be versatile enough to act as efficient suppliers of investment goods as well as manufactured consumer-products. Again, reference to a few examples from the 1980s will suffice to make the point. Mahindra and Mahindra of India became one of the main suppliers of diesel engines to Iran; South Korea supplied her with 20 locomotives and with twenty 42,000-tons bulk-carriers; Daewoo Corp. of Korea won a $106 million contract to build large sections of a major railway-line in southern Iran; the two leading South Korean brewing firms won large contracts for the supply of non-alcoholic beer; Volkswagon do Brasil agreed to supply at least 100,000 Brazilian-made cars to Iraq in a deal worth $630 million in exchange for 200,000-250,000 b/d of crude oil to be taken by Petrobras, having already exported 50,000 Passat cars to Iraq in 1983; in a $181 million deal the Brazilian defence-products manufacturer, Embraer, supplied 80 Tucano training-aircraft to the Iraqi airforce, beating fierce French competition. Other Brazilian military firms shipped over $30 million worth of tanks, rockets, ammunition and light weapons in 1984 alone, and Samsung of Korea won a $132 million order from Kuwait for the supply of six product-tankers.[32] Korean firms' ability to take over the multi-billion dollar, ill-fated Bandar Khomeini Petrochemicals Complex from Japanese concerns by the turn of the 1990s provided the icing on the cake of success for these countries in aggressively attacking the Gulf markets. In so doing not only have they been partially able to offset the higher prices of their petroleum imports, but also to penetrate the rich markets of the Gulf as relatively cheap and efficient contractors, managers and suppliers. This line of attack was in line with their well established export-oriented industrialisation strategies. But by the mid-1980s not only were the NICs penetrating the home markets of the advanced industrialising countries, but they were also recording significant inroads into those markets hitherto regarded as the exclusive domain of the developed countries.

The oil-rich Gulf states, on the other hand, came to regard the expansion of their economic relations with the NICs as both convenient and profitable. They could, for instance, agree to meet the petroleum needs of these countries as payment for business services rendered. So Taiwan, South Korea, Brazil,

Singapore and India all rushed to secure long-term petroleum-delivery contracts with the oil-rich Gulf states in exchange for permission to enter into business partnerships or the right to bid for 'closed' contracts. These sorts of arrangements suited both sides; the oil was sold, the contracts were obtained and if no money changed hands so much the better! It is worth recalling, in this context, that as the leading NICs were forced to pay billions of dollars for their petroleum imports from 1973 onwards, and as their national debts grew, barter arrangements proposed by many of the Gulf states would have appeared to them as a godsend. In the course of their financial expansion, the oil states of the Gulf also began showing interest in the capital markets and the banking sectors of the NICs. They largely, but not exclusively, concentrated on the Far Eastern markets, particularly those of Singapore and Hong Kong. The establishment of the Kuwait Pacific Finance Company, the Korea Kuwait Banking Corporation, the Hong Kong Metropolitan Bank, the Arab Latin American Bank, the UBAN International (Hong Kong), the Arab Asian Bank, Dubai Oriental Finance Ltd, the Banco Brasileiro-Iraquiano and the Arab Brazilian Investment Company are just a few examples of this trend. These and other (joint) ventures have also been particularly active in the Far Eastern equity-markets. Having acquired interests in the NICs' leading corporations, the Gulf states have thus tied their fortunes much more concretely with those of the NICs pole, adding a new twist to the web of interdependence which marks their mutual relations.

Barter arrangements, therefore, meant only one thing: substantial foreign-currency savings.[33] It also gave the NICs access to other rich markets besides the increasingly protectionist and cut-throat markets of the advanced industrialised countries - their traditional markets - without too great a sacrifice of their financial resources. Each side, therefore, appeared to be servicing the needs of the other. In this way the two leading Third World poles had at last come together, and both had managed to bypass their traditional (economic) partners, the Western countries, for a significant part of their respective needs. The two poles' convergence, therefore, was complete by the end of the 1980s, less than twenty years after its inception.

But what are the general and more specific implications of the convergence of the middle in the world economy? The final part of this chapter is devoted to identifying some of the relevant themes.

The Implications of the Convergence of the 'Middle'

I have attempted to show in this chapter that the global order has been changing rapidly over the last twenty years in ways that challenge almost all of our traditional perceptions (both North and South). Due to a number of factors, only one of which is characterised by the political and economic transformations of the Eastern European countries, the post-War global order is changing faster now than ever before. One manifestation of the changing order has been the depolarisation of the world as perceived through the rigid East-West matrix of the post-Korean War era, and its repolarisation through the emergence of new economies and groupings in the international system. But, while we may have witnessed the easy end of one such pole in recent times (the demise of the Eastern European CPEs in 1989), we have also seen the resilience of some of the others. Indeed the disintegration of these CPEs, far from ushering in an end to global polarity, only serves ultimately to strengthen another pole in the system - the highly industrialised countries of Western European. In the current international environment, therefore, disintegration at one end only means absorption and expansion at another.

As we have seen, new poles have emerged, responding in part to the gradual lifting of the stifling pressures associated with the old East-West order, but also as historical realities in their own right; as tangible elements emanating from the inner dynamics of the emergent nations themselves. The loosening of the global structures, I have argued, has not only enabled two important actors within the system to emerge from the ranks of the Third World, but has also facilitated their convergence in global terms, not due to any ideological predispositions or indeed for the sake of Third World 'solidarity', but in fact largely as a consequence of economic expediency and the pursuit of self-interest.

I have already mentioned in this chapter that little consensus exists regarding the emergence and role of the high-income oil-exporters in the international system, but as the discussion inevitably involves an analysis of the contemporary world economy the controversies surrounding the rise of the NICs are greater still. In a compelling book written within the Marxist tradition, entitled *Imperialism: Pioneer of Capitalism*, Bill Warren has forcefully argued that capitalism, as a mode of production, has indeed been spreading its roots in the post-war Third World. Over the years, this capitalism, he has claimed, has received a vital helping-hand from the true inheritors of *laissez-faire* capitalism, the transnational corporations (TNCs) - an argument bordering on heresy as far as the traditional Third World-ists are concerned! Despite the shortcomings of his thesis, if we were to accept his premises then, by extension, the NICs could be regarded as the flag-bearers of this capitalising process; as the natural winners of the 'uneven process of capitalism'.

But, anxious to bury the ghost of the 'dependency theory', Warren makes some rather uncalculated generalisations about the universality of the spread of capitalist relations of production and underestimates its unevenness and the ways in which the system supports the emergence of poles within itself. Others have emphasised this dimension of the world economy through their work on the TNCs. It is argued that the TNCs have led the transformation of the world economy, and essentially through their activities those countries of the Third World with 'potential' have been able to move rapidly up the global ladder from being suppliers of raw materials or consumers of Northern goods and services, to becoming significant manufacturers and exporters of manufactured goods. Ultimately, the argument goes, the TNCs have globalised the production process, rebuilt the world in their own image, and have given birth to the new international division of labour (NIDL). The NIDL hypothesis is probably best represented by Fröbel, Heinrichs and Kreye. In their *The New International Division of Labour* these authors argue that the motor behind the new international division of labour is made up of the rewards embedded in exploiting cheap and reserve supplies of labour on a world scale. The internationalisation of finance and productive capital, in turn, have facilitated the relocation of manufacturing on a global scale. In the words of Fröbel, the NIDL is all about a 'world-wide reorganisation of capitalist relations'.

These controversies and differences of opinion about the nature of contemporary international capitalism further fuel the debates surrounding global dominance/dependence relations. According to Harry Targ, the structure of the international dominance system is virtually analogous with the very hierarchy of the transnational corporation itself.[34]   What are the implications of this view?

Firstly, the dominance/dependence relationship is implicitly regarded as fixed, and is consequently rather rigid. In no uncertain terms, practically all room for manoeuvre by the developing countries is ruled out. To paraphrase Hadley Bull, 'the global system of states' ensures this relationship's longevity. Secondly, as the TNCs are seen as central to the maintenance of the *structure* of power any escape from global dominance/dependence is logically excluded - short of, that is, total planned delinking from the capitalist system of relations. Hardly a serious option these days. Thirdly, this perspective assumes that meaningful change can only occur from above, carried out by those powerful countries at the heart of the system. Finally, it may be argued that due to the tensions that this pattern of power structure generates, the chances of the system being undermined at some future time, are increased. One impact of this scenario is that those Third World countries in a state of flux and 'on the move', so to speak, would be compelled to find allies and consolidate relations with other countries within the system besides the Western states as an insurance policy against the above mentioned destabilising tendencies. If nothing else, the need for the middle to converge may therefore signify their reactions to the global system of dominance/dependence by those countries able and willing to attempt to redefine their relations with that system.

The greatest flaw in the global dominance/dependence perspective, though, is perhaps found in the way that it makes little or no allowance for juxtapositioning and (horizontal and vertical) movement within the system:

The movement of centre nations from industrial to post-industrial economies suggests a new global division of labour whereby 'pre-industrial' and 'industrial' societies extract raw materials and transform them into finished products, while those in nations of power in post-industrial societies make critical decisions about material extraction, production, and the allocation of production outputs.[35]

This kind of analysis, despite its apparent dynamism, fails to take account of the new ways in which the NICs and the capital-surplus oil-producers, for example, interact with the centre states as well as with each other, and is silent furthermore on the implications of these global movements for the important issues of South-South relations.

In addition, the birth, growth and expansion of the NICs' own TNCs since the early 1970s show that the critical decisions regarding 'material extraction, production and the allocation of production outputs' are no longer the sole domain and responsibility of the so-called post-industrial societies. And, that the strategic decisions and policies of the Third World TNCs now very directly affect the fortunes of the centre economies too - much in the same way that the latter's transnationals have for so long been influencing Third World states. The NICs' TNCs have been making decisions on location, plant size and type of operation along similar lines to those of the traditional TNCs, with the difference that it is now the NICs who also choose between sites in the US, Canada, the EC or the liberalising Eastern European countries, amongst other locations in the world. Many of their corporations have grown to such an extent that they have been worthy of listing in *Fortune* magazine's list of the world's 500 largest industrial firms. In its latest listing (30 July 1990), for example, South Korean firms feature very prominently, appearing eighth on the list of the top ten countries with the biggest companies. With a total of 11 companies listed, South Korea appears above both Australia and Switzerland. Her two corporations in the top 50, Samsung (no. 20) and Daewoo (no. 47), registered total sales of $35.2 billion and $19.9 billion respectively for the year, with Samsung beating such established firms as Volkswagen, Siemens, Nestlé, Renault, Honda Motor and Boeing. The two companies' total labour-force stands at 268,003, considerably larger than the combined armed forces of the GCC states of about 166,000. Other NIC transnationals have similar stories to tell, but they are less spectacular and perhaps on a smaller scale in comparison to the South Korean case. But, in my view, there should be little hesitation in perceiving them all as important global actors. The point to be made, however, is the impressive growth and resilience of the expanding capitalist forces in the NICs, with or without foreign assistance, and the ways that these countries have emerged as important actors in the international system, denting rather seriously in the process the underlying assumptions of the global dominance/ dependence school. Here, one can say, are determined and powerful actors who are apparently well equipped not only to change the nature of North-South relations and the traditional asymmetry in the vertical stratification of the world, but also willing to take on the North in both cost and product competition where and when necessary. The capital-surplus Gulf markets of the 1970s with their ambitious planned economic development-drives provided the perfect setting for NIC penetration and a test of their competitiveness. The oil price rises, as we have seen, provided any such further impetus as might have been required.

In a sense, then, the oil-rich Gulf states have complemented the NICs' capitalist intensification drive even though, through their oil price rises, they did threaten to inflict a mortal blow to the NICs' economic expansion strategies. It is precisely the unravelling of this kind of interaction that illustrates best the dynamism of the contemporary system of transnational relations, and the fluidity within the hierarchy. Closer examination of the past two decades of economic history will show that, in different ways and under different circumstances, both the NICs and the oil-rich Gulf states have demonstrated their ability to adapt to, and take advantage of, the changing system. It is this factor which makes them both unique in historical terms and influential as poles within both international and transnational relations. It is not beyond the realm of reason, therefore, to expect that one or both of these poles will, sooner rather than later, effect the breaking up of the pentagonal system of global power alluded to earlier in this paper. If pushed, I would venture to say that, on balance, it may well be the strongest (in both geopolitical and economic terms) amongst the NICs who will break up the current pentagonal mould or enter its ranks, assisted, not least of course, by the changing (and weakening) Soviet empire.

One important indirect consequence, stemming from the oil price rises of the last few years, has been the rechannelling of resources in the NICs away from the financing of oil imports, and towards research and investment into alternative sources of energy. The responses of the NICs have reflected both their state of mind and being. The richer NICs of the Far East, particularly

Taiwan and South Korea, embarked on an impressive nuclear power-generating programme. As early as 1975, i.e. just two years after the first oil-price rises, the South Korean Ministry of Science proposed a new energy policy under which 25 nuclear power plants, costing some $32 billion, were to be constructed to meet 52 per cent of the country's power needs by the year 2000.[36] The Taiwanese government declared similar intentions but on a smaller scale. So, by 1987, South Korea's nuclear-power reactors were generating 37,848 kwh of electricity, and Taiwan's a total of 33,108 kwh, making them the tenth and eleventh largest nuclear electricity generators in the world respectively.[37] In each case nuclear power was providing nearly 45 per cent of the country's energy needs by the second half of the 1980s. By the end of 1990, South Korea, Taiwan, India, Brazil and Argentina would have 29 nuclear power stations in operation, producing nearly 20,000 mw(e) of energy.[38] The urgent need to diversify their energy sources, therefore, seems to have compelled the NICs to undertake huge R&D efforts and investment in costly nuclear-power programmes, in the process adding further expertise to their already considerable industrial capabilities.

India and Brazil seem to have given priority to their domestic oil-production potential in the first instance, followed by investments in a nuclear power capability. Brazil's Petrobras undertook huge investment-programmes in searching for and exploring Brazil's own oil-deposits. In the event, it seems that the exploration efforts paid off quite handsomely. Brazil managed to increase domestic production from no more than 170,000 b/d in 1979 to about 640,000 b/d by 1989, nearly matching her crude-oil needs for that year.[39] India's efforts at increasing domestic oil-production have been equally impressive. Her oil-production rose from 260,000 b/d in 1979 to 690,000 b/d ten years later, managing to maintain a production rate of about twice the country's oil imports throughout the first half of the 1980s.[40] Mexico of course became a major oil-exporter by the advent of the second price-rises, on occasion out-producing many of her Gulf counterparts, and Argentina continued to blend her oil production of (on average) about 450,000 b/d in the 1980s with some imports. But as the reserves are depleted the picture for the 1990s and beyond does appear gloomy for these countries, so there is little sense in them alienating their long-term Gulf suppliers.

Political and military instabilities in the Gulf and the arrival of new suppliers on the scene resulted in virtually all of the NICs choosing to diversify their petroleum suppliers. Taiwan, South Korea and Singapore began looking to South-East Asia, while Brazil ventured into Africa, and almost all of them explored the possibilities of lifting crude oil or processed petroleum from Latin America. The net result of these processes, however, was the same - less dependence on the Gulf oil-exporters.

But the sort of economic alliances forged between the oil-rich Gulf states and the NICs are not solely conditional on the oil factor. While the high price of oil, coupled with the NIC's rising demands, set the convergence-process in motion, the impetus for its continuation comes from the way that the relationship has helped both parties in reaching their respective goals. As poles within the international system they have been observed to have been attracted to one another, but this does not necessarily rule out friction or certain degrees of animosity between (or indeed within) each pole.   They are after all independent poles operating within an hierarchical and highly competitive global system. To give one simple example, the Gulf states' desire to expand their refining capacities and to create petrochemical industries has brought them into direct conflict not only with the OECD countries but also with Singapore, Brazil, India, Mexico, Taiwan and South Korea, who are all operating in the same market. Even though some of the NIC refineries (in Singapore, Taiwan, South Korea and India for instance) may still be dependent on Gulf supplies of crude oil, when the refined products reach the market place they will be in competition with those of the Gulf states themselves.

In recent times the so far mutually-advantageous economic relationship between the two poles has shown signs of spilling over into political and security relations too. The latter, in particular, has been revealed through the transfer of Brazilian-made military hardware to a number of Gulf states and the provision of military expertise extended to both Iran and Iraq, as well as Saudi Arabia and one or two other of the smaller Gulf states in the 1980s.[41]

The military relationship, furthermore, has been consolidated through the transfer of Western-made hardware to the Gulf. The primary advantage of this relationship to the Gulf states lies in its potential to reduce their military dependence on the great and major powers without necessarily compromising too drastically the quality of equipment at their disposal. But the security relationship has also shown political dimensions: it illustrates the increasing ability of the oil-rich Gulf states to find alternative military suppliers, and perhaps even to forge new alliances, without jeopardising their ongoing relations with their erstwhile 'protectors'. Secondly, it clearly demonstrates the coming of age of the NICs and their ability to pursue their 'national interests' in other parts of the world relentlessly, even to the extent of forming military spheres of influence. The role of Brazil in West Africa and that of India in South Asia testify to this. South Korea's plans to go the same way as Brazil and India amongst others, and to produce military aircraft, submarines, warships and missiles by the early years of the next decade, indicate that she too is preparing to protect her interests unilaterally and systematically, even before the Cold War barriers are fully down in Asia - or is she making these plans in spite of the end of the Cold War and the prospects of losing American patronage?

The end of the Cold War in the Europe and the emergence of democracy in a number of the NICs (Argentina, Brazil, South Korea and Taiwan) will also positively influence the economic convergence of the middle. The establishment of democratic institutions, on the one hand, and the distancing of themselves from the 'imperialist' powers, which was so damaging to their interests in the Third World during the Cold War, on the other, may help open up new markets in the Third World to these NICs. But it may also complicate the domestic decision-making process sufficiently for some secretive clients to choose to look elsewhere for diplomatic and security 'favours'. Be this as it may, the long-term impact of the domestic political liberalisation and the rapid improvements in the international climate generally can only assist the NICs in their 'peaceful mission'. This necessarily involves an adjustment in the NICs' foreign-policy orientation too, away from their critically-labelled 'sub-imperialism' and towards a more neutralist global posture. In this respect, at least, the NIC pole may be nearing the position of the 'subsidiary core nations' like Austria, Sweden and Switzerland, even though in economic terms its members are already well placed to overtake them.

Ultimately though, it is hoped that the convergence of the middle may also have spin-offs for the poorer and less fortunate

Third World countries, for, through its own prosperity, this layer in the world economy may well become able to aid the development of the poor countries, through the transfer of both funds and industrial processes with fewer strings attached, and on more favourable terms, than those offered by their Western counterparts.

Table 6.1: The Emergence of the 'Capital-Exporting Countries'

	1964-73	73	75	77	79	81	83	85	87	88
Iran										
A		5,897	5,350	5,663	3,168	1,316	2,442	2,192	2,298	2,305
B		5.6	19.6	23.6	19.2	12.0	19.2	13.0	10.5	8.2
Iraq										
A	1,364	1,932	2,262	2,348	3,477	897	1,099	1,404	2,359	2,740
B	7.3	1.9	7.5	9.6	21.3	10.4	10.0	12.0	11.6	11.0
Kuwait										
A	2,503	2,753	2,084	1,969	2,500	1,130	1,054	936	971	1,340
B	11.8	2.8	5.9	8.9	16.7	14.9	10.0	9.8	7.0	6.3
Qatar										
A	309	570	438	445	508	415	269	290	291	319
B	1.8	0.6	1.8	2.0	3.6	5.4	3.1	3.0	1.9	1.7
Saudi Arabia										
A	3,157	7,596	7,7075	9,200	9,533	9,808	4,539	3,175	3,975	5,086
B	16.7	9.0	29.5	43.3	62.9	116.2	42.8	24.0	19.3	20.5
UAE										
A	578	1,533	1,664	1,999	1,831	1,502	1,149	1,057	1,418	1,510
B	2.2	1.9	6.8	9.1	12.9	18.8	13.8	11.8	9.0	7.4
Bahrain										
A		70	57	58	51	46	42	42	42	43
B		0.050	0.287	0.400	0.530	3.0	2.6	2.4	1.8	1.8
Oman										
A		282	341	339	295	328	389	505	582	617
B		0.177	1.1	1.4	2.2	4.2	3.5	4.2	3.5	3.0

Notes: A = oil exports in '000 barrels.
         B = revenue in US$ billions.

Sources: OPEC, *Annual Statistical Bulletin* (various years); OAPEC data base information; *Petroleum Economist* (various issues); EIU, *Annual Supplement (Oil in the Middle East)* (various years); BP, *Statistical Review of World Energy* (various years); Shell, *Oil and Gas in 1974, 1984 and 1985*; EIU, *Country Profile 1989-90: Oman, the Yemens*.

Table 6.2: Selected NICs' Crude-Oil Imports ('000 b/d)

	1969	71	73	75	77	79	81	83	85	87 88
Brazil	302	421	716	719	836	1,033	871	750	556	636 649
India	225	266	269	277	302	321	323	323	308	307 363
Korea	130	185	240	340	416	502	501	528	543	592 628
Singapore	NA	111	140	363	576	701	721	789	648	665 660
Taiwan	50	80	120	152	272	350	353	375	324	348 355

Sources: BP, *Statistical Review of World Energy* (various years); OPEC, *Annual Statistical Bulletin* (various years); UN, *World Energy Supplies 1950-1974* (N.Y., 1976).

Table 6.3: Total Exports and Petroleum Imports of Three Leading NICs ($million)

	1970	71	73	75	77	79	81	83	84
South Korea									
A	835	1,069	3,225	5,081	10,047	15,055	21,254	24,455	29,245
B	125	174	277	1,271	1,934	3,104	6,376	5,577	5,752
Singapore									
A	1,554	1,761	3,653	5,370	8,241	14,233	20,967	21,833	24,070
B	331	406	657	1,200	2,673	4,445	9,380	8,802	7,946
Brazil									
A	2,739	2,904	6,199	10,670	12,120	15,244	23,293	21,899	27,005
B	266	398	902	3,300	4,201	6,918	11,723	8,888	7,473

Notes: A = Total Exports.
        B = Petroleum Imports.

Sources: IMF, *IFS Supplement on Economic Indicators* (Washington DC, 1985); IMF, *International Financial Statistics* (various years); IMF, *Direction of Trade Yearbook* (Washington DC, 1980).

Table 6.4: Value of Trade in Fuels and Manufactured Goods (% of total)

	1968	69	70	71	72	73	74	75	76	77	78	79	80	81
Argentina														
A	12.3	13.7	14.0	15.2	20.4	22.5	24.5	24.4	24.9	24.0	26.4	24.8	24.9	–
B	7.2	6.7	4.7	6.7	3.8	7.6	14.5	13.2	17.7	16.4	12.4	16.6	10.3	–
Brazil														
A	8.1	9.8	13.4	15.4	19.0	19.8	24.5	25.6	23.2	25.3	33.7	38.2	37.7	39.6
B	14.8	12.9	12.4	14.2	13.5	15.1	23.8	26.2	31.6	34.0	32.9	37.1	43.1	50.5
Hong Kong														
A	92.1	92.5	93.0	93.3	93.2	93.0	92.8	93.4	92.6	93.0	92.7	92.7	92.0	92.3
B	3.4	3.2	2.9	3.2	3.1	2.7	6.3	6.4	6.2	6.1	5.0	5.7	5.5	7.9
India														
A	51.2	55.6	52.7	54.1	55.2	53.1	54.2	49.5	56.5	57.6	62.0	58.7	–	–
B	4.3	4.1	7.7	10.2	11.9	13.9	28.0	22.6	25.7	25.5	26.1	33.2	–	–
South Korea														
A	74.3	77.0	77.4	82.1	84.0	84.3	84.9	81.6	87.7	85.2	88.6	89.2	90.2	–
B	5.1	6.1	6.9	7.9	8.7	7.4	15.4	19.1	19.9	20.2	16.4	18.6	29.9	–
Singapore														
A	24.1	23.6	27.8	33.6	41.2	44.7	40.4	41.8	44.7	43.0	46.0	46.2	48.3	49.6
B	17.2	15.8	13.5	14.3	14.5	12.9	24.0	24.6	27.4	25.6	23.9	25.2	28.7	33.7

Notes: A = value of exports of manufactured goods.
         B = value of fuel imports.

Source: IMF, *International Financial Statistics Supplement Series*, no. 4, 1982.

Table 6.5: Direction of Trade Flows (% of total)

	1966	67	68	69	70	71	72	73	74	75	76	77	78	79	80	81
Argentina																
A	0.3	0.5	1.0	1.3	1.1	1.3	1.0	2.4	4.6	6.0	4.7	5.0	4.5	4.4	3.3	3.4
B	6.5	5.7	5.0	3.9	2.5	3.5	2.3	4.4	10.6	5.8	3.7	5.9	2.4	3.0	5.6	5.4
Brazil																
A	0.5	0.6	0.7	0.3	1.3	1.1	1.2	3.6	7.0	7.6	5.5	6.5	7.2	5.2	7.3	7.3
B	10.0	10.9	10.4	9.9	9.3	10.7	10.8	12.9	21.2	22.6	28.0	30.2	29.1	32.9	36.4	38.1
Hong Kong																
A	8.1	10.0	6.7	5.1	4.5	4.8	4.9	5.3	6.5	7.9	6.8	7.9	8.1	7.3	9.1	9.8
B	2.4	2.4	2.2	2.3	2.3	2.2	1.6	1.3	1.9	1.0	1.2	0.8	0.6	0.9	0.9	0.6
India																
A	3.5	4.2	5.9	5.5	6.5	5.6	5.4	5.6	12.3	17.2	14.7	14.3	13.4	12.3	12.8	12.2
B	2.8	3.3	3.3	3.3	7.1	9.4	11.3	12.8	25.7	20.4	22.8	22.4	21.8	24.5	23.1	16.9
South Korea																
A	0.8	1.6	2.6	1.7	1.9	3.1	2.7	2.4	3.8	6.6	9.3	12.4	10.9	11.1	12.8	13.2
B	2.7	3.3	4.9	6.1	6.5	7.9	9.9	9.5	16.4	18.2	20.8	21.4	17.4	18.4	26.3	23.5
Singapore																
A	2.2	5.5	1.4	1.3	1.3	1.7	1.5	1.8	3.0	4.2	4.2	4.6	5.4	5.8	6.9	7.0
B	13.3	9.7	10.5	9.6	8.2	9.3	10.3	9.5	18.7	19.3	22.4	22.3	20.5	20.3	21.0	25.4

Notes: A = exports to oil-exporting countries as % of total exports.
        B = imports from oil-exporting countries as % of total imports.

Source: IMF, *International Financial Statistics Supplement Series*, no. 4, 1982.

Notes

1   A. W. Clausen, 'Global Interdependence in the 1980s', *Finance and Development*, March 1982, p. 5.

2   Raymond Platig, 'International Relations as a Field of Inquiry', in James N. Rosenau (ed.), *International Politics and Foreign Policy* (Free Press, New York, 1969), p. 13.

3   In a challenging essay entitled 'What about International Relations?' Susan Strange argues that the world has so markedly changed over the last 50 years that 'international' relations can only deal with a narrow range of global issues. Instead, she suggests, scholars must look beyond the strict study of the foreign policy of states and explore more deeply what she terms transnational relations. Transnational relations by definition aim to engage the researcher in understanding forces at play which function alongside and beyond - not above and over - the nation-state. See Susan Strange (ed.), *Paths to International Political Economy* (Allen and Unwin, London, 1984).

4   Since the heady days of the early 1980s crude-oil prices have generally been more 'moderate', bowing to severe downward pressures in the mid-1980s. The price reached a low of $7/b in July 1986 and thereafter was knocking on the door of the $15-20/b price range: most recently of all, on account of the crisis in Kuwait, the price has been more volatile, rising over the $30/b mark.

5   Compiled from OPEC and OAPEC statistics for all but Oman. National sources and the EIU's estimates were consulted for the latter's figures. The value of world trade in 1968 stood at $248 billion, and in 1980 at $1,990 billion. See GATT, *International Trade 1977/78 and 1981/82* (Geneva, 1978 and 1982).

6   Francine Stock, 'Building through Investment', *Petroleum Economist*, Dec. 1982, pp. 504-5.

7   Robert Dixon, *The Foreign Investment Strategy of the GCC Countries 1989-90* (GCSS, London, 1989), pp. 48-9. Kuwaiti investments in the British financial sector include Royal Insurance, General Accident, Royal Guardian Exchange, Commercial Union and the Royal Bank of Scotland.

8   Francine Stock, 'Building through Investment'.

9   Ibid. The Kuwait Investment Office's 17% stake in Siemens, revealed in 1988, can be regarded as another such strategic investment. For details see the *Sunday Times*, 26 June 1988.

10   IMF, *International Financial Statistics* (various years).

11   Data derived from the Arab Monetary Fund estimates and the IMF's *International Financial Statistics*.

12   *Bank of England Quarterly Bulletin*, March 1985.

13   Development-expenditure data for this section has been obtained from EIU, *Oil in the Middle East* (various issues).

14   For details of Iran's Fifth Development Plan see EIU, *Iran Annual Supplement 1975* (London, 1975).

15 Nazih N. Ayubi, 'OPEC and the Third World: The Case of Arab Aid', in Robert W. Stookey (ed.), *The Arabian Peninsula: Zone of Ferment* (Hoover Institution Press, Stanford, CA, 1984), p. 134.

16 James A. Caporaso, 'Industrialisation in the Periphery: The Evolving Global Division of Labour', *International Studies Quarterly*, Sept. 1981, vol. 25, no. 3, p. 355.

17 Caporaso relies on the date from Keesing, *World Trade and Output of Manufactures: Structural Trends and Developing Countries' Exports* (World Bank Staff Working Paper 316, Washington, DC, 1979).

18 G. L. Ingalls and W. E. Martin, 'Defining and Identifying the NICs', in Jim Norwine and Alfonso Gonzalez (eds.), *The Third World: States of Mind and Being* (Unwin Hyman, Boston, 1988), pp. 92-3. The authors add Brazil to their list of NICs in the text and pass Hong Kong as a developed country: 'Hong Kong is not a newly industrialising country but an already quite industrialised city-state'. Their list of near-NICs comprises Malaysia, Egypt, the Dominican Republic, Jordan, Portugal, Mexico and Spain.

19 The data for this section has been compiled from the following sources: OECD, *The Newly Industrialising Countries: Challenge and Opportunity for OECD Industries* (Paris, 1988) and OECD, *The Impact of the Newly Industrialising Countries on Production and Trade in Manufactures* (Paris, 1979).

20 UN, *National Account Statistics* (New York, 1976). Taiwan and Hong Kong obtained manufacturing growth rates similar to Singapore's for the same period.

21 Colin I. Bradford, Jr, 'The Rise of the NICs as Exporters on a Global Scale', in Louis Turner and Neil McMullen (eds.), *The Newly Industrialising Countries: Trade and Adjustment* (RIIA/Allen and Unwin, London, 1982), p. 23.

22 The import bill of the 'middle income' countries, encompassing all of the NICs category, increased from $6.1 billion in 1973 to $26.1 billion in 1977, to stand at $54.5 billion by the second oil-shock of the early 1980s. Incidentally, according to IMF data, the current-account balances of all the non-oil developing-countries worsened significantly during 1973-81 period, from a total deficit of $11.5 billion in 1973 to -$29.6 billion in 1977 and -$96.5 billion by 1981.

23 UNCTAD data reveals that the increase in the exports of the non-oil developing-countries to the OPEC group as a proportion of their total exports rose from 3% in 1972 to 7% in 1978, an increase of 233%. This increase was easily exceeded by a number of the NICs:
Brazil (700%), Singapore (500%), South Korea (400%), Argentina (400%) and India (280%). South Korea's trade with OPEC increased by 7,558% between 1972 and 1978, Taiwan's by 2,710%, Brazil's by 1,770%, Argentina's by 1,075%, India's by 1,026%, Hong Kong's by 706% and Singapore's by 684%.

24 Not unexpectedly, Saudi Arabia and the PRC established formal diplomatic relations recently (on 21 July 1990), dealing a severe blow to Taiwan's foreign policy. The economic and military ties between Peking and Riyadh had been expanding fast in recent years, culminating in the

sale of Chinese-made CSS-2 IRBMs to the kingdom in 1988-9 and the first (60 companies-strong) Chinese trade exhibition in Saudi Arabia in 1989. The Taiwanese, however, have been quick to point out that the extensive economic relations between Saudi Arabia and Taiwan are likely to continue unabated. The two countries have apparently already agreed that Saudi Arabia will continue her crude-oil relationship with Taiwan, and the latter will be allowed to continue participating in the kingdom's industrial, agricultural and scientific projects.

25   *Petroleum Economist*, Jan. 1980, p. 37.
26   *Petroleum Economist*, March 1982, p. 112.
27   *Petroleum Economist*, March 1982, p. 113 and Sept. 1982, p. 390.
28   *Petroleum Economist*, April 1983, p. 149, Sept. 1983, p. 361 and Nov. 1983, p. 439.
29   *MEED*, 31 Aug. 1984 and *MEED*, 'Special Report' on construction, May 1985.
30   *MEED*, 3 May 1984, 5 April 1985 and the May 1985 'Special Report' on construction.
31   Ibid.
32   Ibid.; *MEED*, 4 Jan. 1985, 1 March 1985; *Petroleum Economist*, Feb. 1987.
33   Having said this, it's clear from the data provided elsewhere in this chapter that the countries like South Korea and Taiwan were acquiring market-shares in the Gulf in excess of the total value of their oil-imports. In the case of Korea, her Gulf contracts of some $10 billion in 1983, for example, were more than a match for her oil-imports of $5.6 billion in the same year.
34   Harry Targ, 'Global Dominance and Dependence, Post-Industrialism, and International Relations Theory', *International Studies Quarterly*, Sept. 1976.
35   Ibid., p. 479.
36   *Petroleum Economist*, Sept. 1975, p. 355.
37   CIA, *International Energy Statistics Review* (USGPO, 1988).
38   Vladimir Baun, 'Nuclear Power: Status and Prospects', *Petroleum Economist*, Oct. 1985, p. 361; Vladimir Baun, 'Nuclear Power after Chernobyl', *Petroleum Economist*, Nov. 1987, pp. 395-7.
39   BP, *Statistical Review of World Energy* (various years).
40   Ibid.
41   Brazil, India, South Korea, Argentina, Singapore and Taiwan are amongst those developing countries which also have burgeoning arms-industries, capable of producing a wide range of military hardware. Over the last two decades these NICs, and other countries like Israel, Chile, Pakistan and Egypt, have been seeking export-markets for their weapons, and those countries governed through a civilian-military structure have been well placed to offer military services as well as training to their foreign customers.

7. THE WESTERN EUROPEAN UNION, EUROPEAN SECURITY INTERESTS AND THE GULF

Willem van Eekelen

1. The Origins of the Western European Union

The Western European Union (WEU) was set up by the Treaty of Economic, Social and Cultural Collaboration and Collective Self-Defence signed in Brussels on 17 March 1948, as amended by the protocol modifying and completing the Brussels Treaty, signed in Paris on 23 October 1954.

The signatories of the 1954 Paris Agreements clearly indicated their aims in the preamble to the modified Brussels Treaty: these were, 'to reaffirm their faith in fundamental human rights ... and in the other ideals proclaimed in the Charter of the United Nations ... to preserve the principles of democracy ... to strengthen the economic, social and cultural ties by which they are already united', by co-operating so as 'to create in Western Europe a firm basis for European economic recovery ... to afford assistance to each other ... in resisting any policy of aggression ... to promote the unity and to encourage the progressive integration of Europe.'

The cornerstone of the treaty is Article V, which lays down that,

If any of the high contracting parties should be the object of an armed attack in Europe, the other high contracting parties will, in accordance with the provisions of Article F1 of the Charter of the United Nations, afford the party so attacked all the military and other aid and assistance in their power.

It thus defines a defensive alliance far more binding than the North Atlantic Treaty or any other treaty now in force since it commits the forces of all the member-countries unconditionally in the event of an attack on one of them.

Article VIII of the treaty sets up a Council so organised as to be able to exercise its functions continuously, and deciding by unanimous vote questions for which no other voting procedure has been agreed. The Council's aim is to strengthen peace and European security, and also to promote unity and encourage the progressive integration of Europe. At the request of any of the high contracting parties it may be immediately convened so as to consult 'with regard to any situation which may constitute a threat to peace, in whatever area this threat should arise, or a danger to economic stability'. No limit is placed on the Council's responsibilities and the preamble to the treaty underlines that its aim is to 'preserve the principles of democracy, personal freedom and political liberty, the constitutional traditions and the rule of law' and 'to strengthen, with these aims in view, the economic, social and cultural ties' uniting the signatory countries. In other words, nothing is outside the responsibilities of the WEU.

Article IX sets up 'an Assembly composed of representatives of the Brussels Treaty powers to the Parliamentary Assembly of the Council of Europe' to which the WEU Council has to make an annual report on its activities.

Protocol no. II to the Paris Agreements *inter alia* commits the United Kingdom to maintain four divisions and the Second Tactical Air Force on the mainland of Europe.

According to Article XI, the signatories may decide to invite any other state to accede to the treaty on conditions to be agreed between them and the state so invited.

2. The Organisation of the WEU

The member-countries of the WEU are:
Belgium
France
Germany
Italy
Luxembourg
The Netherlands
Portugal

Spain
The United Kingdom

Organisation

(a) The headquarters of the Organisation is located at its Secretariat-General in London. The present Secretary-General is Dr Willem van Eekelen, formerly Netherlands Defence Minister and State Secretary for Foreign Affairs.
(b) The WEU Council of Ministers (Foreign Affairs and Defence) meets twice a year in the capital of the presiding country. The Presidency of the Organisation rotates annually. France took over the chair from Belgium on 1 July 1990 and will be succeeded by Germany on 1 July 1991, followed by Italy.

The Permanent Council, which consists of the ambassadors to London of the member-states, and an official of similar rank from the Foreign and Commonwealth Office, meets on a regular basis in London at the seat of the Secretariat-General. This Council, which is chaired by the Secretary-General, has set up various working groups, principally involving delegates from the capitals. Regular meetings of political directors of the Foreign Ministries of member-states and senior representatives of the Defence Ministries - the Enlarged Council - are also held. All these bodies are chaired and assisted by the Secretariat-General.
(c) The Assembly of the Western European Union in Paris is composed of 108 parliamentarians of the member-states, and may debate any matters coming within the purview of the modified Brussels-Treaty. It is the only European parliamentary assembly founded by a treaty with competence in defence matters. The Assembly meets twice a year in plenary session and has set up the following committees:

> Presidential Committee
> Defence Committee
> Political Committee
> Technological and Aerospace Committee
> Committee on Budgetary Affairs and Administration
> Committee on Rules of Procedure and Privileges
> Committee for Parliamentary and Public Relations

All of these prepare reports for the plenary session.

(d)   On 1 July 1990, a WEU Institute for Security Studies started work in Paris. Its tasks include:
- carrying out research on behalf of the Council and the Assembly
- promoting a greater awareness of European security issues
- organising meetings with institutes in Western and Eastern European countries.

3. The WEU and European Security-Interests

The WEU is an inter-governmental organisation essentially for European co-operation in the field of security. It aims to establish an ongoing dialogue amongst its member-states in order to arrive at common positions on politico-military issues; in doing so, the WEU contributes to the development within the Atlantic Alliance of a European security identity. The WEU is therefore at the 'crossroads' of European integration and the Alliance.

On 27 October 1987, WEU Ministers adopted a 'Platform on European Security Interests' in The Hague. This document defined the conditions and criteria for European security and the consequent responsibilities of the WEU member-states in respect of Western defence, arms-control and disarmament, the East-West dialogue and co-operation.

Point 2 of the preamble to the Platform states:

We recall our commitment to build a European Union in accordance with the Single European Act, which we all signed as members of the European Community. We are convinced that the construction of an integrated Europe will remain incomplete as long as it does not include security and defence'.

The member-states resolved 'to strengthen the European pillar of the Alliance' (III.a.2). 'Political solidarity and adequate military strength within the Atlantic Alliance, arms-control, disarmament and the search for genuine détente continue to be integral parts of (our) policy. Military security and a policy of détente are not contradictory but complementary' (I.5). Article I.4 underlines the indivisibility of Alliance security:

Under these conditions the security of the Western European countries can only be ensured in close association with our North American allies. The security of the Alliance is indivisible. The partnership between the two sides of the Atlantic rests on the twin foundations of shared values and interests. Just as the commitment of the North American democracies is vital to Europe's security, a free, independent and increasingly more united Western Europe is vital to the security of North America.

Article III.a.4 makes clear:

We remain determined to pursue European integration including security and defence and make a more effective contribution to the common defence of the West.

To this end we shall:
- ensure that our determination to defend any member-country at its borders is made clearly manifest by means of appropriate arrangements;
- improve our consultations and extend our co-ordination in defence and security matters and examine all practical steps to this end;
- make the best possible use of the existing institutional mechanisms to involve the Defence Ministers and their representatives in the work of WEU;
- see to it that the level of each country's contribution to the common defence adequately reflects its capabilities;
- aim at a more effective use of existing resources, *inter alia* by expanding bilateral and regional military co-operation, pursue our efforts to maintain in Europe a technologically advanced industrial base and intensify armaments co-operation;
- concert our policies on crises outside Europe insofar as they may affect our security interests.

The Platform ends by stating that, 'We are determined to do all in our power to achieve our ultimate goal of a just and lasting peaceful order in Europe.'

* * *

Within the last year the political map of Europe has been changed to a degree quite unthinkable at the time of adoption by Ministers of the Platform, or of the WEU's mission in the Gulf in 1987-8. At the hub of these changes have been the drive for democracy in central and Eastern Europe, the process for the unification of Germany, and the collapse of the Warsaw Pact.

Since it stands at the 'crossroads' of European integration and the Alliance, the WEU not only serves as the European dimension of common security, but also has made its own contribution to the building of a new European security order. This it continues to do within the contexts of the future needs of European security and of a new security architecture, of the future role of the Alliance, and of the future European Union.

Thus, the WEU has worked, *inter alia*, to prepare a solid and coherent European input to discussions on the content, implementation and verification of a CFE treaty, and on the post-CFE environment.   In that connection, experts from member-countries are assessing common European requirements as well as existing national capabilities and projects, with a view to setting up a European space-based observation system. Such a system would comprise a satellite component and a WEU agency for the exploitation of satellite images. It would have three goals: to contribute to the verification of conventional arms-control agreements, to monitor crises with security implications (particularly outside Europe), and to monitor environmental hazards.

The 'London Declaration on a Transformed North Atlantic Alliance', adopted on 6 July at the close of the NATO summit in London, heralded the arrival of a 'new, promising era' in Europe and extended the hand of friendship to the countries of Eastern and central Europe. The member-states of the North Atlantic Alliance proposed to those of the Warsaw Pact a joint declaration of non-aggression, and invited all other CSCE member-states to join them in this commitment. A number of important, historic and practical initiatives were also proposed. The highest priority was put on completion this year of the first CFE treaty along with the completion of a meaning CSBM package.   The Alliance's integrated force structure and its strategy will be changed fundamentally. The allies concerned will modify the size and adapt the tasks of their nuclear deterrent forces. In the transformed Europe, the allies will be able to adopt a new NATO strategy making nuclear weapons truly weapons of last resort. A CSCE summit later in 1990 in Paris should, in addition to the signature of a CFE agreement, set new standards for the establishment, and preservation, of free societies and endorse certain CSCE principles, commitments and guidelines.   It should also decide how the CSCE can be institutionalised to provide a forum for wider political dialogue in a more united Europe.

For its part, the WEU will continue to assist in preparing positions to be adopted by its member-states on the broad range of issues relating to their European security concerns. It has also been tasked with establishing contacts for two-way information with the democratically elected governments in central and Eastern Europe. Such a dialogue could increase mutual understanding on security questions, provide another element of stability in Europe and pave the way for new forms of multinational co-operation.

4. The WEU and the Gulf

As we have seen in parts 1 and 3 of this chapter, the modified Brussels Treaty allows for a very far-ranging consultation on 'out of Europe' issues. Past experience shows just how far the WEU's competence with regard to external risks and threats can be an asset both to Europe, as a player on the world stage, and to the Alliance. It provides a framework for concerted European action in the case of a direct threat, or when the security interests of one or more member-states are at stake anywhere in the world.

As part of the WEU's activities with regard to European security interests, political consultations took place within the organisation from the summer of 1987 until early in 1989 on the situation in the Gulf. On 20 August 1987 a meeting of senior officials from the Foreign and Defence Ministries of WEU member-states met in The Hague, at the invitation of the then Netherlands Presidency of the WEU Council, to consider the different aspects of the situation in the Gulf area in the context of the current efforts of the UN to bring an end to the Iran-Iraq conflict. This meeting was held pursuant to Article VIII.3 of the modified Brussels Treaty and the decision taken by Ministers in Rome in October 1984 to consider, whenever appropriate, the implications for Europe of crises in other regions of the world.

At this first meeting it was stressed that Security Council Resolution 598 should be fully implemented forthwith so as to bring the conflict between Iraq and Iran to an end. Member countries of the WEU would continue to support all efforts aimed at achieving this result. In this context they reiterated their support for the efforts of the Secretary-General of the UN. Europe's vital interest required that the freedom of navigation in the Gulf be assured at all times. The member-states strongly condemned all actions contrary to that principle. Participants took note of the measures already undertaken or envisaged by individual member-countries. They agreed to continue to consult each other and exchange information in order to develop further their co-operation. Subsequently, meetings were held at regular intervals at the level of high officials or naval experts in the capital of the Council Presidency, usually followed by press briefings. These consultations within the WEU framework were conducted essentially at three levels: political, at the level of naval contact points in Ministries of Defence, and at the level of base-commanders.

Five (Belgium, France, Italy, the Netherlands and the UK) of the then seven WEU member-states deployed naval forces to the region, while Luxembourg - having no naval forces - made financial contributions and the Federal Republic of Germany, for constitutional reasons, made compensating naval deployments in European waters.

Following the Iran-Iraq cease-fire agreed in August 1988, Operation Cleansweep - the joint European route-check of 300 miles of the most used shipping-lane - was successfully completed early in 1989 and provided additional security for shipping in the region. The objectives of WEU member-states remain to provide reassurance and protection to their shipping, and to demonstrate their commitment to the principle of freedom of navigation. The recent progress in the peace-talks, and the absence of any resumption of hostilities or of any threat to shipping are positive signs. The UK Armilla Patrol remains, however, on station, while France retains an influential naval force in the Indian Ocean.

In this crisis the WEU showed that it could as an institution play a valuable role in concerting member-states' operational plans and presenting a common political line over the non-provocative intentions of their navies in the region. Among the lessons learnt from WEU members' Gulf operations was the effective manner in which WEU members' naval contingents protected shipping of their own nations, and contributed to concerted action against the common threat of mining. The concertation-process was extended to full integration in the case of the UK/Netherlands/Belgian mine-counter-measure contingents. A primary effect of concertation in the Gulf was to create the purpose-built three-tier framework of consultation within the WEU referred to earlier.

As to the possibility of similar developments in the future, should they occur in the Gulf or elsewhere, the WEU stands ready to monitor them at various levels and focus attention on their implications for member-states' security interests. Even in advance of particular crises, however, the WEU can take account of background strategic changes - such as technological developments - which, although not linked to any specific situation of conflict, could affect the background of Europe's security. The proliferation of chemical weapons and conventional ballistic missiles are the paramount current examples of such technological developments.

Overall, the successful experience in the Gulf demonstrated that Europe is capable of facing up to its responsibilities towards the wider perspective of possible security-interests not directly linked to the East-West context. There is no reason to believe that in a future out-of-area crisis WEU countries could not again co-operate successfully and constructively between themselves and with other allies with results as satisfactory as there were in the Gulf. There remains a good case for the active pursuit of regular consultations on out-of-Europe matters within the WEU. It is quite clear, moreover, that Article VIII.3 of the modified Brussels Treaty renders consultation obligatory in the event of a direct threat, or when the security interests of a WEU member-state are affected in any part of the world.

5. An Insight into the Future

While events in central and Eastern Europe continue to dominate the political headlines and bring widespread changes to the wider international framework, including a reduction in the risk that Middle East tension and conflict could lead to dangerous Superpower confrontation, the major problems of the region - for example, the Arab-Israeli conflict, Iran-Iraq, Lebanon, international terrorism, extreme forms of nationalism and Islamic fundamentalism - show every indication of moving forward to even partial resolution much less slowly than the momentous developments in Europe.

The nature and extent of Western European security interests, concerns and policies in the Gulf are clearly of abiding interest and relevance to, and form a logical part of, the other chapters in this book. The relationship of the Gulf region to the new political and strategic environment developing throughout Europe and between the Superpowers, will continue to be vital to the stability of that part of the Middle East. Hopes for a more enduring peace in that troubled part of the world are being raised, if only with an enormous degree of circumspection. Only time will tell whether the intricate and deeply-entrenched politics of the area can be adapted sufficiently to take advantage of this new environment, and to permit the suffering of its grieving peoples to be alleviated so that they too may return to a more peaceful and secure world.

8. JAPAN'S OIL STRATEGY IN THE GULF WITHOUT ARMS DEALS

Susumu Ishida

1. Introduction

Japan is endowed with poor domestic energy-resources. Coal, natural gas and uranium resources are very limited, and whilst her relatively rich hydro-energy resources have now been almost fully exploited, they still only manage to supply a small proportion of the large-scale civil and industrial energy-needs of Japan. In respect of oil resources, in particular, currently the most important energy-source in the world, Japan is almost completely deficient.

In order to recover rapidly from the destruction of the last war and then achieve steady economic development, Japan has badly needed as much energy as possible. During the early post-war years, being isolated from external energy supplies, Japan had to devise her so-called 'priority production policy', which emphasised domestic coal-production, in order to fuel and revitalise steel and other basic industries.

At the beginning of the 1950s, crude-oil import to Japan was resumed and the Japanese oil-industry, which consisted mainly of downstream operations, was gradually revitalised. In the second half of the 1950s, the so-called 'energy revolution' started in Japan, and imported oil replaced domestic coal step-by-step due to the superiority of liquid over solid fuels. The period of high economic growth which commenced in Japan at the same time, and the economic prosperity that followed, have depended for their energy mainly on supplies of imported oil.

2. Primary Energy Supply in Japan

Table 8.1 shows the breakdown of Japan's primary energy supply in five-fiscal-year averages, before and after the oil crises and during the recent oil-glut. Total primary energy supply increased gradually by 25.7 per cent from an annual average of 330,893 billion Kcal during the 1969-73 period to one of 415,768 billion Kcal during the 1984-8 period. But between the periods 1974-8 and 1984-8, the annual average of Japan's primary energy supply increased only by 8.7 per cent.

The breakdown by energy source of the total supply differed slightly between each five-year period. Just before and after the first oil-crisis, crude oil constituted an overwhelming part, or about 65 per cent, of the total primary energy supply in Japan. Coal accounted for 15.1-17.9 per cent of the total, with other forms of energy accounting for less than 20 per cent in all.

The supply of crude oil, after registering a peak during the 1974-8 period, decreased and accounted for less than half of the total primary energy supply during the oil-glut period of 1984-8. In contrast, other forms of energy-supply, apart from hydro-energy, have increased since the first oil-crisis both in volume and in percentage share, thus reflecting Japan's efforts to promote energy conservation and to develop new and substitute kinds of energy: this will be considered hereafter in detail. Although crude-oil supply decreased, it still accounted for 43.9 per cent of the total primary energy supply during the 1984-8 period. If oil products are added to crude oil, their supplies accounted for 57.3 per cent of the total. It is clear that Japan's primary energy supply has been heavily dependent on crude oil and its products.

Table 8.2 shows the extent of Japan's self-sufficiency in the supply of primary energy in five-fiscal-year averages. In Japan's energy statistics, nuclear energy as well as hydro-, geothermal and new energies are counted as domestic production, even though a large proportion of the uranium is imported from abroad. On such an assumption, self-sufficiency in Japan's total primary energy supply was between 11.9 and 17.7 per cent during the periods concerned. Total energy self-sufficiency at once dropped from 14.5 per cent during the 1969-73 period to 11.9 per cent during the subsequent period of 1974-8, but increased after that to 15.3 per cent and 17.7 per cent during the periods 1979-83 and 1984-8 respectively, thanks to a relative increase in supplies of nuclear, geothermal and new energy.

Self-sufficiency in coal, and also in natural gas and LNG, was significantly high, in the order of 36.2 and 65.8 per cent respectively until the first oil-crisis, but after that the figures decreased steadily to 12.1 and 5.7 per cent respectively during the 1984-8 period. Domestic production of the most important crude-oil and oil products was negligible. Due to Japan's poor domestic oil resources, domestic production of crude oil remained very small, even though very great efforts had been directed towards developing indigenous oil-production both onshore and offshore, all of which resulted in a low degree of oil self-sufficiency of less than 0.4 per cent. Self-sufficiency in oil products was less than 0.1 per cent or nearly zero.

3. Japanese Oil-Imports

Table 8.4 shows Japan's crude-oil imports by area and country in five-fiscal-year averages, before and after the oil crises. Total crude-oil imports increased by 20 per cent from 225,373 thousand Kl, during the five-year period just before the first oil-crisis, to 272,430 thousand Kl, during the five-year period just after it; but after that, they decreased steadily by 13.6 per cent to 235,362 thousand Kl, during the 1979-83 period, and by a further 16.3 per cent during the following period, 1984-8, to 197,068 thousand Kl.

Japan has been trying, in particular since the first oil-crisis, to diversify geographically the sources of supply of her crude oil. China, Mexico, in South America, North America and Europe had been expected to become new and important oil-suppliers to Japan, but so far they have only been able to supply Japan with a minor share of her required crude-oil, although oil exports from these countries to Japan have been increasing steadily since the first oil-crisis. Asian countries such as Indonesia, Malaysia and Brunei failed to increase steadily their crude-oil supplies to Japan. Egypt increased its oil exports to Japan, but other African countries including Nigeria, Algeria and Libya decreased them. The USSR supplied only marginal oil-imports to Japan.

Japan has been extremely dependent on the Gulf for her crude-oil imports. The Gulf's share of total Japanese crude-oil imports was 82.1 per cent during the 1969-73 period. After that it decreased substantially, but during the 1984-8 period it still accounted for 68.9 per cent.

Among the Gulf countries, before the first oil-crisis, Iran was the biggest oil-exporter to Japan, followed by Saudi Arabia. The share of other Gulf countries in total oil-exports to Japan was 10.7 per cent or less. During the two five-year periods after the first oil-crisis, Iranian oil-exports to Japan decreased, while Saudi Arabia's increased to become Japan's top crude-oil supplier in place of Iran. The UAE has been increasing its oil exports to Japan, and during the 1984-8 period it became her largest oil-supplier, thereby supplanting Saudi Arabia.

If, in the future, Iran and Iraq can increase their oil-exports to Japan, Japan's oil-imports will be more evenly spread amongst the Gulf exporting-countries. But Japan's heavy dependence on the Gulf for her oil-imports will not decrease drastically in the foreseeable future. There will not, after all, be any reliable oil-exporting countries to take the place of the Gulf exporters in terms of the volume and quality of oil that Japan needs.

4. Japan's Basic Oil-Policy

Since long before the first oil-crisis, Japan has been fully aware of the vulnerability induced by extreme dependence on imported oil. Japan's external oil-policy, aimed at tackling this vulnerability since before the first oil-crisis, has, besides geographical diversification of oil-supply sources, consisted mainly in the promotion of autonomous oil development and an increase in direct oil deals with oil-exporting countries, thereby circumventing the supply-channels of the major international oil-companies.

Thanks to the realisation of OPEC's superiority over the Majors, the so-called D-D and G-G oil-deals increased, and Japan's oil-importing channels were substantially diversified. However, Japan has not been so successful in developing autonomous overseas oil-supplies, except in the case of the Arabian Oil Company, which was the first successful Japanese-owned overseas oil-exploration company in the post-war period. The Arabian Oil Company was established in 1958 for oil exploration in the Neutral Zone between Saudi Arabia and Kuwait, and was fortunate enough to hit oil-resources and started oil-production in 1961.

In the same year, the Japan Petroleum Development Corporation (later the Japan National Oil Corporation) was established to provide Japanese overseas oil-exploration companies with the necessary public financial support. Japan set a target, at that time, to realise 30 per cent Japanese autonomously supplied oil by 1985 (later, in 1978, the target was revised to mean the supply of 1.5 million b/d by 1990). Thereafter, by 1988, the Japan National Oil Corporation had disbursed as direct investments and loans a cumulative total amount of Y1,269.4 billion (in current prices, roughly equal to $8.5 billion: $1=Y150). More than 90 Japanese-owned overseas oil-exploration companies have been established. By 1988, they had invested Y1,859.8 billion ($12.4 billion) in oil exploration and Y1,379.6 billion ($9.2 billion) in oil development (see Table 8.3). More than 75 per cent of the total oil-exploration investment, and more than 90 per cent of the total oil-development investment, were disbursed in the Middle East and in Asia and Oceania.

Table 8.5 shows the growth in Japanese autonomous crude-oil imports, i.e. the results of Japan's efforts to increase her independent oil-supply. Around 10 per cent of Japan's total imported oil during the 1965-88 period was supplied by Japan's autonomous oil, this being far behind the target of 30 per cent by 1985. One of the reasons behind such moderate results, was that the total volume of imported oil rose by a rate a little faster than that of autonomous oil.

Henceforward, Japan will continue her best efforts to augment her supplies of autonomous oil all over the world, however difficult it is to achieve the target, because Japan believes it to be the duty of a very big oil-importer to discover new oil resources and add them to the world oil-market.

Since prior to the first oil-crisis, private Japanese oil-companies had been keeping oil-stockpiles sufficient for 60 days, which were increased to 90 days after the first oil-crisis. In addition, a public oil-stockpile of 30 million Kl was started. Moreover, Japan has greatly endeavoured to develop substitute energies and to promote energy conservation by improving energy-consumption efficiency. Japan's sincere efforts in this field have, since 1973, brought about remarkable results. The total primary energy requirement per unit of GNP was reduced by 36 per cent during the 1973-88 period (see Table 8.6). Japan's GNP has grown steadily with less and less energy consumption.

In order both to improve Japanese living standards and to contribute to the world's economic prosperity, Japan is ready to make great efforts to continue sustainable economic growth until the first decade of the 21st century. Japan is prepared to attain long-term economic growth with the least possible energy consumption, which will be achieved by an elaborate plan of promoting more energy-conservation efforts.

The new energy-conservation plan consists of further improved car-engine efficiency, preventing heat-loss, recovering waste-heat and so on, and aims to achieve by 2010 a second reduction in the total primary energy requirement per unit of GNP equal to that of 36 per cent which was realised during the 1973-88 period. This new exercise in energy-conservation is expected to restrict both Japan's dependency on imported oil and public pollution caused by emissions of carbon dioxide and other harmful substances.

According to Japan's latest long-term energy-demand outlook (see Table 8.7), Japan's total primary energy demand will substantially increase from 482 million Kl in 1988 to 597 million Kl in 2000, a 23.9 per cent increase compared with 1988, finally reaching 666 million Kl in 2010, a 38 per cent increase compared with 1988. Of these total primary energy demands, oil demand will change from 57.3 per cent (276 million Kl) in the base year, to 51.6 per cent (308 million Kl) in 2000 and 46.0 per cent (306 million Kl) in 2010. Oil demand is forecast to increase slightly until 2000, but after that to remain at the same level. Japan will be more dependent on coal, natural gas and nuclear energy. Nevertheless, even in the beginning of the 21st century, Japan has to depend heavily on oil mainly imported from the Gulf. Japan has to continue to pay special attention to the Gulf area.

5. Japan's Relations with the Gulf

In exchange for importing a large volume of oil from the Gulf states, Japan has sought to export as much merchandise as possible to the Gulf. During the 1983-8 period, when the Gulf countries were suffering both from the oil glut and the Iran-Iraq war, of individual countries amongst the major advanced nations, Japan registered as the single most important exporter to the Gulf as a whole. As Table 8.8 shows, Japan achieved the biggest share, or 15.6 per cent, of total exports to the Gulf, with the US and West Germany accounting for the second and third largest shares respectively. As for individual Gulf countries during this period, Japan was the biggest exporter to Saudi Arabia, Kuwait, Qatar and the UAE, and the second biggest exporter to each of the other four Gulf countries.

Moreover, Japan has been doing its best, especially since the first oil-crisis, to establish relations of interdependence with the Gulf, beyond sheer trading. Japan's programme with this end in mind is designed in such a way that the Gulf countries themselves might come to realise how very useful it might be for them to supply her with oil. In other words, Japan has been ready to offer all the economic assistance and co-operation needed by the Gulf countries that Japan's economy, be it healthy on account of adequate supplies of oil being furnished by the Gulf, might be able to yield.

Japan's ODA to the Middle East drastically increased immediately after the first oil-crisis of 1973-4 (see Table 8.9). In 1975 Japan's ODA to the Middle East including the Gulf countries accounted for 10.6 per cent of the total net ODA disbursement, compared with 2.5 per cent in the previous year. In 1977 almost a quarter of the annual total net disbursement of Japan's ODA was allocated to the Middle East. After that until 1980, more than 10 per cent of Japan's annual ODA disbursement was annually allocated to the Middle East. These figures show very clearly how seriously the Japanese government took the matter of economic co-operation with the Middle East including the Gulf countries.

But, as Table 8.10 shows, the activities of Japan's overseas firms in the Middle East are minimal. The number of Japan's overseas firms active in the Middle East is only 1.1 per cent of the total in July 1989.   Even if Turkey and North African countries are included in the Middle East, it makes no great difference.

There are certain reasons why Japan's overseas firms have been prevented from becoming more active in the Middle East, in the Gulf in particular.   These include general unfavourable social, political and military circumstances, limited domestic markets, manpower problems, oil-glut and so on.   Above all, military instability caused by the Iran-Iraq war hindered Japan's economic activities in the Gulf.

The Iran-Iraq war not only prevented Japanese firms from becoming more involved in the economic development in the Gulf, but also caused serious damage to projects receiving their support.   A typical example of a Japanese project damaged by the war is, of course, the IJPC (the Iran-Japan Petrochemical Company Ltd.) project in Iran.   It was a huge joint-venture project between Japan and Iran, which had been initiated during the late Shah's era, and which the Islamic Revolutionary regime had undertaken to complete.   The IJPC project had progressed as far as the completion of more than 80 per cent of planned capacity by the time of the outbreak of the Iran-Iraq war.   During the war itself, the installations were attacked and bombed several times, causing damage.   Construction work was suspended for years.   It was discovered, when a cease-fire was finally agreed upon between Iran and Iraq, that it was impossible to repair the damage.   To Japan's grave regret, then, the project was finally abandoned and left uncompleted.

6. The Gulf's Interests in Japan

There are a number of categories of Gulf interests in Japan. Some Gulf countries could be interested in the conversion as soon as possible of their depleting oil-assets into economic resources capable of regeneration, or in other words they may be interested in the rapid and comprehensive industrialisation of their countries.   If they approach Japan in the hope of accelerating such a process, it will be very warmly welcomed by Japan.   Japan is ready to offer all the necessary assistance, know-how and finance.

Japan has itself designed programmes which the Gulf countries should find of interest.   Programmes such as these, suitable for the Gulf, were, in fact, actually embarked upon. But, unfortunately, some of the projects that formed part of these programmes failed, mainly due to the political and military disturbances that prevailed in the Gulf. However, it is easy for Japan to revive these programmes if the Gulf is prepared to respond to them.

One of the possible misunderstandings which can arise between Japan and some Gulf countries when we seek to pursue economic co-operation projects, seems to stem from a difference in the basic economic systems of the two parties: on the one hand there is Japan, with its private-sector-dominated economic system that depends on the mechanism of the market, and, on the other, there is the public-sector-oriented economic system depending on central-planning which prevails in some Gulf countries. Profit-generating is the most essential criterion for private firms when they make business-decisions even in economic co-operation projects. It is sometimes difficult for public-sector-dominated economies to understand this point.

Problems are, in particular, often encountered in the case of joint-venture projects between private firms and public sector organisations. It is of some importance for a private firm to balance the accounts in a proposed joint-venture project, whilst a public organisation in partnership with a private firm can often aim to balance the accounts not within the framework of the proposed joint-venture project, but within the wider framework of the national economy. Full turn-key projects may be less troublesome in this sense. But it is up to the partner-countries which pattern of co-operation projects is to be adopted. From Japan's viewpoint, joint-ventures may be better for economic co-operation if they are well designed, such that both partners are fully satisfied.

Some other Gulf countries may have interests in Japan other than those mentioned above. These Gulf countries, and some of their citizens, might have sizable funds to be invested in overseas financial markets; they could be interested in the Japanese stock-market. The Japanese financial market has developed rapidly, and has enjoyed progressive deregulation, with an easing of regulations and restrictions, whilst the Japanese yen has appreciated enough to attract more and more foreign funds and Gulf oil-money. Many foreign banks and financial institutions, including some Arab banks, have opened branch-offices in Tokyo in order to maintain a foothold in Japan.

At the same time, many Japanese banks, securities companies and financial institutions have opened branch-offices in Bahrain, in order to attract Gulf funds to the Japanese financial market. It was once said that Gulf oil-funds had a traditional preference for dollar-denominated assets and deposits with banks, and were very reluctant to invest in the Japanese financial market. But recently it has been estimated that more and more Gulf funds from Saudi Arabia, Kuwait and the UAE have been invested in Japanese government bonds and stocks. Being traditionally cautious and conservative, Gulf funds are said to have earlier tended to be invested in fixed-income government bonds, highly secure equities and real estate. During the oil glut, the inflow of Gulf funds into the Japanese financial market is estimated to have been reduced. But it is believed that Gulf investors have not to a great extent drawn on their bank deposits, sold bonds and stocks, or liquidated their Japanese yen assets.

Recently, Gulf funds have become less and less cautious and, as is said, increasingly interested in direct investment in Japanese private firms. According to reports, Gulf funds have just become interested in the Japanese downstream oil-industry, in the same way that they have been in the US and Europe. The Japanese authorities are said to be prepared to accept direct investment by Gulf funds in the downstream operations of the Japanese oil-industry, on the condition that they guarantee the secure supply of crude oil to the downstream companies, and that they refrain from underselling their oil products in Japan, so as not to disturb the prevailing market-order, and, above all, on the condition that Gulf parties accept direct investment by Japanese oil exploration and development companies in their upstream activities.

The more deeply the Gulf funds are involved in the Japanese economy, the more common interests Japan and the Gulf will have. Both sides can find common interests in the secure supply of crude oil by Gulf countries to Japan and in Japan's better economic performance.

7. Beyond the Economy

Japan has sought mainly to establish the strong economic relations of interdependence with the Gulf which are termed in

Japan the co-operation of 'hard-wares'. Although this so-called 'hard-wares' co-operation must be the basis of interdependence with the Gulf, Japan is well aware that 'hard-wares' economic co-operation is not enough to establish and develop a good relationship with the Gulf. Japan is also prepared to offer her so-called 'soft-wares' co-operation, i.e. co-operation with the Gulf in the fields of education and culture.

In the light of the fact that trading and economic relations have developed substantially between Japan and the Gulf, the educational and cultural relations between them are very poor. At a people-to-people level, our mutual understanding is extremely limited. The number of students from the Gulf studying in Japan is very few and vice versa. It is well known that Japan has advantages in the Arab world and the Middle East, including the Gulf, because Japan has had no history of colonial rule there, and at present Japan has no military ambitions in the region. But these advantages have not been made the most of. Japan is going to develop educational, cultural and human relations with the Gulf in order to complement her economic and trading relationship.

8. Conclusion

Japan has been, and will be, heavily dependent on the Gulf for her imported oil supply, although Japan has been doing her best to reduce this dependence. Oil from the Gulf is essential and indispensable, both to Japanese economic growth itself and to the Japanese contribution to world economic prosperity.

Japan has been making serious efforts to establish economic and cultural relations with the Gulf, relations which might also be regarded as essential and indispensable from the Gulf's viewpoint. If it had not been for the Iran-Iraq war, Japan-Gulf economic and cultural interdependence would have been developed so firmly that our mutual needs were by now become inseparable. The Iran-Iraq war has very seriously damaged not only economic development in the Gulf, but also the development of Japan-Gulf interdependence.

In order to achieve economic and cultural prosperity, peace is an absolutely necessary precondition. The Gulf area must be kept peaceful so that prosperous economic and cultural development can be achieved.   However, the Gulf area has recently been a particularly vulnerable part of the world, this the result of militarisation there being pushed beyond the limits of control.   It is almost impossible to keep the balance of power in the highly militarised Gulf.   It is now necessary to try to keep peace in the Gulf by means of demilitarisation. Japan has always refrained from providing the Gulf with weapons in exchange for oil: in other words, Japan has sought to implement its oil strategy in the Gulf without arms deals.   Japan is confident that this policy will be very helpful in keeping the Gulf peaceful.

Japan sincerely hopes, for the sake of keeping the Gulf peaceful, that the Superpowers, together with the newly emerging armaments-powers, will refrain from providing the Gulf with weapons in exchange for oil or financial assistance, and do their best to maintain peace in the Gulf by means of demilitarisation.

Table 8.1: Breakdown of Japan's Primary Energy Supply in Five-FY Averages (Billion Kcal, %)

	1969-1973	%	1974-1978	%	1979-1983	%	1984-1988	%
Coal*	59,286	17.9	57,914	15.1	66,174	17.1	76,906	18.5
Crude Oil	213,449	64.5	253,746	66.4	217,917	56.2	182,354	43.9
Oil Products	31,148	9.4	29,322	7.7	34,270	8.8	55,619	13.4
Natural Gas & LNG	4,152	1.3	11,849	3.1	24,814	6.4	39,644	9.5
Nuclear	1,484	0.4	7,644	2.0	20,589	5.3	37,286	9.0
Hydro-	17,950	5.4	18,230	4.8	19,507	5.0	18,378	4.4
Others**	3,424	1.0	3,688	1.0	4,384	1.1	5,581	1.3
Total	330,893	100.0	382,393	100.0	387,655	100.0	415,768	100.0

Notes: * Including a small volume of other solid fuels
         ** Geothermal and new energies

Source: Tsusho Sangyo Shyo (MITI), Shigen Enrugi Cho (The Resource and Energy Agency), *Sogo Enerugi Tokei* (Comprehensive Energy Statistics), (1989)

Table 8.2: Japan's Self-Sufficiency in Primary Energy Supplies in Five-FY
Averages (Billion Kcal, %)

		1969-1973	1974-1978	1979-1983	1984-1988
Coal*	(A) Supply	59,286	57,914	66,174	76,906
	(B) Domestic Production	21,464	12,653	12,065	9,324
	(B)/(A) (%)	36.2	21.8	18.2	12.1
Crude Oil	(A) Supply	213,449	253,746	217,917	182,354
	(B) Domestic Production	804	637	453	607
	(B)/(A) (%)	0.4	0.3	0.2	0.3
Oil Products	(A) Supply	31,148	29,322	34,270	55,619
	(B) Domestic Production	14	26	19	14
	(B)/(A) (%)	0.0	0.1	0.1	0.0
Natural Gas and LNG	(A) Supply	4,152	11,849	24,814	39,644
	(B) Domestic Production	2,731	2,787	2,316	2,258
	(B)/(A) (%)	65.8	23.5	9.3	5.7
Others**	(A) Supply	22,858	29,562	44,480	61,245
	(B) Domestic Production	22,858	29,562	44,480	61,245
	(B)/(A) (%)	100.0	100.0	100.0	100.0
Total	(A) Supply	330,893	382,393	387,655	415,768
	(B) Domestic Production	47,871	45,665	59,333	73,448
	(B)/(A) (%)	14.5	11.9	15.3	17.7

Notes: * Including a small volume of other solid fuels
         ** Nuclear, hydro-, geothermal and new energies

Source: Same as Table 8.1

Table 8.3: Investment by Japanese-Owned Overseas Oil-Exploration Companies (Billion current yen, %)

		1958-1978	1979-1983	1984-1988	Total	%
Middle East	Exploration	307.1	308.7	69.6	748.4	40.2
	Development	292.0	108.7	110.4	511.1	37.0
Asia & Oceania	Exploration	146.5	283.9	227.7	658.1	35.4
	Development	195.0	298.6	251.6	745.2	54.0
Africa	Exploration	46.6	22.4	103.5	172.5	9.3
	Development	10.4	42.6	40.7	93.7	6.8
North America	Exploration	13.6	102.3	76.7	192.6	10.4
	Development	-	5.6	2.3	7.9	0.6
Middle & South America	Exploration	51.5	13.5	7.0	72.0	3.9
	Development	8.5	-	-	8.5	0.6
Europe	Exploration	-	-	16.2	16.2	0.8
	Development	-	-	13.2	13.2	1.0
Total	Exploration	628.3	730.8	500.7	1,859.8	100.0
	Development	505.9	455.5	418.2	1,379.6	100.0

Source: Sekyu Kodan (The Japan National Oil Corporation) and Sekyu Koguy Renmei (The Petroleum Producers Federation) (eds.), *Sekyu Kaihatsu Shiryo* (Data on Oil Development), (1990)

Table 8.4: Japan's Crude-Oil Imports by Area and Country in Five-FY Averages (1,000 Kl, %)

	1969-1973	%	1974-1978	%	1979-1983	%	1984-1988	%
The Gulf	185,143	82.1	212,866	78.1	169,088	71.8	135,719	68.9
Saudi Arabia	37,280	16.5	76,676	28.1	73,249	31.1	34,032	17.3
Kuwait	19,562	8.7	21,928	8.0	8,648	3.7	6,708	3.4
Neutral Zone	17,454	7.7	13,108	4.8	12,706	5.4	10,707	5.4
Qatar	140	0.1	2,471	0.9	8,102	3.4	10,355	5.3
UAE	16,410	7.3	29,111	10.7	31,086	13.2	38,549	19.6
Oman	5,848	2.6	8,745	3.2	9,145	3.9	15,542	7.9
Iraq	307	0.1	7,239	2.7	7,775	3.3	6,716	3.4
Iran	88,134	39.1	53,572	19.7	18,347	7.8	12,862	6.5
Others*	8	0.0	16	0.0	21	0.0	248	0.1

	1969-1973	%	1974-1978	%	1979-1983	%	1984-1988	%
Asia & Australia	33,411	14.8	47,012	17.3	46,082	19.6	35,005	17.8
China	328	0.2	7,711	2.8	10,109	4.3	14,015	7.1
South & North America	1,394	0.6	368	0.1	6,833	2.9	10,544	5.4
USSR	704	0.3	111	0.0	86	0.0	100	0.1
Africa	4,393	2.0	4,362	1.6	3,113	1.3	1,564	0.8
Europe**	-	-	-	-	51	0.0	121	0.1
Total	225,373	100.0	272,430	100.0	235,362	100.0	197,068	100.0

Notes: * Bahrain and North Yemen
          ** Norway and England

Source: Sekyu Renmei (The Petroleum Association of Japan), *Sekyu Shiryo Geppo* (Petroleum Review)

Table 8.5: Growth of Japan's Autonomous Oil (1,000Kl, %)

Fiscal Year	Imported Autonomous Oil (A)	Total Imported Oil (B)	(A)/(B) %
1965	11,290	87,626	12.9
1966	14,787	104,199	14.2
1967	15,915	125,137	12.7
1968	17,978	146,848	12.2
1969	18,036	174,598	10.3
1970	20,124	204,872	9.8
1971	19,466	224,379	8.7
1972	20,910	246,098	8.5
1973	24,587	288,609	8.5
1974	27,517	275,887	10.0
1975	23,282	262,785	8.9
1976	23,999	275,826	8.7
1977	23,670	277,477	8.5
1978	29,736	270,121	11.0
1979	24,859	277,143	9.0
1980	22,217	249,199	8.9
1981	20,252	230,231	8.8
1982	18,466	207,395	8.9
1983	23,576	212,844	11.1
1984	23,279	212,911	10.9
1985	21,120	197,261	10.7
1986	23,948	187,516	12.8
1987	19,270	187,903	10.3
1988	25,020	199,758	12.5
Total	513,304	5,126,623	10.0
AAGR* %	3.5	3.6	

Note: * Average annual growth rate
Source: Same as Table 8.4

Table 8.6: Japan's TPER*/GNP Ratio (Kl/100 million yen**)

Fiscal Year	TPER/GNP Ratio	Index
1973	224.5	100
1974	225.0	100.2
1975	206.3	91.9
1976	208.6	92.9
1977	198.1	88.2
1978	187.8	83.7
1979	189.8	84.5
1980	176.4	78.6
1981	165.1	73.5
1982	152.3	67.9
1983	154.9	69.0
1984	154.9	69.0
1985	149.1	66.4
1986	144.1	64.2
1987	143.8	64.1
1988	144.1	64.2

Notes: * Total primary energy requirement
         ** Fixed 1980 price

Source: Sho Enerugi Senta (The Energy Conservation Centre, Japan),
          Energy Conservation in Japan (1989)

Table 8.7: Japan's Long-Term Energy Demand Outlook (Million Kl, %)

Fiscal Year	1988(actual)	2000	2010
Total Primary Energy Demand	482	597	666
Energy Source	%	%	%
New Energies*	1.3	2.9	5.2
Hydro-	4.6	3.7	3.7
Geothermal	0.1	0.3	0.9
Nuclear	9.0	13.2	16.7
Natural Gas	9.6	10.9	12.0
Coal	18.1	17.4	15.5
Oil**	57.3	51.6	46.0
Total	100.0	100.0	100.0

Notes: * Solar energy, alcohol fuel and so on
        ** Including LPG

Source: Sogo Enerugi Chosakai (The Comprehensive Energy Investigation
          Committee), *Chukan Hokoku Soron* (a General Interim Report), (June
          1990)

Table 8.8: Exports to the Gulf: a Cumulative Total for 1983-1988 (Million US dollars, %)

Exporter / Importer	Japan	US	France	West Germany	Italy	UK	Others	Total
Iraq	5,256	4,368	3,811	5,687	3,458	3,820	30,033	56,433
%	9.3	7.7	6.8	10.1	6.1	6.8	53.2	100.0
Saudi Arabia	28,854	28,830	9,422	13,493	11,840	14,148	59,325	165,912
%	17.4	17.3	5.7	8.1	7.1	8.5	35.8	100.0
Kuwait	8,351	4,114	2,120	3,356	2,450	2,807	14,786	37,984
%	22.0	10.8	5.6	8.8	6.5	7.4	38.9	100.0
Bahrain	1,380	1,357	299	870	627	1,472	11,848	17,853
%	7.7	7.6	1.7	4.9	3.5	8.2	66.4	100.0
Qatar	1,293	570	436	610	363	1,141	2,947	7,360
%	17.6	7.7	5.9	8.3	4.9	15.5	40.0	100.0
UAE	7,953	4,571	2,292	3,514	2,635	5,070	20,103	46,138
%	17.2	9.9	5.0	7.6	5.7	11.0	43.6	100.0
Oman	2,764	1,086	492	1,180	421	3,202	7,180	16,325
%	16.9	6.7	3.0	7.2	2.6	19.6	44.0	100.0
Iran	9,778	645	1,308	12,838	4,388	4,509	39,750	73,216
%	13.4	0.9	1.8	17.5	6.0	6.2	54.3	100.0
Total	65,629	45,541	20,180	41,548	26,182	36,169	184,772	420,021
%	15.6	10.8	4.8	9.9	6.2	8.6	44.0	100.0

Source: IMF, *Direction of Trade Statistics Yearbook, 1988, 1989*

Table 8.9: Japan's ODA (net disbursement-basis) (Million US dollars, %)

Calendar year	Grand Total (A)	Middle East* Sub total (B)	(B)/(A) (%)
1960-1969	1,938.70	7.86	0.4
1970	371.51	13.48	3.6
1971	432.02	4.99	1.2
1972	477.79	3.83	0.8
1973	765.18	10.59	1.4
1974	880.37	22.25	2.5
1975	850.40	90.41	10.6
1976	752.95	58.98	7.8
1977	899.25	219.99	24.5
1978	1,530.97	347.78	22.7
1979	1,921.22	203.45	10.6
1980	1,960.80	203.61	10.4
1981	2,260.41	190.07	8.4
1982	2,367.33	193.64	8.2
1983	2,425.22	200.53	8.3
1984	2,427.39	249.35	10.3
1985	2,556.92	201.05	7.9
1986	3,846.21	339.82	8.8
1987	5,247.92	526.00	10.0
1988	6,421.87	582.52	9.1
Total	40,338.39	3,670.22	9.1

Note: * Total of 22 countries including Afghanistan, Turkey, Sudan and North
African countries

Source: Gaimusho (The Ministry of Foreign Affairs), Keizai Kyoryoku Kyoku
(The Department of Economic Co-operation) (ed.), *Wagakunino Seifu
Kaihatsuenjo* (Japan's Official Development Assistance), (1989)

Table 8.10: Japan's Overseas Firms by Industry and Area (as of 1 July 1989) (Company, %)

	Total	Asia	Middle East*	Europe	North America	Middle & South America	Africa	Oceania
Total	11,484	4,299	110	2,173	3,286	864	174	578
	% 100.0	37.4	1.1	18.9	28.6	7.5	1.5	5.0
Agriculture	128	46	-	7	18	28	8	21
Mining	137	16	6	5	53	16	5	36
Construction	412	217	26	36	69	31	5	28
Manufacturing	4,220	2,339	30	418	982	316	52	83
Commerce	3,670	924	34	1,043	1,240	203	17	209
Banking & Finance	673	197	2	244	134	59	7	30
Transport, Storage & Communication	525	159	2	66	125	82	70	21
Service	730	218	2	112	289	42	3	64
Others**	989	183	8	242	376	87	7	86

Notes: * Iran, Bahrain, Saudi Arabia, Kuwait, Qatar, Israel, Lebanon and the UAE
         ** Insurance, real estate investment and others

Source: Toyokeizai, *Kaigaishinshutsu Kigyo Soran* (Japan's Overseas Firms), (1990)

9. THE USSR AND THE ARAB GULF: A CURRENT BALANCE SHEET AND FUTURE ASSESSMENT

Vitaly Naumkin

For a long time now, the Arab Gulf has been an arena for the confrontations and clashes of different regional and world forces. The area is vitally important to many great-power interests, whilst some of the great powers uphold relations with some of the Gulf countries on the basis that they constitute a prize (this is at least the US attitude to its relationship with Iran).

The Soviet Union is a novice in the Gulf. Except in the case of Iran, a country adjacent to the USSR, with which Russia had relations of long standing, Moscow has made a very recent, if belated, entry into the region.[1] The three decades from the 1958 Iraqi revolution until today have been tough, complex and eventful. The first two of these saw a rapid growth of relations with Iraq - despite some occasional gloom-casting vignettes. The Soviet Union's dedication to good neighbourly relations with Iran was thwarted by the alliance between the United States and the Shah seeking to oppose Soviet interests there. But then the USSR initiated and expanded its relationship with Kuwait, the first of the Gulf oil-monarchies to experience this. The last decade has been marked by dramatic elements such as the appearance of a new post-revolutionary Iran and the Iran-Iraq war; a further complication, of course, came with the Soviet military expedition into Afghanistan, recently ended. This was also the decade which saw a Soviet diplomatic breakthrough in the Gulf region, brought about by the establishment of relations with some of the other oil-monarchies. Lastly, and unexpectedly, developments in the USSR itself took a no less dramatic course, one that has brought about a fundamental change in the international situation overall. Before long these were to affect the situation in and around the Gulf, making the Superpowers revise their role and policies in the region.

In a review of the past few years, there appear certain distinct major factors that have influenced the Soviet relationship with the Gulf countries. These are as follows:

1. The forgoing of global confrontation with the USA and, more generally, the abandonment of the earlier concept of a world divided into two opposed entities, the capitalist West and the socialist East, whose confrontational posture was projected upon Third World states. The effect has been the renunciation of the 'zero sum game'.

2. By promulgating the principle of de-ideologisation and humanisation in international relations, friendly and mutually advantageous relations became possible *vis-à-vis* those states which had been 'estranged' politically or ideologically and whose 'estrangedness' acted as an impediment this way or that.

3. The Soviet Union developed a keen interest in beneficial economic co-operation with the Gulf countries, one born out of *perestroika* problems.

4. Moscow's traditional friends and partners evinced varying responses to the changes in Soviet domestic and foreign policies, leaving some of them worried and frustrated.

5. National and religious factors became increasingly important and effective in the Soviet Union's relations with the Gulf states. Chief among these is the ever growing urge among the Soviet Moslem community toward the Arab and, broadly speaking, the Moslem world. In turn, several Gulf states were committed to broadening their contacts with the Soviet Moslem Republics and even to encouraging them to become something more lasting and permanent. Some Soviet nations, too, showed a willingness to form special relationships with related nations in the East outside the USSR (e.g. Tajiks with Iranians and Afghan Tajiks, or Azarbaijanis with their counterparts in Iran).

6. The Soviet Union's ties with neighbouring countries (Iran is the prime case in point) began to be assigned higher priorities. One cannot but concur with Oles Smolansky's proposition that 'foreign countries that are contiguous with Soviet territory attract greater attention in Moscow than those which are not'.[2]

Indeed, as the USSR and the USA have progressed from unyielding confrontation to pliant and constructive dialogue, their co-operation in the areas of disarmament and regional dispute settlement has produced a salutary effect in the Gulf region. A look at the future of USSR-USA co-operation shows that it is likely to continue in the longer term. From this perspective, current Third World fears about some 'Soviet-American condominium' seem hardly justified, even given the voices heard sometimes within both Superpowers concerning the need for such a condominium to ensure regional security. The disparity of interests between the USSR and the USA gives staying power to their differences of opinion, precluding the possibility of concerted action by their very existence. On the other hand, the interests of the two powers exist 'on different levels' - they never intersect directly so as to allow a fairly broad field of agreement between them.

In this context, it is relevant to enquire into the proper interpretation of a key thesis underlying the new Soviet foreign policy, that concerning the substitution of balanced interests for the former power-balance. What now looks important in the relationship between the USSR and the USA is probably not only whether they will mutually acknowledge each other's interests in Third World regions, but also how they intend to do so, whether by going for one of the two existing options for such acknowledgement, that is the symmetrical option based on parity, or else adopting the second, asymmetrical, approach. The former consists in recognising a mutual equality of interests and 'rights to be there'. Here, a great deal depends on the view of 'being there' which is held by the other side - whether it is seen as threatening and ominous, or perceived as perfectly normal and not damaging to any of its interests. Peaceful competition, however, is by no means ruled out in this instance.

The alternative approach involves recognition by one side of the other's pre-emptive right to build up relations with a state or a group of states. Thus the Soviet Union should perhaps acknowledge the asymmetry of Soviet and American interests in the Arabian Gulf region, with US oil-imports from the area accounting for an ever greater share of its total consumption. In a move of reciprocity, the USA should accept the Soviet Union's very special interest in furthering its good-neighbourly ties with the countries whose territories are contiguous with its own;

naturally, this is not a licence for the USSR to crowd the Americans out of the area. Balanced interests may go well with an imbalance in presence.

This point is all the more significant in the light of the conceptual changes occurring in the US foreign-policy line. Speaking before those attending a symposium at the Washington Institute for Near East Policy, Les Aspin, Chairman of the House Armed-Services Committee, described major new threats to the United States which are likely to succeed the menace of Soviet expansion as the key determinant of US foreign-policy objectives. One very real successor, he termed 'economic nationalism' - the economic threat looming from Europe and Japan. The Gulf will, without a doubt, rank high on the list of regions where European and Japanese economic interests might grow enough to compete with those of the United States.

There have been significant signs of change in the US attitude to the USSR's Gulf policies. In the West, strong feelings are frequently expressed about the Soviet Union's ability over the years to maintain good relations with Iraq as well as Iran, giving it access to certain possibilities in each. In particular, it was the Soviet Union that offered mediation over the settlement of the conflict and made diplomatic moves in this direction. Not only did the United States never oppose the idea of mediation, as would have been the case some two or three years back, but showed understanding for it. Media reports revealed last May that the mediation proposal would be discussed by the Soviet Deputy Foreign Minister, Vladimir Petrovsky, during his visit to Tehran.[3] To the correspondent who asked him about his Middle East journey to meet the leaders of Iraq, the PLO and Jordan, Petrovsky observed,

The Soviet Union is among the few countries which have normal good relations both with Iran and Iraq, providing us with ample opportunity to offer our good offices to both sides. We stated in Iraq that our assistance could possibly take various forms, including the use of our territory as the venue for the negotiations - whether with our immediate involvement, or without it, on a bilateral basis, is up to the parties to decide.[4]

The Soviet Union stressed it had no intention of interfering with the efforts of the UN Secretary-General and the parties themselves, much less now that the parties seem to have come to terms about an Iran-Iraq summit.

One would be over-optimistic if one thought that the Arab Gulf region will be immune from shocks in the foreseeable future. A clash of interests among the regional powers and political forces may result in new outbreaks of old regional conflicts and spur new ones. Moving away from the means to containment of the Soviet Union, the US Administration, especially in the past two years, has seemed inclined to emphasise a shared concern on the part of the two Superpowers with preventing future regional conflicts and with the settlement of current ones.

In his address to the Foreign Policy Association, Secretary of State James Baker said,

Regional conflicts are likely to be more difficult to contain, more likely to engulf more countries, and more susceptible to escalation. Neither the United States nor a Soviet Union in the midst of *perestroika* has an interest in being drawn into such conflicts... And we have made it clear that we are ready and willing partners - partners who recognise that settling and diffusing regional tensions can diminish the dangers we all face.[5]

A similar view to this is today also characteristic of the Soviet Union.

Over the past decade two stones have been pulling Soviet-Arab, and especially Soviet-Saudi, relations down to the bottom. At first, Soviet military intervention in Afghanistan was responsible; now, it is the exodus of Soviet Jews to Israel. The drastic upsurge in Soviet Jewish immigration into Israel, and the promises that followed from Tel Aviv that it should be relied upon for settlement of the occupied territories, added complexity to this relationship. The Arabs' hurt reaction was largely unforeseen, as Jews from the Soviet Union had left for Israel before and their settlement in Arab territories is nothing new to the Arabs. The Soviet Union can in no way be responsible for this, as it neither instigated nor assisted it. Moreover, the new wave of Jewish immigration by no means gives vent to the desire to settle and make a home in the occupied territories. Although the protests that went up in the Arab world did not have the Soviet Union as their target, repeated attempts were made to divert the criticism toward

Moscow and even to call for acts of retribution to be carried out against Soviet representatives there. Similar criticisms were encountered from the Gulf countries as well. The view was aired that there should be containment of the alleged expansion of 'Jewish capital' into the USSR. Paradoxically, those segments of the Arab world which always embraced anti-Communist attitudes and should, or so it seemed, have welcomed the move to political and economic liberalisation, held *perestroika* and Gorbachev's foreign policy responsible for the rise of hazardous trends on the regional scene. Even the fundamentalists were disgruntled. As Egyptian writer Fahmi Howeidi told a conference which was organised by the London-based Centre for Studies on the Future of Islam, and was attended by forty scholars and political leaders from ten Arab countries, 'the collapse of Communism will weaken, not strengthen, the Moslem world'.[6]

Arab propaganda took to flaunting the myth of some 'Zionist lobby' in Moscow and of the Zionists' influence on Moscow's policy. The flare-up of rhetoric soon began to subside, whereas analysis of the Gulf countries' behaviour indicated that, on balance, they saw the situation in the USSR as favouring broader relations with it. Undisputed advances have since been made in the Soviet relationships with the UAE, Oman, Qatar and Saudi Arabia, where the visit of Vladimir Polyakov, Head of the Middle East and North Africa Department of the Soviet Foreign Ministry, was for the first time covered by the media. Chartered Aeroflot flights delivered a Saudi Arabian gift to Soviet Moslems - over a million copies of the Koran. Continuing progress in the Soviet Union's relations with Kuwait reached a new high in the signing in Moscow last May of an agreement on $US 300 million-worth of credit to the Soviet Union - a fact of much greater political than financial or economic significance. Soviet-Kuwaiti contacts keep multiplying and deepening in the oil and gas industries, health, trade and banking. There are plans to have an agreement to protect mutual investments. In an interview with the newspaper *Izvestia*, the Kuwaiti Ambassador to the USSR called for the lifting of economic relations between the two countries to the level of their political relationship and went on to suggest the formation of Soviet-Kuwaiti joint-ventures in third countries.[7]

In 1990 Soviet Moslems set out on their first mass *hajj* to Mecca, in sharp contrast to before when a few dozen were able to make the pilgrimage. 1,500 people from many cities in the Soviet Union were flown by Aeroflot planes to Jeddah on direct flights chartered specially for them, to gather with a consular group going to Saudi Arabia with the pilgrims for the duration of their sojourn there. There is more vigour now in Soviet-Saudi commercial and economic ties: deals have been struck and visits to the USSR paid for by some major Saudi businessmen.

At meetings taking place these last few months between population-leaders and politicians from the USSR and Arab countries, the latter came up with the idea that Arab entrepreneurs might seriously consider investing in the Soviet Union. On the whole, however, the Arab business community and the Gulf countries' businessmen above all, still display caution and reserve, choosing to wait and see, and, by and large, they are reluctant to invest in the production sphere where the Soviet Union needs it most.

This is not impeding progress in traditional avenues of Soviet trade and economic relations with the Arab Gulf states, amongst which relations with Iraq seem worthy of special discussion. In 1981 Iraq was the leader among the Soviet Union's partners in commerce and trade in the Near and Middle East and North Africa, only to become second-placed after Libya among Arab countries in 1982-6, then advancing into second position after India in commodity turnover among all Third World countries in 1987-8.[8] In their structure, Soviet trade and economic relations with Iraq show two revealing characteristics: first, a large proportion of arms-supplies which, on conservative estimates for 1982-7, stood at about $US 10 billion;[9] second, a major part of the export consisted of plant, equipment and transport-vehicles, accounting for 94.3 per cent in 1987-8, with aircraft topping the list at 41.3 per cent in 1988. Up to the end of 1989 the USSR assisted in the construction work on 98 projects in Iraq, of which 92 became operational.[10] Chief among them were oilfield enhancement, a petro-product pipeline and thermal and hydro-power plants.

At present, boosting relations between the USSR and Iraq is coming up against a number of limitations such as the inadequate financial capabilities of the two countries, restricted Soviet techno-economic potential, and the intense competition of third countries. It may be assumed that economic revival and boosting strategies will give priority to oil and related industries.

Besides the oil and gas industry, the draft economic-development plan drawn up by the Iraqi Ministry of Planning is heavily focused on defence and ferrous metallurgy as the main sectors for restoration and development. The plans for an increase in trade and economic ties with Iraq closely consider its unwillingness to go for turn-key projects, and its demands that new contracts make provision for technology-transfer and maximise the involvement of local building and other companies in the construction of specific projects.

At present, a draft long-term programme of Soviet-Iraqi co-operation is under examination, one which the Soviet parties believe should include among its goals the modernisation of previously constructed projects, the erection of new ones on a compensation-basis through product-deliveries to the USSR, Iraq and third countries, the formation of joint ventures with the participation of Iraqi capital, and shared efforts on third countries' markets. As yet the programme still encounters difficulties in its advancement.

Clearly, in defining the place of Iraq and its relations with external forces generally and the USSR in particular, the following circumstances need to be borne in mind:

1. Iraq possesses the most experienced and best-equipped and -trained army of all the Arab countries, coupled with an evolving war-industry.
2. For a whole number of reasons, Iraq lays claim to the role of Arab leader and, in any case, represents a major and perhaps decisive power in the Arab world.
3. Despite outstanding debts, Iraq's financial potential is indeed great, due chiefly to its oil resources.

It is clear however that Iraq needs time to restore its human and economic potential, and in the short term can hardly be envisaged, as is sometimes done in the West, as presenting a threat to Israel. Yet, in the Arab world today, recourse is frequently made to Iraq as the force capable of providing a counterweight to Israel and its nuclear threat. 'Iraqi chemistry against the Israeli atom' could well be a driving motive and inspiration sufficient to stir up and weave itself into a new wave of Arab nationalism, one in which Iraq is intent on playing first fiddle.

Let us recall that the official Soviet approach to Iraq has at all times been careful and guarded, featuring the desire to avoid anything that might spoil the existing mutual understanding. Soviet leaders, worried as they were by reprisals against the Iraqi Communists during the late 1970s, responded to them with restraint; whilst their assessment by the Communist Party-controlled Soviet media was calm and all too often couched in Aesopian phrases like 'the foes of progressive development in Iraq have once again incited enmity among the progressive forces.' However, the official assessment as conveyed to Iraq through diplomatic channels was much more concrete - as is known, the Soviet leadership did not conceal its concern. The predominant concept at the time, which had been developed by party theorists like R.A. Ulianovsky and K.N. Burtents, rested on the doctrine of unity among the three currents in the national liberation movement - socialist countries, the working-class movement in capitalist countries and the national liberation movement; it allowed 'incorporation into Marxism of revolutionary democrats' and regarded the Iraqi leadership as such. The approach allotted high priority to the political agenda of the day, and its maintenance and expansion was strongly urged, particularly since there existed the conviction that for the Communists to come to power in the East was out of the question on account of a number of objective circumstances.

One should not assume that the Soviet stance towards Iraq was in the past dictated only by the rules of the 'zero sum game', or predominantly determined by Iraq's firm stand against US imperialism and Israeli aggression. The key role was assigned to ideological perceptions as the developmental model of Iraqi society fitted the canons of the 'socialist-oriented way' of development well (although since the latter half of the 1970s the departure from it was *de facto* acknowledged by the Soviet theorists who gradually ceased to mention Iraq as belonging to this group of countries). There were also more, if not totally, pragmatic reasons deriving from the fact that the trade and economic relations with Iraq palpably benefited the Soviet Union.

The Soviet Union's trade and economic relations with the Arab Gulf countries other than Iraq were not considerably advanced for reasons which were partly objective - e.g. the poor competitiveness of Soviet goods in these nations' markets, the USSR's lacking the product ranges they needed, the Gulf nations' orientation towards the West; and partly subjective - the fear these countries had of 'Communist expansion' and the total lack, or poor development, of political relations, relations only being established in 1985 with Oman and the UAE, in 1988 with Qatar, and which are still non-existent with regard to Saudi Arabia and Bahrain. As a result, several Arab states - Iraq, Egypt, Libya, Syria and Algeria - concentrate 90 per cent of their commodity turnover, and 85 per cent of their techno-economic co-operation, with the USSR whose trade with the group of nations that form our immediate concern here is characterised by the principal data contained in Table 9.1.

Table 9.1: USSR Trade with Arab Gulf States (millions of roubles)

	1980		1985		1987		1988	
	exp	imp	exp	imp	exp	imp	exp	imp
Saudi Arabia	30.8	-	15.1	378.8	12.4	-	12.8	12.6
Kuwait	15.2	1.5	3.2	0.4	-	-	-	-
UAE	-	-	-	-	-	-	-	-
Oman	-	-	-	-	-	-	-	-
Qatar	-	-	-	-	-	-	-	-
Bahrain	-	-	-	-	-	-	-	-

Source: *Vneshnaya Torgovlya SSSR* (Moscow), appropriate years.

Commodity turnover with the Gulf monarchies made up between 0.7 and 1.9 per cent of the Soviet Union's total turnover with the Arab community, exports from the USSR forming the main item. The first half of the 1980s stands out because of a dramatic increase in Soviet commodity turnover with the Persian Gulf countries through expanded imports. But the crucial point is that Saudi Arabia and Kuwait were at the time supplying oil to the USSR to make good the former Iraqi shipments, the latter being unable to continue fulfilling its obligations to the Soviet side because of its war with Iran. The principal Soviet export-items included lumber, cement, gas pipes and cars, with oil, petro-products and wheat (from Saudi Arabia) as the main imported commodities.

Economic co-operation proper was going ahead only with Kuwait and even this did not begin to be vigorously pursued until the 1980s. A serious step in this direction was the Soviet Union's consent to lease three tankers to Kuwait and assure their safe passage through the most dangerous stretches of the Persian

Gulf during the Iran-Iraq war.[11] In 1987 a consortium of Kuwaiti banks offered the USSR for the first time on record a loan of US $150 million,[12] followed in May 1990 by a second loan of US $300 million issued to the Soviet Bank for Foreign Economic Affairs (Vnesheconom Bank).[13]

The parties have agreed to create three joint-ventures over the construction of oil-industry projects in the USSR and third countries. The Soviet Union's duties under the agreement concern geological exploration, assessment of reserves, cost-effectiveness estimation of oilfields, assessment of project costs and project lead times; Kuwait has assumed obligations in respect of project financing, recruitment of modern technologies and the provision of markets for product sales from the three joint-ventures.[14] Thus far, however, none of the points agreed upon have been implemented.

Passing, as it is, through a complex period of basic restructuring of its economic system, the Soviet Union needs outside assistance and has recourse to foreign loans in order to achieve it. This serves, naturally, to exacerbate the national debt problem. While the country's indebtedness has been relatively low until recently, it is currently estimated by Western experts to exceed US $50 billion. It may be presumed that the Soviet government will be seeking to diversify its sources of loans and credits, thus avoiding a build-up of debt to one or several states (i.e. Western states for the time being). Hence the likelihood of its turning for finance to yet untapped potential-sources such as the Gulf countries (of which Kuwait has been the first) or Singapore. This is perhaps the right perspective for a proper assessment of the now evolving Soviet contacts with South Korea. Naturally, the oil problem is central to the whole context of Soviet relations with the Gulf states, making a discussion of outlooks for the future very relevant at this point. Even though differing over the details of what might be accomplished by the various oil-companies, the outlooks still agree upon some general predictions for likely developments on the oil-market during the 1990s:

1. Oil production in OECD countries will follow a downturn in the early 1990s with the result, chiefly, of making them more dependent on oil supplies from third countries - from 50 per cent in 1988 to 60 per cent in the year 2000.

2. After steadiness in the oil price at $18 per barrel no price rise is expected until 1992, unless something extraordinary

happens in the political arena so as to cause a drastic policy-change by one of the major oil-exporters or so as to sharpen dramatically the situation in the Middle East.

3. Prices in excess of $20 per barrel, if this level were to be achieved by 1991 in consequence of unforeseen political events in the key oil-exporting countries, would suffer continuous and insistent downward pressure until the strategic reserves now available in the ICCs (industrialised capitalist countries) became depleted and excessive oil production capacities were cut away.

4. In the second half of the 1990s there will be a general upward trend in oil-price variation, reflecting the ICCs' growing demand for oil, which will be the case also in the developing countries, together with an oil-production slump in non-OPEC countries; no 'explosive' price-hike of the kind occurring in the 1970s is any more expected.

5. During the next four to six years oil prices in 1986 dollars will remain at $18-20 per barrel, starting to climb thereafter and reaching $25-35 per barrel by the year 2000.

6. Demand for OPEC-produced oil is going to be as high as 28-30 million barrels per day out of the capitalist world's total of 56-8 million barrels per day.

7. Should oil prices by the mid-1990s achieve a new high at $30 per barrel, the OECD countries' oil-production may be topped by the depleting North Sea resources to the extent of 1.5-2.5 million barrels per day. Lower oil-prices, which render oil extraction in severe regions no longer cost-effective, will reduce the outlay on exploration and geology, the transfer to alternative sources of energy and the design of energy-saving technologies; the OECD countries' reduction in oil output is presumed to be somewhere around the level of 2.5-4 million barrels per day.

8. The oil-price reduction will backfire by boosting the demand for oil from the ICCs. With the formerly high prices it was strongly believed that, on an average daily basis, the demand for oil would be growing at 0.5 to 0.75 per cent annually; contrary to expectations, it in fact reached 2 per cent in 1988-9.

Subsequent to these developments, the situation on the oil-market by the year 2000 may well be as shown in Table 9.2.

Table 9.2: The Oil-Market in the Year 2000 (in million barrels per day)

Consumption		Supplies	
OECD	37-40	OECD	14-15
Other states	16-18	OPEC	26-30
Total	53-8	Other oil-suppliers in developing countries	12-13
		Other states	1-2
		Total	53-60

Thus the OPEC countries will claim from 43 to 57 per cent of total oil-supplies to the world capitalist market for liquid fuel, with the OECD countries' dependence on OPEC oil growing from 40 per cent in 1990 to 50-5 per cent (at currently estimates). This indicator might be higher still if oil prices have fallen below $25 per barrel.

Experts from the Institute of Oriental Studies, USSR (V.A. Isaev and other) estimate that OPEC countries, at the heart of which lie the Arab states, chiefly those in the Gulf region, will retain their significance as the major oil-suppliers to the capitalist market. OPEC at present accounts for 75 per cent of proven world oil-reserves and its Arab member-states for 60 per cent. Iran apart, the Arab countries themselves can go forward as the virtually uncontested leaders in the sphere of oil reserves, be their position measured in any one of the latter's three foremost categories, those of active resources, proven reserves and probable resources which have recently enjoyed renewed growth after a short period of stagnation in the early 1980s. In 1987-8 alone proven oil-reserves in Iraq doubled and they trebled in the UAE; the oil-exporting community was joined by the Yemen Arab Republic and commercial oil-reserves were discovered in the People's Democratic Republic of Yemen.

By means only of production from oilfields with low operating-costs, the Arab countries are able to meet up to 45 per cent of the oil demand of the capitalist world until the middle of the next century.

The Soviet expert V.A. Isaev argues that in all probability by the late 1990s a new and powerful centre of finance and industry, primarily petro-processing and petrochemical, well provided with all the modern production infrastructure, will have become thoroughly established in the Arab Gulf area. The Arab oil-producing states there will maintain a relationship *vis-à-vis* industrialised capitalist states that exhibits an ever greater degree of interdependence; there will still be occasional disagreements between them, but although these may reach a high degree of acerbity on specific issues, such as the price of oil or a Middle East settlement, the parties to a conflict will seek to resolve their dispute through compromise rather than through confrontation.

This is not to rule out a renewal of conflict amongst the Arab states on sensitive issues like oil-production quotas, because non-OPEC countries will probably attempt to boost oil production and oil export in order to maximise their returns from the favourable situation on the world market. One example is Syria and the effort taken by it recently towards a marked increase in oil production and export in an attempt to improve her economic situation - a policy which she has no intention of giving up in the next two or three years. Equally, the Arab countries are likely to fall out with their main competitors, such as Iran in the European market and Nigeria in the African market.

More generally, the 1990s will witness greater tension in the competitive struggles on the world market for liquid fuels, and this will remain a buyer's market. One can project the future appearance of one other factor which distinctly promises to upset the precarious balance obtaining in this market: the USSR, as it is now bent on going beyond the traditional markets in order to earn the hard currency it needs for the resolution of domestic economic problems. Evidence to confirm this intention on the part of the Soviet Union is discerned by Western spectators in the recently adopted series of fuel-saving measures, a probable rise in the internal prices of petro-products and in a willingness to substitute gas deliveries for the oil supplies to East European countries. If this supposition proves right, then oil prices will slump. As counter to this, one needs to consider the Soviet Union's unchanged commitment to the maintenance and expansion of good relations with OPEC member states, and also to the formulation of its trade and economic policies in ways that allow this concern to be taken account of.

Experts from the Institute of Oriental Studies also predict competition for the markets of East European countries, above all those of Yugoslavia, Rumania, Hungary and Czechoslovakia. Plans are already afoot to lay down a pipeline for Libyan oil deliveries to Yugoslavia and Rumania; in a similar move, Kuwait is about to start off-sales of petro-products from its oil refineries in Denmark and Holland to Hungary, Poland and Czechoslovakia. Regardless of Arab oil, even Soviet oil, with its production costs in the 1980s well above the world average, may find itself forced out from these markets. This process of crowding out could speed up if the USSR cuts back, or even keeps up, its present scale of oil supplies to the East European countries, the more so if it starts provisioning them at world prices in freely convertible currency, as some Soviet economists strongly urge.[15] Should this come about, the Arab countries will be quick to offer more lucrative terms for their own oil-deliveries such as the purchase of credits or deferment on payments.

There is still hope, though, that all the problems which are likely to arise from the situation on the oil-market and which affect the interests of the USSR and the Gulf countries will be solved in a spirit of understanding and accord between the two parties. The presumption is further supported by the latter's shared concern for initiating and increasing mutually beneficial economic co-operation and by the trend for political *rapprochement* between the two parties. We feel it is especially important to note the intention, recently stated by the Soviet side, of broadening relations with groups like the Gulf Co-operation Council and the Islamic Conference Organisation.

By and large, the future role of the Soviet Union in the Gulf and the future of its relations with the Gulf nations both seem substantially dependent upon the future and fate of the complex and involved process of change that is now underway in the Soviet Union.

Notes

1   That is, except for the experience of relations with Yemen after 1928 and the more short-lived experience of relations with Saudi Arabia from 1926 until the late 1930s.

2   Manuscript, received from the author, of a report entitled, 'The Soviet

Union and Iraq: a Troubled Relationship, 1980-1990'.

3   *Arab Times* (Kuwait), 8 May 1990.

4   *Izvestia* (Moscow), 25 June 1990.

5   Address by the Honourable James A. Baker III, Secretary of State, before the Foreign Policy Association, New York, 16 Oct. 1989: Dept. of State, pr. no. 192 (17 Oct. 1989), p. 8.

6   *Arab Times* (Kuwait), 6 May 1990.

7   *Izvestia* (Moscow), 2 June 1990.

8   *External Economic Relations of the USSR in 1988* (Moscow, 1989), pp. 10-14.

9   *Argumenty i Facty*, issue 21 (USSR, 1990).

10   Data of the Ministry of Foreign Economic Relations, USSR.

11   This decision, in turn, pushed the Americans to opt for the reflagging of Kuwaiti tankers.

12   *Kuwait Times*, 16 Feb. 1990.

13   *Arab Times* (Kuwait), 8 May 1990.

14   *Arab Times* (Kuwait), 18 Feb. 1989.

15   This does not seem to be a very realistic projection; more probably, the Soviet oil supplies will, in part if not in whole, be delivered on bonus terms.

10. THE USSR'S STATE INTERESTS IN THE RED SEA BASIN AND THE HORN OF AFRICA IN CONNECTION WITH THE GULF ZONE

Alexei Vassiliev

The problem of analysing 'Soviet state interests in the Red Sea and the Horn of Africa' is misleading on account of its apparent simplicity. It might seem that it were enough merely to draw up a hierarchy of the military-strategic, economic, political and other priorities in the USSR's foreign policy in this region for one to arrive at a satisfactory answer within the expected framework. But many of the problems in Soviet foreign policy are still under discussion in our country. The questions raised are as follows:

- What determines the foreign policy of the USSR - a messianic concept of the expansion of the Soviet model of socio-political system as the highest achievement of civilisation, or the pragmatic goals of national interest, such as security and defence?
- What is the meaning of the term 'national interests' now, when the world is moving away from confrontation in the sphere of international relations?
- Do national interests coincide with state ones?

The author of this chapter considers that there is no direct answer to any of these questions. It is true that foreign policy was highly ideologised. But it is also true that sometimes the Soviet government undertook pragmatic, if not cynical, steps. Now Moscow is reconstructing its foreign policy and this process demands the formulation of new methods and principles. We have different attitudes to the past and the future. But the author is not inclined to act as a masochist and thinks that in terms of Soviet-American rivalry all the activities of the Soviet side on the international scene were a mirror picture of the activities of the American side, though sometimes the mirror was curved.

The Persian (Arabian) Gulf zone borders with the southern territories of the USSR. That is why I would specify the geographical factor as one of the most important of those which determine the state interests of the USSR in this region. Peoples who live here and states which are situated in this territory are closely connected with the peoples and republics of the USSR by their mutual historical development, civilisation, and many centuries of cultural and economic ties. The region is rich in natural resources and has great economic potential. It offers great possibilities for mutually advantageous trading, economic, scientific and technological ties with the Soviet Union, its nearest neighbour.

The zone is overburdened with conflicts. Though the eight years of hostilities between Iran and Iraq have been suspended, the conflict has not yet been settled. The war in Afghanistan, which adjoins the Gulf zone, continues and is aggravated by interference from the United States and Pakistan. Many states are involved in the Arab-Israeli conflict. The Middle and Near East region possesses, after NATO and the Warsaw Pact countries, the greatest quantity of weapons and it is also the number one importer of weapons. Missiles and chemical weapons exist in the area and there is a danger that there may be nuclear weapons, too, which means a threat not only to the region but to security and peace in the whole world.

Finally, Western countries have vested interests in the Gulf region, especially the United States of America, whose interests here from the point of view of the USSR may be divided into legitimate and illegitimate ones. The first are trading, economic, political, cultural and other relations including freedom of navigation and stability in oil supplies. The second, illegitimate or imperial interests, which were formed during a period of confrontation, i.e. the desire to prevent the normalisation of relations between the USSR and the countries of the region, are viewed negatively by Moscow.

Among the traditional priorities of Soviet foreign policy, I would point out the problem of security as a regional and global concern. The Soviet Union is interested in guaranteeing that no threat to its borders should come from the south. Until recently, no military threat could arise from the states situated here, but only from the Western powers who might use their territory, the seas nearby and the ocean as a springboard for possible action against the USSR. This was the main reason for the traditionally negative Soviet attitude to all military blocs in the region in which the West participated, such as the Baghdad Pact and CENTO. That is why the Soviet Union was against the establishment of Western military bases in the region, be they an electronic-intelligence station in Iran, US Air Force bases in Turkey, or likewise earlier in Pakistan; be they bases and facilities for the US Navy in the region or the inclusion of this zone into the US Central Command (CENTCOM) area as a possible sector for the actions of the Rapid Deployment Forces (RDF). Naturally, Moscow considers the Indian Ocean basin as a possible link in the encircling of the USSR from the south (the Gulf countries are the most important for its security), and the Red Sea and Horn of Africa region as a part of the Indian Ocean basin, the region being important because of the communications that pass through it.[1]

All these considerations are directly connected with the theme under discussion. I should now like to focus on certain historic aspects of this problem and then make some forecasts for the future.

The Red Sea basin and the Horn of Africa attracted the attention of Russia as a region of state interests soon after the opening of the Suez Canal. After that time, for more than one hundred years, the state interests of Russia (and then of the USSR) underwent considerable change connected with the establishment of new priorities in the foreign policy, global, military-strategic, political and other fields. But St Petersburg, and later Moscow, always kept an eye on this region. In Africa only Egypt, with its exclusively important strategic situation, could compete with the Red Sea region. But they were considered as one, and this was not true of the Persian Gulf. It became a priority in its own right after the discovery and exploitation of enormous oil-deposits in the region.

The Imperial Russian government evaluated the military-strategic importance of the Suez Canal in connection with the geostrategic interests of Russia (though this term didn't then exist). The canal opened up the shortest waterway to the Russian Far East from the European part of the country. There was no reliable and short land-route between the central Russian provinces and eastern Siberia and the Far Eastern Territories. The Trans-Siberian railway and its southern branchline - the eastern Chinese railroad through Manchuria - were built and put into operation only at the beginning of the 20th century. But now, as in the past, the waterway from the Baltic and Black Seas to the Far East passing through the Suez Canal, is the cheapest, though the waterway through the Arctic Ocean has now become navigable. This is the main reason why Russia struggled for the international status of the Suez Canal, trying to defend the sovereignty of Egypt over it and keep Britain away from the area. But London proved to be more powerful and occupied Egypt in 1882.

In Russia's Foreign Policy Archives we found some rather interesting historical information.[2] M.A. Khitrovo, who was appointed as a diplomatic agent of Russia in Cairo in 1883, tried to attract greater attention on the part of the Foreign Office towards Ethiopia. He thought that ties with Ethiopia in the future might become a counterbalance to the British presence in Egypt and Sudan, especially if Russia, as he proposed, rendered diplomatic assistance to Ethiopia to get her own access to the Red Sea. In his opinion, it might afford excellent opportunities for the further military-strategic strengthening of Russia in the region with a foot-hold in Massawa Bay. He wrote:

Involving Abyssinia in the sphere of our political attention could be of great help to our general policy ... earlier or later Massawa must be a port of Abyssinia, which hasn't had its own ports until now. Thus, a *rapprochement* with Abyssinia could provide us in the future with a reliable coal depot and an excellent harbour for our long-distance military ships in the Red Sea.[3]

Building a Russian naval base on the Red Sea coast of Africa would have weakened British control over the Suez Canal and Aden in the event of a military conflict.

M.A. Khitrovo's suggestion was not appreciated in the Ministry of Foreign Affairs but was welcomed in the Navy Ministry. I.A. Shestakov, the head of the navy, was preoccupied by the idea of establishing reliable sea-lines of communication with the Far East.[4] But lack of finance, internal wars in Ethiopia, the occupation of Massawa Bay and the seacoast of Eritrea by Italy, as well as the death of Admiral Shestakov, prevented the fulfilment of this project. Moreover, this plan was at the time opposed not only by Great Britain and Italy but also by France.

N.I. Ashinov, the Russian adventurer known for his anti-British financial swindles in the Middle East, his close ties with Slavophile circles in Russia and his trip to Ethiopia in 1885-6, attempted in 1889 to establish a springboard for Russia on the Red Sea coast of Africa.[5] But Ashinov's attempt, ill-prepared and without any diplomatic protection, failed. The camp of Russian settlers, pretentiously called 'New Moscow' was fired on by a French squadron. The Russian settlers were interned and after a scandal were transferred to the Russian authorities.

However, reports and messages from Lieutenant Mashkov, who visited Ethiopia twice (in 1889 and 1891-2), testify that interest in this country did not diminish. In a supplement to his report about his second trip to Ethiopia he writes:

Strengthening our positions on the coasts of Aden Bay and the Red Sea has another, not less important, reason. When the Suez Canal was put into operation, the coasts of Aden Bay and the Red Sea acquired special significance because the most important waterway for all the colonial and industrial states of Europe lies here. The ports on this seacoast are, even at the present state of Russian navigation, but mostly in the future, important as coal stations ... but they are more important strategically, especially those which are situated in Aden Bay. That is why we must have a sea port on this coast, which would be convenient in spite of its remoteness, because it would rest in friendly Abyssinia. It would be to our advantage if Abyssinia had a free outlet to the sea. On the other hand we need the same ports. The most convenient way to reconcile these demands would be to lease these ports to Russia giving an opportunity to Abyssinia to use them.[6]

Mashkov would point out that the strengthening of Russia in the Red Sea region could be an important factor in her political rivalry with Great Britain.

After the establishment of diplomatic relations with Ethiopia the Russian government undertook efforts to support the Ethiopian Emperor Menelik II, who was striving for an outlet on the Red Sea coast. But, from the end of the 19th and beginning of the 20th centuries, the Russian stand on this issue began changing. When the Trans-Siberian Railway had been constructed, the problem of having a port on the Red Sea coast lost some of its political and strategic importance for Russia.

When Russian foreign policy toward London changed from confrontation to a military-political alliance after the signing of an accord (*Entente*) with Great Britain in 1907, the importance of the Red Sea in its foreign policy drastically diminished.

The October Revolution in Russia in 1917 suspended for several years all direct contacts between Russia and the states of the Red Sea region.   But in the 1920s trade and diplomatic relations were established with the Hijaz, then with Saudi Arabia and Yemen.   In the mid-1930s the Soviet government raised its voice in defence of Ethiopia, which was attacked by Fascist Italy.   Besides moral and political support in the League of Nations, Russia provided Ethiopia with financial, material and military aid.

During the post-war years the Soviet Union gradually returned to the Red Sea region. It was connected both with the establishment of the USSR as a Superpower having almost global interests and with the collapse of the colonial system. This process could be represented in terms of ideology myths about three streams in the revolutionary movement of the modern world - socialist countries, movements of working people in the West, and national liberation movements.

In 1943 the USSR restored diplomatic relations with Ethiopia and Egypt.   In the 1950s the Soviet Union took an active part in the United Nations Organisation in working out the status of Eritrea and Italian Somalia.   At the end of the 1950s and the beginning of the 1960s, the USSR counted on the leftist, anti-Western (anti-imperialist) forces in the countries situated along the Suez - Red Sea waterway - Nasser in Egypt, leftist and Communist forces in the Sudan, national democratic forces in Somalia, South Yemen and North Yemen.

Ideology and mythology greatly influenced Soviet policy in this region.   In these terms the situation in the PDRY and Ethiopia might be an example.   The leadership of both countries voluntarily chose that model of socio-political system which, 'in the third world' (excluding Vietnam and Cuba), is closest to the Soviet one.   Marxist-Leninism, though with some modifications, became the official ideology of the ruling regimes.   Support of these regimes became a necessary component of Soviet policy in the region, though quite often it ran counter to the state interests of the USSR; as, for instance, the support of the PDRY in its confrontation with the YAR and Saudi Arabia, or support for the government in Addis Ababa in its war with separatists in Eritrea and Tigre. It was a price paid for mythology, for the official slogan, 'Socialism is marching over the planet'. The victory of the 'socialist orientation' in Ethiopia was not outstanding, but it was an important argument in favour of the legitimation of the model of socialism created by Stalin and Brezhnev, which was showing more and more flaws and cracks. The 'progressive' character of these regimes legitimised military-strategic confrontation with the USA in the Indian Ocean region.

In terms of this confrontation 'the enemy of my enemy becomes my friend'. As a rule, in regional conflicts, Moscow and Washington were on the opposite sides of the barricade, which intensified the conflicts, but led to a 'draw' situation. Both sides pursued an irrational race to gain local allies for the future, absurd, suicidal but planned 'hot confrontation' between the USA and the USSR.

The Soviet Union was one of the first countries to recognise the independent state of Somalia. It established political and economic relations on a wide scale and rendered considerable assistance in building its national economy and industry. In the mid-1960s military co-operation between the USSR and Somalia was strengthened and after the leftist-radical *coup* of General Muhammad Siad Barre, it expanded considerably. With the assistance of the USSR, Somalia created military forces and a military infrastructure too big for a small country and which apparently exceeded the defensive needs of the country. For example, the modern seaport of Berbera (put into operation in 1970), which was built with the direct assistance of the USSR, could be used as a supply-base for the Soviet Navy in the Indian Ocean region. In the middle of the 1970s, Soviet specialists built a modern airport in Berbera.

A similar situation could be seen in the PDRY. Powerful military forces there created an unbearable burden for this small country; they pushed the leadership of South Yemen towards a rigid foreign policy and led it to political adventures. The USSR used the air-base and port facilities in pursuit of its own geostrategic aims after having established close military-political co-operation with the leftist forces which came to power in the PDRY in the 1970s. This coincided with the creation of the Ocean Navy in the USSR. In 1968 a Soviet Mediterranean squadron was created and Soviet ships could be seen more often in far-away seas.

It seemed that by these means the military-political interests of the USSR in the eastern Mediterranean, the Red Sea and the Indian Ocean were ensured. But the Suez Canal was idle at that time and, when it was put into operation, Egypt, instead of being a Soviet ally, became an American one.

After the overthrow of the monarchy in Ethiopia a strategic parity in the southern part of the Red Sea and on the Horn of Africa was broken. And in 1977 all American bases were withdrawn from the territory of Ethiopia. But the Soviet leadership was unable to prevent the armed conflict of its two 'political allies', Somalia and Ethiopia, and was forced to sacrifice one of them, the weaker - Somalia. This military-political casting was a result of it. A Soviet military presence in Somalia was substituted by an American one. A leftist radical regime, friendly to the USSR, was established in Ethiopia. The USA took steps to strengthen its influence in the Red Sea region. The loss of Iran forced Washington to take some tough, confrontational measures in the Indian Ocean basin. During the Presidency of James Carter, the USA created the Rapid Deployment Forces and established Central Command (CENTCOM) whose zone of activity extended from Pakistan to Kenya.

Both the Gulf region and the Red Sea basin were turned into a hotbed of international tension, fed by the massive military supplies of the two rival military-political alliances. The arms-race could hardly be stopped and exceeded all reasonable limits. The lack of constructive peace-making ideas and the reliance on military solutions to all local ethno-confessional and border disputes, which could not be solved by military means, contributed, in the atmosphere of Soviet-American competition, to the prolongation of the conflicts of the Horn of Africa and to the militarisation of underdeveloped countries. But this region was not a top priority for either the USSR or the USA. The two Superpowers showed enough restraint not to get involved in the excessive escalation of conflicts. During the past few years they have at least not hindered their settlement.

The economic difficulties of Ethiopia and Somalia (including an aggravated food problem) became disastrous and forced the leaderships of the two countries to seek a mutual understanding. In April 1988, Somalia and Ethiopia signed an agreement on the normalisation of relations, which provided for the mutual withdrawal of troops from the borders, the exchange of prisoners of war, putting an end to hostile propaganda and - as a next step - the re-establishment of normal inter-state relations.   Parallel diplomatic efforts by Washington and Moscow, which clearly conveyed to Mogadishu and Addis Ababa the shared interest of the two Superpowers in a relaxation of tensions, played an important role in reaching this agreement.

Despite the fact that the Somali-Ethiopian border lost its status as a frontline, the situation on the Horn of Africa remains complicated (tribal unrest in Somalia, hostilities in Eritrea, Tigre and southern Sudan). In these conditions both the USSR and the USA, which have turned to co-operation on a global scale, now have to reconsider their political assessments of the situation in the region. A considerable Soviet military presence in Ethiopia, as well as its massive military aid to Addis Ababa, correspond less and less to the state interests of the USSR and the new political course of its foreign policy. The Soviet Union urges its friends in Addis Ababa towards a dialogue with the military opposition, in search of a political compromise. But one recalls that the USSR's military involvement in Ethiopian affairs has already gained a considerable momentum, and this makes it hard to reverse the process immediately. The interference of some conservative Arab countries in internal Ethiopian affairs on the side of the separatists, forced the Soviet Union to render military aid to the regime of Mengistu Haile Mariam, in order to maintain the balance of forces favourable to the beginning of talks.   Nevertheless, since 1987, the tendency towards a reduction in the Soviet military presence in Ethiopia and its military aid to the ruling regime has become stable (but we have not got any data from Soviet sources on this issue). This process, however, has a natural impact on Soviet-Ethiopian relations and causes some friction.

What dynamics will changes in Soviet state interests in this region exhibit in the future?

The military-strategic component in the complex of Soviet interests will apparently diminish.   The new conception of 'defence sufficiency' in Soviet military doctrine implies a reduction of the Soviet military presence abroad.   Some unilateral steps in foreign policy (Afghanistan, Mongolia, East European countries) testify to the readiness of the USSR to work in this direction. Apparently this extends to the Red Sea region, including Ethiopia and Yemen.

But a lot will also depend on the behaviour of the other side. The problem of maintaining an approximate military balance between the USA and the USSR implies a danger of upsetting the balance. The obligations of the USSR, in compliance with treaties concluded with the countries of this region (treaties of friendship with Ethiopia, the PDRY and YAR), make the Soviet Union act gradually and cautiously - this, the more so since there is no doubt that Soviet influence diminishes with the shrinking of the military component in her foreign policy.

But the opposite side does not show its readiness to respond adequately, especially in naval armaments. The US has never included the issue of the Diego Garcia base in the talks. Still, it is necessary to point out that the US has reduced its military assistance to the regime in Mogadishu and the scale of its military presence in Somalia. The prolongation of the term of the treaty concerning the base in Berbera is now under consideration in Washington. The internal situation in Somalia has been aggravated (especially in northern Somalia) and there is a possibility of an anti-Siad *coup*. The treaty will expire next year. But if the US loses Berbera, it will have no impact on the military-strategic position of the Pentagon in this region, because in the 1970s and 1980s it established a chain of military bases from Oman to Kenya centring on the Diego Garcia base, the main military base of the USA in the Indian Ocean.

The interests of the USSR in the Red Sea region are determined by close political (inter-state, party) ties with Ethiopia and Yemen in military, economic, cultural and other fields. An immediate Soviet withdrawal could have a negative effect on these ties.

If we follow the frequency of Ethiopian state visits to the USSR and the general tone of joint declarations and discussions, we can see the trend of development in relations between the two countries. The Soviet leader K.U. Chernenko, even during his short stay in power, received Mengistu Haile Mariam 'in a warm comradely atmosphere, in a spirit of friendship and mutual understanding'.[7] The tone of the official communiqué was euphoric. In November 1985 the first meeting of Mr Gorbachev and Mengistu Haile Mariam took place. The speeches were optimistic and traditional: the two leaders praised each other's achievements and were full of enthusiasm about the future.[8]

The tone started to change gradually. But still in July 1988 Mr Gorbachev restated to the Ethiopian leader the 'firm, principled position of the USSR in supporting the unity and territorial integrity of Ethiopia', but wished all success 'in the search for a just settlement of the Eritrean problem within the framework of a multi-national Ethiopian state'. At the same time he expressed, apparently with relief, his support for the normalisation of relations between Ethiopia and Somalia and stressed the necessity for an Ethiopian-Sudanese dialogue to establish relations of trust and mutual understanding between the two countries.[9]   Soviet leaders have more and more frequently laid stress on dialogue, compromise and a political settlement of internal Ethiopian problems. The number of visits has decreased. Both countries have been plunged into their own internal difficulties and reforms.

But the de-ideologisation of inter-state relations, apart from minuses, could also bring some positive results - increasing the prestige of the USSR and the good feelings of the population towards it.   This may result from the more intensive peace-making efforts of the USSR, aimed at the settlement of the Horn of Africa conflict, an additional contribution to curbing the long-lasting civil war in Ethiopia and assistance in the transportation of foodstuffs to the starving people. Taking into account all the existing realities, there may be a need to get rid of an exclusively negative attitude towards the separatist movements in Ethiopia. The political position of the USSR in Ethiopia would be strengthened if the Soviet Union could offer a more constructive basis for the settlement of the conflict between the opposing sides, which both Jimmy Carter and Julius Nyerere have yet failed to do.

The settlement of all the military conflicts in the region accords with the state and national interests of the USSR. First, because these conflicts aggravate international situations and constitute a threat to international security, though on a limited scale. Second, because to some extent they serve as an obstacle to one of the main purposes of Soviet foreign policy - to stop the arms-race and to begin the process of disarmament. Third, because in conditions of regional conflicts, the Western military presence usually increases and it may destabilise the situation with unpredictable consequences. These factors are less typical of the situation in the Red Sea region, but the settlement of the conflict would remove one more reason for the military presence there of the West. And last, but not least, a settlement of these conflicts, which take people's lives, corresponds with the principle of humanistic priorities in foreign policy put forward by the Soviet leadership. Lowering the level of confrontation in the region would give an opportunity to the states involved to concentrate their efforts on socio-economic progress and the supply of food.

The USSR could play a more active role in relations with the united Yemen. The Yemenis are one and the same people, and the reunification of the two parts might speed up socio-economic progress. A long-standing tradition of co-operation with the Soviet Union could be expanded on a de-ideologised basis. Naturally, the political system which will be chosen by the people of Yemen must be indifferent to the USSR, though transition from mythological to real politics could be difficult.

It seems that more attention in the complex of the USSR's state interests should be given to economics. But it will not happen in the very near future. The Soviet economy is in crisis. Without deep renewal and reforms, including changes in the system of foreign economic activity, we cannot expect a breakthrough. But there is potential for co-operation. A large part of industry in Ethiopia, Yemen and Somalia is based on Soviet equipment, which is still used though in need of renewal. This is why these countries need Soviet technology and 'know-how'. Soviet industrial equipment is cheaper than its Western counterpart. And the modernisation of national enterprises will not require the radical break in the technological process which could happen if they decided to replace outdated Soviet with Western equipment.

While pursuing economic co-operation with the countries of the Red Sea region and the Horn of Africa, the USSR will probably concentrate its efforts on the fields where definite success has been hitherto achieved, where some experience has been gained and where it can get considerable feedback.

We are talking about cotton-supplies, tropical agricultural products, coffee, bananas, animal-breeding products, fish and some consumer goods in exchange for Soviet industrial equipment. So, in circumstances of drastic change in the international situation, and a transition from confrontation to co-operation, the state interests of the USSR will correspond to that state's real national interests. These may be defined as follows:

- the desire to guarantee freedom of navigation in this region through political co-operation (not through a military presence) with its constituent countries as well as with the USA, the countries of the EEC, and Japan and China, under the auspices of the United Nations Organisation;
- a gradual reduction of the Soviet military presence and commitments to arms-supplies to the region, bearing in mind existing state-ties;
- the de-ideologisation of the USSR's relations with the states of this region on the basis of mutually balanced interests;
- the maintenance and later increase of economic co-operation with the states of the region, introducing new forms such as joint ventures, trade companies, etc.;
- the maintenance and development of ties in the fields of education, science, culture, sports and tourism.

It is obvious that ensuring the USSR's state interests in the light of new political thinking will not be an easy task. The state interests of the USSR and Western countries could hardly coincide completely and be mutually complementary. We cannot exclude peaceful competition. But it is difficult to find even one aspect where the state interests of the USSR and of the countries of the region would contradict each other. On the contrary, they are mutually complementary. And, moreover, if we consider the USSR and other countries not belonging to the Red Sea region, in spite of all the differences in their approach to existing problems, we will see that they have no alternative, if they once exclude the use of force, but to find a balance of interests on the way to co-operation .

Notes

1   Naturally enough Iraqi aggression against Kuwait has changed a lot of old perceptions. Advocating a political solution of the crisis, Moscow shows understanding, if not to say approval, of the deployment of the US and other Western military forces in the region.

2   This was found with the help of the Research Fellow from the Institute of African Studies, USSR Academy of Sciences, Andrei Khrenkoff.

3   Archives of the Foreign Policy of Russia (AFPR), F. Politarchives, OP 482, D. 1999, L. 89.

4   Central State Archives of the Navy (CSAN), F. 26 (I.A. Shestakov), OP, L. 81.
5   From a letter from K. Kireev to I Shestakov, AFPR, F. Politarchives, OP 482, EDHR, 20. 30/1, L. 22.
6   AFPR, F. Politarchives, OP 482, D. 2009, L. 62, 63.
7   *Pravda*, 3 April 1984.
8   *Pravda*, 2 Nov. 1985.
9   *Pravda*, 27 July 1988.

11. UNITED STATES POWER-PROJECTION CAPABILITIES IN THE GULF AND SOUTH-WEST ASIA: CHANGING FORCES FOR A CHANGING WORLD

Anthony H. Cordesman

For at least two decades, the United States has been the only Western power that can intervene in a moderate to high level conflict in the Gulf and South-West Asia, the Red Sea, and the Horn of Africa. Other Western states have been able to play an important, and sometimes critical, role in low-intensity conflicts, peace-keeping, advisory missions, and arms supply. Nevertheless, the US has been the only nation capable of projecting true carrier task-forces, sustainable division-sized forces capable of engaging heavy armour, and massive amounts of tactical and strategic air-power.

The term 'Superpower', however, has always been something of a misnomer. US power-projection capabilities have been critically limited by the availability of bases and facilities in the area, and by the difficulties in deploying heavy army units capable of engaging threats with large amounts of armour. The size of the forces the US could commit to the Gulf has also been severely restricted by the limitations on its strategic air and sea lift, and by the risks inherent in redeploying US forces from other regions.

Since the late 1970s, the US has reacted to these challenges by making significant improvements in its power-projection capabilities. It has steadily improved the forces it can commit to the Gulf and South-West Asia, which are tailored to regional needs and contingencies, improved its strategic lift, and improved the anti-armour capability of its lighter forces. At the same time, the US has sought to build up prepositioned equipment and stocks in the Gulf to minimise the strain on its strategic lift, and improve its access to the bases and supply capabilities of friendly southern Gulf states so it can concentrate on building up US combat-forces, rather than creating bases and support facilities.

The US will continue many of these policies in the 1990s, but it already faces a new political and strategic situation in the Gulf and South-West Asia, and fundamentally different challenges in shaping its global force posture. The US no longer faces a major risk of a sudden massive conflict in central Europe, or of a strategic nuclear engagement with the USSR. The Soviet bloc has shifted from the main focus of American military planning to the key arena for arms control and gradual disengagement from the confrontations of the past. While Soviet and Warsaw Pact military capabilities remain strong, they are rapidly diminishing and the chances of any conflict are diminishing even faster.

At the same time, the US faces a new challenge from peaceful global economic competition. There are strong pressures to provide a massive 'peace dividend' by cutting US military expenditure, and providing the resulting benefits to the American taxpayer and to US industry in improving its global competitiveness. These pressures have already reached the point where US defence expenditure has fallen in real terms for the last six years. Even the highest projections of future defence expenditure call for a 2 per cent real annual cut over the next five years, and General Colin Powell, the Chairman of the Joint Chiefs of Staff, has talked of planning for real cuts in defence spending that would reduce the FY1996 spending level to 75 per cent of that of FY1990.[1]

The scale of the resulting cuts may well mean cutting the US Army from 18 active divisions to between ten and twelve; it would mean cutting the combat strength of the Marine Corps by roughly one-third, cutting the Air Force from 36 active tactical wings to 25, and cutting US carrier and battleship battle-groups from 19 to 12. Similar cuts are likely to take place in reserve forces.[2] As a result, the US must simultaneously adapt to a different strategic situation and make major cuts in its military forces. It must make hard choices between contingency capabilities for Europe and North-East Asia, and power projection for the Middle East and other lesser contingency requirements. No one can predict the future, but US military planners have no alternative other than to try.

THE CHANGING STRATEGIC SITUATION AFFECTING US MILITARY CAPABILITIES TO PROJECT POWER IN THE GULF AND SOUTH-WEST ASIA

The pace of strategic change in the Gulf and South-West Asia, the Red Sea, and the Horn of Africa has reached the point where it is difficult to summarise all of the factors the US must consider in reshaping its power-projection capabilities in the region. This is particularly true because trends are not realities: they are reflections of the most probable course of events, and not predictions of what will actually occur. As such, they tend to be written on sand - if not oil. American military planners cannot, however, wait for change to occur. They already must make hard trade-offs between future investments in given types of forces. From an American perspective, this means reacting to the following shifts in the strategic situation:

The Soviet Union is collapsing inward, rather than expanding as a military threat

In a few short years, the USSR has been transformed from a Superpower that has steadily sought to expand its global power to an inward-oriented state whose primary goal is economic reform. While the USSR has not yet cut its naval forces - in fact it set new records for the tonnage of new surface-vessels and submarines it constructed in 1989 - it has begun to cut its naval activity in the Indian Ocean, Gulf, and Red Sea area.

The USSR provides arms and assistance to Algeria and Libya on a cash basis, and has no apparent strategic ambitions in North Africa. It has taken a more viable approach to reaching an Arab-Israeli peace settlement, has encouraged Syria to adopt a defensive military posture, and operates on a cash basis for most arms sales to Syria. It has withdrawn from Afghanistan, largely disengaged from the PDRY, and ended most of its advisory role to Ethiopian combat forces. The forward deployment facilities it developed in Ethiopia and Yemen now exist only at token levels, and it has cut back much of its presence in Cam Rahn Bay - its major staging-base for power projection into the region. It has begun to make significant cuts in the total forces it can deploy against the Gulf and South-West Asia, and faces a significant series of ethnic problems from Islamic and other minorities in the Soviet republics in the relevant border area that may yet take the form of separatism.

The United States no longer needs to size its forces to treat the USSR as its primary contingency threat in the region, and can structure its forces primarily to deal with lesser contingencies involving local threats

US and Soviet relations have not evolved to the point where the US can totally ignore Soviet military capabilities in the Middle East and South-West Asia, but US planners see the primary threats in the region as being a renewal of regional conflicts like the Arab-Israeli conflict and the Iran-Iraq War, a threat by a regional power to a US friend or ally, a crisis or conflict threatening US or Western interests and citizens, or the escalation of local conflicts so as to threaten the flow of oil exports and commerce. Given the growing proliferation of weapons of mass destruction in the region, such threats can require anything from demonstrative uses of force to high intensity regional conflicts. But the risk of nuclear or horizontal escalation that was inevitable in any conflict with the USSR or a Soviet proxy has largely been removed.

The US is now firmly committed to a regional presence based on informal co-operation with friendly states like Morocco, Egypt, Israel, Bahrain, Kuwait, Oman, and Saudi Arabia, backed by over-the-horizon reinforcement

The currently planned cuts in US forces will not materially reduce US power-projection capabilities for most contingencies involving co-operation with friendly states in the region, but will reduce 'forced entry' capability, and make US military action increasingly dependent on some form of partnership with local forces. As a result, US planning increasingly calls for co-operation with local forces in defensive operations in virtually every contingency, except those cases where American citizens are directly threatened. US planning no longer seeks formal bases in the area, and has sharply reduced its past emphasis on forced entry.

The basic political and military structure for such co-operation is already in place. The US does not need facilities in most Maghreb countries for most military contingencies, but has good relations with Morocco and Tunisia. It has conducted numerous joint exercises with Egypt and can co-operate with Egypt in dealing with contingencies ranging from a threat to Tunisia to defence of the Red Sea. The US has long had the ability to reinforce Israel rapidly, as well as a high degree of standardisation with Israeli forces.

The US has ceased to seek a formal headquarters or basing presence in the Gulf as a result of the negotiations it conducted with southern Gulf states during its deployment of naval forces into the region during Operation Ernest Will in 1987. During the course of 1989 and 1990, it has largely abandoned contingency planning for forced intervention in the northern Gulf on the grounds that any kind of Soviet invasion of Iran no longer is credible enough to require such efforts.

The US has, however, developed considerable over-the-horizon capability. It has completed the creation of a major staging-base at Diego Garcia, and has deployed stocks and equipment for army and air units, and prepositioned ships with major combat equipment and stocks for an entire Marine Expeditionary Force (MEF). The US has also completed a smaller prepositioning effort at Masira, off the coast of Oman, and has developed a contingency base on that island. It has developed informal working arrangements with the military forces of Bahrain, Kuwait, Oman, and Saudi Arabia. The coming cuts in US power-projection forces that seem likely as a result of cuts in the US defence budget will not materially reduce US power-projection capabilities for most contingencies in the southern Gulf, but will further reduce any 'forced entry' capability, and make US military action more dependent on some form of informal partnership with local forces.

Changes in military politics and internal security

The character of the rivalries in the Middle East and South-West Asia is changing, and US contingency-planning is changing accordingly. Friendly regional states are less threatened by external political pressures and radical movements. Arab socialism no longer poses a significant threat of subversion or insurgency, and the Islamic revival does not seem likely to create outside military threats to friendly states. Internal rivalries and tensions continue to exist in virtually all states in the region, but domestic political movements tend to demand democratic evolution and/or increased adherence to Islam, rather than revolutionary change. Gulf states face far less of a risk from a 'man on horseback' from within their own military forces, and are willing to put more trust in military professionalism - although there has been little reduction in the surveillance of the military by internal security forces.

The changes in the Arab-Israeli conflict, and in the character of Arab politics, have sharply reduced the possibility that any of the Gulf states will become militarily involved in some future Arab-Israeli conflict, and the political problems each Gulf state faces in dealing with the Palestinian movement

Egypt's commitment to peace, the emergence of a strong Arab liberation movement on the West Bank and Gaza, and Syria's growing problems in financing its military forces make it steadily less likely that a major Arab-Israeli conflict will occur - particularly a conflict that involves states other than Israel and Syria. All of the Gulf states continue to support the PLO and other Palestinian groups, but the prospects of being dragged into some form of direct military action are far smaller than in the past. In spite of Iraq's emergence as a conventional military power that could have a significant impact on the Arab-Israeli balance, it is the proliferation of long-range missiles, strike aircraft, and weapons of mass destruction that seems most likely to engage Gulf states in an Arab-Israeli conflict, and even that possibility seems to have limited probability.

Iraq's emergence as a regional 'Superpower'

Iraq has strikingly reversed the balance of power in the Gulf. During the period between February and August 1988, it conducted a 'battle of the cities' with aircraft and long-range missiles that left Iran virtually unable to defend itself or retaliate, and decisively defeated Iran's ground forces, capturing or destroying at least 40 per cent of their armour and major combat equipment. At the same time, Iraq built up a relatively effective air-force, massive long-range missile capabilities, and an effective chemical-corps. Since the partial cease-fire in August 1988, Iraq has imported nearly three times as many arms as Iran, steadily adding modern weapons and technology to a battle-proved force structure that suffered only minimal losses during the final phase of the Iran-Iraq war. Iraq has also aggressively sought biological, more advanced chemical, and nuclear weapons, and missiles and aircraft capable of delivering weapons of mass destruction anywhere in the region. Iraq's only major remaining limitations in military capability lie in its lack of naval, amphibious, and power-projection forces and ability to sustain large-scale military forces outside its own borders.

Iran's emergence as the 'sick man' of the Gulf

Long before its climactic military defeats in 1988, most of Iran's air force and heavy surface-to-air missile forces had ceased to be operational. It had lost most of the armour and helicopter forces it possessed under the Shah - both because of combat and because of a lack of spare parts. Much of its navy had ceased to be fully operational, and its remaining inventory of Western-supplied missiles had aged beyond its rated shelf-life. During 1987 and 1988, Iran lost most of the new land-force equipment it had been able to obtain from North Korea and the PRC. Its navy suffered severe losses to the US, and its forces became even more divided because of conflicts between and among its revolutionary and regular forces. Iran has been able to do almost nothing to change this situation since the cease-fire. Its economic problems consume most of its resources, it has not been able to fund major arms-imports or find a supplier of advanced modern weapons, its remaining Western inventories average more than fifteen years in age, and require massive rebuilding - not simply spare parts. Its limited chemical warfare and missile capabilities do not approach those of Iraq, and it still lacks an effective military organisation and anything approaching a cohesive concept of force modernisation.

Saudi Arabia has not emerged as a balanced military power, but it has had nearly two decades in which to build up the core of a modern air-force, effective active and passive air-defences, a strong coastal navy, and mechanised land-forces

Saudi forces can scarcely match those of Iraq, but they have significant self-defence capabilities and the ability both to provide significant air-support to its smaller conservative neighbours and to dominate the southern Gulf. Saudi Arabia has become both protector of, and potential threat to, the other southern Gulf states. The tensions been Saudi Arabia and its neighbours have been most serious in terms of Saudi and Omani relations, but even these tensions have not gone beyond low-level political rivalry.

The smaller southern Gulf states remain weak, but have made some efforts at collective security

Bahrain, Kuwait, Oman, Qatar, Saudi Arabia, and the United Arab Emirates (UAE) have increased their strategic and military co-operation, and they banded together to create the Gulf Co-operation Council (GCC) in 1981. Their military co-operation is still far more limited than the rhetoric of the GCC sometimes implies, and many traditional quarrels between ruling families and over border issues still divide them. Nevertheless, the southern Gulf states are gradually developing a potential capability for collective defence. The smaller southern Gulf states do, however, have only limited military capabilities and many of their forces and procurements are poorly organised and lack effectiveness. While their forces are now far better manned and trained than a decade ago, their steady increases in military technology and advanced-weapons strength continue to strain their capabilities seriously, and few Western arms-sales have actually resulted in a high level of military capability or effective technology transfer.

The potential threat from the Yemens and Red Sea states is less significant

Significant border-clashes have taken place between Saudi Arabia and the PDRY in the last year. Nevertheless, the civil war in the PDRY in the late 1980s, and growing Soviet disengagement from the PDRY, left a regime that was forced to abandon Marxism, allow political parties, and largely free its press. This regime reached a unity agreement with the YAR on 22 May 1990.[3] The YAR, in turn, has maintained a surprising degree of political stability, and the military build-up in both states has slackened significantly since the early and mid-1980s. As for the other states in the Horn and Red Sea, Somalia has never been a significant threat and is consumed in a growing tribal civil war. The Sudan is an economic and military basket-case wrapped up in its own civil war and with negligible chances of becoming a regional military power. Ethiopia is equally sick in economic terms, and has lost most of its recent military encounters with the rebel groups in the north. Where Ethiopia threatened to become a major regional military power in the mid-1980s, it is now a decaying military power that has lost most of its Cuban and Soviet support.

Changes in weapons capability and technology

The military forces in the region now include large numbers of first-line weapons that are roughly equivalent to those of most NATO and Warsaw Pact countries. While command, control, communications, and intelligence (C^3I) capabilities do not rival those of NATO and Pact forces, they are steadily improving. Some countries - most notably Iraq - have developed effective logistic and support forces to match their strength in weapons. All of the larger Gulf-states have acquired, or are doing so, significant numbers of modern strike-aircraft capable of long-range missions, and most now have advanced air-ordnance. Most Gulf states have at least a token strength of long-range anti-ship missiles, and some have considerable military capability. Many Gulf states have large armoured forces equipped with modern main-battle-tanks. Naval strength is more erratic. Iran has the ship numbers, but most Iranian ships have limited capability to operate their sensors and missiles. Iraq has never taken delivery of most of the modern combat-ships it ordered from Italy before the Iran-Iraq war and will take years to develop significant naval capability. Saudi Arabia has a significant number of modern combat-ships, but its navy still has only limited effectiveness.

The proliferation of weapons of mass destruction

The Iran-Iraq war triggered an arms race between Iraq and Iran to acquire chemical, biological, and nuclear weapons, and long-range missiles, that led to major Iraqi chemical-warfare attacks on Iranian forces in 1984, and to a missile war in 1987. Saudi Arabia acquired its own long-range missiles in 1988, and Iraq and Iran have since continued actively improving their chemical-warfare capabilities, deploying effective biological-weapons, and developing the ability to produce nuclear weapons. Iraq already has the capability to strike virtually any target in the Gulf with long-range missiles that will soon have chemical and biological warheads, if they do not already possess them. Many peripheral states are actively involved in some form of proliferation: these states include Egypt, India, Israel, Libya, Pakistan, Syria and the Yemens. Many of these efforts are covert or limited, but the efforts of India, Israel, Pakistan and Syria have already resulted in significant military capabilities. As a result, an increasing number of states can reach a wide range of highly vulnerable targets in the Gulf, including oil facilities, water facilities, power-plants, population centres, and military bases.

Oil has growing strategic importance, and the Red Sea is increasing in importance as a trade-route, although oil prices and external dependence on Gulf oil continue to fluctuate

In 1990, the Gulf region had roughly 77 per cent of the Free World's proven oil reserves and over 50 per cent of all the proven oil-reserves in the world. Free World dependence on the region was indicated by the fact the US imported 11 per cent of its oil from the Gulf, Europe imported 27 per cent, and Japan imported 62 per cent. This percentage seems almost certain to increase, since virtually all of the oil-exporters in other areas have, or soon will have, declining reserves. During 1989, US dependence on oil imports increased by 5 per cent. Europe already imports 66 per cent of its oil, and Japan imports 100 per cent.[4]

The overall importance of Gulf oil exports is illustrated by the fact that over 20 per cent of the world's oil consumption passes through the Strait of Hormuz at the mouth of the Gulf, or through pipelines from the Gulf area to the Mediterranean or the Red Sea. Iraq can deliver another 1.7 million b/d of oil to the Mediterranean via pipelines through Turkey. The Saudi Petroline to the Red Sea has a capacity of over 3 million b/d, and Iraq has a parallel pipeline with a capacity of 1.65 million b/d. The Saudi Petroline will be expanded to a nearly 5 million b/d capacity by the late 1990s. Additionally, some 20-30 major ships transit the Strait of Hormuz each day, and 40-55 major ships transit the Red Sea and Suez Canal.[5]

THE DYNAMICS OF THE MILITARY BALANCE IN THE GULF AND SOUTH-WEST ASIA

Many of the strategic trends in the Gulf and South-West Asia are relatively favourable. US planners must, however, be concerned with military capabilities as well as current political intentions. Few of the more than 200 contingencies where the US has deployed military force since World War II could have been predicted in advance, and Iraq's emergence as a Gulf 'Superpower' and the growing proliferation of weapons of mass destruction, at least create the possibility of major military threats to the southern Gulf states, and to the flow of oil. The US cannot dismiss the possibility of some kind of renewal of the Iran-Iraq war, or of a local conflict in the Red Sea leading one of the participants to try to use its ability to strike at shipping as means of influencing the outcome. The US also cannot ignore the military build-up in the region.

The recent trends in the military balance in the Gulf are shown in Table 11.1, and provide a summary picture of the relative military power of each Gulf state, and each Gulf nation's

Table 11.1: The Military Build-Up in the Gulf - Part One

Defence Expenditure in $ Millions

	1978	1979	1980	1981	1982	1983	1984	1985	1986	1987
Iran	23,510	14,700	12,540	13,820	15,570	13,590	18,960	21,120	17,000	17,000
Iraq	8,823	10,000	17,460	21,680	22,090	22,260	22,850	16,710	16,500	16,500
Iran-Iraq Total	32,333	24,700	30,000	35,500	37,660	35,850	41,810	37,830	33,500	23,500
Saudi Arabia	9,629	12,390	14,990	18,410	22,040	24,800	20,400	21,340	17,290	10,490
Kuwait	649	806	939	903	1,179	1,473	1,505	1,606	1,369	1,330
Bahrain	108	143	157	215	281	166	148	151	161	160
Qatar	260	475	604	720	948	1,790	1,213	2,308	1,800	1,800
UAE	822	1,197	1,724	2,090	1,980	1,973	1,932	1,901	1,580	1,700
Oman	687	699	1,057	1,355	1,510	1,742	1,891	1,935	1,728	1,516
GCC Total	12,155	15,710	19,471	23,693	27,938	31,944	27,089	29,241	23,928	16,996
Gulf Total	44,488	40,410	39,471	59,193	66,598	67,794	68,899	67,071	57,428	50,496

Trends in Arms Imports in $Current Millions

	1972	1974	1976	1978	1980	1982	1984	1986	1988	1990	1992	1994
Iran	525	1,000	2,000	2,200	410	1,600	2,400	2,200	1,550	2,100	1,800	2,000
Iraq	140	625	1,000	2,400	2,500	6,500	9,300	3,800	4,800	3,700	4,000	4,100
Iran-Iraq Total	665	1,625	3,000	4,600	2,910	8,100	11,700	6,000	6,250	5,800	5,800	6,100
Saudi Arabia	100	340	440	1,500	1,800	3,100	3,100	3,800	3,300	3,400	3,500	3,500
Kuwait	5	10	80	320	40	110	450	130	550	600	640	690
Bahrain	2	2	4	6	40	5	40	50	80	70	70	75
Qatar	3	2	5	20	90	270	200	80	190	230	240	260
UAE	10	50	100	60	170	50	190	30	190	180	170	170
Oman	5	10	10	270	100	130	310	10	240	230	230	250
GCC Total	125	414	639	2,176	2,240	3,665	4,290	4,100	4,550	4,710	4,850	4,945
Gulf Total	790	2,039	3,639	6,776	5,150	11,665	15,990	10,100	10,800	10,510	10,650	11,045

Source of Arms Imports By Major Supplier during 1983-1987 in $Current Millions

	Total	USSR	US	France	U.K.	F.R.G.	China	Poland	Czech.	Italy	Bulgaria	Other
Iran	8,865	100	10	-	70	-	1,800	20	40	-	650	5,610
Iraq	29,865	13,900	0	4,800	40	700	3,300	460	700	370	625	5,000
Iran-Iraq Total	38,730	14,000	10	4,800	110	700	5,100	480	740	370	1,275	10,610
Saudi Arabia	18,320	0	7,200	6,400	2,400	0	0	0	0	320	0	2,000
Kuwait	1,275	240	220	525	110	170	0	0	0	0	0	10
Bahrain	425	0	230	60	5	120	0	0	0	0	0	10
Qatar	555	0	10	525	20	0	0	0	0	0	0	0
UAE	610	20	320	0	220	0	0	0	0	20	0	30
Oman												
GCC Total	21,185	260	7,980	7,510	2,755	290	0	0	0	340	0	2,050
Gulf Total	59,915	14,260	7,990	12,310	2,865	990	5,100	480	740	710	1,275	12,660

The Military Build-Up in the Gulf - Part Two

Trends in Military Manpower

	1975	1976	1977	1978	1979	1980	1981	1982	1983	1984	1985	1986	1987	1988	1989
Iran	385	420	350	350	415	305	660	640	640	735	745	705	700	654	480
Iraq	155	190	140	362	444	430	392	404	434	788	788	845	1000	1000	750
Iran-Iraq Total	540	610	490	712	859	735	1052	1044	1074	1523	1533	1545	1700	1654	1230
Saudi Arabia	75	75	75	75	79	79	79	80	80	95	96	97	95	95	95
Kuwait	25	25	10	10	11	12	12	13	13	15	16	18	20	21	22
Bahrain	2	2	2	2	2	2	2	2	2	3	3	3	4	4	4
Qatar	5	5	5	5	6	6	6	6	6	6	7	9	11	12	12
UAE	21	27	25	25	25	44	44	44	44	44	44	43	44	44	44
Oman	12	12	12	12	13	15	15	15	20	25	25	26	27	28	28
GCC Total	140	146	129	129	136	158	158	160	165	188	191	186	201	204	205
Gulf Total	680	756	619	841	995	893	1210	1204	1239	1711	1724	1731	1901	1858	1435

Trends in Military Equipment

	Main Battle Tanks						Combat Aircraft					
	1973	1979	1982	1984	1989	1992	1973	1979	1982	1984	1989	1992
Gulf												
Iran	920	1735	1110	1000	900	1250	159	447	90	95	70	110
Iraq	990	1800	2300	4820	5500	5400	224	339	330	580	513	535
Iran & Iraq	1910	3535	3410	5820	6400	6650	383	786	420	675	583	645
Bahrain	0	0	0	0	54	70	0	0	0	0	12	18
Kuwait	100	280	240	240	275	290	34	50	49	49	36	50
Oman	0	0	18	18	39	50	12	35	37	52	63	70
Qatar	0	12	24	24	24	30	4	4	9	11	13	20
Saudi Arabia	85	350	450	450	550	600	70	178	191	203	179	219
UAE	0	0	118	118	136	160	12	52	52	43	65	72
Total GCC	185	642	850	850	1078	1200	132	319	338	358	368	449
Total Gulf	2095	4177	4260	6670	7478	7850	515	1105	758	1033	951	1094

Source: Estimated by the author using various editions of the IISS, *Military Balance*, and ACDA, *World Military Expenditures and Arms Transfers*.

military expenditures, force levels, and arms-imports. Even if one ignores qualitative factors and proliferation, these statistics reflect a continuing arms-race that could make a future conflict far more intense and provide a growing challenge to US power-projection capabilities.[6]

In spite of the changing strategic conditions affecting the Gulf, the patterns reflected in Table 11.1 do not seem likely to undergo radical change in the near future - although they remain highly dependent on oil prices and the flow of revenues from oil imports.[7] If the Iranian threat has decreased, the Iraqi threat has increased, and no smaller state can predict whether Iran will re-emerge as a major threat. If the Soviet threat has decreased, Saudi Arabia continues to need the US as a counterbalance against Iraq and the smaller Gulf states need the US as a counterbalance against both Iraq and Saudi Arabia. The regional arms-race will be driven by the ongoing competition between Iraq and Iran, the dominant role of Saudi Arabia in the southern Gulf, and the need of each smaller southern Gulf state to develop some independent military capability while finding some kind of balance with the need for reinforcement from the US and/or Saudi Arabia.

Qualitative Factors Affecting the Military Balance

The US cannot ignore the fact that the rate of technology-transfer to the Near East and South-West Asia has increased to the point where many states have first-line weapons roughly equivalent to those in US forces. The shifts taking place in the conventional weaponry available to Gulf powers are summarised in Table 11.2, and they include a wide range of systems the US can only deal with by using high-technology counter-measures and/or substantial amounts of force.

A decade ago, there was usually a 5-10 year lag between the initial deployment of major new weapons systems in US, NATO, Soviet, and Warsaw Pact forces, and any large scale sale of such arms to the developing world. That lag is now being eliminated. Western Europe is selling aircraft, armour, and ships to developing nations at the same time that it introduces such systems to its own armed forces. For example, the USSR not only has sold its new MiG-29 fighters to India, Iraq, and Syria, it has sold co-production rights to India. Soviet SS-21 missiles appeared in Syrian forces almost at the same time they became fully operational in Soviet forces in East Germany. The same patterns have emerged in US and European arms transfers.

The current rate of technology transfer is indicated by the fact that the US estimates that 40 countries are now significant arms-producers. In addition to the vast increase in modern jets and armour discussed earlier, 41 countries now have diesel submarines and there are now nearly 250 such submarines deployed in the Third World. Over 40 countries have a naval mining capability, 102 countries now have some form of cruise missile, and US experts estimate that at least 15 countries will be producing their own ballistic missiles by the year 2000.[8]

This pace of qualitative change has also had several important side-effects on the friendly forces with which the US would co-operate in most contingencies. First, it has kept them dependent on outside resupply and technical advice. Second, it has kept their forces in a constant state of military flux, and prevents effective training and organisation. Far too large a percentage of the force structure of the southern Gulf states is receiving new equipment and has to be retrained and reorganised.

Coupled with force expansion, the end result is almost constant turbulence. Officers, NCOs, and technicians are constantly being rotated and retrained. Units are constantly changing in structure. In many cases this turbulence has gone on for over a decade and many units have never enjoyed enough stability to operate as coherent forces. Finally, this pace of change makes effective manpower-management virtually impossible. The impacts on the manpower pool of changes in force structure and equipment are compounded by low administrative standards. Personnel are often trained without adequate language skills or education. Trained personnel are mis-assigned. Insufficient career incentives are provided for trained personnel. Traditional discipline cannot adjust to the creation of highly skilled NCOs and junior officers and the need for highly skilled enlisted men.

Table 11.2: Key Near-Term Trends in the Technology of Arms Sales to the Middle East during 1990-1997

Weapon/Technology	Impact
Challenger, AMX-40, M-1, T-80	Advanced tanks with 3rd and 4th generation fire control systems, spaced and other advanced armour, and advanced 120mm guns. Will be matched by advanced types of other armoured fighting-vehicles.
TOW-2, IHOT, Dragon 2, Hellfire, AT-8, AT-6, AT-7	Advanced anti-tank missiles with full automatic tracking or fire-and-forget capability.
MRLS, BM-24, BM-25, ASTROS	Western and Soviet multiple rocket launchers capable of firing advanced submunitions and 'smart' minelets at ranges beyond 30 km.
Night Vision Devices	Widespread use of night vision devices. '24 hour' infantry, helicopter, and armoured combat.
Secure, Switched, Communications	Conversion to advanced secure communications with automated advanced tactical message traffic and battle-management capabilities.
SA-10, Patriot, Improved Hawk, SA-12	Advanced surface-to-air missiles which cannot easily be suppressed with current weapons and electronic-warfare means. Many will be netted with advanced sensor and battle-management systems and linked to advanced short-range systems.
SHORADS: SA-14, Stinger-POST, etc.	Next generation short-range crew and man-portable surface-to-air missiles and radar-guided AA guns with far better tracking and kill capability and greater ranges. Many will be 'netted' into an integrated battlefield and point defence system.
E-3A (Imp), E-2C (I), IL-76, SUAWACS	Airborne warning and control aircraft capable of managing large-scale air wars using radar and electronic support measures (ESM) equivalent to NATO-level capabilities.

F-15, MiG-29, SU-27, Lavi, F-16C, EFA, Mirage 200, Tornado, MiG-35, A-12, F/A-18	Next-generation air-combat and attack fighters with far more accuracy and up to twice the range payload of existing fighters.
Aim 9L/M, Phoenix, Mica, AA-8, AA-X10, AA-X-P2, Super 530, Python III, AMRAAM	Advanced short and long-range multi-aspect air-to-air missiles which greatly improve the air-to-air combat capability of all modern fighters.
Durandal, Paveway, ERAM, ACM, SUU-65, WASP, J-233	Advanced air-to-surface munitions including runway suppression, anti-armour, anti-hardpoint, anti-personnel, anti-radar, and other special mission point and area weapons with far more lethality than current systems. Many will use stand-off weapons like glide bombs or advanced dispensers for low-altitude single pass penetrations under radar.
RPVs, IMowhawk, MiG-25 (I)	Improved airborne sensor and reconnaissance platforms which can provide advanced targeting, intelligence, and battle-management data.
PAH-2, AH-64, Mi-24	Next-generation attack helicopters with much longer ranges, improved air-to-air missiles, 3rd or 4th generation launch and leave anti-tank guided missiles, and air defence counter-measures. Will be supported by steadily improved troop-lift helicopters with improved protection and fire-power.
Peace Shield, Project Lambda, Lion's Dawn and C^{3}I/BM Systems	Air sensor and battle-management systems equivalent to NATO NADGE-level systems for integrating fighter and SAM defences. Many with advanced attack mission control capabilities.
Maritime Patrol Aircraft	More advanced versions of E-2C-type aircraft armed with ASW weapons and air-to-surface missiles.
Silkworm, and other land-based anti-ship missiles	New longer range and more accurate land-based anti-ship missiles with improved sensors and target finding capability and ranges capable of covering the entire Gulf.

FAC(M), Missile Frigates: Saar 5, Lupo, F-2000, etc.	Next-generation missile patrol-boats and corvettes with Improved Harpoon and other moderate-range advanced ship-to-ship missiles.
Sea Skua, Harpoon II, Exocet II, Gabriel III/IV, AS-4, AS-6, AS-7	Advanced ship, shore, and air launched anti-ship missiles with advanced sensors and electronics, and far more lethal payloads. Can kill war ships and tankers far more effectively than today.
Coastal Submarines	Advanced diesel submarines with excellent silencing, moderate cruise ranges, and smart torpedoes.
SS-22, SS-23, CSS-2, Jericho 2	Advanced surface-to-surface missiles with ranges of up to 1,500 miles.
Nerve Gas	Widespread stocking of single or binary nerve-gas agents and limited CBW defence-capabilities.
Nuclear Weapons	Wider proliferation adding nuclear weapons capability to Iraq, Iran, and possibly other regional states.

The Proliferation of Weapons of Mass Destruction

The US also must consider the impact of proliferation. According to recent US estimates, 14 countries in the world now have chemical weapons and 11 countries are suspected of delivering them.[9] Three countries now have biological weapons, and 15 countries are suspected of delivering them. Other sources indicate that at least 10-12 developing countries are actively developing nuclear weapons or have shown a significant interest in such development.[10]

The search for weapons of mass destruction is scarcely new to the region. Israel first began examining nuclear options in the 1950s, and Egypt used poison gas against the royalists during the Yemeni civil war in the 1960s. Israel had acquired a significant stockpile of nuclear weapons by 1967. Egypt and Libya sought both nuclear weapons and long-range delivery systems, and Egypt and Syria were heavily equipped with chemical defence gear when they attacked in 1973.

Nevertheless, six recent politico-military developments have interacted with the patterns shaping the conventional arms race to accelerate the regional search for weapons of mass destruction. The first such development is Iraq and Iran's use of poison gas in their war and Iraq's use of poison gas against its rebellious Kurds. The second development has been a series of revelations about the size of the Israeli nuclear effort, and the fact that Israel may be developing missiles with IRBM ranges. The third development has been Syria's response to Israel in the form of the development of a capability to produce and deliver nerve gas and other chemical weapons. The fourth development is the possible Soviet use of chemical weapons in Afghanistan. The fifth is India and Pakistan's development of nuclear weapons, and the sixth is Libya's possible use of poison gas during the final phases of its war in Chad and its creation of a massive facility for the production of weapons of mass destruction.

This race to proliferate has interacted with similar arms-races in other regions: for example, with efforts like those of Argentina and Brazil to develop long-range missiles and the capability to make nuclear weapons, with similar efforts at proliferation in Asia, with South Africa's nuclear weapons and long-range missile effort, and with the search of various Western European firms and the PRC to enter the market for missiles, nuclear components, and the equipment needed for chemical and biological weapons.

The end result is that Iran and Iraq are locked into a major arms-race to acquire biological and chemical weapons, and that Iraq, Iran and Saudi Arabia have already acquired long-range missiles. A wide range of states on the periphery of the Gulf have, or are seeking to acquire such weapons, and no one can guarantee that a future conflict will remain conventional. It is true that past estimates of the probable rate and consequences of the proliferation of weapons of mass destruction have often been over-pessimistic. However, Table 11.3 shows that this new aspect of the regional arms-race is all too real.

Table 11.3: The Race for Weapons of Mass Destruction

NORTH AFRICA

Mauritania

- No resources of its own and no signs of any development activity.

Morocco

- No indications of any organised activity.
- No advanced long-range delivery systems
- Holdings of CS gas.

Algeria

Delivery Systems

- 18 Su-20 Fitter C fighter ground attack.
- 60 MiG-23BM fighter ground attack.
- Multiple rocket launchers and artillery.

Chemical Weapons

- Basic technology and industrial infrastructure for production of nerve, mustard, and cyanide gas present in country.
- No indications of any organised activity.

Biological Weapons

- Moderate research capability.
- No indications of any organised activity.

Nuclear Weapons

- Limited research capability.
- No indications of any organised activity.

Libya

Delivery Systems

- Possible purchase of PRC-made M-9 missile with 200-600 kilometre range, or alternative system with MRBM/IRBM range.
- Al-Fatih missile with 300-450 mile range reported to be under development with aid of FRG technical experts.
- 48 FROG-7 rockets with 40-kilometre range.
- 80 Scud Bs with 190-mile range. In service since 1976.
- Several active missile-development programmes. One is a West German design with a 500-kilometre range.

- Considering Brazilian Orbita MB/EE missile with 600-kilometre range?
- Considering OTRAG missile?
- 6 Tu-22 bombers
- Su-24 long-range strike fighters with limited refuelling capability using C-130s. Seeking higher capability jet tanker.
- 58 Mirage 5 fighter ground attack.
- 14 Mirage F-1D fighter ground attack.
- 44 MiG-23BM Flogger F and 14 MiG-23U fighter ground attack.
- 90 Su-20 and Su-22 Fitter E, J. F fighter ground attack.
- Tube artillery and multiple rocket launchers.

Chemical Weapons

- May have used mustard gas delivered in bombs by AN-26 aircraft in final phases of war against Chad in September 1987.
- Nerve and mustard gas production in industrial park at world's biggest chemical weapons plant at Rabta - with capacity in excess of 1.2 tons per day. Plant built beginning in January 1985, with some Japanese corporate assistance. There are probably two other research/batch production facilities. Plant seems to have started test runs in mid-1988. Rabta plant may have suffered a massive fire in March 1990, but damage is not confirmed.
- Stocks of chemical bombs and rockets with mustard and perhaps non-persistent nerve gas.
- Unconfirmed reports of shipments of chemical weapons to Syria and Iran do not seem valid.

Biological Weapons

- Some research activity.
- No evidence of production capability.

Nuclear Weapons

- Has actively sought to create a development and production capability, but no evidence of any real progress or success.

Chad

- No resources of its own. Libya may have used poison gas in Chad during final phases of fighting in 1987.

Tunisia

- No indications of any activity.

Egypt

Delivery Systems

- Possible co-operation with Iraq in paying for development and production of 'Badar 2000' long-range missile. This is also reported to be a version of the Argentine Condor II or Vector missile. Ranges have been reported from 820-980 kilometres, with the possible use of an FAE warhead. Egyptian officers were arrested for trying to smuggle carbon materials for a missile out of the US in June 1988.
- Possible co-operation with Iraq and North Korea in developing the Sakr 80 missile, with ranges of 80 kilometres.
- Reports of development of a capability to produce an improved version of the Scud B, possibly with North Korean co-operation.
- 9 Scud B launch units with 300-kilometres range.
- 12 FROG 7 rocket launch units with 40-kilometres range.
- 9 Tu-16 bombers.
- 32 F-4E fighter ground attack.
- 54 Mirage 5 fighter ground attack.
- 14 Mirage 2000EM fighter ground attack.
- SAKR-80 rocket with 50-kilometres range, and other multiple rocket launcher weapons.
- Tube artillery

Chemical Weapons

- Produced and used extensive amounts of mustard gas in Yemeni civil war in 1960s, but agents may have been stocks British abandoned in Egypt after World War II. Effort was tightly controlled by Nasser and was unknown to many Egyptian military serving in Yemen.
- Completed research and designs for production of nerve and cyanide gas before 1973.
- Seems to have several production facilities for mustard and nerve gas. May have limited stocks of bombs, rockets and shells.
- Unconfirmed reports of recent efforts to acquire feedstocks for nerve gas. Some efforts to obtain feedstocks from Canada.
- Industrial infrastructure present for rapid production of cyanide gas.

Biological Weapons

- Major laboratory and technical base.
- No evidence of major organised research activity.

Nuclear Weapons

- Low-level research effort. No evidence of more than basic research since the 1960s.

LEVANT

Israel

Delivery Systems

- Up to 50 'Jericho I' missiles deployed in shelters on mobile launchers with up to 400-miles range with a 2,200 lb. payload, and with possible nuclear warhead storage nearby. Unverified claims that up to 100 missiles are deployed west of Jerusalem (claims seem too high).
- 'Jericho II' follow-on missiles are under development. These seem to include a single stage follow-on to the Jericho I and a multistage longer-range missile. The latter missile seems to have a range of up to 900 miles with a 2,200 lb. payload, and may be a co-operative development with South Africa. (Extensive reporting of such co-operation in press during 25 and 26 October 1989)
- A major test took place on 14 September 1989. It was either a missile test or failure of Ofeq-2 satellite.
- The Shavit I launched Israel's first satellite on 19 September 1989. It used a three-stage booster system capable of launching a 4,000 lb. payload over 1,200 miles or a 2,000 lb. payload over 1,800 miles.
- Work on development of TERCOM-type smart warheads. Possible cruise-missile guidance developments using GPS navigation systems.
- F-15, F-16 and F-4E fighter-bombers capable of long-range refuelling and of carrying nuclear and chemical bombs.
- 160 Lance missiles with 130-kilometres range.
- MAR-290 rocket with 30-kilometres range believed to be deployed
- MAR-350 surface-to-surface missile with range of 56 miles and 735 lb. payload believed to have completed development or to be in early deployment.
- Arrow ATBM with slant ranges of up to 40 kilometres, speeds of up to Mach 9, plus Rafale AB-10 close-in defence missile with ranges of 10-20 kilometres and speeds of up to Mach 4.5. Tadiran BM/C^{3}I system.
- Israel seeking supercomputers for Technion Institute (designing ballistic missile RVs), Hebrew University (may be engaged in hydrogen bomb research), and Israeli Military Industries (maker of 'Jericho II' and Shavit booster).

Chemical Weapons

- Mustard and nerve gas production facility in the restricted area in the Sinai near Dimona established in 1982. May have additional facilities. May have capacity to produce other gases. Probable stocks of bombs, rockets and artillery.
- Extensive laboratory research into gas warfare and defence.
- Development of defensive systems includes Shalon Chemical Industries protection gear, Elbit Computer gas detectors, and Bezal R&D aircrew protection system.
- Extensive field exercises in chemical defence.

- Gas masks stockpiled, some distributed to population on test basis.

Biological Weapons

- Extensive research into weapons and defence.
- No evidence of active production effort.
- Warhead delivery capability for bombs, rockets, and missiles, but none believed to have been equipped with chemical gas.

Nuclear Weapons

- Estimates differ sharply.
- At least a small stockpile of plutonium weapons. May have well over 100 nuclear weapons assemblies, with some weapons with yields over 100 kt, and some with possible ER variants or variable yields. Stockpile of up to 200 weapons is possible.
- Director of CIA indicated in May 1989 that Israel may be seeking to construct a thermonuclear weapon.

Syria

Delivery Systems

- 36 SS-21s with 100-120 kilometres range. May be developing chemical warheads.
- 18 Scud Bs with 310-kilometres range. Believed to have chemical warheads.
- Short range M-1B-missiles (up to 60-miles range) seem to be in delivery from PRC.
- 18-28 Su-24 long-range strike fighters.
- 50 MiG-23BM Flogger F fighter ground attack.
- 19 Su-20 fighter ground attack.
- 28 Su-17 fighter ground attack.
- 24 FROG-7 rockets.
- Possible order for PRC-made M-9 missile (185-375 miles range) in August 1989.
- Multiple rocket launchers and tube artillery.

Chemical Weapons

- Major nerve-gas, and possible other chemical-agent production facilities north of Damascus. Two to three plants.
- Unconfirmed reports of sheltered Scud missiles with Sarin or Tabun nerve gas warheads.
- Shells, bombs, and nerve gas warheads for multiple rocket launchers.
- FROG warheads under development. Reports of SS-21 capability to deliver chemical weapons are not believed by US or Israeli experts.

Biological Weapons

- Extensive research effort.
- Probable production of botulism and other agents.

Nuclear Weapons

- Ongoing research effort.
- No evidence of major progress in development effort.

Jordan

Delivery Systems

- 32 Mirage F-1D fighter ground attack.
- May be buying Tornado or Mirage 2000 fighters with long-range strike capability.

Chemical Weapons

- Technology base is present, but no signs of development activity.

Biological Weapons

- Technology base is present, but no signs of development activity.

Nuclear Weapons

- No indications of any effort.

Lebanon

- No confirmed indications of proliferation.
- No advanced air-strike systems. Iraq seems to have sent FROG-7 missiles to Maronite forces.
- Maronite Christians began exploring possible purchase of poison gas in 1984.
- Hizbullah may have tried to produce an agent called 'metallic nitrogen' (probably nitrogen mustard gas) at a laboratory in West Beirut.

GULF

Iran

Delivery Systems

- Scud B (R-17E) missiles with 230-310 kilometre range. Missiles provided by Libya and North Korea.

- Possible order for PRC-made M-9 missile (280-620 kilometres range).
- Iranian-made IRAN 130 missile with 150+ kilometres range.
- Iranian Oghab (Eagle) rocket with 40+ kilometres range.
- New SSM with 125-mile range may be in production, but could be modified FROG.
- F-4D/E fighter bombers.
- HY-2 Silkworm missiles.
- Multiple rocket launchers and tube artillery.

Chemical Weapons

- At least two research and production facilities.
- Stockpiles of cyanide (cyanogen chloride), phosgene and mustard gas weapons. Include bombs and artillery.
- Production of nerve gas seems to have started.

Biological Weapons

- Extensive laboratory and research capability.
- May be involved in active production.

Nuclear Weapons

- Has revived nuclear-weapons production plant begun under Shah.
- Significant West German and Argentine corporate support in some aspects of nuclear weapons effort.
- Stockpiles of uranium.
- Facilities heavily damaged by Iraq in final months before cease-fire.

Iraq

Delivery Systems

- Tu-16 and Tu-22 bombers.
- Acquiring MiG-29 fighters.
- Mirage F-1, MiG-23BM, and Su-22 fighter attack aircraft.
- Su-24 long-range attack aircraft.
- Probable orders of Mirage 2000.
- Extensive deployment of extended-range Scuds called al-Husain (600-kilometres range)
- Have deployed al-Abbas missile (900-kilometres range) at three fixed sites in northern, western, and southern Iraq. At least 12 missiles deployed. Can hit targets in Iran, Gulf, Israel, Turkey, and Cyprus.
- Development of the Tamuz liquid-fuelled missile with a range of over 2,000 kilometres, and a solid-fuelled missile with similar range.
- FROG 7 rockets with 40-kilometres range.
- Multiple rocket launchers and tube artillery.
- Iraq may be seeking a long-range missile test site in Mauritania.

Chemical Weapons

- Massive production facilities and stockpiles of mustard and Tabun and Sarin nerve gas.
- Now seems to have persistent nerve-gas agents.
- Warheads for missiles, rockets, bombs, and shells. Have spray dispersal systems.
- At least three major research and production facilities at Salman Pak, Samarra, and Habbaniya.
- Extensive stocks of defence equipment.

Biological Weapons

- Major research effort.
- Production has probably begun of at least one highly lethal agent. Degree of weaponisation unknown.
- Laboratory capability to make anthrax, botulism, tularemia, and other biological agents.
- Possible bombs and missile warheads.

Nuclear Weapons

- Osiraq reactor was probably designed for weapons production. No major production capability since Israel destroyed most of Osiraq, but considerable research. Has major stockpiles of uranium and possibly some illegal enriched material. Interested in centrifuge and laser isotope separation.
- US blocked some shipments of centrifuge technology in 1989, but Iraq may have obtained magnets from PRC and some additional technology from Netherlands.
- Massive purchasing effort in Europe. Up to $1 billion in unauthorised loans arranged through Georgia branch of Banca Nazionale del Lavoro (BNL).
- US and UK intercept shipment of high-voltage military-specification capacitors designed solely for use in triggering nuclear weapons in March 1990.

Saudi Arabia

Delivery Systems

- PRC-made CSS-2 (DF-3A modified) surface-to-surface missiles with IRBM ranges (2,620-3,050 kilometres).
- 34 Tornado strike fighters.

Chemical Weapons

- Low-level research effort began in 1984. No evidence of efforts to acquire actual agents.

- Plastics plants and oil facilities provide much of the equipment needed for production of chemical weapons.

Biological Weapons

- No indications of organised effort.
- Laboratory capability to make simple biological agents.

Nuclear Weapons

- Slight indications of financial ties to the Pakistani nuclear-weapons effort, but no serious evidence of such ties.

Kuwait

- Acquiring A/F-18 with medium-range strike capability.
- No indications of any interest in weapons of mass destruction.

Bahrain

- No indications of any interest in weapons of mass destruction.

Qatar

- No indications of any interest in weapons of mass destruction.

UAE

- No indications of any interest in weapons of mass destruction.
- Has recently acquired Scud missiles.

Oman

- No indications of any interest in weapons of mass destruction.

RED SEA

North Yemen

Delivery Systems

- 15 Su-22 fighter ground attack.
- SS-21 missiles.
- 65 BM-21 multiple rocket launchers.
- Tube artillery

Chemical Weapons

- May have limited stockpiles of mustard gas captured from Egypt in the 1960s.

Biological Weapons

- No indications of organised effort.

Nuclear Weapons

- No indications of organised effort.

South Yemen

Delivery Systems

- FROG-7
- Scud B
- 15 Su-20/Su-22 fighter ground attack.

Chemical Weapons

- No indications of organised effort.

Biological Weapons

- No indications of organised effort.

Nuclear Weapons

- No indications of organised effort.

Sudan

- No indications of organised effort.

Ethiopia

Delivery Systems

- 40 MiG-23 fighter ground attack.
- 78 MiG-21 fighter ground attack.
- BM-21 122mm multiple rocket launchers, and tube artillery.

Chemical Weapons

- Possible limited use of chemical weapons supplied by Soviets or Cuba against EPLF in Eritrea in early 1980s.

Biological Weapons

- Reports of use of mycotoxins or other toxins supplied by Soviets or Cuba seem to be untrue.

Nuclear Weapons

-   No indications of organised effort.

Djibouti

-   Nature of French stockpiles, if any, are unknown.
-   No local effort or capability.

Somalia

-   No local effort or capability.

OTHER RELATED

Turkey

Delivery Systems

-   95 F-4E fighter ground attack.
-   100+ F-104 fighter ground attack.
-   Tube Artillery.

Chemical Weapons

-   Fully capable in terms of technology and industrial infrastructure.
-   No indications of organised effort.

Biological Weapons

-   Fully capable in terms of technology and industrial infrastructure.
-   No indications of organised effort.

Nuclear Weapons

-   No indications of organised effort.

India

Delivery Systems

-   40 Mirage 2000H fighter ground attack.
-   44 MiG-29 fighter ground attack.
-   95 MiG-23BN Flogger H fighter ground attack.
-   24 MiG-27 Flogger D/J fighter ground attack.
-   120 BM-21 122mm multiple rocket launchers.
-   Tube artillery.
-   Prithvi and longer-range missiles under development. The Prithvi is a 150-kilometres range missile with a 500+ kilogramme warhead and

inertial navigation. It is scheduled to be ready by 1993, and orders for production were placed in September 1989. A successor system is now in early development.

- SLV-3 space vehicle could be adapted into long-range surface-to-surface missile with 1,640-2,540 kilometres range. Longer range ASLV and PSLV boost vehicles are in development. Four-stage Polar Satellite Launch Vehicle was successfully tested in October 1989. Can lift 420-600 lb. satellites into polar orbit.

- Agni system is under development with ranges up to 2,500 kilometres. Can lift 500+ kilogramme warhead. Tested successfully at 625-miles range with one-ton payload on 22 May 1989. Was tested again on 27 September 1989.

Chemical Weapons

- No evidence of production or stockpiling. Research complete on production of nerve, mustard and cyanide gas. Rapid deployment and stockpiling capability for cyanide gas. Status of nerve and mustard gas production capability unknown, but all basic industrial infrastructure is present.

Biological Weapons

- Research effort. Laboratories actively involved in development of biological agents. No evidence of production.

Nuclear Weapons

- Tested nuclear device in 1974.
- Active nuclear-weapons development and production effort in spite of denials. Research into fusion weapons, but initial production is likely to be fission weapons in the 100-kt range and possibly enhanced radiation weapons.
- Known stockpiles capable of rapidly producing at least 20-35 weapons. Some experts believe has produced enough plutonium to build up to 100 bombs. Seems to have greatly accelerated production of fissile material in late 1980s.
- In May 1989, Director of CIA reports indications that India is working on a hydrogen bomb.
- Currently arguing with US that two reactors India imported from US and constructed at Tarapur do not involve restrictions on their plutonium production.
- Seeking supercomputers from US for use at Indian Institute of Science and Indian Institute of Technology. Both deeply involved in missile efforts. Inspection and use restrictions seem likely to be ineffective.

Pakistan

Delivery Systems

- 39 F-16 fighter ground attack.
- 16 Mirage IIIEP fighter ground attack.
- 50 Mirage 5PA3 fighter ground attack.
- BM-21 122mm multiple rocket launchers.
- HATF 1 (King Hawk) missile with ranges up to 70 kilometres in development. Tested on 11 February 1989.
- HATF 2 (King Hawk) missile with ranges up to 350 kilometres in development. Tested on 11 February 1989.
- New missile programme with ranges in excess of 500 kilometres announced on 14 October 1989.
- Tube artillery.

Chemical Weapons

- No evidence of stockpiling. Research complete on production of nerve, mustard and cyanide gas. Rapid deployment and stockpiling capability for cyanide gas. Status of nerve and mustard gas production capability unknown, but all basic industrial infrastructure is present.

Biological Weapons

- Research effort. Laboratories actively involved in development of biological agents. No evidence of production.

Nuclear Weapons

- Seems to have acquired enough fissile material for one device in 1985. Centrifuge production of highly enriched uranium seems to have started in this year.
- Active nuclear-weapons development and production effort nearing completion in spite of denials.
- Research into enhanced radiation and fusion weapons, but initial production is likely to be fission weapons in the 100kt range.
- Can probably rapidly assemble 2-11 uranium-fuelled weapons.

Afghanistan

- No local effort or capability.

- USSR may have used lethal chemical weapons, and there are highly uncertain reports of the use of biological agents. Long-range delivery systems are reported to have included artillery, helicopters, fighter-bombers and bombers.

NOTE: The above data are estimates based on press reports and other unclassified sources, and do not represent official positions of the US government. See John S. McCain, 'Proliferation in the 1990s', *Strategic Review*, summer 1989, pp. 9-20; *New York Times*, 3 July 1988, p. 3; *Christian Science Monitor*, 15 July 1988, p. 1; 'A Deadly New Missile Game,' *Time*, 4 July 1988, p. 38; *Washington Post*, 27 March 1988, p. C-1 and 5 April 1988, p. A-1; 'Ballistic Missile Proliferation in the Developing World' in *World Military Expenditures and Arms Transfers, 1988* (ACDA, Washington, 1989), pp. 17-20; and 'Ballistic Missile Proliferation Potential of Non-Military Powers', CRS-87-654 SPR, 6 August 1987, and working updates by the CRS.

MEETING THE CHALLENGE OF CHANGING FORCE REQUIREMENTS

The US will not find it easy to deal with this changing strategic situation. It faces the prospect of major force-cuts as it reacts to the reduction in the Soviet and Warsaw Pact threat, and the risks of large-scale or 'close in' conflicts in the Middle East and South-West Asia are all too real. Nevertheless, the US will retain a wide range of tools it can use, and each of its four military services provides unique capabilities that are not matched by any regional state or potential aggressor from outside the region. While any given military capability is limited, and will almost certainly be cut during the next five years, the US can draw on the following pool of resources:

Naval power-projection forces

These forces consist of carrier battle-groups, which can project both air attack and air defence capabilities, long-range conventional cruise-missiles, and amphibious lift assets. They also include mine warfare, escort and convoy, anti-ship missile protection, and sealift forces.

Marine Corps expeditionary forces, of which the largest unit is a Marine Expeditionary Force (MEF) to the Gulf

An MEF is equivalent to a self-sustainable light mechanised division plus an integral air wing. Marine Corps forces are organised primarily to conduct amphibious operations or to rely on naval support, but can operate independently in any mission calling for infantry or light mechanised forces. They are capable of 'forced entry' operations using helicopters and landing craft. They have attack helicopters, AV-8 VSTOL attack fighters, and F/A-18 fighters. The amphibious ships they deploy on are operated by the US Navy. Major amphibious ships include a naval crew and complement of Marines, plus whatever Marine combat units are embarked.

Rapidly deployable US Army units

Typical US Army rapid deployment forces include airborne and air assault forces, a mechanised division, and armoured or air cavalry regiments. Airborne units are paratroop forces capable of rapid deployment by air, mid-intensity combat, and surgical attack operations with little or no warning. Air assault units are heavier, but must stage from some nearby forward area. Both types of forces require resupply. The mechanised forces are lighter variants of the mechanised divisions the US deploys in NATO.

Substantial additional land-forces if more than 30-60 days is available in which to deploy

The US currently has a total of 18 active divisions, and the total US Army and Marine Corps forces now in service include 19 active and 9 reserve divisions. Given sufficient time, the US can deploy and sustain armoured and heavy mechanised divisions to the Gulf in formations similar to the Corps-sized forces deployed in NATO. What is more practical in many contingencies, is selectively deploying key force elements such as attack helicopters, armoured battalions, etc.

Special forces

Special forces or special operations units are capable of elite infantry operations, but their main purpose is intelligence-gathering, 'commando'-type operations, deep strikes, operations in hostile territory, sabotage, mine-clearing and assault-zone preparation, demolition, and the other highly specialised missions assigned to such forces by most countries. Special operations aviation units exist that can conduct long-range, clandestine operations in support of SOF.

As many tactical air wings from the US Air Force as friendly nations in the region can base and support

In virtually all currently foreseeable contingencies in the Gulf region, the USAF can rapidly fly in more fighters than local facilities can shelter, arm, maintain, and support with effective command, control, communications, and intelligence (C^3I).

Long-range strike aircraft and bombers

The US can use any part of its long-range bomber force, including the B-52, B-1B and eventually the B-2, with a high probability of penetration and sufficient effectiveness to destroy most area targets. The B-52 and B-2 can use the HAVE NAP system to provide precise strikes against land targets, and the B-52s can use Harpoon air-to-surface missiles for long-range strikes against enemy ships. All US bombers are capable of dropping large numbers of mines, and can quickly interdict hostile waters, ports or offshore facilities.

Strategic lift

US strategic air and sealift are essential to deploying and supporting US forces, to most arms-transfer efforts, and often to providing allied or friendly third nations with the mobility they need to support friendly states.

Global command, control, communications, and intelligence assets

The US has a steadily improving ability to provide electronic and imagery intelligence on the region, and can provide such support to its friendly as well as its own forces. With some exceptions, such US capabilities are far superior to those of most states in the region.

Arms transfer and military assistance efforts

The US can rapidly deploy large amounts of weaponry, military technology of all kinds, and technical and other advisory teams. In many cases, the assistance of friendly forces allows the US to project power before a crisis or conflict, and to minimise the need for the actual commitment of US forces. In other cases, the ability to project power by proving equipment and advisory support is critical to allowing an effective partnership with local forces, and to correcting the main defects in their training and equipment.

The threat or reality of retaliation using chemical and nuclear weapons

The threat of US retaliation may increasingly be the only means some friendly states - or even US forces - have of deterring or countering the use of weapons of mass destruction. The US does, however, have the additional option of highly precise long-range missile attacks on high-value targets using conventional warheads. Given the potential impact of such conventional attacks on key oil, power, industrial, or leadership targets, there is nothing axiomatic about a US need to escalate to weapons of mass destruction in response to the use of such weapons by a Third World state.

Many of the elements of this pool of forces, including virtually all maritime, strategic air and strategic lift forces, are general purpose forces that can be used in a wide range of missions. Each element has its own strengths and weaknesses, and each can be used with the others in a wide range of combinations - often in ways that are synergistic. In fact, it is US ability to draw on a very wide range of different force elements and military capabilities from each of its four military services, rather than sheer numbers, which is the greatest strength of US power-projection capabilities.

The US has limited capability to operate without support from friendly states in the region, but it can deploy and sustain major amounts of force if it has such support. Similarly, US forces have a potential 'force multiplier' effect: the US can rapidly provide over-the-horizon reinforcements of most of the capabilities that friendly states lack and are likely to need most in a given contingency.

US Military Capabilities to Deploy Forces For Contingencies in the Gulf and South-West Asia

An estimate of the pool of forces the US is most likely to draw upon in deploying forces for a contingency in the Gulf, South-West Asia, the Red Sea or the Horn is shown in Table 11.4. The US Navy forces in the pool are largely forces now in the Atlantic and Pacific fleets. US naval forces deployed in the Indian Ocean have not previously been assigned to USCENTCOM, although they may be so assigned in specific contingencies.

Most of the land and sea forces in Table 11.4 are earmarked to the US Central Command (USCENTCOM) for contingency planning purposes, and organise and train to operate in the Gulf and South-West Asia, as well as in other missions.[11] No combat units are assigned to USCENTCOM in peacetime. Forces are allocated to its command for specific contingencies in a crisis or conflict. USCENTCOM was originally formed in March 1980, in response to the fall of the Shah of Iran, the fear of a Soviet invasion of Iran, the Soviet invasion of Afghanistan, the Iranian hostage-crisis, and the fear of the economic consequences of a major interruption of US oil-supplies. USCENTCOM has its headquarters at Macdill Air Force Base in Florida. It is the only major US regional command that is not headquartered in its primary area of operation.

The pool of forces available to the US Navy and USCENTCOM could provide massive naval and air power by regional standards. All of the US forces shown in Table 11.4 are far better tailored to such missions than in the late 1970s and mid-1980s, and are now specially trained and equipped to operate in the region - something that no longer is true of most other Western and Soviet power-projection forces. The scale of the training involved is illustrated by the annual Bright Star exercise in 1987, which involved 12,700 men ashore and 15,000 afloat, together with four sealift ships and 205 airlift missions. The US also conducts major special operations, field training, mobility, and command post exercises.

This does not mean, however, that the US Navy or USCENTCOM would find it easy to operate in the Gulf or Red Sea region in medium to high intensity combat or that their forces are without many limitations and flaws. Effective US operations would be highly dependent on long-range bombers, or on access to friendly bases and the support of friendly states. US forces have deficiencies in support, readiness, supply, and C³I, and the total pool of land forces available to the US lacks anything approaching the strength of the Soviet land forces still deployed to the north of the region, and would have serious problems in defending a southern Gulf state against an all-out attack by the land forces of Iraq or Iran unless it had strategic warning.

This situation would be different, however, under conditions where the US could react to warning over a period of several months. The forces shown in Table 11.4 are only part of the story. The US can deploy up to two more heavy army-divisions, and a total of three carrier battle-groups and two surface-action groups, three Marine Corps Expeditionary Forces, 25 tactical air squadrons, seven strategic bomber squadrons, and 20 airlift squadrons. Any US operations in the Gulf would still, however, be limited by the actual or potential need for US forces in other regions - and by the availability of factors like strategic lift, bases and support facilities, munitions and stocks, and the quality of allied support.

Table 11.4:   US Forces Available for Power Projection to the Gulf and South-West Asia in Mid-1990

Force and Element	Manpower
US Central Command Headquarters (MacDill Air Force Base, Florida)	1,100
US Navy Forces	123,000
Headquarters, Pearl Harbour, Hawaii	
2-3 Aircraft Carrier Battle Groups[a]	
1-2 Surface Action Groups	
3 Amphibious Groups	
5 Maritime Patrol Squadrons	
US Middle East Task Force (Bahrain)	

US Marine Corps Forces	50,000-70,000
Headquarters (Camp Pendleton, CA)	
- Marine Expeditionary Force (MEF),	
including	
1 Marine Division	
1 Marine Aircraft Wing[b]	
1 Force Service Action Group	
- Marine Expeditionary Brigade (MEB),	(8,000-18,000)[c]
including	
1 Marine Regiment (reinforced)	
1 Marine Air Group (composite)	
1 Brigade Service Support Group	

US Army-Central Forces Command   142,000
Headquarters US Third Army (Ft. McPherson, Georgia)
    XVIII Airborne Corps Headquarters
    82nd Airborne Division including the
        3rd or 73rd Light Armoured (Sheridan) Battalion
    101st Airborne Division (Air Assault)
    24th Infantry Division (Mechanised)
    10th Mountain Division
    194th Armoured Brigade
    XVIII Airborne Corps Artillery
    20th Engineer Brigade
    16th MP Brigade
    35th Signal Brigade
    18th Aviation Brigade
    11th Air Defence Brigade (HAWK)
    6th Cavalry Brigade (Air Combat)

    1st Corps Support Command

US Air Force, Central Command Air Forces
        (9th Air Force)   33,000
    7 Tactical Fighter Wings[d]
    3 1/3 Tactical Fighter Wings
        (available as attrition fillers)
    2 Strategic Bomber Squadrons[e]
    1 Airborne Warning and Control Wing
    1 Tactical Reconnaissance Group
    1 Electronic Combat Group
    1 Special Operations Wing

US Special Operations Command-Central (SOCCENT).   4,500
Headquarters, USSOCOM
        (Macdill Air Force Base, Florida)
    5th Special Forces Group
    Naval Special Warfare Task Group

Ranger Regiment
Special Operations Squadrons

TOTAL   372,600

Notes: a) A typical active navy carrier-wing consists of ten squadrons
           (approximately 86 aircraft): two F-14 fighter squadrons, two F/A-18
           light attack squadrons, one A-6/A-12 medium attack squadron, plus
           supporting elements for airborne warning, anti-submarine and
           electronic warfare, reconnaissance, and aerial refuelling operations.
           These include 10 EA-6, 4 E-2, 10 S-3, and 6 H-3/H-60 aircraft.
        b) An active Marine Corps air wing typically consists of 23-5 squadrons
           (338-70 aircraft) with: four fighter attack squadrons, two or three light
           attack squadrons, one or two medium attack squadrons, plus
           supporting elements for electronic warfare, reconnaissance, aerial
           refuelling, transport, airborne assault, observation, and tactical air
           control.
        c) The MEB is currently the only element of the MEF which has
           prepositioned equipment in the Gulf area.   All   MEFs have
           prepositioned equipment on ships, although the other two sets are
           deployed for missions in NATO and Asia.
        d) Each Air Force Wing typically contains three squadrons of 24 aircraft
           each. (Combat support units, such as those composed of EF-111
           electronic warfare aircraft, are generally organised into squadrons of
           18 to 24 aircraft) By the end of FY1989, the US had the equivalent of 40
           tactical fighter wings-27 active and 13 Air National Guard and
           Reserve.
        e) There are a total of 7 B-52G squadrons assigned to general purpose as
           well as nuclear missions. These have a strategic reconnaissance and
           anti-shipping mission as well as a conventional land bombing role.

Source: Data furnished by USCENTCOM, and in the Department of Defence,
          Annual Report, FY1986, p. 212, and FY1988, pp. 223-33; Kurt Beyer, 'US
          Power Projection Capabilities in the Gulf,' NSSP Georgetown
          University, 7 May, 1990, p. 9; and Aaron A. Danis, 'US Power
          Projection Capabilities in the Persian Gulf Region,' NSSP Georgetown
          University, 1 May, 1990, pp. 3-4.

Naval Power-Projection Forces

While much of the public analysis of US power-projection
capabilities in the Gulf region focuses on USCENTCOM's land
and air forces, it is US naval forces which have dominated US
power-projection activities in many post-war contingencies.
Military historians differ over the exact number of times the US
has deployed military forces to deal with crises or other
contingencies since World War II, and the data currently

available may understate the role of US Army and US Air Force units.

According to a recent study by the Centre for Naval Analysis, however, the US used military force at least 240 times between January 1946 and December 1989. The study estimates that 202 of these cases - or 84 per cent - involved the use of naval forces.[12] In 59 per cent of the cases analysed, or 129 cases, the US used carrier task-forces. It used amphibious ships 53 per cent of the time, or 108 cases. The US Marine Corps was used 54 per cent of the time, or in 108 cases, and US Marine Corps aviation was deployed on carrier forces in 21 cases. If one looks at the total use of the Marine Corps, it was deployed 56 per cent of the time, or in 115 cases. The importance of co-operation between the four military services is illustrated by the fact that the US Army was deployed in 18 per cent of the cases the Navy studied (36 crises) and the US Air Force was deployed in 30 per cent (60 crises). If any accurate count of the uses of US Army and US Air Force uses of force were available, it seems likely that these figures would be substantially higher.[13]

It is interesting to note, given the historical emphasis on the Cold War and combat, that only a small percentage of US uses of force were either related to a confrontation with the Soviet Union or led to actual fighting. Only 18 out of 240 cases between 1946 and 1989 involved any kind of confrontation between US and Soviet military forces (about 8 per cent of the total) and none led to combat. Only 12 out of 240 cases escalated to combat involving any other forces, and only 7 per cent of the 202 uses of naval forces escalated to combat. In virtually every case, forward deployed forces acted to deter or to limit actual combat.

The overall patterns in the US projection of significant amounts of naval force are shown in Table 11.5. While these data are complex, they show that the number of these cases involving contingencies in the Indian Ocean and Persian Gulf has increased over time. For example, the US has used naval forces 32 times in the Indian Ocean/Persian Gulf area out of a total of 196 uses of force between 1946 and 1989. This was 16 per cent of the time. In contrast, the US has used naval forces 10 times in the Indian Ocean/Persian Gulf area out of a total of 52 uses of force between 1980 and 1989. This was 20 per cent of the time. The average size of the US naval forces deployed to the region in each contingency was 1 carrier battle-group during the entire peacetime period, but increased to 1.4 battle-groups during 1980-9.

In terms of overall deployment rates, annual US carrier-deployments in the Indian Ocean fluctuated between zero and 0.5 during 1975-8, jumped to a peak of 2.5 during the time of the fall of the Shah of Iran in 1979-80, and fluctuated between 0.5 and 2 during 1981-6. During the 1987-8 crisis in the Persian Gulf, for example, the US deployed up to 18 ships and 16,000 naval personnel into the region.

The average crisis shown in Table 11.5 may appear to have involved the use of a small fraction of US naval forces, but the cases involving the use of force in the Indian Ocean and Persian Gulf took a massive effort. At the slow cruise-rates the US uses in peacetime, the Persian Gulf is 43-days steaming from Norfolk on the east coast of the US if US ships move around the Horn of Africa. It is 22-days steaming from Japan, 32-days steaming from Hawaii, and 39 days from San Diego on the west coast of the US. Put differently, if one attempts to deploy a carrier task-force continuously in the Indian Ocean, and still attempts to keep cruise times limited to maintain peacetime tours of duty and maintenance and service schedules, it takes a total force of seven carriers - counting the ones which will be in major maintenance and modernisation.[14] It is also important to note that the US is a global power. It must reserve the bulk of its forces for other contingencies, and in a number of the cases shown in Table 11.5, crises occurred simultaneously in different parts of the world.

The practical problems involved in deploying and maintaining a global naval force are illustrated by the overall pattern of deployment of US naval forces. The US now has 562 major ships. On average, these include 15-18 ballistic missile submarines, three carrier battle-groups and one battleship battle-group (roughly 40 ships in total), 48 attack submarines, and 64 maritime patrol aircraft which are constantly on patrol or deployed on a daily basis. At any given time, 75 per cent of these 562 ships are at sea or are prepared to go to sea, but only about half are actually at sea. In May 1990, 44 per cent of the total were at sea (26 per cent were forward deployed, 18 per cent were in home waters), 31 per cent were in port for training and routine maintenance or overhauls, and 25 per cent were in major overhauls, being rebuilt, or undergoing major modernisation.[15]

The activities of this force during the previous 18 months had involved 10 crisis contingency deployments, 2,000 ship-days of counter-narcotics operations, 600 exercise deployments, and humanitarian deployments to 44 countries involving some 68 ships and the delivery of over two million lbs. of material.

Table 11.5:   US Naval Power Projection in the Post-War Era - Part One:
The Use of Force Between January 1946 and December 1989

Reason for Use of Force

Region	All Uses	Freedom of Navigation	Regional Stability	To Protect US Citizens/ Anti-Terrorism
Mediterranean	60	2	36	22
Indian Ocean/ Persian Gulf	32	4	13	15
Latin America/ Caribbean	50	0	31	19
Africa	18	3	7	8
Asia and Pacific Rim	36	0	23	13

Type of Force Used

Region	Average Carrier Battle-Groups Use Per Event	Events Using Other Forces		General Purpose Ships
		Amphibious	Marines	
Mediterranean	1.8	37	36	9
Indian Ocean/ Persian Gulf	1.0	6	5	10
Latin America/ Caribbean	1.9	26	25	10
Africa	1.3	3	3	7
Asia and Pacific Rim	2.1	17	18	7

Table 11.5:   US Naval Power Projection in the Post-War Era - Part Two
The Use of Force Between January 1980 and December 1989

Reason for Use of Force

Region	All Uses	Freedom of Navigation	Regional Stability	To Protect US Citizens/ Anti-Terrorism
Mediterranean	23	2	7	14
Indian Ocean/ Persian Gulf	10	4	6	0
Latin America/ Caribbean	7	0	6	1
Africa	9	2	6	1
Asia and Pacific Rim	5	0	3	2

Type of Force Used

Region	Average Carrier Battle Groups Use Per Event	Events Using Other Forces		General Purpose Ships
		Amphibious	Marines	
Mediterranean	1.5	10	9	1
Indian Ocean/ Persian Gulf	1.4	3	2	2
Latin America/ Caribbean	1.2	5	5	0
Africa	1.8	0	0	2
Asia and Pacific Rim	1.3	3	3	0

Source: Provided to the author by the US Navy, May 1990

The total forces in the US Atlantic and Pacific fleets are shown in Table 11.6, and the strength of typical US Navy and

Marine Corps air wings is shown in Table 11.7. The key elements of these forces for most US contingencies in the Gulf and Indian Ocean include the carriers and the ships capable of using cruise missiles, the mine-warfare ships and the amphibious ships. The largest nuclear power Nimitz-class carriers displace up to 95,000 tons and the US now has an active force of 14 carriers, one of which is in long-term overhaul. These carriers are deployed in battle groups which in the 1990s will typically include two Ticonderoga-class guided-missile cruisers with Aegis guided-missile defences, two Arleigh Burke-class destroyers with Aegis defences, two Spruance-class destroyers for anti-submarine warfare, 1-2 escorting nuclear attack submarines and a large number of support vessels.[16]

These carrier task-forces are unique: no other nation now has a single carrier task-group capable of all-weather deployment of modern fixed-wing combat aircraft, or capable of self-defence against a modern air-force or missile attack. No foreign carrier-group is normally equipped to support land or air operations against an enemy equipped with modern combat aircraft and tanks. Given the limits on all other foreign carriers now under construction, the USSR is the only nation which may be seeking to create such forces during the 1990s.[17]

The strike power of these carriers consists of the US Navy or US Marine Corps air wings deployed upon them. These air wings make a natural team, and can be reinforced by US Air Force tactical combat aircraft and long-range bombers. The US Navy force provides long-range all-weather air defence as well as long and medium range attack aircraft. The US Marine Corps' air assets have an air combat capability, but their major mission is to provide strike and close support sorties in support of US Marine and Army forces. Even the US Navy wings, which emphasise air defence relative to attack power, can deliver 17.5 tons of ordnance per hour in an alpha strike or 26 tons per hour during carrier cycle operations.

Amphibious ships provide sea bases from which to conduct a variety of operations, including forcible entry to seize and hold objectives such as airfields or ports for follow-on forces. Amphibious ready groups (ARG's) are routinely forward-deployed to provide ready crisis response. US carrier and amphibious forces train and often operate together as amphibious strike forces. This combination of the US Navy-

Marine Corps team offers a powerful range of power-projection capabilities. Amphibious forces also operate independently and are capable of simultaneously landing forces by sea and air using organic transportation. Amphibious forces relay on carrier and battleship battle-groups, US Air Force strike-forces, and friendly airpower for air and surface fire support.

US carrier and amphibious forces are currently supported by two battleships. While these ships are sometimes referred to as obsolete, and have experienced recent problems because of an accident involving the use of their 16" guns, they can deliver up to 40,500 lbs. of ordnance in one minute at ranges of up to 23 miles, and up to 1,458 tons of ordnance per hour.

The battleships also are primary platforms for sea-launched cruise-missile delivery. Each battleship has eight quadruple armoured box Tomahawk missile-launchers. These missiles can deliver 1,000 lb. warheads. The anti-ship version can attack ships at ranges greater than 300 nautical miles. The land-attack version can hit static targets with precision at ranges in excess of 700 nautical miles. The land-attack version of such cruise missiles can be used to suppress fixed air-defences and allow the carrier or land-based aircraft to penetrate. It can be used to strike surgically at high-value military targets, or to destroy key economic targets like refineries and power plants with minimal loss of civilian life. As such, the SLCM, or bomber-delivered ALCM, may make an ideal counter to the proliferation of weapons of mass destruction in the region, since it enables the US to strike or retaliate without using similar weapons.

It now appears that the US Navy will cut its active carrier-strength from 14 to between 10 and 12 carriers by 1997, and it could retire all of its battleships from service by this date. These cuts will be the result of both budget pressures and the ongoing decline in the Soviet threat. This will have an effect on US power-projection capabilities, but its impact on the number of carriers the US can deploy to the Indian Ocean in an emergency will be moderated by the fact that the need to keep carriers elsewhere has been reduced by the changes taking place in the USSR and the Warsaw Pact. The US will retain ample cruise-missile delivery capability for regional contingency needs on its CG-47 guided-missile cruisers, DDG-51 and DD-963 guided-missile destroyers, SSN-688 nuclear submarines, and long-range strike aircraft.

Potential-threat nations will almost certainly improve their air and anti-ship missile capabilities during the period when the US is making these force cuts. In fact, many of the countries in the Indian Ocean, Gulf and Red Sea areas already have long-range anti-ship missiles.[18] The US will, however, substantially upgrade the air-defence capabilities of its F-14 long-range air-defence fighters, and deploy the new A-12 long-range strike fighter, which has many 'stealth' characteristics. These improvements in aircraft performance should permit the US Navy to maintain a substantial qualitative edge over the combat aircraft in the region, and to strike at considerably longer distances. The US will deploy a new generation of ASW and special-purpose aircraft, and will deploy a new type of air-defence fighter beginning around the year 2000. Equally importantly, the US Navy will continue to upgrade its surface-based air and missile defences, and electronic warfare and counter-measure capabilities.

The most significant deficiency in US naval capabilities in the region during the 1990s may be in mine warfare. At the time the *Bridgeton* was hit by a mine during Operation Ernest Will, the US had only 21 30-year-old minesweepers (MSOs) in service.[19] All but three of these minesweepers were in the Naval Reserve Force. The three active ships were assigned research duty and were not ready to perform their mission. They were augmented only by seven active-duty 57-foot minesweeping boats (MSBs), and 23 Sea Stallion RH-53D helicopters, four of which were also allocated to the naval reserves.[20] The MSOs were 830-ton vessels with a maximum speed of 14 knots. They had sonars with mine-hunting capability, but lacked the ability to simulate the magnetic or acoustic image of larger tankers so as to detonate modern influence mines. The MSBs were only 30-ton vessels which could often make only seven knots in the open sea. Only one of the MSBs had a sonar to prevent hunting before sweeping. None of the vessels had the electronics and sweeping equipment to be fully effective against modern acoustic and magnetic influence mines or sophisticated mines like the Soviet 99501 combination bottom and influence mines that Libya had used in mining the Red Sea approaches to the Suez Canal.[21]

The US had begun a $1.5 billion programme in the early 1980s to replace its 1950s-vintage minesweepers, and to build 14 large wooden-hulled Avenger-class minesweepers, and 17 small high-technology fibreglass coastal minesweepers. The Avenger-class ships were designed as fully modern 224-foot mine vessels with a size of 1,040 tons and SQQ-30 variable-depth mine detection/classification sonars, Honeywell mine-neutralisation vehicles, and acoustic and magnetic sweeps. The programme ran into major problems, however, and the first ships only entered active service in 1988.[22] The initial order of coastal minesweepers had to be cancelled in 1986 - in part because the fibreglass hulls peeled under the simulated shock of nearby mine-explosions. The US then had to order a new type of ship from Italy's Intermarine and Hercules Power at a cost of $120 million. Work on the first of these MCC-51s began in November 1987.[23]

The US did use the SH-2 helicopters on its surface ships to help spot and destroy 10 of the mines found off Kuwait. These helicopters were not, however, capable of detecting deep mines or of mine-sweeping. The Navy's only dedicated heliborne minesweeping assets were three squadrons with a total of 23 RH-53D Sea Dragon helicopters, which had serious structural reliability problems, were only usable in daylight and shallow water, and had relatively limited endurance. New Sikorsky MH-53E AMCM helicopters are replacing them which are designed to provide night-operations capability, a major increase in range payload, a 50 per cent increase in towing capability, improved hot-day performance, an on-station mission time of more than four hours, improved coverage for the AQS-14 towed sonar, and more effective use of dual acoustic and magnetic minesweeping sleds. The MH-53Es have lagged badly in delivery, however, and Sikorsky has been penalised for slow progress.[24]

These programmes are gradually leading to improvements in US capabilities. No US mine-warfare resources are normally deployed in the Indian Ocean, Gulf, and Red Sea areas, however, and the US experience in the Gulf in 1987 and 1988 showed that mine-warfare capabilities normally take so long to mobilise and deploy that it is unlikely they would arrive in a contingency where time was critical.[25]

The capability of US forces will also be uncertain when it does arrive. By the time of the cease-fire in the Iran-Iraq war, the entire Western minesweeping effort in the Gulf had found a total of 89 moored mines in seven different minefields.[26] These mines included 79 M-08 Soviet mines and 10 Iranian-made Myam mines which were smaller contact mines. In addition, there were large numbers of floating mines. The total number of mines neutralised was 176, including 89 moored and 87 floating, and a total of 83 M-08s and 95 Myams. These figures clearly demonstrate that Third World states can and will take the risk of challenging Western powers, even Superpowers. This is particularly true when the West either lacks any effective way of striking directly at their leadership elites, or when those leadership elites have a deep anti-Western political or ideological commitment.

The West succeeded in its mine-warfare efforts during 1987-8 largely because all of the mines involved were older types that are comparatively easy to detect. None of the minesweepers that any Western nation deployed to the Gulf would have been quickly and reliably able to sweep more modern non-magnetic or influence mines, particularly ones which could be set to operate at fixed intervals or become active only when approached by given sizes of ship.[27] If Iran had used the more sophisticated mines it was rumoured to have bought from Libya, it might well have created a far more serious problem, and one that would have required weeks of additional sweeping and the interdiction of virtually all naval traffic out of Iran. In 1982, for example, when mines were discovered in the Red Sea, it took a British minesweeper six days to identify, disarm and neutralise a sophisticated 1,500 lb. mine.[28] Far more sophisticated mine-warfare threats are likely to occur in the future, and even the latest US mine-warfare forces will experience serious problems in rapidly clearing such mines from the Gulf, the Gulf approaches and the Red Sea.

Table 11.6: Active Strength of US Naval Forces as of 30 April 1990

Ship Type	Total	Atlantic Fleet		Pacific Fleet
		Total	In Mediterranean	
Ballistic Missile Nuclear Submarines (SSBN)	33	25	0	8
Carriers Attack (CV)	8	4	1	4

Nuclear Attack (CVN)	6	3	0	3
Total	14	7	1	7
Battleships (BB)	4	2	0	2
Guided Missile Cruiser (CG)	33	15	2	18
Nuclear Guided Missile Cruiser (CGN)	9	4	1	5
Destroyer (DD)	31	16	1	15
Guided Missile Destroyer (DDG)	28	16	3	12
Frigate (FF)	39	20	1	19
Guided Missile Frigate (FG)	35	22	1	13
Total Surface Combatants	179	95	9	84
Conventional Submarines (SS)	1	0	0	1
Nuclear Submarines (SSN)	94	54	4	40
Guided Missile Patrol	6	6	0	0
(LOC)	2	1	0	1
(LHA)	5	2	1	3
Amphibious Assault (LHD)	1	1	0	0
(LKA)	5	2	0	3
(LPD)	13	6	1	7
(LPH)	7	4	0	3
Landing Ship Dock (LSD)	11	4	0	7
Landing Ship Tank (LST)	18	9	2	9
Total Amphibious	62	29	4	33
Ammunition (AE)	12	5	1	7
Stores (AF)	NA	NA	NA	NA
Stores-Submarine (AFS)	7	3	0	4
Oiler (AO)	5	3	0	2
Oiler and Ammo (AOE)	4	2	1	2
Oiler and Repair (AOR)	7	3	1	4
Total Combat Logistic	35	16	3	19
Submarine Tender (AS)	4	4	1	0
Submarine Support Ships (AK)	37	29	2	8

Source: US Navy Computer Print-out

Table 11.7: Strength of Typical US Navy and Marine Air Wings

Aircraft Type	Function	Squadrons	Aircraft Numbers		

A. Carrier Air Wing

Aircraft Type	Function	Squadrons	C	T	R
F-4, F-14 (TARPS)	Fighter (Reconnaissance)	2	24	20	20
F/A-18	Light Attack	2	24	20	20
A-6/A-12	Medium Attack	1	14	16	20
KA-6D	Tanker	1	0-4	-	-
S-3A	ASW (Fixed Wing)	1	10	8	10
SH-3/H-3/H-60	ASW (Rotary Wing)	1	6	6	6
EA-6B	Electronic Warfare	1	4	5	5
E-2C	Airborne Early Warning	1	4	5	5
		10	86-90	80	86

B. Marine Corps Air Wing

Aircraft Type	Function	Squadrons	Aircraft Numbers
F-4, F-18	Fighter	4	48
A-4	Light Attack	1	9
AV-8B	Light Attack	2	40
A-6	Medium Attack	1-2	20
KC-130	Tanker/Transport	1	12
EA-6B	Electronic Warfare	1	8
RF-4 or F/A-18	Reconnaissance	1	8
OV-10	Observation	1	12
AH-1	Attack Helicopters	1	24
CH-53	Transport/Utility Helicopters	6-7	48
UH-1	Helicopters	-	24
		27-30	313

Source: DoD, Annual Report, FY1988, p. 188; US Navy print-out, May 1990; United States Marine Corps, Concepts and Issues (US Marine Corps Headquarters, Washington, DC, Feb. 1989)

Note: C = Conventional; T = Transitional; R = Roosevelt.

Marine Corps Expeditionary Forces

Important as seapower is, it cannot defend friendly territory, seize hostile areas, occupy the land, or perform all of the same missions as land-based airpower. The other key elements of US power-projection capabilities are the Marine

Corps, Army and Air Force. These components of any power-projection forces the US deployed to the Gulf, Indian Ocean, Red Sea and the Horn would come under the command of USCENTCOM. It is important to stress that the relative contribution each service would make would depend on the nature of a given contingency, and it is as impossible to rank the relative importance of the contribution each service - or each type of force - would make as it is to predict the future.

All of the amphibious forces in the US force structure are provided by the US Marine Corps, and these forces are designed for large-scale 'forced entry' into a hostile country and self-sustaining operations as an expeditionary force. Marine forces are highly flexible, however, and can be deployed to fight at any intensity of combat short of nuclear engagement.

The key building-blocks of Marine Corps forces that USCENTCOM would draw upon in deciding on the forces it needed for a given contingency include a Marine Expeditionary Force (MEF), a Marine Expeditionary Brigade (MEB) and a Marine Expeditionary Unit (MEU). The Marine Expeditionary Force (MEF) is the largest type of unit and includes some 50,000 Marines and US Navy personnel, about 160 tanks, and some 5,000-6,000 other vehicles. It may range in size from less than one to several infantry divisions and aircraft wings. It is capable of a wide range of contingency operations and is designed to deploy with 60 days of support and supply for sustained operations ashore.[29]

There are now three combat-ready MEFs. The most likely unit to go to the Gulf is the 1st Marine Expeditionary Force, which is deployed in California. It includes the 1st Marine Division, the 1st Force Service Support Group, the 3rd Marine Aircraft Wing, and the 5th and 7th Marine Expeditionary Brigades - which also have a training role.   The 2nd Marine Expeditionary Force is deployed in North Carolina. It includes the 2nd Marine Division, the 2nd Force Service Support Group, the 2nd Marine Aircraft Wing, and the 6th and 10th Marine Expeditionary Brigades - plus the 4th Marine Expeditionary Brigade in Norfolk. Additional Marine Corps forces in the Far East include the 1st Marine Brigade and the 24th Marine Aircraft Group of the Fleet Marine Force Pacific at Kaneohe Bay in Hawaii; the 1st Marine Aircraft Wing which is headquartered in Okinawa, and the III Marine Expeditionary Force in Okinawa.

The latter force has the 3rd Marine Division, 9th Marine Expeditionary Brigade, 3rd Force Service Group and 36th Marine Aircraft Group.[30]

The Marine Expeditionary Brigade (MEB) is a smaller unit, with 4,000-18,000 personnel. It is designed to suit a given task, but it is normally built around a reinforced infantry regiment and a composite Marine aircraft group. It is commanded by a general officer and is capable of amphibious assaults and follow-on operations ashore. During a crisis, an MEB can be forward deployed afloat for an extended period to provide rapid response. An MEB has 30 days of sustainability, and may be supported from its sea base, facilities ashore, or a combination of both. MEBs can serve as the forward element of a deploying MEF.

An MEB can have up to 53 tanks and 1,200 other vehicles of assorted types. Its fixed-wing air is ferried to the region while its helicopters are air-deployed with the rest of the MEB. These include UNH-1 utility helicopters, Cobra attack helicopters, CH-46 transport helicopters which can carry 24 troops each, and CH-53 heavy-lift helicopters, each of which can carry one light armoured vehicle (LAV).[31]

A Marine Expeditionary Unit is the smallest air-ground task force the Marine Corps organises and has 1,800-4,000 men. It is normally built around a reinforced infantry battalion and a composite helicopter squadron reinforced with fixed-wing assets and an MEU service support group. It is commanded by a Colonel, and is routinely deployed in forward afloat assignments. MEUs are often afloat in the Atlantic/Mediterranean and Pacific/Indian Ocean. The MEUs deployed in amphibious shipping carry 15 days of sustainment, but they normally require external support, and would not be deployed for independent amphibious assaults. The MEU is special-operations capable and can be embarked aboard 3-5 amphibious ships.

The Marine Corps uses dedicated Maritime Prepositioning Forces to provide strategic mobility. The Corps has 13 ships, organised into three squadrons. The first squadron (MPS-1) operates in the Eastern Atlantic, the second (MPS-2) operates at Diego Garcia in the Indian Ocean, and the third (MPS-3) operates in the Western Pacific.[32] The major equipment and stocks for the 7th Marine Expeditionary Brigade are prepositioned aboard ships at Diego Garcia and can reach the Gulf in seven days.[33]

The Marine Corps forces are capable of reinforcing friendly states to the point where they can deal with virtually any limited war contingency in the Gulf and Red Sea regions short of a major civil war, or a land conflict involving substantial Iranian or Iraqi forces. It is important to note, however, that this capability is dependent on substantial support from friendly states in many contingencies.   Marine Corps forces have substantial anti-armour capability, but they are not organised, trained and equipped for major fluid armour-battles, and their 'forced entry' capability is limited. Their effectiveness and self-sustainment capability increase sharply if they can obtain access to ports, and if they can operate out of airports and permanent air-facilities with friendly support. They have only moderate capability for urban warfare, and they are combat troops. They are not intended to operate as an occupation or security force in the face of popular opposition.

The Marine Corps also faces a number of challenges because of the cuts taking place in the US defence budget. It could lose as much as one full MEF out of its force structure by 1995. It faces serious problems in funding the modernisation of its amphibious forces, some of which will encounter serious block obsolescence in the period between 2002 and 2008.[34] Equally importantly, there is a serious risk that the Marine Corps will not get the new V-22 VTOL aircraft, or the numbers of air-cushioned landing craft (LCAC) that it wants. The V-22 has a 400-mile combat radius compared to about 250 miles for the CH-53E without in-flight refuelling. It would provide the Corps with the ability to close from 400-miles offshore and strike anywhere along a 1,000-mile coast within a 24-hour period.[35] The LCAC is a long-range amphibious ship capable of speeds of 40 knots, compared with 10-12 knots for the current landing-craft. It is less vulnerable to mines, and can operate on 70 per cent of the world's beaches, compared to 17 per cent for current landing-craft.

US Army Power-Projection Forces

The US Army provides substantial numbers of land combat units that USCENTCOM can use in its contingency planning.

These forces are most likely to be taken from the XVIII Airborne Corps which includes the 82nd Airborne Division at Fort Bragg, the 101st Airborne Division (AASLT) at Fort Campbell, the 24th Mechanised Division at Fort Stewart, and the 10th Mountain Division at Fort Drum. The 7th Infantry Division, which is being relocated at Fort Lewis, is not part of the XVIII Airborne Corps, but is attached to it for specific contingencies. As Table 11.4 has shown, there are a number of additional brigades and support units. The Army units that can be assigned to the Corps also include large-scale civil affairs and psychological warfare forces, and long-haul logistics forces - capabilities that are not part of Marine Corps forces.

These forces are designed to be highly flexible in adapting to specific contingencies. Each division has Division Ready Brigades (DRB) which are an all-arms task-force with its own combat, combat support and service support capabilities. Each division can form as many DRBs as there are brigades in the division and one DRB is always ready for immediate deployment. These brigades generally include three infantry battalions. In addition to the infantry battalions, they can be organised into task forces with armour, artillery and special-forces units, and sufficient combat support to be self-contained fighting units. The army can also provide command and control assets with global communications capabilities from corps and division levels to operate as a joint task-force headquarters with other services.[36]

The Division Ready Brigades vary by division according to the parent division's mission, and provide a wide range of options. For example, the 82nd Airborne Division is a relatively lightly equipped paratroop force, with three brigades of about 5,000 men each, which is capable of forcible entry by parachute into distant areas of operations. Its DRB has air-droppable M-551 Sheridan Armoured Reconnaissance/Airborne Assault Vehicles. The DRB which is most combat ready can begin deployment in as little as 18 hours, and all three DRBs can deploy to the Gulf in less than five days if sufficient airlift is available. Each DRB can be task-organised to include whatever combat elements are needed, but all are dependent on resupply, and rapidly deployable DRBs would have to be augmented to strengthen their air-defence and anti-armour capabilities for mid-intensity combat against many of the potential threats in the region.

The 101st Airborne Division is a heavier unit of about 17,900 troops. It is more heavily equipped than the 82nd Division, but would take roughly 30 days to reach the Gulf by sea and 12-17 days by air. Its DRB contains a large number of Blackhawk UH-60 armoured utility helicopters, and it has AH-64 all-weather attack helicopters which have ferry ranges in excess of 1,000 miles with add-on fuel tanks. Both of these divisions, and selected light infantry divisions - including the 7th Light Infantry Division - can begin movement by air only 18 hours after an initial alert notification. In Operation Just Cause, for example, forces flew 2,000-3,000 miles from different locations in the US in 200 different aircraft and struck the same night at nearly 30 different targets.

The 24th Mechanised Infantry Division's DRB is a mix of M-1 Tanks and Bradley M-2 Infantry Fighting Vehicles. Unlike the previous divisions - which move by air - it would move to the port of Savannah and use fast airlift and sealift. The 24th's DRB can move to port within 18 hours of an alert and fit the equipment for its DRB aboard one fast sealift ship. On a recent exercise, a single SL-7 (TAKR) fast sealift ship deployed 58 M-1 tanks, 60 Bradleys, a Hawk surface-to-air missile unit, and over 100 additional tracked and wheeled vehicles. Other divisions have different capabilities, but all possess significant anti-armour capability, have artillery and other indirect fire weapons, and all have about the same mix of engineer, signal, intelligence, logistics and medical support. Additional combat and support elements can be added to each division, most of which are air-droppable.

All of the major combat units in the XVIII Airborne Corps, and several additional selected light divisions are combat-ready, and they have equipment and supplies prepositioned at Diego Garcia as part of the Afloat Prepositioning Force. Unclassified briefing data provided by USCENTCOM in the late 1980s, however, indicates more than 50 per cent of the combat support and service support units it planned to use in a high-intensity conflict were reserve units. These included 49 per cent of the combat support units and 59 per cent of service support units. Although the readiness of some of these forces has since been improved because of the crisis in the Gulf and the operation in Panama, the full-time active combat support units in USCENTCOM may still have only about 83 per cent unit-readiness and the reserve units about 62 per cent readiness.

The full-time active service support units that USCENTCOM planned to use in a high-intensity conflict had 78 per cent unit-readiness in 1987, and the reserve units had 57 per cent readiness. Current unclassified data are not available, but it is clear that there are still serious shortfalls in specialised skilled manpower, in total manning and in senior NCOs. The support units available to USCENTCOM also probably still have equipment problems. In 1987, the full-time active combat support units in USCENTCOM had 89 per cent of their equipment on hand and the reserve units had 83 per cent. The full-time active service support units in USCENTCOM had 93 per cent of their equipment on hand, and the reserve units had 80 per cent.[37]

It is unclear how serious these readiness shortfalls now are, or how important they would be in any real-world contingency, particularly now that the US faces far less risk of having to keep most of its forces assigned to help defend NATO if it does face some major contingency in the Gulf. The total US Army now includes a total of 28 divisions and 22 brigades, and 18 of the divisions are active. In addition to the XVIII Airborne Corps forces discussed earlier, the US Army has ranger and special forces, and six tank and four mechanised divisions.

The Army also has a total of five light divisions, each with approximately 10,800 soldiers, nine infantry battalions, three 105mm towed artillery battalions, and one 155mm towed 155mm howitzer battalion. Three of the light divisions are active with some reserve 'round outs', and two are in reserve. However, these light divisions are not normally considered for scenarios in the Gulf. Two - the 6th and 25th - are tailored for specific geographic assignments outside the region.[38]

The US Army has a total of more than 5,000 actives assigned to special-forces units, and 14,000 more in the reserves. It has units like the 75th Ranger Regiment which is a 1,800-man unit designed for either direct action in support of other forces or independent action deep in hostile territory. The army can draw upon large numbers of civil-affairs units and psychological-operations units for use in the Gulf and Red Sea region. Finally, the army forces in the US include the III Corps with five divisions. Three are active divisions with Army National Guard 'round outs' and two are reserve units.[39]

Like the other services, however, the US Army is likely to experience significant cuts during the coming decade. It might shrink from 18 active divisions today to as few as 10 in the year 2000, and from a current active manning level of about 769,000 to as little as 500,000.[40] Most of these cuts, however, will take place in forces now designed largely to meet the Warsaw Pact threat in the Central Region of Europe. The US is likely to retain more active-force strength for power-projection purposes than it can deploy and support in a Gulf or Red Sea area contingency.

Accordingly, the primary problems the US Army is likely to encounter are not sufficiency of force, but the ability to deploy and sustain it. To the extent that there will be a qualitative shortfall in such forces, it will probably lie in the ability to deploy heavy armour. Even if the US deployed the entire 24th Mechanised Infantry Division and the US Marine Corps 7th MEB - the maximum tank-force it can probably deploy and sustain within 14-21 days - it would still have only 216 Army and 53 Marine Corps Tanks. This deficiency would, however, be offset if the US deployed large numbers of AH-64 Apache and Super Cobra attack helicopters. The AH-64 can also ferry directly to the Gulf in an emergency if it is granted overflight and refuelling rights.[41]

US Air Force Power-Projection Forces

It is almost impossible to pick out the specific tactical and strategic air units that the US Air Force would use in a contingency in the Gulf and Red Sea areas. These would be tailored to a given contingency, and the US Air Force now has approximately 260 strategic bombers, 47 conventional B-52G long-range bombers, 1,710 active fighters and attack fighters, and 828 reserve fighters and attack fighters.[42] The USAF can deploy more wings than any given contingency is likely to require. Its actual force levels are likely to be determined by the needs imposed by a given contingency, by the number of aircraft friendly states in the region are willing to base and support, and by any limitations in the number of aircraft local facilities can shelter, arm, maintain, and support with effective command, control, communications, and intelligence (C^3I).

Like seapower, airpower has great flexibility because large amounts of force can be rapidly deployed and sustained at long ranges and in very short periods of time. The flexibility of US air power is illustrated by a list of a few typical USAF power-projection missions during the 1980s:

- January 1980: USAF B-52s overfly Soviet naval vessels in the Arabian Sea as a demonstration of US capabilities.
- August 1983: A force package of AWACS, tankers and F-15s is sent to Khartoum in response to Libyan attacks on Chad.
- 1986: A raid is launched on Libya by air and naval forces supported by strategic tankers.
- December 1989: Airlift supported by tankers air drops 82nd Airborne and Ranger troops into Panama during Operation Just Cause.
- 1980-1989: USAF AWACS, strategic lift aircraft and tankers provide surveillance, supplies and fuel.

USAF tactical air units include a wide range of highly advanced air defence, strike/attack, reconnaissance, electronic warfare, battle management, and other special-purpose aircraft, plus aircraft with low observable or stealth features like the F-117. The USAF has electronic warfare and AWACS capabilities that are vastly superior to any regional power. In additional to B-52 forces fully dedicated to conventional strike missions, the US can use any part of its long-range bomber force, including the B-1B and eventually the B-2. These bombers are capable of all-weather long-range strikes that can be delivered with a very high probability of penetration and with sufficient effectiveness to destroy most area targets, including hardened facilities like air bases. They are also capable of precision strikes, mining operations, and anti-ship missile strikes.

It is difficult to put the resulting capabilities into perspective, but if one examines only ordnance delivery capability, a single F-15E wing can deliver about 500 tons of ordnance per day at a 500-nautical-mile radius. A single carrier-wing can deliver about 175 tons at the same radius. Depending on the scenarios, and the facilities available, the land-based aircraft can also sustain prolonged operations while there are obvious limits to how long a carrier can service and arm its aircraft without major replenishment. All of these aircraft have more lethal munitions available than any aircraft in the region, and the Tornado is the only strike aircraft now in the region which has attack avionics and all-weather mission capabilities roughly equal to those of US strike-aircraft.[43]

Long-range bombers offer major strike-capabilities as well as a great deal of freedom from dependence on local bases, and their bases may be less vulnerable in dealing with the sophisticated threats that may develop in the 1990s than carrier battle-groups. All US Air Force long-range bombers can operate from Diego Garcia. Beginning in 1983, the US has conducted exercises showing that its B-52s could fly out of bases in Egypt and reach virtually any target in the Gulf. This range puts bomber bases outside the strike range of most countries in the region, although the proliferation of long-range missiles may change this situation in the mid to late 1990s.[44]

Bombers also have tremendous carrying capacity. Thirteen B-52s can deliver roughly 175 tons per day over a 3,000-nautical-mile radius, and eight B-1Bs or B-2s can deliver the same amount. The HAVE NAP systems on the B-52 and B-2 give them an ability to launch extremely precise conventional strikes against land targets. B-52s can deliver mines in larger amounts and more rapidly than any other weapons system in the world. Each B-52 can carry eight Harpoon anti-ship missiles. Flying at 450 knots, a single B-52 can carry out armed surveillance over an immense area. For example, two B-52s can survey 448,000 square miles of ocean on a standard maritime patrol sortie - an areas the size of the South China Sea.[45]

While the B-2 is normally thought of as a strategic nuclear bomber, and its expense may limit its use in some contingencies, it also offers the ability to deliver very high payloads from bases far outside the normal strike range of countries in the region with little risk of losing an aircraft to hostile forces. Six B-2s, operating from the US with the support of six tankers, could conduct an operation like the 1986 raid against Libya. The actual Libyan raid utilised two carrier battle-groups, an Air Force F-111 squadron, and numerous supporting assets. All in all, it involved 119 aircraft and 20 ships, and the B-2s could operate without reliance on forward bases and overflight rights.[46]

Given these USAF capabilities - and those of US Navy carrier aviation and US Marine Corps air units - the US could rapidly help any friendly Gulf state establish air superiority over any potential regional threat in a matter of days, and establish a significant advantage in air attack capability. US Air Force tactical aircraft would, however, need to operate from friendly air bases, and they would be most effective if these bases had suitable sheltering and air defences. Much would also depend on whether the US had time to prepare and deploy its land-based and naval air forces. Warning would be critical to giving US air reinforcements both deterrent and combat value, as would the availability of stocks of US munitions, parts, and aircraft service facilities - although the Air Force has equipment and supplies prepositioned at Diego Garcia as part of the Afloat Prepositioning Force.

US long-range bombers can operate from Diego Garcia. However, if USAF tactical aircraft were forced to deploy suddenly to bases without protection and interoperable stocks and facilities, their effectiveness would be far lower - perhaps by a factor of 50 to 70 per cent, depending on the quality of the attacking air force and problems in deploying to an inadequate friendly base. This could be critical in a contingency in the Upper Gulf because the F/A-18 and AV-8B lack the range to operate effectively in the area from carriers deployed in the Gulf of Oman, and the A-6 and A-12 would face severe operating constraints. As regional anti-ship missile and air capabilities improve, the US may also be forced to deploy its carriers further from the entrances to the Red Sea or away from land in the Gulf of Oman and Arabian Sea.

The US would face some other problems in deploying land-based aircraft. There currently are some shortfalls in the ability of assigned aircraft to fly all-weather and night missions, however, and these will not be corrected until the mid-1990s, when the F-111D is upgraded with PAVETACK and the F-15E and F-16 with LANTIRN are deployed. The tactical air control equipment used to co-ordinate between land and air units is 25-years old, bulky, and limited in information-processing capability. While munitions are being upgraded with improved BLU 109/8 2,000 lb. bombs, HARM anti-radiation missiles, and IR Maverick, SFWs, AGM-130Bs, and a number of classified systems, budget cuts will probably delay or cancel some advanced systems and reduce planned purchase-levels significantly.[47]

More broadly, the US Air Force faces the same force cuts as the Navy, Marine Corps, and Army. It could lose up to one third of its active strength between 1990 and 1995. The actual rate of decline will be heavily dependent on a continued improvement in US and Soviet relations, but major force cuts do now seem likely. At the same time, significant cutbacks and delays have already occurred in the procurement of new tactical aircraft and weaponry. The Air Force has delayed procurement of the ATA, a new long-range strike aircraft which is a variant of the Navy's A-12, and has delayed procurement of the ATF - an extremely advanced air-defence fighter with many stealth features. Procurement of the B-2 has already been cut back from 132 to 75 bombers, and the programme may be cancelled. These shifts could eventually reduce US contingency-capability in terms of both numbers and technical superiority, but it is too early to be sure what effect they will actually have.

US Strategic Lift Forces

The US now has substantial strategic and theatre lift assets it can use in deploying forces to the Gulf and Red Sea area. In mid-1990, US inter-theatre lift assets included 66 C-5As, 44 C-5Bs, 234 C-141s, 57 KC-10A tankers, with four new C-17s in production. These aircraft are all capable of deploying large air-cargoes across the Atlantic or Pacific. US intra-theatre lift assets included 444 C-130s. The Air Force can also augment its strategic lift assets with civil airliners in the Civil Reserve Air Fleet, which make up 30 per cent of its cargo and 95 per cent of its total potential lift assets. The total force consists of over 400 active, reserve and National Guard aircraft, and approximately 480 CRAF aircraft. It can lift up to 48 million ton miles of cargo per day, while meeting all passenger lift requirements.[48] The Navy and Marine Corps have a total of 92 tactical support ships, including eight fast sealift ships. The US has 27 tankers and 39 cargo ships in its active fleet, and a large number of additional ships in its Ready Reserve Force (RRF). The Ready Reserve Force is managed by the Maritime Administration and is composed of 96 militarily useful and specialised ships maintained in a 5, 10 and 20 day activation status. These ships include break bulk ships, roll-on/roll-off ships, crane ships specially modified for operations in unimproved ports, handy-size product tankers, and barge carriers that are critical to sustained mid-intensity combat. The RRF provides about 25 per cent of all US strategic sealift capacity and over 50 per cent of its ability to move military unit equipment by sea.[49] The US is seeking to build up the RRF to a force of 105 ships, but only provided 63 per cent of the required funds in 1990.[50] There is also a large National Defence Reserve Fleet (NDRF) but these are much older and less ready ships whose value lies largely in providing attrition fillers in a protracted conflict.

These lift assets are impressive, and it is interesting to note how important they can be in supporting all forms of US power projection. For example, USAF tankers flew over 300 sorties during Operation Ernest Will to refuel US Navy carrier aircraft over the Strait of Hormuz. These flights allowed US carrier aircraft to operate further away from the Gulf and reduce the threat of any Iranian attack.[51]

Nevertheless, strategic lift still imposes significant limits on what the US can and cannot do. In 1988, the US concluded that it only had 57 per cent of the strategic or 'inter-theatre' airlift it needed to deploy and support the power-projection forces it required for the most demanding global contingency used for force planning.[52] These shortfalls are now far less significant because USCENTCOM no longer plans for a worst case like a Soviet invasion of Iran. Current plans to improve US strategic airlift should provide at least 8,000 tons of strategic lift per day for a Gulf contingency, which should be adequate for any situation other than a high intensity conflict involving armoured forces.[53]

The situation in regard to intra-theatre lift is different. The US has only about 55 per cent of the Cold War goal for intra-theatre lift of 13,500 tons per day that it set for intra-theatre lift when it was still planning for a major conflict in Europe, and there are serious limits on the C-130's cargo size capacity and speed of handling. These demands seem to be easing as the USSR and Warsaw Pact decline in offensive capability, and the US should strongly improve its intra-theatre lift beginning in the mid-1990s, but *only if* the C-17 is deployed in significant numbers.

The C-17 is a new strategic lift aircraft that has great potential. One C-17 payload is equal to 172,200 lbs., compared with 86,100 lbs. for the C-141B and 38,000 lbs. for the C-130. It also has about three times the tonnage per ramp cycle of the C-141B. The C-17 is also capable of fundamentally different missions from any existing strategic lift aircraft. Unlike the C-5 and C-141 strategic lift aircraft, which must operate out of major airports, and then their cargo be transferred to smaller planes for intra-theatre missions, the C-17 can fly strategic missions and then land on relatively limited runways in the forward area.   It can swing directly from the inter- to the intra-theatre role - replacing both the C-141 and C-130 without off-loading or refuelling.

This swing capability of the C-17 sharply reduces the total number of aircraft required for any given mission, reducing dependence on long runways, and reducing load and re-load times.   To put this in perspective, the C-17 can can deliver 167,000 lbs. of cargo into a 2,700-by-90 foot runway and it requires only 7,600 feet of runway for take-off at maximum take-off gross weight.   This performance allows the C-17 to operate in and out of over 10,000 airfields in the free world outside the US, versus only 850 airfields for the C-5 and 3,500 for the C-141.   It also can transport outsize cargo that only the C-5 can now transport, is capable of far more efficient use of space than the C-5 or C-141, and its reverse thrust capabilities allows it to make far more efficient use of ramp space and to load and offload far more quickly.   Further, it will be the only aircraft in the US fleet capable of outsize airdrops.[54]

Unfortunately, the C-17 has run into cost and time problems.   The US cut its planned purchases substantially in April 1990, and the continuing delays and increases in cost have put the programme in danger of outright cancellation.   Such a cancellation would have a considerable impact on US contingency capability.   The C-17 was originally planned to provide a major portion of US strategic lift, and 60 per cent of all intra-theatre lift, by the year 2000.   The US also has no clear alternative to the C-17.   The C-141B, the backbone of the current USAF fleet, is an aging aircraft that is rapidly reaching the end of its service.   No programme can credibly keep the C-141 alive at its present strength much beyond the late 1990s.

The situation in regard to sealift is equally complex.   Some studies indicate that sealift will deliver approximately 95 per cent of the dry cargo and 99 per cent of all petroleum products in a high-intensity conflict scenario.   Other studies show that over 95 per cent of USCENTCOM tonnage-requirements move by sealift in a high-intensity conflict.   The navy is now close to meeting its goal of 1 million short-tons worth of capacity for USCENTCOM, and will be at about 89 per cent of its goal during FY1986-92.   It has already reached its goal for fast sealift ships and maritime prepositioning ships.[55]   At the same time, the availability of commercial US sealift continues to decline, and the withdrawal of US forces from Europe after CFE could impose new demands on US sealift resources. The US maritime fleet has dropped from 894 ships in 1970 to 423 in 1989, a reduction of 53 per cent. Some projections indicate it will drop to less than 200 ships by the year 2000.[56]

Further, USCENTCOM lacks the assets it needs to offload ships and carry them across beaches. Unless it has ready access to a port in the rear combat zone, it will have only 44 per cent of the US Army Logistics Over The Shore (LOTS) assets it needs for the high-intensity conflict it uses for planning purposes. The army needs air-cushion vehicles, lighters, better landing-craft and ferries. If currently planned funding is provided, this lift will be available by FY1996, but USCENTCOM can now only move 9,300 short tons a day versus a goal of 21,000.

USCENTCOM may also be short of its goals for shore-based equipment prepositioning. The US does have 12 vessels with afloat prepositioning deployed in the Indian Ocean and Western Mediterranean, plus 13 Maritime Prepositioning Ships deployed in three locations in the world, and each carries the equipment and supplies for three Marine Expeditionary Bridges. Even so, USCENTCOM once had a goal of 300,000 short-tons worth of prepositioned supplies and equipment for a high-intensity conflict. In 1986, only 20 per cent of this goal was available afloat and another 13 per cent ashore. USCENTCOM only had 77 per cent of its goal of 150,000 tons worth of prepositioned ammunition, all of it afloat. It had 41 per cent of its goal of 12 million barrels worth of prepositioned petroleum, oil and lubricants (POL), with 5 per cent prepositioned on shore in the area, 8 per cent afloat, and 28 per cent stored out of the USCENTCOM area.[57]

USCENTCOM may face similar shortages in prepositioned sustainability. In 1986, it had only 60 per cent of its requirement of supplies and equipment; only 50 per cent of its requirement for petroleum, oil and lubricants (POL), and 36 per cent of its requirement for munitions. This situation may well have changed. Some estimates indicate that USCENTCOM had 80 per cent of its requirement of supplies and equipment, 70 per cent of its requirement for POL, and 40 per cent of its requirement for munitions in 1988.[58] Most of these stocks were located on land, although 20 per cent of USCENTCOM's requirement of supplies and equipment, 25 per cent of its requirement for POL, and 31 per cent of its requirement for munitions seem to be afloat.

Current USCENTCOM reporting does not provide statistical data on either of these possible shortfalls, but also does not highlight them as major problems. This may reflect the fact the US has steadily built up its capabilities during the 1980s, and no longer has to plan for a worst case as demanding as a Soviet invasion of Iran.[59] This same reporting indicates that the Bright Star 90 exercise was used to test the value of prepositioning and it was found to be a vital substitute for sea and airlift. This reporting also indicates that, 'We are now in the process of re-evaluating and validating our prepositioning requirements. Initial studies indicate that some prepositioning requirements can be reduced, while shortfalls exist in selected commodities.' This reporting also indicates that USCENTCOM continues to preposition about 3,000 tons of material a year, and that sustainability has improved strikingly since the mid-1980s, and continues to be improved by three major programmes. These include the Logistics Over The Shore (LOTS) programme to allow US forces to reduce their need for ports, compensate for a lack of facilities, and bypass mined areas.   The second programme is the South-West Asia Petroleum Distribution Operational Project (SWAPDOP) to provide fuel supplies in areas lacking major supplies, and the third is a series of water programmes to produce, purify, store and distribute water.[60]

At the same time, all of the issues affecting US strategic lift, prepositioning and sustainability relating to Gulf, Red Sea and Horn of Africa contingencies are currently being re-examined as the US rethinks its requirements in the post-Cold War era. On the one hand, continuing to size forces for a worst case, principally a largely unsupported defence of Iran against a Soviet invasion now seems to make little sense. On the other hand, the primary threat to the flow of oil and to friendly states in the Gulf and Red Sea area is likely to be one of the northern Gulf states, and Iraq is a major military power. Any serious contingency requiring US support of Kuwait and/or Saudi Arabia could require major amounts of strategic and intra-theatre lift, and predeployed and rear area equipment and stocks. It is unclear whether current or planned US lift and war reserves will meet such a requirement.

US Arms Transfer and Military Assistance Efforts

The US would benefit greatly if friendly nations in the Gulf and Red Sea area bought US equipment, and US forces could draw on their equipment and munitions if they deployed to their aid. However, the US has had at least one major incident in which it failed to meet the arms requests of every state in the southern Gulf. The end result has inevitably been that friendly Gulf states have turned to other suppliers whose equipment and munitions are generally not interoperable with those of US forces. Through no fault of US military planners, the US has done little to take advantage of its capability for arms transfer and military assistance efforts to improve its contingency capabilities in the region since the early 1980s - when it sold the E-3A AWACS to Saudi Arabia. The US Congress has often failed to support Presidential requests for major arms-sales, and the US has failed to be a reliable supplier to friendly Gulf states.

Some examples of the arms sales cases and aid problems that have prevented the US from making effective use of its arms transfer and military assistance capabilities include:
- Insistence in 1987-8 on Stinger buy-back arrangements when the US transferred these missiles to Bahrain, although Bahrain agreed to all US security protection arrangements and the missile requires regular US maintenance to remain militarily effective.
- Failure to sell Kuwait Stingers after Iranian air attacks on Kuwait in the mid-1980s, leading Kuwait to make massive air defence purchase from the USSR. Inability during most of the 1980s to assure Saudi Arabia that the Congress would permit a sale of US tanks to replace its obsolescent British tanks. This was followed in 1988, by an embarrassing Congressional debate over the purchase of F/A-18 fighters that forced Kuwait to agree publicly to drop Maverick missiles from the arms package that it had bought as a result of proposals by the US.
- Failure to provide Stingers to Qatar in 1987-8, which led Qatar to buy missiles Iran had seized from the Afghan Mujahidin. US demands for return of the missiles have effectively blocked military co-operation with Qatar although the missiles are no longer reliable enough to be used for most military purposes.

- Refusal to sell Saudi Arabia 40 F-15E fighters, leading Saudi Arabia to buy 72 modern Tornado fighters from Britain, and the largest single arms package ever sold. Inability during most of the 1980s to assure Saudi Arabia that the Congress would permit a sale of US tanks to replace its obsolescent AMX-30s.
- Denial of Stinger sales to the UAE after one of its oil-platforms was attacked by the Iranian Air Force. The USSR immediately sold the UAE several times more equivalent SA-14 missiles. Inability to assure the UAE during the mid-1980s that the US could obtain Congressional permission to sell US fighters, which helped lead the UAE to buy Mirage-2000 fighters from France.
- Failure to provide significant military assistance to Oman, and go beyond the limited level agreed to when the US first obtained prepositioning and contingency basing-rights following the fall of the Shah.
- Failure to keep the level of military assistance to the YAR at a significant value, virtually yielding the field to Soviet military assistance efforts in spite of the YAR's largely pro-Western politics. US aid to the YAR was $1 million in FY1988, and dropped to only $500,000 annually in FY1989 and FY1990.

The broad trends in the financing of US military assistance efforts also present serious problems. Total US military assistance to the entire area covered by USCENTCOM remained relatively constant in current dollars from the mid-1980s to 1990. US security assistance aid totalled $1,735 million in FY1985 and was $1,610 million in FY1990. Virtually all of this aid was earmarked to Egypt and Israel, however, and these countries have only a peripheral impact on Gulf and Red Sea security. As a result, US military assistance to all the other countries in the region dropped from $235 million in FY1985 to $148 million in FY1986, $65 million in FY1987, $39 million in FY1988, $14 million in FY1989, and $12 million in FY1990. This is a 95 per cent decline in US aid in current dollars and a far more substantial drop in constant dollars.[61] It is also striking that, in spite of cutbacks in Soviet personnel deployed to the region, the US had only 248 military personnel in the region in January 1990, and the USSR had 4,470.[62]

The political and military effect of these cuts in US aid has been partly deferred by the fact that, (1) many of the nations involved have nowhere else to turn to in the West or the Gulf; (2) Bahrain, Kuwait, Qatar, Saudi Arabia and the UAE finance all their own arms-purchases and military assistance needs; and (3) the impact of cuts in US training has been minimised by selective use of aid or direct funding. Nevertheless, these cuts may ultimately have a critical impact on US contingency-capabilities in the Gulf.

The impact on Oman, the Red Sea states and the Horn has been more drastic. The cuts in aid to Oman, coupled with the fall in its oil revenues, left it with very limited funds for modernisation, and may eventually produce the kind of backlash that could deprive the US of its most important staging-site and prepositioning point in the region - particularly since Mauritius and India are stepping up their campaign to persuade Britain to push the US out of Diego Garcia.[63] The cuts in US aid to the YAR have left a programme so small that the US aid programme between 1974 and 1988 only totalled two per cent of the aid the Soviet Union has provided the YAR since 1980. The MAP programme was cut another 49 per cent in FY1987, and left at that level in FY1988. This has virtually abandoned the military aid effort to the USSR.

US aid to Somalia has been cut to the level where it has virtually deprived the Somali armed forces of their ability to modernise, or even maintain existing equipment - although the degeneration of Somalia into civil war has now made any aid effort problematic. The cuts in US aid to the Sudan have been so serious that they have left the country open to Libyan and Ethiopian pressure. Cuts in aid to Kenya have left no funds for modernisation, and even basic maintenance activity has had to be cut back. In contrast, the USSR has provided over ten times as much military assistance to Ethiopia over the past ten years as the US has to Kenya, the Sudan, Djibouti, and Somalia, the four surrounding states.

The total patterns of arms sales to the USCENTCOM area reflect a similar pattern. Arms sales to the Gulf, Red Sea and Horn countries, by countries other than the US, remained relatively constant at around $12 billion annually during 1985-90. US sales were in excess of $4 billion in 1987. When the US failed to provide arms to the southern Gulf states in response to the expansion of Iranian attacks to cover the southern Gulf, however, US sales to the region dropped to a little over $2 billion in 1988 and have continued to drop since, in spite of a few major sales. US sales to the region are estimated to be below $2 billion in 1990, and US sales have dropped from around 25 per cent of all arms transfers to the region in 1987 to around 14 per cent in 1990. In contrast, Soviet sales have risen from around 24 per cent of all sales in 1985 to 42 per cent in 1990.[64]

US ability to change this situation during the 1990s will be a critical factor in improving strategic relations with friendly states, compensating for its force deployment and sustainment problems, helping to compensate for its force cuts, and ensuring contingency access to bases. The key to the problem lies almost solely, however, in changing the behaviour of the US Congress. The Carter, Reagan and Bush Administrations have fully recognised the potential value of military aid and arms transfers for nearly two decades.

US Command, Control, Communications and Intelligence Efforts

The US has a tremendous advantage over regional powers because of its ability to provide airborne regional surveillance, its vast superiority in electronic warfare and counter-measure technology, and its constantly improving ability to provide electronic and imagery intelligence on the region, and it can provide such support to its friendly as well as its own forces. These technologies give the US a major advantage in warning, tactical intelligence, targeting, damage assessment and battle management. In most cases, the US would be the only power in the region capable of looking beyond line of sight for visual or electronic devices.

The US does, however, have problems. It does not have the human intelligence resources of friendly states, or states with a long history of relations with given countries - for example, the British in Oman. Technology does not provide political intelligence, and has many shortcomings in dealing with guerrilla, insurgent and urban warfare. The US is still in the process of deciding how best to use its national technical means to support commanders in regional operations, although major improvements are now taking place.

USCENTCOM will complete installation of a new imagery receipt and processing system in FY1990 which will provide imagery intelligence results within hours of an event. A high-quality secondary imagery system, combined with the Scalable Transportable Intelligence Communications System (STICS) will move imagery and data to operational levels within minutes. The Deployable Intelligence Data Handling System (DIDHS) will also be fielded in FY1990, and will greatly increase the ability to manage, store and manipulate large amounts of intelligence information. USCENTCOM is, however, still seeking long-range RPVs to improve its tactical collection assets.[65]

The creation of effective communication-nets is also a problem. The Defence Communication System effectively stops at Turkey in the west and the Philippines in the east. There is only limited commercial capability, and it would be hopelessly inadequate in combat. The DCS system is slowly being extended into the area, and an initial operational capability was achieved in June 1987. It will be some years, however, before a fully adequate system is deployed. Fortunately, tactical satellites now are available to cover the 7,000 miles between the theatre and the US, and automated secure communications are steadily improving. Efforts are also being made to implement a new theatre-wide intelligence architecture, and deployable intelligence data handling systems will be deployed in FY1989. There have been intelligence satellite imagery processing facilities in the theatre since 1986.[66]

US Capabilities to Counter the Use of Weapons of Mass Destruction

The prospects of a regional state using biological, chemical or nuclear attacks on friendly forces and targets, or US forces, are now all too real, but the US has major regional contingency capabilities to deal with weapons of mass destruction. It has a vast superiority in nuclear weapons and the threat of US retaliation to any use of chemical and nuclear weapons is a major deterrent to the actions of any state in the region. In fact, the threat of US retaliation with chemical or nuclear weapons is likely to be the only means most friendly states and US forces have of deterring or countering the use of weapons of mass destruction.

The US also does not have to retaliate in kind and has the option of retaliating with high-technology conventional weapons. It can use surgically precise air or long-range missile attacks to destroy high-value targets using conventional warheads. Given the potential impact of such conventional attacks on key oil, power, industrial, or leadership targets, there is nothing axiomatic about a US need to escalate to weapons of mass destruction in response to the use of such weapons by a Third World state.

These US capabilities to wage a chemical, nuclear or biological war in the Gulf and Red Sea area do not mean, however, that such a war might not produce major US casualties. Medical readiness might then be a problem. USCENTCOM only had 60 per cent of the hospital beds it needed for conventional combat in FY1988, although it plans to have 95 per cent in FY1991. The readiness of medical personnel is a problem: in 1988, it was 85 per cent for active personnel and 78 per cent for reserve personnel. Only about 36 per cent of its goal for prepositioning key medical items had been met in 1987, and recent budget cuts mean this situation may have improved slowly, if at all.

These medical problems could be particularly serious in the event of chemical warfare - something that seems all too possible in the Gulf. USCENTCOM has 79 per cent of the required individual protection gear, 50 per cent of the collective protection gear, 83 per cent of the decontamination capability, and 90 per cent of the detection systems.

THE NEED FOR ACCESS TO FRIENDLY BASES AND PORTS IN THE GULF AND RED SEA AREA

The final factor shaping US power-projection capabilities in the Gulf and Red Sea area is US access to friendly bases and facilities - a factor that is shaped as much by the attitudes and plans of friendly states as by US desires and intentions. There is no doubt that most US power-projection capabilities are militarily impressive. At the same time, it is clear from the preceding analysis that the US cannot keep its forces over-the-horizon in peace-time, and not be dependent on support from friendly states in a crisis.

While US Navy carrier task-forces, US Marine Corps amphibious forces, US Army airborne forces, and USAF long-range bombers can operate without access to friendly territory, the effectiveness of all US power-projection forces will be heavily dependent upon the actions and support of friendly states in most contingencies. Naval forces need ports for repair, supply, and resupply of heavy cargo by air from the US. Marine Corps forces need ports and air bases for resupply and to provide effective air support. US Army forces are far more effective if they can deploy to friendly ports and bases and count on friendly lines of supply.

This is particularly true of US armoured forces. No matter how well the US meets USCENTCOM's evolving requirements in the 1990s, it will still take several weeks for the US to deploy the equivalent of a two-division force to the Gulf and Red Sea area, and a month to six weeks to deploy three full divisions. These forces will still be lightly armoured compared to the major powers in the northern Gulf. The US also faces the practical reality that carriers are vulnerable in Gulf and Red Sea waters, or anywhere else where they cannot operate a long-range air and missile defence screen and enemy operations can strike from nearby air-bases or the terrain-masking provided by land.

Any US effort to conduct major land-force operations will be heavily dependent on friendly local forces, and good staging-facilities. US ability to use strategic sea and air lift will be critical. This means US, strategic-lift aircraft must have free access to critical NATO and Middle Eastern staging facilities such as those in the Azores, Morocco, Egypt, and Oman. The struggle to conduct successful operations half a world away from the US will be difficult at best. These limitations on US capabilities help explain why Western access to bases and facilities in the southern Gulf could be so critical in a conflict, and why the quality of US military relations with friendly Gulf states are so important to protecting the Gulf's oil supplies.

The tactical elements of the US Air Force will be almost totally dependent on access to friendly air bases. Its effectiveness will also be heavily dependent on having sheltered, defended, well stocked and interoperable facilities with suitable C^3I/BM capabilities. Such bases now exist only in Spain, Morocco, Italy, Greece, Israel, Egypt, Turkey, Oman, and Saudi Arabia, and contingency access is uncertain and scenario-dependent.

Table 11.8 shows the full range of US contingency-bases affecting US capabilities in the region, and these capabilities are now very significant. The US spent some $1.1 billion just on military construction in the USCENTCOM area - and on en route support facilities in Morocco, Lajes, and Diego Garcia - between FY1980 and FY1988. These facilities are now virtually complete, and spending has been drastically reduced since FY1985. It dropped from a peak of around $250 million annually in FY1980-2, to less than $50 million in FY1985-8. The only major projects still underway are an Intermediate Staging Facility (ISF) in the Horn of Africa, and a Theatre War Reserve Facility (TR2). The US Army portion of these programmes was completed in FY1989, and the USAF portion will be completed in FY1991.

Yet, for all the contingency facilities listed in Table 11.8, the US only has four sets of bases or basing facilities it can use to defend the Gulf, and the only other Western bases in the entire region are the French facilities in Djibouti in the Red Sea. The US learned during Operation Ernest Will that it must rely on the additional facilities that friendly states like Bahrain, Egypt, Kuwait, Oman, Saudi Arabia and the UAE can provide in a crisis, and it seems virtually certain that any future US operation in the Gulf, the Red Sea or the Horn would be equally dependent on the availability of forward area and staging facilities from nearby states.

Table 11.8: US Military Contingency Facilities in the Near East

Base	Status
NORTH AFRICA AND STAGING POINTS	
Morocco	Total Cost of Military Construction in FY1980-8 was $58.6 million.
Slimane	Agreement signed in May 1983. A former B-47 base closed in 1963 which is now being modernised to support C-141 and C-5 operations.
Navasseur	This base or Rabat may be given similar modernisation later.

Liberia

Monrovia   Agreement signed in February 1983, to
                            allow US to make contingency use of
                            international airport for stage air
                            operations. US will fund expansion of
                            airport to allow use of C-5s, C-17s, and
                            C-141s.

Portugal

Lajes   Negotiations were completed in 1983-4 to
                            keep Lajes as a major air staging-point
                            for US air movements. The fuel, runway
                            and other facilities at this base in the
                            Azores are being upgraded. The total
                            cost of military construction in FY1980-8
                            was $66.6 million.

EASTERN MEDITERRANEAN AND RED SEA AREA

Egypt

Suez Canal   The US has been granted tacit permission
                            to move warships through the Canal.

Cairo West   The US shares an unnamed air base with
                            Egypt, and normally deploys about 100 men
                            on the base. It has been used for joint
                            F-15 and E-3A AWACS operations.

Ras Banas   Still under negotiation. Ras Banas would
                            provide basing capabilities for C-5
                            aircraft, and for unloading and transit
                            of SL-7 and other fast sea-lift ships.

Djibouti   Access agreement and arrangements with
                            French allow port calls and access to
                            maritime patrol aircraft.

Turkey

Mus   The US has informal arrangements to use
Batman   three Turkish air bases near the Soviet
Erzurum   border, Iran and Iraq. These are NATO
                            bases and are being funded to allow the
                            deployment of US heavy lift aircraft and
                            fighters.

GULF AND RED SEA

Diego Garcia	Used through a long-term 50-year lease from the UK signed in 1965. The base provides 12,000-foot runways and facilities suitable for B-52 and heavy airlift facilities, and is where seven US prepositioning ships in the Gulf are now deployed. The total cost of military construction in FY1980-8 was $542.9 million.
Seychelles	Satellite tracking and communications base with NASA and air force personnel.

Kenya

Mombasa	Provides a potential staging-point, maintenance facilities, and port call. Access agreement signed in mid-1970s.
Nanyuki Airport	Facility expansion programme completed in 1983. The total cost of military construction in FY1980-8 was $66.6 million.
Kenya Naval base	US spent $30-million dredging harbour to allow it to be used for carrier port-calls.

Somalia

Mogadishu Airport	Staging facilities for US air and sea movements. Limited repair capability. Expansion completed in 1983. The total cost of military construction in FY1980-8 was $24.4 million.
Berbera	Somalia is 1,400 miles from the Gulf and facilities could be used for sea control and intermediate staging. Its use is increasingly uncertain because of the growing civil war in the country.

Oman	Total Cost of Military Construction in FY1980-8 was $270.3 million.
Khasab	Small air-base in the Musandam Peninsula near Goat Island and Strait of Hormuz.

	Limited contingency capability. Largely suited for small maritime patrol aircraft.
Masira	Island has been expanded to a major $170 million air and naval staging-point, with limited deployment of prepositioning ships. Some $121 million worth of equipment is prepositioned, including food, trucks, air-traffic electronics, artillery shells, and air-to-air missiles.
Thumrait & Sib Air bases	Contingency air-base facilities. Used by US maritime patrol aircraft during Operation Ernest Will.
Saudi Arabia	No formal basing agreements, but the US has deployed F-15s, KC-10 and KC-135 tankers, and E-3As to Saudi air bases in emergencies, and operates E-3As from Riyadh and Dhahran. All Saudi major air-bases have the sheltering and facilities to accept extensive US air reinforcements and/or support US deployment of heavy-lift aircraft. Saudi Arabia and Bahrain have also supported the US 'barge base' called Hercules that the US has used as a forward staging-base in the Gulf since 1987.[67]
Bahrain	US Middle East Force deploys in Bahrain, although formal agreement has lapsed. A 65-man US support unit is present. The US has spent $2.6 million on military construction. In addition to port and airfield facilities, Bahrain provides extensive petroleum storage facilities.

Source: Adapted from Antony H. Cordesman, *The Gulf and the West* (Westview, Boulder, 1989), pp. 137-41.

The main factor limiting US operations in the region is that the only permanent fully active Western base in the Indian Ocean and Gulf area is on the British island of Diego Garcia in the southern Indian Ocean - which the US now leases from Britain and where the US now prepositions much of

USCENTCOM's equipment. This base is so far to the south, however, that it is nearly as far away from the key strategic areas in the upper Gulf as is Dublin, Ireland. The US is also helping Turkey strengthen its bases in eastern Turkey, but Turkey has firmly stated that it will not provide contingency bases for USCENTCOM, and that it must make defence of its territory against the USSR its primary concern. The bases in Turkey are also useful primarily for contingencies involving a Soviet invasion of northern Iran.

The US has contingency bases in Oman - the one Gulf state whose internal and external politics allow it to grant such facilities with minimal risk to its security. Oman provides important staging-facilities on the island of Masira, allows the US to fly maritime patrol aircraft from its soil, and has supported contingency arrangements to allow US tankers to stage out of Omani airfields and refuel US carrier aircraft flying from the Indian Ocean. Oman, however, is too far east to allow US forces to defend most of the Gulf oilfields and key oil-nations like Kuwait efficiently.

The US also has *de facto* access to Bahrain for a number of contingency purposes. The US Middle East Force is home-ported in Bahrain, and there is a small USCENTCOM headquarters on a ship in this force. Bahrain's willingness to allow the US to use its facilities was important during the US intervention in the Gulf during Operation Ernest Will, and Bahrain provided important support and repair capabilities for the US Navy during its operations in the Gulf.

Bahrain agreed to provide large fuel storage facilities, and some prepositioning facilities. It also allowed US personnel and military cargoes to transit into the Gulf via its international airport during Operation Ernest Will, and allowed relatively free use of its ports and anchorages by US naval forces. It also allowed the US to deploy a large barge called the Hercules just outside its territorial waters. This barge acted as a base for Task Force 18, and provided a location for special forces, attack helicopters, radars, air defences, and intelligence-sensors during the crisis in the Gulf in 1987 and 1988. The helicopters on the barge included the OH-58D, a configuration of the OH-58 which was rapidly created in the mid-1980s for use in the Gulf, and which has improved night-vision, 2.75' rocket pods, and can carry pods with Hellfire air-to-surface missiles, Stinger anti-air missiles and .50-calibre machine guns.[68]   The barge also contained an underwater breathing bottle, and 30-foot caving ladders - light aluminium roll-up ladders that can be suspended below a helicopter for use in picking up downed crews. Nevertheless, Bahrain is a small and divided state. It cannot base or support large air or land forces and it is vulnerable in both political and military terms.[69]

Kuwait could base a substantial number of US troops or aircraft, but it has no strategic depth, and its air, naval and co-operable support facilities are acutely limited if the US should have to deploy for a low-level war involving Iran or Iraq. It would take several weeks to build up enough US forces in Kuwait to sustain large numbers of combat sorties or deploy land troops to help Kuwait defend its territory.

Kuwait did agree to allow the US to deploy equipment to protect it from Iranian Silkworm attacks and small elements to support its tanker escort effort in late 1987. Kuwait has also bought F/A-18 aircraft and US air munitions, and this indicates that Kuwait might accept larger US forces in the face of an immediate threat to Kuwait. Nevertheless, Kuwait is in a highly vulnerable position in terms of any threat from the northern Gulf states, and has recently bought large numbers of Yugoslav copies of Soviet T-72 tanks and Soviet armour - systems US forces cannot operate. Any US deployment to Kuwait, except in the face of a direct and publicly apparent threat to Kuwait's security, would make it highly vulnerable to political attacks from radical Islamic states and Arab political movements. Kuwait might well accept deployment of US forces in an absolute emergency, but only for its national defence. Even if it did, it might well delay until US reinforcements would find it impossible to deploy sufficient forces in time, and the US would need other bases in the region to secure its access to the Gulf in virtually any contingency - including an attempt to defend Kuwait.

All of these factors make Western access to Saudi bases like the ones at Dhahran and Hafr al-Batin critical in any major defence of the Gulf against a threat from Iran, Iraq or the USSR. In fact, USCENTCOM probably cannot function in its most critical contingency-roles without Saudi co-operation and wartime access to Saudi bases and facilities. While Diego Garcia, Djibouti, Turkey and Egypt provide useful contingency-facilities on the periphery of the Gulf and lower Red Sea, they cannot make up for the range and reinforcement problems the West would face in defending its critical oil-facilities in the upper and central Gulf.

Saudi Arabia has never formally agreed to provide the US with contingency bases. The politics of the Gulf preclude Saudi Arabia from overtly granting base-facilities without a clear and immediate threat. It would be accused of neo-colonialism, of supporting an ally of Israel, and of having brought Superpower confrontation into the region. Saudi Arabia has, however, quietly consulted US defence planners and senior USCENTCOM officers regarding US use of Saudi facilities in an emergency, and it has made USCENTCOM over-the-horizon reinforcement capabilities one of the mainstays of its defence planning.

Saudi Arabia has, however, sought US deployments in past contingencies, and these have recently included detachments of US minesweeping forces, USAF F-15s, and USAF E-3A AWACS aircraft. Saudi Arabia still has US E-3A AWACS aircraft deployed on its soil which were first requested early in the Iran-Iraq war, and a small USAF detachment operates in a joint headquarters at Dhahran, and shares data on developments in the Gulf, as it did on the Iran-Iraq war.

The Saudi Air Force's past reliance on US equipment has also given it some capability to conduct joint operations with US forces, to support USAF reinforcements, and to provide C³I and support facilities. The Saudi Air Force now operates 57 F-15C/Ds, and nearly 114 F-5E/Fs and RF-5Es. It uses US training and maintenance standards, and many Saudi squadrons now approach USAF proficiency and qualification levels. Saudi Arabia also has the largest and most modern air-bases in the Middle East, with bases in the Gulf (Riyadh, Dhahran, and dispersal facilities at Hafr al-Batin), and in the Red Sea area (Ta'if, Khamis Mushait, Sharura, Jeddah, and Tabuk).[70]

These air bases have extensive shelter-facilities, and those in the Gulf and lower Red Sea areas are equipped to support US-made F-15 and F-5 aircraft. They are also defended with Hawk missiles, and will soon have the new Peace Shield command, control, communications, and intelligence (C³I), and air control and warning (AC&W) system using US E-3A AWACS aircraft and advanced ground radars and electronics. Large amounts of US air power could deploy to these bases in 48-72 hours, and operate over virtually any areas in the Gulf or lower Red Sea. Such Saudi air facilities could base up to two wings of USAF fighters, and give them full munitions and service support. The US still has large numbers of contract personnel servicing Saudi equipment in the air force, army, National Guard, and navy, and large numbers of Saudi military and civilian personnel have had US training and can operate with, or support and service, US military equipment.

Further, the US experience in deploying naval forces to the Gulf during Operation Ernest Will showed that Saudi bases are located in areas where US carriers cannot operate their aircraft effectively without moving into the Gulf. The Gulf is a highly vulnerable area for such operations. Hostile states like Iran have anti-ship Harpoon missiles and can launch suicide air-attacks with only limited warning, and Soviet attack fighters and bombers can launch air-to-ship missiles after taking advantage of the terrain-masking provided by the mountains in Iran and with far less chance of detection than in the open sea.

Saudi Arabia has equally modern naval facilities and ground bases. These bases have extensive stocks of parts and munitions, and service and support equipment, which can be used by USCENTCOM forces. The Saudi base at Hafr al-Batin (which is located in the critical border area near Kuwait and Iraq) will also have two full brigades equipped with US armour.[71] Saudi army and naval bases have some of the most sophisticated infrastructure and service facilities in the world, and can both speed the deployment of US forces and make them more effective once they arrive.

THE IMPLICATIONS OF GIVEN TYPES OF FUTURE CONFLICTS

US strategic objectives in the Gulf, the Red Sea and the Horn are clear: they are to ensure the flow of oil and trade, to maintain regional stability and the security of friendly states, to ensure the safety of American citizens, and to ensure no local or outside power dominates the region. There is little point, however, in examining all of the possible contingencies which might require the US to project power to the area to ensure that these strategic objectives are met. The previous analysis has shown that US power-projection capabilities are fully capable of coping with limited missions like establishing military presence, limited-intensity conflict, minor engagements at sea, and the host of other low and medium intensity crises and conflicts that characterise most uses of military force in the real world. It has also shown that these US contingency-capabilities are likely to remain high through the 1990s, and to be limited more by the particular regional political conditions affecting a given crisis than by US military capabilities.

The key issue from a military viewpoint is the limits the US would face in projecting power in a medium or high intensity conflict, and how US capabilities are likely to change in the near term - the only length of time for which anyone can now make reasonable predictions. Once again, the particular political circumstances shaping a given crisis are likely to be at least as important as military factors, and history has shown with grim regularity that such political circumstances tend to be highly unpredictable. Nevertheless, there are several 'worst case' military scenarios that - regardless of their political realism - illustrate the strengths and limits of US power-projection capabilities.

Case One: A Major Popular Revolution

The US has ample military capability to help any state in the region to deal with a military *coup* unless the *coup* seizes and consolidates power within 24-48 hours, to deal with any level of border incident with the exception of the Iraqi-Kuwaiti border area, and to deal with foreign-supported insurgency. It is important to note, however, that the US could not and would not save any regional ruler from a popular revolution or his own people. Managing political evolution in a way that ensures the rights of the people in any given country, and their economic well-being, is a task for local regimes and one where they must be successful on their own to survive.

Regardless of how hostile a revolutionary movement may be to the West, the whole pattern of political change in the region - including the fall of the Shah of Iran - demonstrates that it is pointless for an outside power to try to intervene militarily when a ruler or ruling elite cannot maintain a reasonable level of popular support and legitimacy. Even assuming that the US could help such a ruler regain control of a capital or some part of his territory, the resulting military victory would be pointless, and simply hurt American interests in the long run. Even the most oil-rich state will soon resume exports after a revolution and Iran and Libya's conduct over the last decade has shown that oil has no ideology, only a price tag. Finally, the improvements in US and Soviet relations are reducing the risk that revolutionary movements will align themselves militarily with a hostile outside power, and have already reduced the US incentive for military action in any kind of internal struggle for power.

Case Two: A Major Arab-Israeli Conflict

There is little serious prospect of a major Arab-Israeli conflict that requires US military intervention. Syria's attempt to achieve parity with Israel virtually collapsed during 1988-90, and it now has the shell of an offensive force without the resources to provide the training, sustainability, or modernisation to support anything like its present forces. Soviet modernisation of the Syrian Air Force and Syrian surface-to-air missile defences have not kept pace with the advances in Israeli military capabilities, and Syria is more vulnerable today that it was in 1982.

The main risk that could occur in an Arab-Israeli conflict would be that a war might spread to include Iraq and/or weapons of mass destruction. In the event such a war remained conventional, Israel could almost certainly cope with the resulting land and air threat, and could count on massive US military resupply in a matter of days. US ability to deploy large amounts of military equipment rapidly has improved strikingly since 1973. At the same time, the US would not support Israel in any offensive operations against an Arab state and would immediately seek to reach a cease-fire.

The use of weapons of mass destruction would be a different story. Assuming a successful first strike against Israel, the US would almost certainly deploy its carrier and power-projection forces to support Israel and threaten immediate retaliation of some kind against the power involved. The same, incidentally, would be true of any such Libyan attack on Egypt or any similar use of weapons of mass destruction against a close friend or ally of the US.

In the case of Israel, however, such a contingency is unlikely. It is much more likely that if Israel believed it was about to be attacked with weapons of mass destruction, it would pre-empt this by using nuclear weapons to attack and destroy the military forces of the attacking state. It is extremely unlikely that the US would be consulted or have time to intervene. If a state like Syria or Iraq did succeed in using such weapons to produce significant Israeli casualties, or on an Israeli population centre, it is likely that Israel would retaliate by destroying all the major population centres of the attacking state. Such a scenario would be an unmitigated disaster for the entire region, but it is one where the US is much more likely to find itself attempting to create a cease-fire and involved in using its power-projection capabilities for aid purposes, than in military conflict.

Case Three: A Soviet Invasion of Iran

No one can reject the possibility of a clash between US and Soviet interests in the region, or even a limited clash between US and Soviet forces. Such contingencies, however, now seem unlikely. Both powers will probably continue to jockey for influence, and to use arms transfers and aid as a means of achieving it. They have little real reason, however, to take sides in regional quarrels - particularly to the extent of aiding any state or outside political movement to seize control of another state by force.

In many ways, US and Soviet interests begin to coincide the moment that the USSR ceases to try to enforce a political system on the region. No method of allocating oil can be more effective than the market, and any outside effort to seize the oil resources in the region would lead to an endless guerrilla war. The US has no reason to want to see minor ethnic mini-states emerge out of the republics in the southern USSR as long as the USSR continues its democratic and economic reforms. The creation of such mini-states would be virtually certain to lead to major ethnic conflicts and abuses of human rights. Similarly, neither the US nor the USSR has any reason to want to see regional boundaries changed by force, or to see new examples of the kind of 'institutionalised' civil war that is taking place in Ethiopia, Somalia and the Sudan. Both powers have strong incentives to seek ways to end the growing proliferation of weapons of mass destruction.

The most likely reason that a military clash could occur between the US and the USSR under these circumstances would be if regional states or factions dragged the Superpowers into regional quarrels under conditions that got out of control for reasons beyond the control of the US and USSR. Such contingencies seem unlikely, particularly given the low strategic value of having a given side win most such quarrels. If they did occur, however, the US would have a significant military advantage in every contingency except a major conflict in the northern Gulf - always depending on the balance of local forces.

The worst case example of such a northern Gulf contingency is a Soviet invasion of Iran. This was the key planning scenario that the US used in shaping USCENTCOM during the early and mid-1980s.[72] The US has not, however, regarded such a contingency as a serious risk since the mid-1980s, and no longer shapes its forces to deal with such a case. US planners feel that the Soviet experience in Afghanistan persuaded the USSR that such an invasion would be a political and military disaster long before ethnic unrest in the southern USSR made such a contingency seem even more unlikely. If such an invasion did occur, the US would be far more likely to respond by providing the kind of support for local forces provided to the Afghan Mujahidin than to try to meet Soviet forces in a major conflict near the Soviet border.

Case Four: An Iraqi Attack on Kuwait[73]

The true strengths and weaknesses of US power-projection capabilities become clearer from a review of another worst case: an Iraqi attack on Kuwait. Kuwait is militarily the most vulnerable of all the Gulf states. Kuwait is a small state with vast oil wealth and limited forces, and whose territory offers Iraq greatly improved potential access to the Gulf. Its two northern islands - Bubiyan and Warba - block Iraq's access to the Gulf out of Umm Qasr.

While Iraq has not openly threatened Kuwait in recent years, Iraq has made repeated attempts to acquire Bubiyan and

Warba and to improve its access to Gulf since the late 1960s. Iraq made new attempts to obtain or lease the islands in 1984, and even sent troops across the border. This border incursion led to a sudden visit to Baghdad by Kuwaiti Prime Minister Sa'd Al Sabah on 10-13 November 1984. This visit seems to have resulted in a substantial aid-payment by Kuwait to Iraq, and Iraq limited itself to creating a hovercraft base across the river from Warba.[74]

Iraq has not made any overt threats since the cease-fire in the Iran-Iraq war, but it has put considerable political pressure on Kuwait to at least grant it a channel it can use to move warships freely from Umm Qasr to the Gulf. In any case - if one considers military capabilities, rather than political intentions - Iraq could almost certainly seize Kuwait in a matter of days unless Kuwait sought immediate American military support. In spite of the rhetoric surrounding the Gulf Co-operation Council, and the forces at Hafr al-Batin, Kuwait would be forced to try to defend its territory with little more than its own land-forces. Yet, Kuwait has a total military manning of only 20,300 men. It lacks the forces to defend its two northern islands - Bubiyan and Warba - which block Iraq's access to the Gulf out of Umm Qasr. Kuwait has only one significant defensive barrier - the Mutla' Ridge just north of Kuwait Bay and Kuwait City. This position can be flanked by an armoured attack to the west and does not effectively shield Kuwait's main air-base at Ali al-Salim.

Iraq could overwhelm such defensive positions in a matter of days with two corps of two to three divisions, and could simultaneously send in its elite Republican Guard forces to occupy Bubiyan and Warba with an amphibious attack. Once Iraq took Kuwait, Iraqi forces could go even further. Iraqi armoured units would be able to move rapidly down the eastern coast of Saudi Arabia and occupy the key oilfields and facilities in Saudi Arabia's Eastern Province. Neither Kuwait nor Saudi Arabia now have the armoured strength, or forward deployed forces, to check an all-out Iraqi attack without external support.

The key shortfalls in Kuwaiti capabilities would lie in armour and anti-armour capability, airpower and air defence. Kuwait's 16,000-man army now has only one mechanised division (with two armoured and one mechanised brigades), which is based north of Kuwait city, and a FROG and headquarters unit based at al-Jahra. The army has a total of 245 operational tanks, which are a mix of 143 Chieftain, 70 Vickers, and some obsolete Centurion tanks.[75] It has 50 BMP-2 armoured fighting vehicles, some AMX-13s, 90 Ferrets, Some V-150s, and about 280 other armoured personnel-carriers, with a mix of M-113s and Saracens. Its artillery consists of a mix of 36 155mm M-109 self-propelled howitzers, 40 AMX-F-3 towed 155mm howitzers, 16 105mm M-101 towed howitzers, 60 122mm towed guns and 12 FROG rocket-launchers. This mix of equipment badly needs upgrading and standardisation. Kuwait needs a modern main battle tank, and a major increase in artillery fire-power, to offset the advantage its neighbours have in weapons numbers.

Kuwait is actively examining options to buy new tanks from the US, USSR, Brazil and Western Europe, and the possible purchase of the MLRS multiple rocket system from the US.[76] It is also reported to have ordered 245 BMP-2s from the USSR, and 200 M-84 Yugoslav tanks (a T-72 variant with 125mm guns), although such reports are uncertain, and Kuwait has been slow to implement many of its past procurement plans.[77] In any case, it is unclear how Kuwait can build up a force of more than one true division equivalent unless it introduces true universal military service, and Kuwait's army is already heavily dependent on foreign contract personnel for service support and logistic functions and has limited to moderate military effectiveness.

Kuwait has bought a wide range of anti-tank guided weapons, including the AT-4, BGM-71A Improved TOW, HOT, M-47 Dragon, and Vigilant, and it has 56 M-901 ITV armoured TOW carriers. It has 4,000 Improved TOW missiles on order. Kuwait also has 84mm Carl Gustav rocket launchers and 24 106mm recoilless rifles. This is a good mix of anti-tank weapons, but the Kuwaiti Army training and support effort to use such weapons is of only mediocre quality and they cannot be used as a force multiplier to compensate for Kuwait's lack of tanks.

Accordingly, Kuwait would need all of the US land force and air capabilities it could absorb to deal with an Iraqi invasion. In the case of land forces, the key issue would be strategic warning and the amount of support the US and Kuwait could get from Saudi Arabia. The US would need at least two weeks in which to deploy several divisions in support of Kuwait, and to deploy air units with all the munitions and stocks it needs, and to improve Kuwait's air and missile defences. It also would benefit greatly if it could stage out of Saudi and Bahraini ports and air bases, and make use of the facilities, stocks, and equipment that Saudi Arabia has at Hafr al-Batin.

Kuwait would require massive air reinforcement from the US - a level of reinforcement that would present major problems even with strategic warning. Kuwait's two air-bases, at Ahmad al-Jabir and Ali al-Salim, would be difficult to defend from armoured attack and are not designed and equipped to support massive reinforcement by other countries. Hafr al-Batin does not have a major operating air-base, and there is no other major and well sheltered air-base in the area just south of Kuwait.

Kuwait's 2,200-man air force is slowly improving in effectiveness, and it now has 70 combat aircraft and 18 armed helicopters. It has 24 A-4KU/TA-4KU attack fighters in combat-ready service. The air force does not, however, have any aircraft which are now in service with US forces, and is experiencing problems with its 34 Mirage F-1BK/CK fighters. The Mirage F-1 aircraft have proved hard to maintain, Kuwait has lost several of the aircraft to accidents, and the 55-kilometre air-intercept range of their radars has proved too short to meet Kuwait's operational needs. This has led Kuwait to discuss replacing them with Mirage 2000s with France, but there is no indication of such an order.[78] Kuwait is now forced to use its A-4 attack aircraft in the combat air patrol role when it needs to create an air defence screen.

This situation will change in the early 1990s. Kuwait ordered 40 US F/A-18 fighters in July 1985, at a cost of $1.9 billion. This sale will also include 120 AIM-9 Sidewinder air-to-air missiles, 200 AIM-4 Sparrows, 40 AGM-84 Harpoon anti-ship missiles, and 300 Maverick AGM-65G anti-ship/anti-hard point missiles.[79] This US sale only came after a bitter fight between the Reagan Administration and Congress. Not only did the sale come close enough to collapse for the USSR seriously to offer Kuwait the MIG-29, but in order for the Administration to win approval of the sale, Kuwait had to give up its effort to order 200 IR Maverick AGM-65D anti-tank missiles, agree to base the F/A-18s only in Kuwait, not to acquire a refuelling capability and to exchange one A-4KU for every F/A-18 delivered to Kuwait. It also has to accept a slow delivery schedule: the F/A-18s will only begin delivery in January 1992, and Kuwait will not receive its full active strength of 28 fighters and eight fighter-trainers until June 1993. Its remaining four F/A-18s, which will act as an attrition reserve, will only be delivered after 1994.[80]

Even so, the US sale of the F-18 will eventually give Kuwait an advanced air-defence/air-attack fighter, and advanced munitions and support facilities which are standardised with those used by the US Navy and US Marines. The F/A-18 sale will significantly improve US ability to provide Kuwait with over-the-horizon reinforcements.[81]

The US could also immediately deploy the kind of AWACS and maritime patrol capability Kuwait now lacks. Kuwait's capabilities now consist of the Westinghouse Low Altitude Surveillance System (a modified AN/TPS-63 radar suspended from aerostats) and its system is not fully integrated into the C^{3}I system of any other Gulf state. Kuwait does benefit from data exchanges with Saudi E-3As, but the quality of the data links between them and Kuwait's French-designed KFAD air control and warning system is uncertain. It is far from clear that the Kuwaiti Air Force can react quickly and effectively enough to deal with Iranian or Iraqi intruders into Kuwait's air space.[82]

Further, the US could rapidly deploy improved army and air force land-based air defences. Kuwait now has too many diverse types of air-defence weapons, and poor training in operating them. Like all the southern Gulf countries, it suffers badly from the lack of an integrated system or belt, and from efforts to standardise training and support around a common system of weapons, sensors and command centres. Kuwait's Air Force does, however, already have 12-24 US-supplied Improved Hawk surface-to-air missile launchers, and these are organised into six batteries with two launchers each in three sites surrounding Kuwait City, and three SA-8 surface-to-air missile batteries. In an emergency, the US could make the IHawk units fully effective in a matter of days.

As for other threats, Kuwait lacks significant naval capabilities, and cannot defend itself against direct naval attacks, anti-ship missile attacks, or mine warfare. It has created a 2,100-man naval force to replace its coast guard, and has two battalions of naval commandoes.[83] The navy is based at Kuwait City and Ra's al-Qulaica and its core consists of eight Lurssen guided-missile patrol-boats. Two of these boats are FPB-57s, and six are TNC-45s - which have 76mm OTO Melara guns, twin

40-mm guns, and four Exocet MM-40 missile launchers each.[84] These patrol boats have some important limitations common to virtually all GCC naval vessels. They lack air-defence capability, and while their voice communications are good, they cannot be integrated into a data-link exchange network.[85] Kuwait received four 55-metre South Korean missile patrol boats in August 1987, and these are based in Kuwait's offshore islands. They have anti-ship missiles, helicopter pads and a hovercraft docking facility. The ships are not fully combat-ready, but increase Kuwait's shallow-water defence capability. With limited strategic warning, the US could deploy the kind of air power necessary to ensure that Iraq could not use assault craft and small craft to seize Bubiyan and Warba and to halt any action like a mining of Kuwaiti waters.

In spite of its lack of ability to deploy major amounts of armoured forces, this mix of US capabilities indicates that the US could probably deploy enough force to deter an Iraqi invasion if it had enough strategic warning and access to the facilities of Saudi Arabia and Bahrain. US success in an all-out military confrontation with Iraq would be more uncertain. With sufficient time to deploy, the US could probably dominate the sea and air, but would have major problems in dealing with a massive Iraqi armoured attack. Much would depend on the result of a major conflict between advanced anti-armour systems like the AH-64, A-10, and TOW and Iraqi Soviet-supplied armour - a type of engagement that has never been fought previously. The balance of US-Kuwaiti and Iraqi capabilities would be radically different, however, if Kuwait buys the M-1 tank and M-2 Infantry Fighting Vehicle. This would effectively give the US the option of drawing on prepositioned equipment.

If Iraq launched an all-out surprise attack, the US would face a far more drastic situation. It might well be limited to securing the western border of Saudi Arabia and hoping that political negotiations would lead to an Iraqi withdrawal. The US would, however, have the option of 'horizontal escalation'. Unlike Iran, the US can sharply reduce or halt Iraqi oil exports for an extended period using limited numbers of conventional cruise missiles, and do so within hours or days after it deploys the necessary ships. Its strategic bomber forces offer a similar set of options, and Iraq would find it difficult to escalate without losing much of the value of its intended conquest. Such an option is scarcely desirable, or without risk, but it does exist.

THE FUTURE IMPACT OF US POWER-PROJECTION CAPABILITIES ON THE GULF, THE RED SEA AND THE HORN

Political analysts and regional experts tend to be impatient with the details of military force. Unfortunately, the 'devil' really does lie in such 'details'. In the real world, strategy and political intentions are only part of the story. It is the ability to deploy given kinds of military force in a given time that determine whether a given nation can deal with a given contingency. The post-war history of the US has also shown US planners that they cannot shape their power-projection forces for a narrow range of the most probable contingencies, count on political or strategic warning, or rely on time-consuming deployments from the US as substitute for forward deployments and a rapid deployment capability. It has shown them that they must develop regional and global flexibility, and they must do so in a way which takes account of political and budget constraints, as well as military effectiveness.

The end result of these lessons is the mix of evolving US power-projection capabilities discussed earlier. These capabilities are not tailored to any one contingency, and offer great flexibility in dealing with limited to medium intensity conflicts. At the same time, the term 'Superpower' is highly misleading. The US remains dependent on the support of friendly states. It cannot act as a regional policeman or force an end to many regional conflicts. It neither has the capability nor the desire to prevent political change, although it can help ensure that such change has popular legitimacy and is not the result of a *coup* or the outside use of force.

For all its 'Superpower status', the US is also more likely to be driven by local political conditions than to shape the situation with military force. It will always have to react to the political conditions shaping particular crises and shape its use of military force accordingly. At the same time, the events of 1987 and 1988 have shown just how real and immediate the need for the unique character of American power-projection capabilities capabilities can be. In an ideal world, the region might not have any need of such outside military capabilities, but such an ideal world now seems just about as probable as the end of history.

Notes

1   *Washington Post*, 7 May 1990, p. 1.
2   *Washington Post*, 19 May 1990, p. 1; *New York Times*, 20 May 1990, p. 1.
3   The new nation will have 13 million people (10 million coming from the YAR) and be the poorest state in Arabia. The President will be General Ali Abdullah Salih, the former President of the YAR. The Prime Minister will be Haidar al-Attas, the former President of the PDRY. The political capital will be San'a' and the economic capital will be Aden. Approximately two million Yemenis work abroad. *The Economist*, 26 May 1990, p. 45.
4   General H. Norman Schwarzkopf, 'Witness Statement before the Senate Armed Services Committee' (USCENTCOM, Washington, D.C., 8 Feb. 1990), p. 9.
5   *Jane's Defence Weekly*, 31 March 1990, pp. 588-90; 'Statement and Testimony of the Director of the Central Intelligence Agency, William H. Webster, before the Senate Armed Services Committee', 23 Jan. 1990; and telephone conversation with US Department of Energy, International Affairs.
6   The defence expenditure and arms-transfer data shown in Table 11.1 represent estimates by the CIA, as reported in the US Arms Control and Disarmament Agency (ACDA) document, *World Military Expenditures and Arms Transfers, 1989* (GPO, Washington, 1989). These data are generally more accurate than those produced by the IISS and SIPRI, but have several important uncertainties. They do not reflect loans or off-budget accounts. The Gulf states have very large accounts based on oil revenues that do not show up on central government budgets. Several countries, particularly Iraq and Saudi Arabia, have massive military debts that do not appear in ordinary government reporting. The total Iraqi war debt, for example, is often reported as equalling $60 billion, although much of this went to civil expenditures and is drawn from loans by southern Gulf states that are unlikely ever to be repaid. The arms-import data represent the estimated dollar-value of actual imports and not orders or the prices actually paid.
7   The flow of oil revenues has generally been the key factor setting a cap on Gulf state military and arms expenditures. Total OPEC oil revenues rose from $20 billion in 1973 to nearly $220 billion in 1980, and then fell to $60 billion in 1986, as world demand fell and OPEC developed a net surplus. World demand for oil has increased at roughly 2% annually since the collapse of world oil-prices in 1986, and OPEC now produces about 21-2 million b/d. Many projections indicate that demand will rise to the point where OPEC will need to produce about 33 million b/d in the mid-1990s, which could lead to major price-rises. Such predictions have, however, been made for years and prices have not risen to anything like the level

predicted. (*A Survey of the Arab World*, (*The Economist* Publications, 12 May 1990), pp. 17-18.)

The oil revenue patterns of the Gulf states are shown in Table 11.9. They provide a good picture of each state's relative buying-power.

Table 11.9: Petroleum Exports Income for Selected Middle Eastern Countries: 1980-1988[a] (In billions of nominal dollars)

Country	1980	1984	1985	1986	1987	1988
Bahrain[b]	1.2	1.2	1.1	0.8	0.7	0.7
Iran	13.3	12.3	13.1	7.2[e]	10.5[e]	8.2[e]
Iraq	26.3	9.4	10.7	6.9	11.4[e]	11.0[e]
Kuwait	17.7	10.7	9.8	6.4	7.5	6.3
Oman[c]	3.0	3.7	4.3	2.7	3.3	2.8
Qatar	5.4	4.4	3.1	1.7	1.8[e]	1.7[e]
Saudi Arabia	105.8	34.2	24.2	17.0	19.3	20.5[e]
U.A.E.	19.6	13.0	11.8	7.4	8.7[e]	7.4[e]

Notes: (a) Estimates provided by Dario Scuka, Congressional Research Service, 15 March 1990.

(b) Revenue from total exports. Bahrain relies heavily on imports, notably from Saudi Arabia. Bahrain is not a member of OPEC.

(c) Estimates are calculated by the Congressional Research Service and are drawn from CIA un- classified data.

e = estimate.

8   'Statement of Rear Admiral Thomas Brooks, US Navy, Director of Naval Intelligence, before the Seapower, Strategic, and Critical Materials Subcommittee of the House Armed Services Committee on Intelligence Issues', 14 March 1990; and US Navy briefing, May 1990.

9   US Navy briefing, May 1990.

10   Estimates differ, but various press reports indicate such countries may include Argentina, Brazil, Egypt, India, Iran, Iraq, Israel, Libya, Pakistan, North Korea, South Africa, South Korea and Taiwan.

11   USCENTCOM was originally formed in March 1980, and was called the Rapid Deployment Joint Task Force (RDJTF). The RDJTF was redesignated as USCENTCOM in January 1983.

12   Adam B. Siegel, 'The Use of Naval Forces in the Post-War Era: US Navy and US Marine Corps Crisis Response Activity, 1946-1989' (Centre For Naval Analysis Paper 90-0355, Alexandria, Virginia, 22 Feb. 1990).

13   The US Army and US Air Force both note that the Siegel study is oriented primarily towards the study of seapower and involves some very low level or demonstrative uses of force. For example, the CNA figures do not include crisis-related deployment of army MTTs, communications teams, etc.

14   US Navy briefing, May 1990.

15   The US has a goal of keeping an average of 50.5% of the fleet deployed. The present 44% compares with 56.6% during the fall of the Shah of Iran in 1989, 58.6% during the Lebanon crisis in 1980, 55.5% during the Nicaragua crisis in 1983, 60% during the invasion of Grenada in 1984, 50% during the

US strike on Libya in 1985, and 54% during the Persian Gulf crisis in 1987-8.

16   *New York Times*, 22 May 1990, p. 1.

17   A great deal of confusion surrounds the use of the word carrier. Some US amphibious ships are counted as carriers by foreign sources although they have no catapults, and cannot sustain either air-defence or air-offensive operations. These ships are designed to carry amphibious forces and ships. They do not have the catapults necessary to launch fixed-wing US fighters, or the arresting-gear necessary to land them. They can carry and launch a small number of US Marine Corps AV-8B VSTOL fighters, but are not designed to serve as a platform for such fighters in any form of extended combat. From a US perspective, a true carrier must be able to launch and land fully modern fixed-wing fighters in all weathers and regardless of wind speed. No current NATO allied, Soviet, or Third World carrier can do this. The best are limited to VSTOL fighters or 1960s generation fighters. The USSR may have up to three such carriers in trials or planned for construction. The new French carrier, the De Gaulle, will approach such capabilities, but will be too small and too slow to provide all of the operational capability the US requires in a carrier.

18   Bahrain has the Exocet; Egypt has the Otomat, Harpoon, and SS-N-2; Ethiopia has the SS-N-2; India has the SS-N-2, SSC-3, SS-N-7, and Sea Eagle; Iran has the Harpoon, Sea Killer, and HY-2 Silkworm; Iraq has the Exocet, SS-N-2, and HY-2 Silkworm; Israel has the Gabriel and Harpoon; Kenya has the Gabriel and Otomat; Kuwait has the Exocet; Oman has the Exocet; Qatar has the Exocet; Saudi Arabia has the Otomat, Harpoon, and AS-15; Somalia has the SS-N-2; the UAE has the Exocet; and the Yemens have the SS-N-2, SSC-1, and SSC-3. 'Statement of Rear Admiral Thomas Brooks'; and US Navy briefing, May 1990.

19   *Washington Times*, 3 Aug. 1987, p. 1.

20   To put these numbers in perspective, classified studies have indicated that it would take a minimum of 25 modern minesweepers to keep the Gulf ports open, assuming a 1,200-metre wide channel is explored every 48 hours. *Jane's Defence Weekly*, 22 Aug. 1987, p. 296.

21   Department of Defence sources indicate that the USSR only has three ships designed specifically for mine-laying operations, but has 125 vessels which can lay mines, as well as aircraft and submarines. US experts estimate that it has stocks of some 100,000 moored contact-mines, and 200,000 magnetic/acoustic fused mines. The Tango-class submarines, the oldest Soviet type in service, can carry 30 mines. The USSR has some 300 submarines with at least limited minelaying capability.

22   The Avenger programme was funded in FY1986 at a cost of $256.6 million, with $297.3 million requested in FY1988. Ships are also being built by Marinette Marine. The MHC programme was funded at $120.1 million in FY1986, but no money was requested in FY1987, and the House vetoed a request of $297.3 million in FY1988. The Administration plans to request $199 million in FY1989. *New York Times*, 18 Aug. 1987, p. 6

23   *New York Times*, 29 July 1987, p. A-1; and *Defence Technology Viewpoint*, 31 Aug. 1987, p. 8.

24   The US had an active strength of 21 RH-53D Sea Stallions. It took delivery of the first squadron of 12 on 26 June 1987, and had obtained three more by 1 July 1987. Its plans then called for 35 MH-53E Sea Dragons to be in service by 1990. See Scott Truver, 'Airborne Mine Countermeasures in the US Navy's Front Line', *International Defence Review*, Oct. 1987, pp. 1353-9.

25   David M. Ransom, Lt. Colonel Lawrence J. MacDonald, and W. Nathaniel Howell, 'Atlantic Cooperation for Persian Gulf Security', *Essays on Strategy* (National Defence University, Washington, DC, 1986), p. 102.

26   Two fields were in the lower Gulf, with the rest strung out over the convoy routes. The mines were often poorly moored and had no safety devices.

27   The US and UK are working on improved methods and software to detect influence mines. Current progress is classified.

28   James D. Hessman, 'Mine Warfare: The Lessons Not Learned', *Sea Power*, Oct. 1988, pp. 37-45.

29   Most of the technical data used in this section on US Marine Corps unit and force size, and equipment, is taken from General A.M. Gray, *US Marine Corps Concepts and Issues, 1989* (US Marine Corps, Washington, Feb. 1989). Also see General A.M. Gray, 'Statement before the House Armed Services Committee Defence Policy Panel on the Subject of Contingency Forces', 14 March 1990.

30   US Marine Corps Briefing Sheet, March 1990.

31   Anthony H. Cordesman, *The Gulf and the West* (Westview, Boulder, 1988); Robert Haffa, *The Half War, Planning US Deployment Forces to Meet a Limited Contingency, 1960-1983*, (Westview, Boulder, 1984), pp. 238-46; Kurt Beyer, 'US power-projection capabilities in the Gulf,' NSSP (Georgetown University, 7 May 1990), p. 11; and Aaron A. Danis, 'US Power-Projection Capabilities in the Persian Gulf Region,' NSSP (Georgetown University, 1 May 1990), pp. 3-4.

32   Gray, *US Marine Corps*, pp. 1-8 to 1-9.

33   Cordesman, *The Gulf and the West*; Haffa, *The Half War*, pp. 238-46; Beyer, 'US Power Projection', p. 11; and Danis, 'US Power Projection', pp. 3-4.

34   These include some 38 ships, largely LPHs, LPD-4s, LKAs, LSD-36s, and LCCs.

35   Gray, *US Marine Corps*, pp. 1-14 to 1-15.

36   Most of this information is taken from General Carl E. Vuono, 'Statement before the House Committee on Armed Services Defence Policy Panel on Contingency Forces', 14 March 1990.

37   Most of readiness and strength data on USCENTCOM in the text of this section are taken from unpublished USCENTCOM briefing material dated Feb. 1988 and Feb. 1989.

38   Vuono, 'Statement before the House Committee'; and 'The United States Army Posture Statement FY90/91', (Department of the Army, Washington, Feb. 1990), pp. 23-5.

39　Vuono, 'Statement before the House Committee'; and 'The United States Army Posture Statement', pp. 23-5.

40　*Washington Post*, 19 May 1990, p. 1; *New York Times*, 20 May 1990, p. 1.

41　Cordesman, *The Gulf and the West*; Haffa, *The Half War*, pp. 238-46; Beyer, 'US Power Projection', p. 11; and Danis, 'US Power Projection', pp. 3-4.

42　Secretary of Defence Frank Carlucci, *Annual Report, FY1990* (Department of Defence, Washington, Feb. 1989), p. 232.

43　USAF Briefing Chart, Feb. 1990; US Air Force, *The Air Force and US National Security: Global Reach - Global Power, A White Paper* (US Air Force Press, Washington, June 1990), p. 9.

44　US Air Force, *The Air Force and US National Security*, p. 8.

45　US Air Force, *The Air Force and US National Security*, p. 10.

46　US Air Force, *The Air Force and US National Security*, p. 8.

47　Most of readiness and strength data on USCENTCOM in the text of this section are taken from unpublished USCENTCOM briefing material dated Feb. 1988 and Feb. 1989. The data on stock levels are based on the Department of Defence's FY1991 budget request.

48　General Hansford T. Johnson, Commander-in-Chief, US Transportation Command, 'Presentation to the Committee on Armed Services Subcommittee on Projection Forces and Regional Defence', 19 June 1990, pp. 7-12.

49　'Statement of Mr. David Berteau, Principal Deputy Assistant Secretary of Defence (Production and Logistics) before the Committee on Armed Services Subcommittee on Projection Forces and Regional Defence', 19 June 1990, p. 6.

50　Carlucci, *Annual Report, FY1990*, p. 233. Secretary of Defence Richard Cheney, *Annual Report, FY1991*, (Department of Defence, Washington, Feb. 1989), p. 77; Johnson, 'Presentation to the Committee on Armed Services', pp. 7-8.

51　US Air Force, *The Air Force and US National Security*, p. 12.

52　Jeffrey Record, 'The Plan to Defend Iran', *Baltimore Sun*, 7 March 1990, p. 15A.

53　Unless other major contingencies required US airlift at the same time as a Gulf contingency.

54　A C-17 can carry a double row of 5-ton vans, up to 18 463L pallets, 11 463L pallets and 54 troops for airdrops.

55　The 17 prepositioning ships now deployed carry some 165,000 short-tons of ammunition and supplies. To put this into perspective, this is equivalent to more than 6,100 C-141 sorties.

56　Johnson, 'Presentation to the Committee on Armed Services' pp. 11-12.

57　These and the following shortfall statistics are taken from the FY1987 USCENTCOM Command Briefing as provided by USCENTCOM, and General George B. Crist, *Status of the United States Central Command*, 22 Feb. 1988, pp. 83-4.

58　FY1987 USCENTCOM Command Briefing as provided by USCENTCOM, and Crist, *Status of the United States*, pp. 83-4.

59   Schwarzkopf, 'Witness Statement'.
60   Schwarzkopf, 'Witness Statement', pp. 59-60.
61   Schwarzkopf, 'Witness Statement', pp. 50-3.
62   Schwarzkopf, 'Witness Statement', p. 38.
63   *New York Times*, 4 Jan. 1988, p. 10.
64   Schwarzkopf, 'Witness Statement', p. 52.
65   Schwarzkopf, 'Witness Statement', pp. 59-62.
66   Crist, *Status of the United States*, pp. 83-4.
67   *Washington Post*, 1 Aug. 1989, p. A-22.
68   *Washington Post*, 1 Aug. 1989, p. A-22; and *Washington Times*, 23 May 1990, p. 5.
69   USCENTCOM briefing and *Christian Science Monitor*, 19 Jan. 1988, p. 1.
70   Saudi Arabia originally planned a base at al-Kharj, near Riyadh, for its E-3As. This base expansion has been cancelled due to funding reasons, but may be reinstated because of the problem of securing Riyadh airport against terrorism.
71   This base was originally designed for three brigades, and has considerably better equipment storage and support facilities than its normal deployment strength of two brigades indicates. Saudi Arabia has also discussed the possibility of converting one brigade to a 'Gulf brigade' which would include forces from other GCC countries.
72   *Baltimore Sun*, 7 March 1990, p. 15A.
73   The estimates made in this section are drawn primarily from interviews in the region, in London and in Washington; press sources and computerised defence data bases, and the relevant country chapters of International Institute for Strategic Studies, *Military Balance, 1989-1990* (Brassey's, London, 1989); Shlomo Gazit and Zeev Eytan, *The Middle East Military Balance, 1988-1989* (Westview Press, Boulder, 1990); The 'International Navies' issue of *Proceedings* (Naval Institute Press, Annapolis, March 1990), pp. 138-43; Tony Bank (ed.), 'JDW Country Survey: The Gulf States', *Jane's Defence Weekly*, 31 March 1990, pp. 583-602; Arms Control and Disarmament Agency, *World Military Expenditures and Arms Transfers, 1989* (GPO, Washington, 1989).
74   *Washington Post*, 19 Dec. 1987, p. A-27.
75   Kuwait is considering upgrading the Chieftains to fit the RO/RARDE 120mm L30 CHARM gun, a new engine or power pack, additional armour, a new fire-control system, and passive night-vision. The existing Chieftain is now Kuwait's most advanced tank, but it has shortcomings in power, firepower and armour. *Jane's Defence Weekly*, 18 Nov. 1988, p. 1254.
76   Kuwait has been examining such options for some years. It tends to shift between US, Soviet, and Brazilian options depending on the politics of the day. The US candidate is the M-1A1. The European candidates include the AMX-40, the Challenger, and possibly the Leopard 2. The Brazilian candidate is the Osorio EE-T1. The Soviet candidate is the T-72S, and its purchase may be somewhat more likely in view of Kuwait's reported tank-purchase from Yugoslavia. The T-72S has provisions for adding reactive

armour, an improved engine and suspension, and a 125mm gun that can also fire a laser-guided projectile. *Jane's Defence Weekly*, 18 Nov. 1988, p. 1254; 15 April 1989, p. 627; 15 July 1989, p. 65; 2 Sept. 1989, p. 369.

77   Kuwait bought the BMPs and other defence equipment as part of a $300 million order from the USSR in July 1988. Kuwait is reported to have ordered the 200 M-84 tanks, 14 command vehicles, 15 armoured recovery-vehicles, ammunition, logistical support, anti-tank weapons and training from Yugoslavia in July 1989. The resulting deal is said to have been worth $800 million and to have occurred because Yugoslavia could not pay its debt to Kuwait for past oil imports in any other way. *Jane's Defence Weekly*, 15 April 1989, p. 627; 15 July 1989, p. 65; 2 Sept. 1989, p. 369.

78   *Jane's Defence Weekly*, 17 Dec. 1988, p. 1549.

79   *Defence News*, 3 Oct. 1988, p. 12.

80   *Defence News*, 8 Aug. 1988, p. 7; *Jane's Defence Weekly*, 13 Aug. 1988, p. 246; *Washington Times*, 25 July 1988, p. 1; *Newsweek*, 25 Aug. 1988, p. 47.

81   *Defence News*, 8 Aug. 1988, p. 7; *Jane's Defence Weekly*, 13 Aug. 1988, p. 246; *Washington Times*, 25 July 1988, p. 1; *Newsweek*, 25 Aug. 1988, p. 47.

82   *Jane's Defence Weekly*, 3 Feb. 1990, p. 203.

83   *Jane's Defence Weekly*, 31 March 1990, p. 597.

84   I am indebted to Lt. Commander Jerry Ferguson, one of my students at Georgetown University, for much of the research, and many of the insights, on Gulf naval and air forces presented in this chapter.

85   The 76mm and 40mm guns can provide some air-defence, but with little lethality. The TNC-45s have very complicated electronics, virtually all of which are maintained by foreign technicians. The voice network system used by the TNC-45 is so slow that it is virtually hopeless for air-defence operations and generally creates confusion and increases delay and vulnerability if any attempt is made to use it.

12. US INTERESTS IN THE GULF: IMPLICATIONS FOR AMERICA'S REGIONAL POLICY

Richard W. Murphy

America's interests in the Gulf have traditionally been threefold: to assure non-discriminatory access to Gulf energy sources for itself and its allies, to support the security and stability of its Gulf friends, and to contain the expansion of Soviet influence there. Washington demonstrated a related concern during and after its major naval deployment of 1987-9: its unwillingness to allow a regional power to impose its hegemony on the other Gulf states.

Soviet Influence

In the light of the generally improved US-Soviet dialogue, is it still appropriate to proclaim containment of Soviet influence in the Gulf as a major US-interest? Much of US strategic planning in this area after the Second World War was shaped by America's reading of Soviet ambitions. Washington perceived that its interests required, in company with its friends and allies, the blocking of any Soviet move to improve its political and military positions in that region. The rapid pace of change in Soviet foreign policy during the past two years has led the US to begin to rethink some of its own positions. For example, only recently did the US Central Command, the Defence Department's military command responsible for the Gulf, decide that it was no longer a realistic goal to develop the capability to stop Soviet troops in the Zagros mountains in a scenario which postulated Moscow's military thrust into Iran.

Today it is much harder to define how much we should worry about the expansion of Soviet influence in the Gulf. To many Americans it sounds quaint, even reactionary in view of *perestroika* and *glasnost*, to continue to cite the need to contain the Soviets. But one should approach any contemplated changes in national strategy with care and deliberation. To be worthy of the name, a national strategy is developed carefully and takes into consideration a number of variables. The case can be made that although we have a better understanding with the Soviets on many fronts, there remains an adversarial quality to our relations which it would be unwise to overlook, particularly in an area such as the Gulf where Western interests are truly vital.

As recently as the autumn of 1986, however, there was no national debate about US Gulf-strategy. We were very clear in our minds that we had to counter the expansion of Soviet influence. Against the background of intensifying Iranian attacks on Kuwait-bound shipping, the government of Kuwait had asked both Moscow and Washington in October 1986 what each would do to assist the safe passage of its oil through the Gulf and the Strait of Hormuz. The Soviets answered first, saying they would protect the tankers. Not wanting to see the Soviets play a security role in the Gulf other than that of protecting their own shipping, we in turn said that we would do the job. That was the backdrop of President Reagan's decision in March 1987 to agree to reflag a number of Kuwaiti tankers and put them under US naval escort. Our decision-making unfortunately took nearly three months, but we then agreed to put eleven Kuwaiti tankers under the US flag, leaving Moscow the role of chartering three Soviet tankers to Kuwait.

Moscow, which had answered Kuwait both positively and significantly more rapidly, may today agree that it erred in appearing so eager to move into a major Gulf security-role because of the alarm this aroused in Washington. The US described its naval mission as being to defend the principle of freedom of navigation, and to assure our moderate Gulf friends of our support by sending a clear signal to Tehran that we stood against any expansion of its conflict with Iraq. These were serious positions. However, the position which the American public most easily understood was that we were standing up against the threat of Soviet expansionism, as we had done in many other regions since World War II. The public had widely approved the Carter Administration's reaction in 1979 to the Soviet invasion of Afghanistan. The Reagan Administration adopted Carter's policy on Afghanistan and implemented the position Carter set forth on the Gulf in his farewell State of the Union message of 1981.

In the mid-1970s there had been some public debate in the United States about the need for US military intervention to protect its Gulf interests, but this was largely confined to US academic circles. In the aftermath of the oil crisis brought on by the 1973 Arab-Israeli War, American scholar Robert W. Tucker sharply raised blood pressure in the Arab Gulf states by arguing that since Persian Gulf oil was a vital Western interest, the US government should seriously consider the possibility of applying the threat of force and/or its use to resolve any crisis which might threaten its supply. He pointed out that no American official or academic completely ruled out the use of force, and that the debate should revolve around what circumstances would justify it. He dismissed the moral arguments against the use of force - military unfeasibility, the reactions of other countries, domestic public opposition on moral grounds, and the availability of other means - as simply not compelling. He concluded that there could be a contingency under which the United States would have to deploy its forces in the Gulf to safeguard Western interests.

Of course, that had been the basic justification for our small naval presence in the Gulf since World War II and the debate of the 1970s subsided. In 1987, twelve years after Tucker's article appeared, Washington deployed major fleet-units to the Gulf. The US rapidly increased its presence from the three to five ships assigned to the region since the 1950s to about fifty, including those operating in the Arabian Sea just outside Hormuz. That number stayed engaged in the Gulf operation for over one year. Its mission, stimulated by the Kuwaiti request, evolved in close co-operation with the Gulf states.

At the working level in the Departments of State and Defence, the President's decision was doubly welcome. Officials there had grown weary of hearing Gulf friends attack Washington as unreliable, and express doubts that they could rely on the US to come to their defence should their security be seriously threatened. We were accused of having abandoned the Shah in 1979 and having aggravated the Lebanon crisis in 1984 by the withdrawal of the US Marines. The President's decision to reflag the Kuwaiti tankers demonstrated publicly the seriousness of American intent to stand by its long-standing policy and pledges. Even so, the Gulf leaders questioned whether we would stay the course. They warned Washington that if it was not ready to see the crisis through, it had better not get militarily involved.

The American Congress was initially puzzled by the President's naval commitment and unhappy that the Administration seemed ready to do so much more to protect Western interests than were our European and Japanese allies. The Congress correctly noted that those states, whose dependence on a secure supply of Gulf oil dwarfed that of the United States, were hanging back.

Iraq's attack on the USS *Stark* in May, in which it used French Exocet missiles, raised Congressional alarm that the President's decision had been ill considered. They talked of reviving the debate on the War Powers Act which had halted when the Marines were withdrawn from Lebanon. Congressional uneasiness ended only when Belgian, Dutch and Italian ships undertook minesweeping operations in the Gulf later that summer, adding a broader European presence to the British and French ships which had long been active.

As the war continued there was a subtle, steady change in regional attitudes towards the United States' military force. Washington had for years represented a safety net for the Gulf states in their security planning. But, they had insisted that our military remain 'over the horizon' where it would cause them less domestic political embarrassment. They gradually came to accept that a major naval campaign simply could not be run from over the horizon. Having successfully carried out its commitment, Washington may have achieved a new acceptance by several of those states of the need for joint planning and joint logistics facilities. Both sides remain, however, sensitive to the need for discretion.

Energy Dependence

Whatever the future may bring in terms of improved US-Soviet relations and however that may assist resolution of regional conflicts, there is no doubt that the United States will consider assured Western access to Gulf oil an overriding priority. Two thirds of the world's proven reserves are there and world demand grows steadily. Kuwait, Saudi Arabia and the UAE are expanding their production facilities. They will try to increase crude supplies to meet the demand, probably encountering some technical problems along the way which will fuel consumer-country anxieties. While the US will continue to fret over its vulnerability to imported oil and price volatility, more analysts are making the point today that dependency on imports need not equate with vulnerability. With that in mind, I submit that the balance-of-trade effect of America's oil imports may soon become the primary focus of US policy-makers' attention.

America will become a net oil-importer by the mid 1990s. Pressured by rapidly escalating prices in the 1970s we went on a strict energy-diet and managed to drop our oil consumption by about 19 per cent. But since 1985 oil consumption has risen by more than 12 per cent. In those five years, with our domestic production falling, our annual net imports of oil grew by 66 per cent. Although the US is amongst the lowest in the OECD in its rate of oil consumption growth, the stark fact remains that with only 4.7 per cent of the world's population, the US now consumes over a quarter of the world's total crude-output.

As recently as 1985, the US imported only about 4.5 million barrels a day. We expect to increase our imports by about 2 million more barrels per day by the mid-1990s and another million or so by the year 2000. This means a projection of US annual oil-imports at about the level of 9-10 million barrels per day, assuming no import restraints.

Given that our trade deficit is already a major cause of concern, the $64 question, or rather some enormous multiple thereof, is how we will pay for this oil. Our non-oil net export accounts would need to swing in the range of $200 billion or so just to achieve a balanced current account in 1995. So our trade and balance-of-payments accounts will be of mounting concern.

Soon the Gulf will not only be America's major supplier but that of much of the rest of the world. Leaving aside Soviet production, which currently is so uncertain as to defy medium-term forecasting, by the end of this decade probably only six countries will have significant excess capacity to export and thereby real power in the market place. The list may in fact shrink to only Saudi Arabia, Iraq, the UAE and Kuwait. Their reserves are massive: as one measure, a recent discovery in Saudi Arabia, if proved to be a single field, may add what some estimate to be a further 30 billion barrels to the Saudis' proven reserves. This incremental increase to the already vast Saudi reserves gains significance when one considers the US situation. Our total proven reserves, including those in Alaska, amount to only about 27 billion barrels (a figure which ongoing discoveries has kept fairly steady for the past several decades).

Another Boycott?

Whether the concentration of production in such few hands will tempt those producers to use the oil weapon again as they did in 1973 is an often-posed question. For at least two reasons, such a boycott in the foreseeable future is improbable. First, for several years to come the producers in the Gulf Co-operation Council will need all the oil income they can attain to fulfil their development plans and, in Iraq and Iran, to pay their reconstruction bills. Second, the 1973-4 boycott proved a clumsy and ineffective weapon. It caused some damage to the United States' and other Western economies, perhaps more from our own mishandling of the boycott than anything else. But, relatively speaking, it was more destructive to the non-oil-producers of the Third World whose good will the Gulf producers try to cultivate.

US-Gulf Relations

While one should not exaggerate the possibility that oil supply in the coming decade will be subject to political influence, it would be equally unwise to concentrate only on the economics of oil. The character of US relations with the Gulf states will play a role.

America currently enjoys close ties with the six member-states of the Gulf Co-operation Council. Our support for their security during the Gulf War enhanced those relations: we demonstrated that we would be there when needed. Historically, our oldest ties are those with the sultanate of Oman, whose first emissary visited our republic in the 1830s. A century later we began to forge ties with the newly established kingdom of Saudi Arabia when King Abd al-Aziz Al Saᶜud awarded an exploration concession to the Americans in preference to British and European companies. His reported comment that 'Americans know the oil business and are farther away' succinctly summarised his assumption that we would be less likely to interfere in the kingdom's political affairs than the British and French who had intervened in the region with such verve during the first quarter of this century.

Thus the kingdom of Saudi Arabia established its first ties to the US through the group of US oil-companies later known as ARAMCO. The degree of respect of the Saudi leadership for ARAMCO's contributions to the kingdom's development was later demonstrated by its handling of the nationalisation which ARAMCO underwent, beginning in the 1970s. There has been no gentler example in our time.

American ties expanded in the post-war years to include diplomatic exchanges and a major educational programme bringing over thousands of young Saudis for college and postgraduate training. We established a military training mission in the 1950s and until recently were the kingdom's major supplier of military equipment. We handed that role over to Britain in 1985 when the Reagan Administration decided it could not convince the US Congress to agree on the sale of US fighter-aircraft to Riyadh. That decision will have long-term implications not just for the US but also for the region. For present purposes, suffice it to record that no other arms-seller has shown the same degree of interest as Washington in preserving a Middle East arms-balance.

Some observers argue that the regimes of the Arabian Peninsula are unstable and lack legitimacy. They describe these regimes as archaic in their political structures, and so awash in the oil revenues which have prompted rapid economic change that they are certain to undergo drastic political upheavals, and soon. These observers note that the youth whom these states have sent abroad for higher education have been exposed to revolutionary ideas of political and economic development. Certainly it would be foolish to deny that some of those graduates would like to see changes in their systems of government. But the sweeping conclusion that the peninsula is on the brink of revolution is overdrawn. These are not police states.   Their citizens enjoy major benefits in respect to education, housing and medical care.   And the ruling families enjoy a legitimacy, deriving from more than their ability to finance generous social-welfare programmes, which seems to escape their critics.

Often it is safer and more dramatic to make negative predictions about Third World political prospects.   But commentaries about the non-viability of peninsula regimes have been fashionable for more than a generation.   In the Shah's time, Iranians were fond of commenting about the inevitability of early upheavals in the Arabian Gulf states, whose regimes they viewed as utterly unequipped for the modern world.   The question remains, why have these regimes survived while so many others, including Iran's, have foundered?

There is a resilience in the political structure of those states which is difficult for the outsider to comprehend.   One explanation is that in these six states the rulers have preserved remarkably open communications with their subjects.   Each has maintained a variant of the *majlis* system where, outside normal bureaucratic channels, any citizen can approach senior governors and members of the ruling family to petition for redress of grievances, to seek favours or simply to exchange views on national issues.

Iraq and Iran

US relations with Baghdad and Tehran are obviously of a very different quality from those it enjoys with the countries of the GCC.   Our dialogue with Iraq, however thin at present, is nonetheless better than that with Iran.

Iraq is not an easy partner in dialogue.   It sharply reacted to criticism of its human rights record and use of chemical weapons as constituting unacceptable interference in its internal affairs.   Sensitivity to American criticism may have provoked the Iraqi President's public attack on the continued presence of the US Navy in the Gulf, even though Baghdad had welcomed it during the war and despite the fact that the number of US Navy ships has long since returned to the level approximating that in the Gulf since the 1950s.

Washington forthrightly criticised Iraq for its use of poison gas both before and after the 1988 cease-fire.   It welcomed Iraq's pledge in 1988, repeated at the Paris Conference on Chemical Weapons the following January, to forswear future use of this weapon. Baghdad's use of chemical weapons during the last years of the war was viewed by competent military observers as an unnecessary, although admittedly successful, intimidation-tactic against Iran, at a time when Iraq enjoyed superiority both in the air and on the ground. Worthy of note is the fact that no Arab state ever criticised Iraq's use of chemical weapons.

This is not to suggest that our dialogue with Baghdad is restricted to human rights and chemical weapons. During the course of the Gulf War we developed good rapport with Iraqi officials in drafting what became Security Council Resolution 598 calling for the cease-fire. We also worked out practical measures with the Iraqi military in 1987-9 to avoid having our navy pulled into the conflict, or into a repetition of the mistaken attack on the USS *Stark*. Iraq, in company with the Gulf Co-operation Council states, credited our naval involvement, our diplomatic efforts and America's 'Operation Staunch', a programme to deny US military equipment to Iran, as having accelerated the end of the war. (This comment is not intended to gloss over the misguided episode of Irangate)

In recent years, our trade with Baghdad has grown substantially. In terms of agricultural credits we have had one of the largest programmes worldwide with Iraq. We are mindful that with its oil structures still not fully mapped, Iraq has reserves second only to Saudi Arabia. Endowed also with water and good soil it could with proper management become self-sufficient and even possibly a net exporter of foodstuffs, furthering its emergence as a major economic power in the region.

For all these reasons, Iraq has attracted the interest of several major US corporations. Some have hesitated to get involved because of the country's current economic difficulties, especially its heavy war-debts which are wildly estimated to range between $80 and $150 billion. Baghdad has been consistently reluctant to provide details of its finances, including its debt situation, thereby adding to uncertainty in international circles about its economic condition. Most observers, however, agree that the country should have restructured its debts and be creditworthy within five years.

Concerning Iran, there is still no clear signal from Tehran of a serious intent to move relations with the US beyond their currently poisonous state. Iranian officials fondly rehash the wrongs that they insist were committed against Iran by the US during the Shah's time and later against the Islamic Republic. Their inability to maintain the initial approval which the revolution brought Tehran in some countries of the region has perversely added to the Iranian animus towards the United States.

For its part, the American public continues to harbour bitterness because of the humiliation it suffered by Iran's seizure of our Embassy in 1979 and its holding our officials hostage. The subsequent US-Iranian military confrontation during the Gulf War did nothing to alter the public conviction that the regime of the Ayatullah Khomeini was implacably hostile to American interests. Since Khomeini's death, the continued detention of American and other Western hostages in Lebanon by factions known to be responsive to Iranian direction does not help the case of those who argue that the US must work to improve relations with Iran. To date, explicit statements by the Bush Administration about its desire to see better relations and its willingness at The Hague to speed up settlements of outstanding claims at the International Tribunal have not stilled the voices of Iranian officials who still find it useful to portray Washington as an enemy to their public.

Iranian authorities may one day adopt a more coherent and restrained view of the US than has yet been the case. But their awareness of the benefits to Iran in terms of reconstruction assistance from such institutions as the World Bank, where a co-operative American attitude could be useful, has not yet served to move them in any significant way towards a more conciliatory approach.

Implications for Future US Gulf-Policy

As stated, and to recapitulate, we committed a major component of our navy to the Gulf in 1987, acted to defend freedom of navigation, to block Soviet expansion in the Gulf and to reassure the Arab states of the Gulf that we were serious about our long-stated policy in support of their security. Today the cease-fire is holding well, although negotiations for an Iraq-Iran peace remain stalled. Whether President Saddam Hussein's recent overtures to President Rafsanjani for direct negotiations will be productive remains unclear.

Might the latest American naval intervention have been the last of its kind for the US in the Gulf? In 1987 we responded to a Kuwaiti request, with the quiet approval of the other GCC-states. Are future contingencies conceivable in which we might again intervene, even if not invited to do so? Certainly it would be far easier both in terms of regional and American public opinion for Washington to intervene only when invited. However, if the conflicts in the area were to spill over into the Gulf and threaten the supply of oil, it is conceivable that the option to use force, invited or not, would again be considered.

But we did not respond militarily to the oil boycott of 1973-4, and military intervention to preserve American and Western interests need not be America's only policy option. We can also discourage actions hostile to our access to Gulf oil resources by stepping up research in alternative energy programmes, by diversifying our supply sources, by increased government stocks and by developing quicker response mechanisms to oil supply disruptions.

Another way to enhance the stability of international oil-supply is to develop greater awareness in the Gulf region of the economic interdependence between the Gulf producers and Western consumers. The stronger the perception of shared interests between producer and consumer, the less likelihood of politically-motivated actions to cut off the flow of oil. Specifically, we might encourage Gulf state investment in downstream operations of the West's refining and distribution networks. The US already has such Kuwaiti and Saudi investment, although Washington sensibly refrains from officially proclaiming an open-door policy in order to avoid a xenophobic reaction.

We owe it to ourselves and to our friends worldwide to try to ensure that there be no disruption of oil supplies. Since most of us are so heavily import-dependent, the industrialised nations will suffer from any serious disruption of oil supply, wherever it occurs. A disruption of Western European or Japanese supplies would seriously affect the export earnings, prices and employment levels of all. Our common, overriding goal should be to assure that no power, in or outside the region, succeeds in inhibiting the market-induced production levels of the Gulf states or interferes with their international shipments.

Our task will be to pursue policies which convincingly reinforce the growing perception of economic interdependence between the US and the Gulf region, and if possible to achieve normal relations with both Iraq and Iran. To this end it will also be desirable for the US to keep security-assistance ties with the Gulf states and, where possible, with others in the region.

On regional issues, Washington must be under no misconception that the Gulf states are indifferent to the goal of a comprehensive settlement of the Arab-Israeli conflict. Palestinian rights do matter to them, and they regularly raise this issue with US authorities. Undoubtedly these states will continue to urge that Washington use its leverage with Israel to push the peace-process forward. There has always been the converse proposition that the US should use its 'privileged' relations with Saudi Arabia and other GCC states to press them harder to support the 'peace-process'. The fact is that neither approach has worked or will work in any crude straight-line fashion. The Arab Gulf states do not see themselves as frontline states in the Arab-Israeli conflict. They have channelled the greatest share of their support to the moderate Arab-states and, as far as concerns the PLO, to support of Arafat's leadership rather than to that organisation's radical elements. They have been impatient with what they perceive as a lack of American energy in the peace-process, but support American efforts, provided those efforts remain within the framework of Security Council Resolution 242 and the 1982 Reagan Initiative.

We have today a multifaceted relationship with the Gulf, and it will be essential to keep it that way. We cannot afford to neglect any single element in our dialogue, be it the peace-process, the security of the Gulf states and their investments, or oil supply. They see these questions as interrelated and so must we.

13. EXTERNAL INTERESTS AND INTERNAL PROCESSES OF MILITARISATION IN THE GULF REGION

Rolf Müller-Syring

As long as money and armies continue to exist, arguments will rage about the quantities of material, financial and human resources which are appropriate for the purposes of the military. Determining the position of the border separating reasonable and legitimate defence expenses from destabilising and wasteful overspending represents perhaps the most difficult problem in this century-old worldwide debate. A general answer is, of course, impossible. But because it will always remain - at least partially - a matter of subjective judgement, even a case-by-case approach is not necessarily the way to reach conclusive results on the point where an increase in quantities can bring about a qualitative change, from defence to militarisation. This chapter defines militarisation in contemporary times in Third World countries as follows:

1. The integration of the developing countries in global arms-circulations. The armament efforts in quantitative and qualitative terms and the increase in military power (arms-spending, arms imports, and internal arms-production) exceed by far the frontiers of self-preservation and defence against attack. The armaments machine goes beyond social and political control.

2. Military technical considerations and predominantly military-inspired security doctrines overshadow political reason. The political instructions to the military are directed more towards the achievement of military superiority in peace and to victory in wartime than to the legitimate protection of people and territory.

3. Militarisation therefore represents a permanent cause of regional tensions and conflicts and tends more to enhance

than to diminish the role played by outside powers in the areas concerned.

4. The intensification of international military entanglement is accompanied by the rise of the military's influence at a national level. It plays a decisive role in the economic and political life of the country. Military goals, values and norms increasingly dominate national culture, education, the media, religion, and even the daily behaviour of the citizens at the expense of civilian institutions.

5. The military penetration of everyday life undermines any democratic development and represents a real threat to human rights. It may (but need not necessarily) lead to the erection of an open military dictatorship.

To follow this attempted definition implies acceptance of the fact that necessary general standards, capable of determining the position of that ominous point where 'too much' for a reasonable national defence capability begins, simply do not exist. Sometimes this may be deplorable, but in some cases it is not actually necessary to fix the diffuse frontier between day and night exactly, because it is precisely midnight.

Some Features of Militarisation in the Gulf

The Gulf has for nearly twenty years been the most rapidly militarising region of the Third World, outpacing the arms-race even in conflict-laden areas such as the Near East, the Horn of Africa, and the Northern Tier and Indian Ocean area. While military spending in the Gulf climbed in the mid-1980s to a peak of more than $53 billion, it still exceeded $30 billion in 1988 after a long, damaging war, and in a situation of financial and economic exhaustion.[1]

The Saudi defence budget, which had already increased more than tenfold in the 1970s, stabilised in the 1980s between $20 and 25 billion per year - comparable with the size of the French, West German or British defence budgets.   These amounts represent about 20 per cent of GNP or between a quarter and a third of central government expenditures. The smaller Gulf states - with a population of about 6 million people each - spent between $5 and 6 billion each year on defence in the 1980s, roughly the same as Spain.[2]   The average defence expenditure per soldier in the Gulf comes to about $80,000, in Saudi Arabia to more than $200,000, and in the United States to about $50,000.[3]

A considerable part of the defence budget has been used to import weapons and equipment, and for the installation and improvement of the military infrastructure. The figures in Table 13.1 refer only to major weapons, ignoring the substantial disbursements on the military infrastructure, amounting to dozens of billions of dollars in the case of Saudi Arabia alone.

Table 13.1: Import of Major Weapons by Gulf States (Bahrain, Iraq, Iran, Kuwait, Oman, Qatar, Saudi Arabia and the UAE)*

1950-9	98.9 million
1960-9	697.8 million
1970-4	2,796.8 million
1975-9	4,684.4 million
1980-4	5,795.6 million

Note: *Figures are at constant 1985 US$ prices and represent five- or ten-year averages.

While exact figures for the second half of the 1980s are not yet available, the drop in military spending at the end of the decade seems not to have had a strong impact on the weapons flow to the Gulf. Between 1984 and 1988 Iran, Iraq and Saudi Arabia alone imported weapons worth $5,737 per year (yearly average over the five-year period).[4] This time the Gulf accounted for about 30 per cent of the total arms-imports of the Third World.[5] The weapons bought for this money filled the storehouses of the Gulf states. In 1972 they were able to field 1,825 main battle tanks, by 1980 the number had risen to 5,019, and in 1988 the figure was 6,584. The number of combat aircraft at the disposal of the Gulf states doubled during this period from 477 to 919.[6]

To put these numbers into perspective it is useful to note that the Gulf states possess the equivalent of about the total tank inventory of the NATO central region, and that Iraq alone (with at least 4,500) has many more tanks than the Germans had in 1943 on the entire eastern front (3,000), or considerably more than twice the British tank force.

Impressive as the quantitative arms build-up in the Gulf may be, it is surpassed by the speed of qualitative changes. The Gulf states now command conventional weapon systems which are the most modern available to the Superpowers themselves. They have even procured ballistic missiles (Iran, Iraq and Saudi Arabia) and state-of-the-art combat aircraft which are capable of serving as delivery-systems for nuclear weapons. Iraq and, to a lesser extent, Iran acquired and used chemical weapons in the Gulf War and it seems likely that at least Iraq is trying to develop nuclear and biological weapons.

What are the reasons for this massive military build-up? The rulers of the Gulf states and scores of security experts from all over the world point at the precarious situation faced by the region. There are at least four different levels:

1.   *International instability*: Although the Gulf states are rightly considered to be wealthy, the internal social, economic, political, religious and security situation is not at all stable. These countries are undergoing a deep-seated process of modernisation and of socio-economic transformation in a time-span lasting a few decades, which, for instance, in Europe lasted more than two centuries. Ethnic, demographic, religious, cultural and mental peculiarities together imbue the process with a truly formidable degree of complexity. The unusually high proportion of foreign to native labour (in the case of Saudi Arabia, Kuwait, Bahrain, Qatar and the UAE the size of the foreign labour force exceeds that of the native labour force) is only one illustration of this.

2.   There exists a lot of deep-rooted mistrust, and a large number of conflicts which have led fairly often to armed clashes, and, in the case of Iran and Iraq, to the most destructive and devastating war ever waged between Third World countries.

3.   The Gulf is surrounded by an arc, or rather by a circle, of instability of its own: the Arab-Israeli conflict lasting more than forty years to the north, the volatile situation on the Horn of Africa to the west, and the war in Afghanistan and the India-Pakistan rivalry to the east.

4.   The geo-strategic importance of and the key role played by the Gulf due to its huge oil and gas reserves have attracted the close attention of the Superpowers. After the retreat of

the British from 'east of Suez' in the late 1960s the Gulf has become a playground for rivalry between the Superpowers.

The menacing scenario produced by this diversity and volatility results, under contemporary circumstances, almost automatically in the seizure of military protective measures, and therefore in an arms build-up. Even a cursory look at the history of this tremendous regional arms-race reveals the important role played in the process by the Superpowers and, to a lesser extent, by some European and, in the last few years, by some Third World countries. The early 1970s seem to have been a certain starting-point. In 1972 Nixon and Kissinger offered the Shah in Tehran a blank cheque for conventional arms deliveries. The resulting huge inflow of arms bolstered the Shah's ambitions as 'guardian of the Gulf' as well as the main strategic aim of the 'Nixon Doctrine', which consisted of enabling the 'new influentials' in the Third World to share at least partial responsibility for containing the assumed Soviet expansionism and the anti-Western-orientated states or movements. Officially the United States pursued a 'twin-pillar strategy' in the Gulf, but in reality the second 'pillar', Saudi Arabia, received only second-class treatment in military terms as long as the Shah ruled in Tehran. The Soviet Union did not hesitate in countering the attempt by the United States at filling the power-vacuum left by the British retreat with pro-American forces. Already a month before Nixon's visit to Tehran took place it signed a treaty of friendship and co-operation with the Iraqi government which included an article on common endeavours to strengthen defence capabilities. Military procurements by the Soviet Union for Iraq lagged behind the quantitative and qualitative levels of the American-sponsored Iranian armaments.

Nevertheless, in 1980 the Iraqi leadership estimated its arsenal, stemming almost exclusively from the Soviet Union, to be sufficient to overwhelm its arch-enemies in Iran.

The Soviet invasion of Afghanistan was followed by the Carter Doctrine under which it was proclaimed that 'any attempt by any outside force to gain control over the Persian Gulf region ... will be repelled by any means necessary, including military force.'[7] Carter initiated the establishment of a Rapid Deployment Force which was enlarged under President Reagan and transformed into the (new) US Central Command with a potential operational area of nineteen African and Asian countries.

The subsequent concentration of considerable parts of the US Navy in the Arabian Sea near the Gulf was accompanied by the deployment of a comparable Soviet fleet in this area. Although the Superpowers bear no direct responsibility for the devastating Iran-Iraq war, they didn't distinguish themselves in vigorously re-establishing peace during the greater part of it. On the contrary, they delivered weapons and/or important military information to one or the other combatant, sometimes even to both, or tolerated such deliveries by their respective allies. This kind of fuelling of the war came to a halt when the Iraqi policy of internationalisation of the Gulf War began to bear fruit. The US and the Soviet Union now hurried to contain a war which had become a threat to their interests.

Taken altogether these well known facts illustrate that the policy of the Superpowers in the last two decades did not dampen but stimulated the internal processes of militarisation already existing in the Gulf region.   They supplied huge amounts of increasingly sophisticated arms and the necessary military know-how during peace and wartime.   Their own behaviour seemed to rest in many respects upon military patterns: a supposed threat or even challenge aroused in or around the Gulf almost inevitably caused a military response. But also the lack of ideas and of the political will to settle the Arab-Israeli conflict and the Palestinian problem strengthened at least the psychological foundations of the armaments in the Gulf.

Assessing Various Aspects of Militarisation in the Gulf

Even if one shares these evaluations, one might draw completely different conclusions. Indeed, are the developments outlined above detrimental and dangerous or simply business as usual, or even positive endeavours intended to create military equilibrium, enhancing stability and security? Did the processes of militarisation in the Gulf, fuelled from the outside, really cause any remarkable hardship for the people in the Gulf? Are they not in a better position than any other Third World region to pay the military bills? Was not the Gulf region in military terms extremely weak in the early 1970s, so that the support in this field provided by the great powers seemed to be merely a kind of life insurance? And did there really exist any reasonable alternative in the world we are used to?

In the following thesis this chapter suggests an answer to these and similar questions:

1. Bearing in mind the huge amounts in cash the weapons-exporters received for their products, altruism should be excluded in the assessment of the external aspect of militarisation in the Gulf.

2. At least some doubts remain when regional, or general, supra-regional, international or vital security interests are mentioned as forming the decisive background for the military build-up in this volatile region. 'Everybody's Doing It' was the title *Time* gave to an article in 1987 countering European condemnations of the immorality of US military support to Iran at a time when a US-initiated arms embargo was in force against that country. And indeed the list of the arms-exporters to the Gulf during the war is so long that it would be rather difficult to detect the respective security interests: France, Sweden, Britain, Czechoslovakia, Portugal, Spain, Italy, Poland, East and West Germany, Rumania, China, Brazil, Switzerland, North and South Korea, etc.[8]

3. A bold and unbiased approach clearly backs the assumption that militarisation did not solve any of the existing problems of the Gulf states, but has rather been successful in aggravating them and in creating scores of new difficulties. The billions of dollars yearly spent on tanks, combat aircraft, mortars or the military infrastructure reveals that in this way large economic, financial and human resources are being diverted towards unproductive fields. None of the arguments (which are anyway strongly disputed) lauding armaments and military spending as an effective instrument in the development-process succeed in holding true in this case, where financial means are in abundance. On the other hand this money might instead contribute much more than is currently possible to such useful things as economic development, environmental protection and social improvement in the neighbouring countries of the Gulf, where affluence by no means prevails. Economic disorder, social eruptions and environmental pollution in these countries would affect the Gulf too - and

military power will not provide an appropriate means of defence against that kind of threat. Given the chronic shortage of skilled manpower in the economy, infra- structure and administration of nearly all the Gulf states, the attraction of a considerable proportion of the well- educated and motivated who are in the best physical condition to serve in the armed forces would seem to be a luxury.

Furthermore the dynamics of militarisation inevitably enhance the role of the military in politics. According to Anthony Cordesman's evaluation,

every Gulf state is thus forced to be as worried about the potential internal threat from its military forces as about the threats posed by foreign military powers... The most important military balance in most Gulf nations is often the one that prevents their own military forces from seizing power.[9]

The stockpiling of arms has obviously not promoted general political restraint in the Gulf, but an inclination to solve intricate questions by military means. An example of this kind of behaviour was the beginning of the Iraq-Iran war. The war started at a point where the political possibilities of preserving peace were clearly not yet exhausted. Neither side, for instance, made any attempt to call in the UN Security Council.

The history of more than twenty years of the arms-race in the Gulf indicates that there is a strong temptation to cut the Gordian knot by the sword it if is big and sharp enough. Under these circumstances a compromise, which by definition can never be a glorious victory, achievable only by long, painstaking and unspectacular negotiations, seems to be a much less attractive option.

Gavin Kennedy refers to the fact that having a strong and well equipped defence-force in being means a relatively low entry-cost to war. Because the economy has already paid for the personnel, consumables and equipment, this cost does not constitute a strong restraining factor in the initial stages of decision-making about war.[10]

It is as remarkable as it is fatal that the Superpowers, who pursued a course of *détente* in their bilateral relations in the early 1970s, carried out the militarisation-fostering policies that they did in the Gulf.

4. Up to now there has been no evidence of the falsity of Altaf Gauhar's well known saying of 1982 concerning the results of the arms-race in the Middle East: 'Two decades of profligate arms-spending did not resolve any dispute in the region, nor did any country acquire a greater sense of security. All that happened was that oil was converted into guns.'[11] Some countries in the Gulf, or adjacent to it, currently command armed forces comparable in numbers and in other quantitative terms with those of medium European powers, but although it is dubious, to say the least, whether these enormous armaments have positively influenced intra-regional security, it can be taken for granted that the risks of destruction in case of war have risen dramatically. Thus it appears to be unreasonable to expect a productive correlation between stability, security and conflict-settlement from an arms-race of the size and speed, and increasingly of the quality, of that which has been witnessed in the conflict-laden region of the Gulf, where military strategies and tactics are all-encompassing so as to include the various elements of *blitzkrieg*, surprise, attack, offensive strikes and pre-emptive action.

Dangerous Climax and Prospective Decline of the Role of Military Means in the Gulf

Military means are also increasingly losing their functional capabilities in regional conflicts, thereby becoming dysfunctional. The Gulf War teaches us a clear lesson: the huge destructive power, the ferocity of the troops engaged, the ability to sustain prolonged fighting, the capability to mobilise internal resources and external allies - all normally good and valuable military virtues - were not what was needed, in either country, to save the land and its inhabitants from death and destruction. What was supposed to be defended was destroyed, and despite the heavy losses in Iraq and Iran, no combatant was able to attain decisive victory. The price which has to be paid by the people of both countries for non-defence and non-victory in eight years of war has been immense:

- according to SIPRI estimates, the combatants, taken together, may have spent $170-200 billion on military activities and an additional $27 billion on arms imports;
- the losses caused by damage to the infrastructure and production systems reach possibly some $500 billion;
- to these sums ought to be added the costs created by human loss - the killed, wounded and those crippled for life - and the financial means required to compensate the families of the dead.

Oil constitutes for Iran as well as for Iraq the paramount export commodity. All the oil exported by Iran and Iraq from 1919 and 1931 respectively up to the end of the war, therefore, could easily add up to double the amount both countries have earned in decades.[12] (All figures are in constant 1985 prices)

Qualitatively new developments in the Middle East arms-race not only constitute a deadly threat to the Gulf, but imply serious repercussions for other continents as well. Solid information on ABC-weapons (atomic, i.e. nuclear, biological and chemical weapons) in the Gulf, on their development in or their import into the region, is as rare as can be. Speculation, as well as data from various intelligence sources, which is not verifiable, contrasts with strongly worded official denials; but the fascinating guessing game of 'are they trying to get the bomb, and, if so, how far have they got?' produces only poor results. What about the facts?

1.   An arms race has been taking place in the Gulf for many years, exhibiting what is an inevitable tendency of this kind of process, namely the escalation to ever higher quantitative and qualitative levels of armaments. As both history and the present show, this upward trend, and not a sudden halt, is the norm for an arms race.

2.   The results of militarisation processes in the Gulf have proved conclusively that the states of this region have tried to obtain the most modern, destructive and sophisticated weapons or weapons-systems either by purchase or by indigenous development and production.

3.   A considerable part - and this should not be confined to Iraq - of the political and military leadership in the Gulf and in adjacent countries has obviously come to the conclusion that a 'credible deterrence capability' based on weapons of mass destruction is an indispensable attribute of a (prospective) major power at a regional or global level.

4. Certain kinds of mass destructive weapons are already deployed in the region[13]. Serious doubts are no longer raised about Israel's status as a nuclear power, and the possession (and even the use) of chemical weapons by several Middle East countries is a matter of fact.

5. Nearly all of the Gulf states have formidable delivery-systems for weapons of mass destruction at their disposal. There are several types of high-performance aircraft systems capable of carrying nuclear weapons (F-15, F-16, SU-24, Mirage 2000, etc.) and of surface-to-surface ballistic missile systems. Two countries, Israel and Iraq, have entered the club of the space powers by successfully launching space rockets. At least three Middle East states (Israel, Iraq and Saudi Arabia) have ballistic missiles with a range of more than 1000 kilometres at their disposal, either by indigenous production or by import. More developments in this field are underway, for instance in Egypt and Syria.

6. In some states situated in or around the Gulf a great deal of research and development with potential civil and military use is being carried out. So called dual-use devices include, for example, the Krytrons seized by British customs in March 1990 while on their way to Iraq. They could serve as an extremely high precision timing-switch in laser-technology or to set off the chain reaction in a fission bomb. Bio-reactors - which are freely available - can synthesise bacteria and fungus-cultures for medical purposes and the food industry, or a brand of toxic germs such as milt inflammation, typhus or cholera. The case is very similar concerning chemical raw materials and the necessary processing machinery. Even within the weapons sector, dual-use questions are of considerable interest: is a missile equipped with conventional or nuclear/chemical/biological warheads?

7. The advice to be cautious about taking calming denials for granted should not be misinterpreted as worst-case thinking. Firm and repeated official denials could make sense not only to cover developments under way, but also to perform an absolute requirement where a bomb-in-the-basement strategy - as executed successfully by Israel - is being pursued. With regard to these facts and real

developments, and bearing in mind the extreme tensions in the Gulf region, it seems at the very least to be doubtful whether the Gulf states and their neighbours are going to dissociate themselves at this crucial point from the regional arms-race. Economic and technological barriers might prohibit the acquisition of certain types of weapon only for a time. They are by no means an insurmountable obstacle, especially if sufficient funds are available.

What will be the consequences of the likely proliferation of weapons of mass destruction in the Middle East and in the Gulf? Could it foster stability by creating a deterring balance of fear or undermine security further by increasing the temptation to launch the final, victorious blow against the enemy?

It is risky to try to answer hypothetical questions, but too much optimism could be a bad adviser. The technical dynamics inherent in the character, range and destructive capability of ABC-weapons would necessarily result in fatalities because of the then inseparable interlinking of at least two conflict-ridden, unstable regions, i.e. the Gulf and the eastern Mediterranean area. There have always, of course, been connections between the two regions, but the consequences of the existence of substantial stocks of weapons of mass destruction would intertwine the disputes, and even the local conflicts of each area, and transform them into a matter of regional importance. The potential number of enmities and adversaries could well be doubled; the possibilities of alliances and counter-alliances, and other imponderable developments, would as surely increase as the stability would decrease.

The further these hypothetical thoughts go into detail, the less attractive a Middle Eastern version of deterrence looks. The East-West deterrence emerged and developed in a predominantly bi-polar world with two military alliances, each with one Superpower on the commander's bridge and with the ability to secure the necessary harmony inside the respective camps. With the exception of the early post-war years the balance of power between the two blocs oscillated around a rough military equilibrium.

A certain intellectual and material safety mechanism has been incorporated in the East-West confrontation, including formalised security doctrines, agreements on the prevention of accidental or non-authorised attack, a 'hot line' between

Washington and Moscow, diplomatic and economic relations, and negotiations and agreements on arms reduction or limitation. All these security-enhancing and, to a certain extent, confidence-building measures were possible only because neither adversary left the common ground where the opponent had a right to exist and therefore some legitimate interests too, even in the military field.

A steadily-developed national electronic surveillance capability, state-of-the-art command, control, communications, intelligence systems (C^3I), the deployment of nuclear weapons on submarines, in fixed silos, or on board strategic bombers, all these succeeded in diminishing the dangerous feeling of vulnerability, as did the geographic distance between the main opponents.

The fact that none of these stabilising mechanisms - relative as they may have been - exist in the Middle East/Gulf region either now or, possibly, in the future, needs no explanation. Given the past and present situation in the Middle East, the question arises of where restraint, also a requirement in this region for survival in the age of possible mass destruction, could emerge. The area is characterised by at least two main conflicts, several other almost equally acute sub-conflicts, various wells of internal instability, the diverging interests of some would-be leading regional powers and the Superpowers behind the scenes, and, finally, an historical experience yielding the important lesson that wars are possible and can be won. The world, and especially an over-armed and conflict-ridden area like the Middle East, has become too small and too fragile for nuclear, chemical or biological weapons; but even if this assumption were to be disproved and it became possible to create a set of deterrence-schemes in the eastern Mediterranean, the Gulf and notably also in other Third World regions, especially in South Asia, would this be the master plan for peace and stability in the world of the 21st century? How much would it cost and how many years would it take? How many resources, human, material and financial, would have to be invested in the different C^3I systems and the relatively safe deployment of ABC-weapons?

The long and winding road of the two blocs appears to lead to disarmament, peace and co-operation after all, but it has been an extraordinarily expensive, dangerous and, in nearly every respect, unique and roundabout way which is not easy for completely different partners to copy under changed circumstances.

In Search of an Alternative

The question remains: Is there, in the contemporary world, and especially in the hostile environment of the Gulf, any realistic alternative to relying on the military, i.e. on soldiers and modern weapons, to defend the integrity of a given country and to protect the physical security of its people? Could a peaceful, but unarmed and therefore unsheltered, country survive in a region armed to the teeth?

Before going into details, two remarks should be made. First, this chapter does not favour a lofty and simplistic anti-militarism. 'Down With Weapons' may be a good slogan, but it has not got even a tiny chance of receiving any attention from the decision-makers in the Gulf, and the response of the people would surely also be a weak one. The military and military-based security have gained an important place in all societies in the world and rest on strong and solid interests. This historically grown and socially deep-rooted phenomenon could not and should not be eradicated immediately.

Secondly, on the other hand, it should be noted that the role of the military in the history of human civilisation has been relatively stable but not static. The most dramatic changes occurred after World War II. The hyper-successful development in military technology as regards range, destructive power, sophistication, etc., has deprived the military of one of its most important functions: it could no more serve as a mere extension of politics because this would mean the end of any forms of politics in the world. This chapter shares the opinion of those who think that this prediction is also gaining more and more validity in regional wars in the Third World and, consequently, likewise in the Gulf. The impossibility of achieving any reasonable political goal, gaining victory or effectively defending a land and people, as became manifest in the Iraq-Iran war, may support this assumption.

Kuwait, for example, could never be defended by military means against an - hypothetical - Iraqi or Iranian attack. 90 per cent of the population live in the capital, approximately 100 kilometres from the Iraqi border and less than 15 minutes flying-time away from the nearest Iranian air base, situated directly on the coast of the Gulf. There is no shelter from an air, land or sea attack, should one of the neighbouring giants decide to launch one.

The Gulf states, especially the smaller ones, are uniquely vulnerable should the nuclear-chemical threshold ever be crossed. The search for non-military schemes of security, or at least ones with diminished military elements, represents an imperative task. What could be done in this respect?

The situation requires determined efforts in the field of arms control and disarmament on a regional and global level, and a productive interaction between them:

1. An international conference under the auspices of the United Nations (maybe in co-operation with regional organisations) should gather all the states which import or export weapons to the Gulf and the Middle East or produce them inside the region. The aim of such a conference would be first to stabilise the intra-regional balance and then to explore ways and means of bringing down the levels of armaments.

2. A parallel or subsequent measure might consist of an agreement by the Gulf states to decrease their arms spending and to envisage a long-term programme of restructuring their armed forces. The task is to strengthen the defensive capabilities of the Gulf armies relative to the offensive power of all sides. This can best be achieved by relatively small, mobile, a-centrally led units preferably equipped with light or medium arms.

3. The discussion in the UN framework about a nuclear-weapons-free zone (NWFZ) in the Middle East should be resumed. In 1980 the UN General Assembly adopted, by consensus, an Egyptian resolution on the establishing of a NWFZ in the region. The Israeli attack on the Iraqi nuclear reactor Osiraq in 1981 prevented any further development in this direction. Nevertheless this consensus achieved ten years ago has not been suspended by any party concerned and could therefore serve as a basis for concrete negotiations to ban nuclear, chemical and biological weapons in the Middle East. Because of the deadly threat

posed by these weapons, first and foremost to the civilian population, this question should be given paramount priority.

4. There are spiritual obstacles to be overcome in the effort to introduce steps towards substantial de-militarisation in the region and to diminish the danger of war. The public perception of the arms race and its consequences in the Gulf and in the Middle East generally, as well as the lessening of the Middle Eastern states' chronic distrust of each other, are seen to be critically important in this respect. It would be very helpful to establish a mechanism for the systematic exchange of information on military manpower and arms stockpiles, plans for arms acquisition, military expenditure etc., and to make the most of the key data available to the public.

5. Mutually acceptable non-military conflict-resolution instruments should be revitalised or initiated in the Gulf and adjacent areas. The UN and/or regional institutions might fulfil tasks in the manifold verification processes that arise once disarmament has started. The International Court could found regional subsidiaries to avoid the fatal step from stalemate in negotiations to war by interposing with impartial arbitration as an additional non-violent means. Furthermore, several kinds of joint commissions and regional peacekeeping forces could be envisaged that might provide non-violent possibilities for discussion, and even allow for consensual and peaceful change of a *status quo*-situation which has become untenable or intolerable.

It is highly improbable that the possible moves to stability by disarmament in the Gulf/Middle East outlined above could be undertaken successfully without fundamental changes in the overall political environment, both regionally and globally.

First and foremost, any attempt to reduce the armament levels in the region substantially must be seconded by serious efforts to settle the political disputes underlying military confrontation and the arms race. The region's countries and organisations, as also the world community and its institutions, must be requested to intensify activities to bring the Arab-Israeli conflict, the Palestinian question and the Iraqi-Iranian confrontation closer to a solution.

Progress toward substantial disarmament in the Gulf, therefore, seems to be very unlikely under the current volatile conditions. Secondly, the Superpowers bear a special responsibility in this respect. Without their active participation, or even if they display an attitude conducive to procrastination, no results can be achieved. This responsibility also entails a distinct change in the political behaviour of the United States and the Soviet Union. Their rivalry, in a regional context, in quest of influence or bases, and their policies directed towards 'controlling' certain areas or preventing their control by their opponent, have turned out to be obsolete in the last decade of the 20th century and in some cases even dangerous, and they should therefore be abandoned. The pretended necessity for not suffering the shameful defeat of the weapons they had supplied has constituted an element which has fuelled and delayed armed conflicts, and was suited to transforming local disputes into global confrontation. Further, the 'vital interests' claim, like similar pretensions, implied a readiness to intervene, as practised several times by each of the Superpowers; but, of course, only by removing the danger of foreign intervention or military domination could arms be made superfluous in a region like the Gulf.

A crucial role in the process of damping down and stopping the arms race, let alone implementing a disarmament scheme in the Gulf/Middle East, depends on the will and ability of the major powers to reduce their arms spending, their arms stockpiling and their arms production. Of course, the readiness of the Soviet Union and of the United States drastically to decrease their nuclear weapons, and to abandon their chemical weapons, represents the most critical element. Determined, far-reaching and irreversible steps towards disarmament by the military giants are a decisive prerequisite for substantial arms-reduction on a regional scale, 'not only because the United States and the Soviet Union account for more than half of global military expenditures and control by far the largest arsenals', says Michael Renner,

but also because an unfettered arms race between them indirectly lends legitimacy to other countries' efforts to acquire nuclear weapons. As long as possession of a nuclear arsenal seems to have political or military value, conferring special status and diplomatic leverage, it is of little surprise that countries such as Argentina, Brazil, India, Iraq, Israel, Pakistan and South Africa have crossed or seek to cross the nuclear threshold.[14]

Conclusion

It may be that this chapter will be charged with having been naïve and illusory. It is, of course, up to the reader to decide whether or not the main evaluations and conclusions are based on reality. The research efforts which preceded the elaboration of this study brought the author to the conclusion that it would indeed be illusory to assume that a copy of the prevailing military-oriented security policy could form a suitable instrument to achieve security, stability and peace in Third World regions, for example in the Gulf. Militarised thought and action in the East and the West which has swallowed trillions of dollars, led mankind several times to the brink of a nuclear holocaust, contributed to cementing a world order under which one part was armed to the teeth, while another part was fighting for physical survival, is being given up bit by bit by its main proponents. It will disappear slowly because practically nobody can afford the enormous costs it requires and because it can only fulfil its task, to preserve (an ever fragile) peace, less and less efficiently. Alva Myrdal's statement that 'all countries are now buying greater and greater insecurity at higher and higher costs,'[15] describes a fact which is valid for the Gulf region as well.

The facts, figures and reflections provided by this chapter suggest that wishful thinking is undertaken by those who want to proceed with the hazardous 'zero sum game' in the regional arms-race. A new realism is required, which is oriented towards the objective tasks of guaranteeing the future, and not just at the conventional wisdom, the current prejudices and the extent of the political imagination of the day.

Two short reservations are to be added. A clear distinction should always be made between the necessity and the reality of regional disarmament. This matter is not of course - although urgent enough - on the list of priorities of the decision-makers in the Gulf either today or tomorrow; but it represents a strategic imperative and a necessary orientation for all the Gulf states, and for the Superpowers and their allies who have contributed so actively to the militarisation of the region.

In addition, any kind of demonisation of militarisation-processes should be avoided. This would imply *inter alia* an idealisation of the possible results disarmament might provide. The problems and sorrows of the Third World in general, and the Gulf in particular, did not start with the weapons inflow and will not disappear with their reduction, but some of them probably will; and because militarisation is intertwined with other urgent problems, steps to reduce armaments in the Gulf would necessarily include tackling scores of grievances which are harassing the people and the governments of the Gulf. Going into further, deeper details, analysing backgrounds and interrelationships, synthesising general theoretical knowledge and formulating adequate proposals for proper solutions, all these seem to constitute a formidable but also a rewarding subject for research.

Notes

1   SIPRI, *SIPRI Yearbook 1989: World Armaments and Disarmament* (Oxford University Press, New York, 1989), p. 184.

2   Ibid., pp. 183-4; SIPRI, *SIPRI Yearbook 1987*, pp. 135-6; A.H. Cordesman, *The Gulf and the Search for Strategic Stability: Saudi Arabia, the Military Balance in the Gulf, and Trends in the Arab-Israeli Military Balance* (Westview, Boulder and Mansell, London, 1984), pp. 202, 224.

3   Cordesman, *The Gulf*, p. 501.

4   M. Brzoska and T. Ohlson, *Arms Transfers to the Third World 1971-1985* (Oxford University Press, New York, 1987), pp. 338-48; SIPRI, *SIPRI Yearbook 1989*, pp. 210-11.

5   Ibid., p. 196.

6   Cordesman, *The Gulf*, pp. 152-3; The International Institute for Strategic Studies, *The Military Balance 1988-1989* (London, 1988), pp. 97-118.

7   Wireless Bulletin from Washington (USICA Bonn), 24 Jan., 1980.

8   G. Russel, 'Everybody's Doing it', *Time* (New York), 16 March 1987, p. 33; W. Zank, 'Wundersame Wege des Pulverclubs', *Die Zeit* (Hamburg), Nr. 46, 6 Nov. 1987, pp. 30-1; SIPRI, *Information Sheet on the Iraq-Iran War 1980-1988* (Stockholm, 1988), p. 5.

9   Cordesman, *The Gulf*, pp. 494-5.

10 G. Kennedy, 'War Economics', in R.E. Harkavy and S.G. Neuman (eds.), *The Lessons of Recent Wars in the Third World*, vol. II (Lexington, Lexington, Mass., 1987), p. 97.

11 A. Gauhar, 'Weapons go where the money is', *South* (London), July 1982, p. 11.

12 SIPRI, *SIPRI Yearbook 1989*, pp. 165-6; SIPRI, *Information Sheet*, pp. 2-3.

13 As far as ABC-weapons are concerned, the area under scrutiny may not be

limited to the Gulf region. Due to the wider range of these weapons, at least the eastern Mediterranean has to be included.

14   M. Renner, 'National Security: The Economic and Environmental Dimensions', *World Watch Paper 89* (Washington, DC, 1989), p. 55.

15   A. Myrdal, 'The Game of Disarmament', in R.E. Jolly (ed.), *Disarmament and World Development* (Oxford University Press, New York, 1978), p. 85.

14. THE INEVITABILITY OF CHANGE: THE UNDERTOW OF POLITICAL TIDES IN THE GULF[1]

John Townsend

There are three strong political currents converging on the shores of the conservative Arab oil-producing states of the Gulf. The purpose of this chapter is to examine whether the existing bulwarks of Gulf society can hope to withstand the strongly flowing tides that threaten it in the last decade of the twentieth century. These political forces are, first, populist Islam, second, the spirit of the *Intifada* in Palestine, and third, the example of the successful undermining of the socialist autocracies of central and eastern Europe.

These three political ideas have a common base: they are popular, of the people. They are grass-roots political movements which have evolved and thrown up leaders. Khomeini's success in Iran was only possible because he expressed the will of and spoke for the popular spirit of the times. Each of these three political ideas has a positive and dynamic, albeit a very different, ideology. Although there are substantial contradictions between the ideologies, each of them has an identical primary objective: the removal of apparently well-entrenched governments which are seen, rightly or wrongly, to be autocratic, authoritarian, manipulative, increasingly unrepresentative and often corrupt and their replacement by a government ultimately answerable to the people.

The governments of the six conservative Arab oil-producing nations of what is commonly termed 'the Gulf' - Bahrain, Kuwait, Oman, Qatar, Saudi Arabia and the United Arab Emirates - have every reason to be nervous of these populist movements. The windfall affluence of surplus oil-revenues has permitted these essentially paternalistic governments to bring extraordinary and far-reaching changes, and tangible and visible benefits to their peoples. Effectively, there has been an obvious economic and at the same time, a profound social revolution.

Within little more than one generation, societies which had been amongst the poorest and most deprived in the world became, at least in terms of gross domestic product per head of population, amongst the richest. Profound social changes for individuals and society inevitably followed.

In the centuries before oil, these societies, with the questionable exception of Oman, did not exist as separate, coherent nations. It might be argued that Oman had a national entity long before oil was discovered, in spite of substantial tribal differences and civil wars. There is some truth in this, but the fact remains that as recently as the late 1960s, the typical Omani community was like the typical community in virtually any other part of the Arabian Peninsula: small, numbered in hundreds of souls, isolated, cut off from its neighbours by extremely poor and difficult communications. In common with communities throughout the Arabian Peninsula, those in Oman permitted survival at a subsistence level only. The poor communications in an especially harsh environment made anything approaching a market economy virtually a non-starter.

Less than 20 years ago, in Oman, the author of this chapter was privileged to be invited by an Omani friend to visit his village, some 150 miles from Muscat. The journey took all day in a Landrover, following near-impassable tracks through some very rugged country. In the evening, over the ritual coffee, a villager asked: 'How long did your journey from Muscat take?'

'Ten hours.'

'Ten hours? Last time I went to Muscat, it took seven days on a camel'.

A mere twenty years ago, that was the norm throughout the Arabian Peninsula. There was a sprinkling of wealthy people, rulers and their families and merchants, in cities and towns, but they were the few. The many knew only poverty. A man considered himself blessed by Allah if he survived forty summers, a woman if she survived her second confinement. Parents expected that three out of every four children born to them would die within the first 12 months of their lives. Easily eradicable diseases such as trachoma, caused by a vitamin-deficient diet and spread by flies, were widespread. There were neither schools nor hospitals. People were oppressed by the tyrannies of poverty, ignorance and isolation. The overriding communal objective was survival; an individual could not survive on his or her own. Only through the community could survival be ensured - and only through adherence to basic rules which were at once immutable and inflexible.

In such societies, political systems had to be conservative. The community was led by a man who would ensure that the basic rules were not broken and to whom the community delegated the task of defending it against enemies. Enemies would invariably be people from similar communities who, driven by poverty or cupidity, or a mixture of both, would seek to rob their neighbours merely to ensure their own survival. Although communal decisions were arrived at wherever possible by consensus following often lengthy discussion and argument, the demands of communal survival meant that communal leaders could only be effective and themselves survive if they had a strong right arm, a good sword, an authoritarian personality and exceptional manipulative political skills.

In such societies, there could be no challenging of basic social rules, because any such challenge would put the survival of the community at risk. It takes nothing away from a respect for and appreciation of the enormous spiritual strengths of Islam to say that Islam provides also a code for personal and communal survival in a naturally harsh environment in which people feel constantly threatened. Thus a politically intelligent ruler will inevitably invoke Islam in ensuring that the community he rules ensures its own survival by following the rules. Naturally, such a policy helps ensure the political survival of the ruler.

A politically intelligent ruler can continue to ensure his own political survival by being seen to have impeccable Islamic credentials. After his father, King Abd al-Aziz, no ruler or leader in the Arabian Peninsula in the twentieth century was respected as much as King Faisal. Faisal was seen throughout the peninsula as both a great ruler and an outstanding Moslem.

At a personal level in the traditional societies of the peninsula, there was very little room for personal choice by individuals. To European ears, the expression 'traditional society' could imply a society in the remote past but in the Arabian Peninsula, any man or woman now aged 25 or more was born in the 'traditional society'. It was the traditional society that moulded the social attitudes of his or her parents.

In the marginal and extremely harsh environment of these societies, any degree of personal choice, any marked independence of spirit, simply could not be countenanced. Such education as existed was primarily centred on the conformity necessary for group survival. Boys and girls had to learn a skill which permitted them to be immediately useful members of the community. Marriages were arranged with the concept of the best interests of the community - and family betterment, naturally enough - being uppermost in the minds of the parents of the bride and bridegroom.

When surplus oil-revenues permitted investment, most Gulf governments built roads, followed by schools and hospitals. But roads were of paramount importance: they were instrumental in removing the tyranny of distance and poor communications, and, by making internal trade physically possible, permitted a cash economy to take the place of the old subsistence economy and thus conquer the tyranny of poverty. This was when the economic revolution began to filter down to the remoter parts of the peninsula. Hospitals and a national health care service caused dramatic improvements in the health and life expectancy of men, women and children, and schools permitted the introduction of a policy to which every Gulf government has given priority: manpower (and womanpower) development.

The sudden shift from centuries of struggle for survival has inevitably produced a corresponding social revolution. The priority given to manpower development during the windfall affluence period of the oil-boom years and the concomitant transformation of Gulf societies from rural subsistence to wealthy urban communities has created a substantially new social environment. Some 60 per cent or more of Gulf citizens are aged 20 or less; they are the children of the oil-boom years. They have no personal experience of the long centuries of poverty and hardship that moulded and tempered the lives of countless generations of their predecessors. Young Saudis, young Omanis, young Kuwaitis, young people throughout the Gulf have become aware of the possibility of choice, a privilege of fundamental importance. This is a concept that their parents and grandparents could never have envisaged and with which many still have great difficulty. An education is no longer a question of acquiring skills related to something of obvious and immediate specific relevance to the community - making coffee and herding camels, for example - but implies a much wider national and international perspective.

Some of the young Saudi men or women, for example, who have studied outside the kingdom and obtained a good postgraduate degree, are less than happy to return to a society where personal choice remains trammelled by tradition. One of the more striking - and often poignant - examples of young people demanding the right to exercise choice is provided by the growing number of young Saudi women who refuse arranged marriages.

But contrary to what might be imagined by their Western contemporaries, not every young Gulf citizen seeks to choose freely a career and lifestyle. Very often, the most fervent Moslems among the younger generation of Gulf citizens are those who have studied in Europe or the United States and who have returned home apparently determined to show their peers that they have in no way been corrupted by the material and venal lures of the West. But a growing number accept established norms less easily. Some take drugs and tend to drop out. Others question increasingly the apparent direction in which their nation is heading. With the exception of Kuwait, there is probably nothing in any Gulf country which could be termed an organised political opposition; nor is there any apparent coherence in dissenting views. Yet up and down the Gulf, the voices of criticism and dissent are growing.

Many younger Gulf citizens criticised national economic policies in the wake of the first oil price collapse in 1986. These voices were heard again in 1988, when the oil-market weakened once more. There are rumblings again in the earlier part of 1990 as oil prices experience another cyclical fall. There is a temptation to sweep much of this criticism under the carpet as being the verbal expression of disappointed expectations of effortless capital-accumulation by the age group that just missed the easy financial pickings of the boom years. Yet, having made every allowance for the majority of young Gulf citizens who accept without too much difficulty the conservatism of their elders, for those who resent having to work for a living, for the disappointed, for the drug-takers and the drop-outs, there is a growing number of young Gulf citizens - men and women - who increasingly ask a basic question:

We have been given a wide and international education. An essential element in this education has been encouragement to think for ourselves and to challenge conventional norms. A modern scientific education means the ability to mount intellectual challenges and to question basic assumptions. Why should we not now be permitted to question and to challenge the way in which our country is governed? This is not to say that we seek radical change, but we need to know more about how basic economic policies are being made, and above all, about policies that touch immediately upon the lives and the well-being of our families. The government tells us very little. Published statistics are sometimes two years out of date, and can be misleading. In short, we need a national forum where national economic policies can be debated.

What is noteworthy about this statement (an amalgam of a number of statements to the author over the last 12 months) is its reasonableness. There is no questioning of basic constitutional arrangements, no request for information on defence and security arrangements, no apparent dispute on foreign policy, no challenging the right of the ruling family to rule. There is simply a request for more information and for an effective forum where national economic policies may be debated.

When statements such as this are put to officials in Gulf governments by concerned outsiders, there is a small number who concur and who appear to be deeply preoccupied both about the way their country is being governed and the implication of where certain key government policies are leading. But for each aware and concerned official, there must be at least ten who regard the question as impertinent, and as yet another attempt by foreigners to 'say bad things about our country and about the Arabs'. Of the small number of this group who are prepared to listen and to talk, a not unreasonable view is that intellectuals in all countries tend to be somewhat politically naïve and that quasi-political questions emanating from a very small number of Gulf citizens who have studied abroad have very little relevance to the furtherance of overall national policies. This view holds that the 'silent majority' of

Gulf citizens, irrespective of their nation, respect their rulers and their government, that they would not wish any other form of government, that they are uniformly and universally grateful to their government for the very great benefits of the oil-boom years, and that everything is now for the best in the best of all possible Saudi (or Omani, or Kuwaiti, or other Gulf nation) worlds, and will continue to be so for all time, due praise be given to Allah.

They may be right. When foreigners counter that there is no historical precedent in the records of mankind for a small non-representative oligarchy or plutocracy succeeding in holding on to political power *in perpetuum*, they risk the 'saying bad things' accusation. A somewhat more intelligent response from Gulf, and especially Saudi, citizens is that a government based on Islam is, by definition, near-perfect and hence, by Allah's giving, will survive. As a corollary, those who hold this view are led inevitably to criticise bitterly the alleged obsession with material values by large numbers of Gulf citizens who profess none the less to be good Moslems.

Defensively, governments in the Gulf argue against this small group of educated and sometimes vocal younger citizens and aver that the existing consultative mechanisms are adequate. Stressing that the groups who argue for any sort of change are small and unrepresentative, senior members of Gulf governments sincerely (in many cases at least) believe that they really do command the unswerving support of the great majority of their citizens.

An Economist Intelligence Unit publication, *Arabian Peninsula*[2], says:

rulers and citizens alike have retained an innate conservatism which has merely been reinforced by external factors such as war and revolution. On the whole it is as strong among the emerging middle class of merchants, technocrats and civil servants as among the traditional shaikhly class. It translates into an extreme deference towards the ruling families of the peninsula which, given the trappings of late 20th century society, distance ruler from people. The openness between shaikh and tribesman of traditional Arabia was attractive to outsiders and was often upheld by nationals as a more valid form of democracy than the various versions adopted in the West. It did not, of course, guarantee a remarkable degree of stability in the past; rulers have been ousted or assassinated in most Gulf states. Yet the modern, somewhat more remote form of government saw fewer *coups*.

In fact, those rulers who have been either ousted or assassinated in the past were in almost all cases victims of family feuds or rivalries. It is difficult to find an historical precedent for a successful challenge to a ruling family coming from outside the family.

As to the modern form of government itself, the publication quoted above continues:

Gulf rulers surround themselves with a circle of advisers composed almost exclusively of family members. Each also has a cabinet where the major ministries - defence, interior, foreign affairs, sometimes finance, sometimes oil - will be held by the ruling family. Some family members may be extremely able but the system does not insist on merit. The family often provides its head with his only links to his people, through the *majlis*, an informal gathering at home of men who drop in, usually in the evening, with a comment, a complaint or a request...

In Kuwait the majlis has developed into a slightly more formalised *diwaniya*. Most leading families will patronise these huge weekly gatherings, usually on Thursday evenings, to discuss events, policies and personalities far into the night.

Kuwait used to have a parliament, a parliament elected, it is true, on a very restricted franchise, but a parliament for all that, a forum which was marked by spirited (if at times somewhat cynical and ill-informed) debate on national issues. This parliament has been dissolved by the ruler twice, the last time being in 1986. Having tasted the heady wine of free (more or less) political debate, Kuwaitis want their parliament back. But the Kuwaiti ruling family, which has the support of ruling families up and down the Gulf on this issue, is extremely reluctant to open the Pandora's box of political liberty once again.

On achieving full independence in 1971, Bahrain established a national assembly elected from a small electorate, very much along the lines of Kuwait. Debates in this assembly were seen by the ruling family to be unduly critical, and the assembly was abruptly closed in 1972.

Both the United Arab Emirates and Oman have consultative assemblies the members of which are appointed by the ruling family and by other establishment interest groups. The Emirates assembly survives because in the federal structure of the UAE, criticism of the Federal government is not regarded as being such a serious matter as similar criticism of any one of the ruling families in the seven constituent members of the Federation.

As far as the Omani consultative assembly is concerned, informed comment is not possible mainly because sessions are not open to the public. There is no encouragement of public debate of national issues.

Although Qatar has a consultative assembly, nominated by the ruler, Saudi Arabia does not and there is no formal forum in the kingdom in which national issues may be debated.

A broadly sustainable generalisation on the representative and consultative political structures of the conservative Arab oil-states of the Gulf would be that these states have political forms evolved out of a centuries-old survival, imperative in a naturally harsh and marginal environment. The generalisation would continue that the windfall affluence of surplus oil-revenues over the space of rather more than one generation has permitted ruling families to add considerable strength to their essentially patriarchal and manipulative political skills; in essence, political support can and has been obtained by the age-old practices of benefits and favours bestowed.

It is probable that the Gulf countries collectively will be able to count on oil revenues for at least another decade. Natural causes will inevitably bring new rulers, and new rulers will probably introduce some degree of political innovation. A critical question is whether the shaikhly system - that is, a self-perpetuating system of government by a ruling family and a plutocracy in which dynastic survival has the highest national priority - will remain unchallenged?

The union of the two Yemens provides a new element in the political configuration of the Arabian Peninsula. Both Yemens have a history of formal colonial domination, revolution and civil war which their neighbours to the north and east have not known. These neighbours, Saudi Arabia, Oman and the other conservative Arab states of the Gulf, believe that they can look at Yemeni unification with a degree of equanimity. There may also be a certain nervousness, if only because in terms of numbers, there are more relatively hungry Yemenis in the peninsula than there are relatively comfortable Gulf and Saudi citizens.

The new Yemen Republic has an elected parliament. But it would be difficult to find a Saudi or a Gulf citizen today who would deign to consider that the conservative oil-states can learn anything politically from Yemenis. The experience that most citizens and officials have of Yemen and Yemenis is of hordes of unskilled immigrant workers, almost a helot class, and of a suppliant nation. Yet in terms of popular participation in government and a degree of political accountability, the Yemen Republic, for all its many weaknesses, is in advance of these conservative states.

But what about neighbouring Jordan, and more distant Algeria? In both these countries, the rumblings of popular pressure for substantial political change are becoming louder. In both countries economic pressures are behind much of the political agitation, but there are also social pressures pushing for change. In both countries a growing class of urban poor, under-privileged and often unemployed, is registering its discontent. In each country, this group is providing fertile ground for Islamic populists and extremists. In each country, the government is engaged in a belated effort to create an effective dialogue with the people and to amend and develop the institutions of government so that a dialogue may be started before reaching the point of rupture which, to some at least, seems inevitable.

In Algeria, in local government elections on 12 June 1990, the Islamic Salvation Front polled nearly 65 per cent of the popular vote in an admittedly low poll. Nearly 6 million Algerians, men and women, voted in protest against the policies of their government. Many observers regarded the following comment from an ordinary Algerian in his mid-thirties who voted for the Islamic Salvation Front[3] as both typical and underlining the basic problem of the Algerian government:

In this country, if you are a young man ... you only have four choices: you can remain unemployed and celibate because there are no jobs and no flats to live in; you can work in the black market and risk being arrested; you can try to emigrate to France to sweep the streets of Paris or Marseilles, or you can join the Front and vote for Islam.

A protest vote against the government and for Islam was undoubtedly an important factor in Algeria's first free elections. For some Algerians, even more important was the fact that they were, for the first time ever, permitted to engage in a free and far-ranging political debate.

In Jordan, King Hussein, keenly aware that dynastic survival is the issue, permitted a national election in November 1989. The June 1990 issue of *Saudi Arabia Monitor* said:

King Hussein's democratic experiment, initiated in response to trans-Jordanian anti-government riots in April 1989, has led to real political reforms. The King's immediate aim was to prevent further violent outbreaks, to respond to popular demands for political participation and to share responsibility with parliament for the unpopular policy choices to come. His long-term aim, however, is to both legitimise and guarantee Hashemite rule. This April, King Hussein appointed a 60-member Royal Commission, comprising representatives from all political trends, to draw up a National Charter. The Charter is expected to secure allegiance for the monarchy within an agreed political structure - including the legalisation of political parties.

The fact is that democratisation is working for stability in Jordan. The King has in effect co-opted the opposition on the basis of a promised return to the 1952 Constitution; and today there is no significant opposition wanting to remove him. The internal debate is over the shape of Jordan's future political order, and the new Hashemite partnership with the people is helping to strengthen popular identification with the state and define Jordan's identity at a time when growing numbers of right-wing Israelis want to establish a Palestinian state in Jordan.

The result of the King's chosen democratic path is official tolerance - within limits - of a range of political activities. There is a freer press; secular political parties, though still formally banned, are now openly active...

It can be argued that the experience of Algeria and of Jordan has little relevance to the wealthy states of the Gulf. Maybe. The obvious rejoinder is one word: 'Kuwait'. In Kuwait, the Kuwaiti citizens agitating for a restoration of their parliament are neither poor, unemployed nor insecure.

But before considering what is happening in Kuwait, it is worth looking at the Intifada in Palestine. Does this popular uprising, an extraordinary expression of political opposition, have any lessons for Gulf governments?

The Intifada is many things. This chapter is not an appropriate vehicle for an attempted analysis of cause and effect. Perhaps less surprisingly than may be thought, some of the best analysis has come from certain Israeli sources. In a recent balanced and scholarly book entitled *Intifada*[4], Ze'ev Schiff and

Ehud Ya'ari point to a number of lessons to be learned by governments, officials and people not only in Israel but in the Arab world as well. Governments which become complacent, which lose touch with the people, are at risk. They risk an explosion of popular anger which can sweep them away. (This is what happened in the countries of central Europe). Schiff and Ya'ari say:

The Intifada was an assertion of defiance which bubbled up from below, a statement by the legions of Palestinian youth who felt bereft of a future; the high school and university students doomed to choose between indignity and exile; the tens of thousands of labourers who made their living in Israel but were expected to remain invisible; the veterans of Israeli prisons who were more convinced than ever of the justice of their cause but saw their people sinking deeper and deeper into hopelessness. In short, it was the work of the Palestinian masses, and that is why it surprised everyone: the   complacent Israeli authorities, the overconfident Jordanians, the self-satisfied PLO leadership, and even local Palestinians regarded as influential figures in the territories. A popular revolt with all the hallmarks of a genuine revolution, it erupted suddenly and created a new strategy for the Palestinian struggle that confounded both the PLO establishment, scrambling wildly to keep up with events from afar, and the native leadership, whose constituents were suddenly spinning out of control.'

Again, it can be argued that, as important as the Intifada is in the Arab world, it really has very little relevance in those best of all possible worlds, the wealthy and conservative Arab oil-producing states of the Gulf. But again, a warning note is sounded by the experience of Kuwait.

Some people have said that in Kuwait it is the Shiᶜa population that is behind the popular pressure and occasional demonstrations for political change. There may be some grounds for this, but the relatively small Kuwaiti Shiᶜa community has no monopoly in seeking political change and in any case is closely watched by the authorities. Others say that it is the large Palestinian population in Kuwait seeking to make trouble for the Kuwaiti government. The truth is that Kuwait's Palestinian community, taken as a whole, has much to lose and tends to be conservative. The reality is that the pressure for a reconvening of the Kuwaiti parliament and for new elections comes from Kuwaiti citizens. Yet, no one can say that Kuwaitis are oppressed by a brutal and insensitive occupation, that they suffer great economic hardship, that they are under-privileged, that they have to seek employment outside Kuwait to keep their families alive.

Nor is it the Kuwaiti business establishment that seeks a broadening of the political base in the state. In general, Kuwaiti businessmen are closely allied to the ruling family, with which they have a close identity of purpose and objectives. The Kuwaiti business community is, naturally enough, conservative and has no wish to change the *status quo*. It is in general young Western-educated Kuwaitis who are demanding a greater say in national decision-making. It is this group which points to the reality of the tumbled regimes of central and eastern Europe. These regimes were outwardly paternalistic and manipulative, but in reality acted in cynical disregard of the common good by abusing the system for financial advantage, personal aggrandisement and power lust.

Young Kuwaitis are quick to recall the *Suq al-Manakh* affair in 1986 and the resignation of a Minister of Finance on a matter of principle linked to his attempt to find a just solution to a serious national problem, a solution which came up against certain high-placed vested interests in Kuwait.

Young Kuwaitis see also, as does virtually every thinking and politically aware adult in the world, that governments in central and eastern Europe lost contact completely with the people, in spite of having elaborate and greatly feared internal-security organisations. Lord Acton's adage that power tends to corrupt and absolute power corrupts absolutely was amply demonstrated in central and eastern Europe. It could be said also that unchallenged rulers, who gather around them sycophantic advisers and whose contacts with the people they govern become tenuous, tend to become complacent, and this complacency will ultimately spell political doom.

Senior Gulf ministers and officials argue that events of this kind could not happen in the Gulf because of the strength of the links between the ruling families and the people. Most observers would sincerely hope that this will prove to be the case. The Shah of Iran was convinced that his links with his people were deep and permanent, as was President Sadat. In each case, the world considered that Islamic activists stirred up the opposition. This is not disputed, but it can be argued that

Islam formed an ideal rallying-point for popular distress and a general lack of confidence in rulers, especially in situations where political opposition is not encouraged or is immature. The mosques form a network and an organisation which a politically ambitious and unscrupulous cleric, playing on popular frustrations and feelings of insecurity, can manipulate to his own advantage.

This brings the discussion back to Kuwait. Quoting the April 1990 *Saudi Arabia Monitor*,

Demands to restore the National Assembly have been strong and will not go away. The opposition - the groups that want to restore parliament - are concerned that, amongst other things, public account-ability has deteriorated since the assembly was suspended in 1986 and that opposition groups have no forum for expressing their views and complaints. While the big meetings have died down, discussion of the assembly has not; most probably, the Al Sabah, whose shrewd understanding and experience of the country have kept them in power for 200 years, will acquiesce in the autumn, but to a somewhat different format. The Al Sabah apparently want to deal with the assembly issue on their own, and have warned off other senior Kuwaitis from taking an active role in the political discussions on the grounds that ruling Kuwait is their patch. Not by any means all sophisticated Kuwaitis are keen to see the assembly restored: some prefer government by the Al Sabah to the pro-assembly groups, whom they see as greedy and expedient.

The first agitation for a new assembly, which emerged during autumn 1989, came from the radicals, and then other groups, such as the fundamentalists and Shiᶜa, joined the bandwagon. The use of the evening assemblies, the diwaniya, for holding large meetings was a new tactic in Kuwait, though similar in style to the mass meetings in eastern Europe. The changes in eastern Europe cannot be discounted as a stimulus, but Kuwaitis are swift to say there is no direct time-link between the two. The stirrings of democracy in the Arab world - e.g. in Jordan, Tunisia and Algeria - have also had an effect.

The ruling family, usually so skilled in its dealings with Kuwaitis, seems to have reacted clumsily to the political discontent. Some people suggest that the Al Sabah have not been too canny in their choice of ministers; that some ministers are weak and have tended, especially in the recent political fracas, to tell the Emiri family more what they wanted to hear than the true nature of the position. The Al Sabah, no doubt under pressure from their neighbours not to accede to another assembly, are probably playing for time - which is really not in their interests; they should be proactive, not reactive. When an assembly is finally formed, the Al Sabah will want its terms of reference changed, and here will run up against a Catch-22 situation: the terms for the assembly cannot be changed without changing the constitution; the constitution cannot be changed without ratification from the assembly.

Some Kuwaitis are puzzled that the ruling family has not grasped the simple principle - absence of representative government is fine when citizens' economic needs and aspirations are being met. But when this is no longer the case, as now, and in a country that already has a tradition of some popular representation, an assembly becomes genuinely necessary.

It is possible to envisage some dramatic evolutionary political changes in Kuwait within the next one-to-two years. It is conceivable that these changes - if they take place - would be of a generally peaceful nature. It is certain that the other conservative Arab states of the Gulf will seek to insulate themselves from political developments in Kuwait.

Should there be radical political developments in Saudi Arabia, it is scarcely conceivable that the other Gulf states could remain unaffected. It becomes therefore important to consider Saudi Arabia and examine those forces which might act as a catalyst for substantial political evolution.

The Saudi government's position has been - at least since the death of King Faisal in March 1975 - that it had drawn up plans for the establishment of a Consultative National Assembly, a *Majlis al-Shura*, and that it would implement these plans 'at the right time'. A building to house the projected Majlis al-Shura was in fact constructed in Riyadh during the oil-boom years.

The key word in Saudi Arabia may well be 'accountability'. The nature of the political contract between the ruling family, the Al Su\c{c}ud, and the people is that the people have in essence delegated all political power, including the formulation of detailed economic and social policies, to the ruling family. The family from time to time may seek to explain its policies, but is never called upon to justify them. 'Trust us; we know best what is good for you' would seem to be the essence of the family's message to the people.

In as much as the concept of 'we know best what is good for you' has been translated into undeniably substantial material benefits, the people have had little incentive to question government policies. Provided that this flow of material benefits continues, there would seem to be little reason for any significant call from the people for a change in the relationship, or for a call to the government to account for its actions.

Thus a key question in addressing the 'inevitability' of political change in Saudi Arabia is whether or not the rising expectations of the people can continue to be met. Popular expectations are rising, if for no other reason than that the population of the kingdom is increasing so very rapidly. On present rates of population growth, the population of Saudi Arabia - whatever is conjectured about its real total today - will double within 18 years.

There are two current issues on which the Saudi government's apparent refusal to discuss its policies openly and its *penchant* for secrecy could act to its detriment. These two issues are, first, the question of the nation's finances and its financial reserves, and second, its water supplies. Failure to be effective in handling either or both of these issues would inevitably activate a strong popular desire for greater governmental accountability in general. Both issues are vital to the future of the nation.

If it is accepted that substantial largesse on the part of the government is an essential element in the government-people relationship, and that injections of cash are effective lubricants to counter any friction in this relationship, then it becomes vital for a government always to have enough money. The importance of water in the Arabian Peninsula does not need to be stressed.

It requires no great prescience, no special awareness, to appreciate the fact that the Saudi nation - government and people - has been prodigal over the last 15 years with both financial and water resources. This would not matter if either resource was limitless. But there is an immediate problem: the nation as a whole does not know the extent of either its financial resources or its water resources. A few senior members of the government doubtless have this information, but they make no attempt to make it public.

'Trust us; we know best what is good for you' is a classic paternalistic and manipulative political policy statement. It implies a continuing and unquestioned complete delegation of policy- and decision-making by the people to their rulers. It implies that searching questions are not considered necessary, and that any formal accountability by the government to the people is an irrelevance. This can be an effective policy for as long as the government gives the people no cause for complaint about its stewardship. It is, however, an open invitation to cover up any errors which governments may have made. It might also tempt governments to a degree of coercion if too many people start asking too many awkward questions.

As far as Saudi Arabia's financial position is concerned, published information is generally up to two years out of date, and tends to be very general. Any interested Saudi citizen who studies this published information is likely to find manifest anomalies and even contradictions. There is no formal or informal mechanism for asking intelligent questions aimed at elucidation or clarification. It is possible to deduce from the published information that the Saudi government appears to be spending substantially more each year than it earns. The government is certainly borrowing from banks in the kingdom and from the Saudi private sector. It appears to have run down its external financial reserves substantially. The government's financial policies appear to be based on the expectation - or hope - that oil revenues will increase as the decade progresses and that eventually the excess of expenditures over revenues will be corrected. In the meantime, a mixture of tough budgetary control, running down reserves and borrowing will ensure that basic public sector financial commitments will be met and, most important, the expectations of the fast-growing Saudi population will not be disappointed.

This is carrying the 'trust us - we know best' concept to an extreme. It is a policy which gives rise to rumour and still more rumour. It is not difficult to find people in Saudi Arabia who will tell you that the Saudi government will face a serious financial crisis within the next one-to-two years. The government could scotch these rumours at the stroke of a pen by publishing up-to-date details of its financial situation, something that governments in most countries in the world feel, or are, obliged to do. No Saudi citizen would expect his government to do more than what other governments equally prominent in the International Monetary Fund would do as far as published national accounts are concerned. But failure to publish sufficiently detailed and meaning figures leads to rumours that the government has something to hide, that it is trying to cover up its own past errors. An extreme version of these rumours holds that the government faces a crisis for which it has itself no convincing solution. It is rumoured that external financial assets have been run down to a bare minimum, that gold has been sold in an attempt to meet international financial commitments linked with major defence purchases. It is said that the government's longer-term financial strategy is no more than the Micawberish 'something will turn up'.

It cannot be emphasised enough that the suggestions in the preceding paragraph are rumours. It is certainly possible that the Saudi government does not have a serious financial problem at this juncture. If this is the case, there would seem to be no reason why the government should not publish far more detailed national accounts and in so doing, take the Saudi people into its confidence, thus demonstrating a possibly acceptable degree of accountability.

As with national finances, so with water. There is one major difference, however: money can be borrowed, water cannot. In a number of areas of the kingdom, central pivot (and other) irrigation systems installed for wheat production have caused dramatic falls in the water table. It would seem that water consumption from natural aquifers, in certain areas at least, is substantially in excess of replenishment from natural causes. It is said that Saudi Arabia is sitting on an enormous underground reservoir, and that the kingdom is, in essence, mining water, in other words, treating water as a non-renewable resource.

In the recently published summary of the Fifth Five-Year Development Plan, to run from 1990 to 1994, the Saudi government recognises that its estimates for water consumption have, in the past, been too low. Again, the information provided by the government on the 'trust us - we know best' basis is inadequate and gives rise to rumour. Most Saudi citizens prefer not to think of a national water-crisis. The significant majority now living in cities and towns tends to shrug its shoulders and suggest that there will always be enough water from desalination to meet urban domestic needs.

They may be right. But, once again, it seems to outsiders that the Saudi government would have nothing to lose by taking its citizens into its confidence, by demonstrating that it trusts their collective common sense and maturity, and by publishing the detailed information at its disposal on the nation's water resources and the rate of depletion and replenishment.

If there is no possibility of a Saudi Arabian financial problem nor of a water supply problem in the next decade, everyone could only rejoice. But if a serious problem does arise, it is possible to envisage the Saudi people becoming very angry indeed with their rulers, who would have been seen to have broken their side of the political contract and, in doing so, to have lost political and personal credibility.

To revert to the title of this chapter, 'The Inevitability of Change' and to the reference in the opening paragraph to three strong political ideas lapping at the shores of the Gulf - populist Islam, the spirit of the Intifada and the spread of democracy from Europe - it has to be asked whether political change in the Gulf countries is inevitable? Will the undertow of political tides become so strong in the decade ahead that the traditional political relationships will undergo profound change and that governments will find themselves unable to avoid becoming more accountable to the people for their actions?

Consider populist Islam. The expression 'populist' has been used in preference to the more usual 'fundamentalist', because many Gulf citizens, Wahhabis in Saudi Arabia and *Ibadis* in Oman for example, have considered themselves fundamentalist for centuries, long before the Western press picked up the expression. Populist (of the people) is considered a better description of a process whereby the masses, increasingly insecure in a fast-changing world, seek to hold on to formal and unchanging social rules. For example, eighteenth and nineteenth century England and France saw similar movements of popular reaction to drastic economic and social change.

Present-day populist Islam is to a great extent a rejection by the masses of the materialism of the West, a materialism seen as corrupting and destructive of family life, one of main the pillars of Islam. This mass feeling of insecurity may open the door to ambitious, self-seeking and unscrupulous individuals, enabling them to appeal to the masses through Islam and thus create coherent political movements.

Although Moslems argue that Islam is a religion of moderation, its history has many martial episodes. The world is witnessing the emergence in Islam of charismatic leaders, some of them schooled in the thesis of Frantz Fanon that violence is a catharsis for subject peoples seeking to throw off real or imagined alien yokes. Khomeini, whose proclaimed constituency was the down-trodden and oppressed of Islam, used this implicit appeal to violence with great effectiveness.

The down-trodden and oppressed of Islam are perhaps too quickly identified with the Shiᶜa. Observers looking at potential political opposition groupings in the Gulf tend to point at once to the Shiᶜa communities. Apart from Bahrain, the Shiᶜa population in the conservative Arab states of the Gulf is a small percentage of the total population. Shiᶜa groups are frequently in opposition to the establishment but could never hope to form an alternative government. They are a political irritant and a potential source of terrorist attacks on property and individuals, but do not represent a substantive political threat to the established order.

The Saudi Arabian leadership, and indeed, leaders throughout the Gulf, were shocked by the attack on the Grand Mosque in Mecca in November 1979. This was an attack emanating from a direction never hitherto envisaged. The internal security institutions of the Gulf states were directed towards Arab Baᶜth Socialism and towards Palestinian organisations. An attack on the defenders of Islam from within did not come within the compass of political risk assessment by governments at that time.

Governments in the Gulf are not likely to be taken by surprise by such an attack from within again. Yet the fact remains that each one of the six is ideologically on the defensive. King Fahd's assumption of the title of Defender of the Two Holy Mosques can be seen as a form of ideological counter-attack. But throughout the recorded history of mankind, any political group which has been unable to meet the threat of new and evolving ideologies has found itself under increasing pressure.

For a number of years, Western analysts have regarded a hypothetical political challenge to any one of the six conservative Arab states of the Gulf, emanating from and built around a charismatic individual with impeccable Islamic credentials, as being one which would be most difficult to counter effectively. Such an individual would most probably - but by no means certainly - be a member of a ruling family and an officer in the armed forces. He would be able to carry a large section of the armed forces with him and his political attack on the established government would be built around the Islamic credentials of those in power as well as around their perceived lack of competence in managing the nation's resources.

The spirit of the Intifada is to be taken into account, not because of its more obvious manifestation of young and unarmed Palestinians mounting a moral threat to an insensitive and brutal occupation, but because this 'shaking off' is the ultimate despair of a people which has lost contact with its leaders. The reaction to the Intifada in some Gulf capitals has been at least ambiguous: the last thing that conservative Gulf governments wish to see is large numbers of angry young people demonstrating in the streets for political change. This has already happened in neighbouring Jordan and, to a very limited extent, in Kuwait.

Finally, the overthrow of the authoritarian regimes of central and eastern Europe in generally peaceful popular movements has underlined the fact that governments which are not representative, which have lost their contact with the people, and which have to rely on coercion, are putting their political survival at risk. Perhaps the Soviet Union forms the most telling example. In spite of a formidable and ruthless internal security apparatus, a government which became ideologically bankrupt and which at the same time demonstrated extraordinary incompetence in managing the nation's resources has lost the confidence of the people and is extremely unlikely to survive in its present form.

If there is political change in the Gulf, it will not result in Western-style democracy. Political systems evolved by a nation to meet its own needs can rarely, if ever, be successfully translated into a system to meet the needs of another nation. Western-style democracy is in any case not homogeneous. The understanding of democracy in the United States, for example, can hardly be compared directly to that of other federations, for example, Switzerland. This is equally true of Britain, France, or Germany. But what all democratic forms do offer is a substantial degree of accountability by governments to the people.

As Abraham Lincoln said: 'you can fool all the people some of the time, and some of the people all the time, but you cannot fool all the people all of the time.'

Lincoln also said: 'What is conservatism? Is it not adherence to the old and tried, against the new and untried?' The problem with conservatism, however, is that it becomes increasingly difficult to sustain in a fast-changing world. Within the space of one generation, the nations of the Gulf have ceased to be extremely poor rural subsistence-economies and have become rather rich urban societies.   In short, there has been a fundamental and far-reaching change in economic and social structures.   Ultimately, no matter how competent individual ruling families in the Gulf may be, they will have to evolve new political forms to ensure a political adjustment commensurate with the sweeping changes in the social and economic fabric of their nations.

This change does not have to be violent, nor does it have to be revolutionary. But if any ruling family in the Gulf is seen by the people to be putting dynastic survival ahead of overall national interests and in doing so emphasises its lack of accountability to the people, then that family will assuredly be ousted.

Notes

1   This chapter is based on and developed from material written by the author which has already been published in Business International's 'Saudi Arabia Monitor' and in the Saudi Arabian volumes of the joint Business International/Economist Intelligence Unit Middle East Forecasting Services.   Specific references in the text to these and other Business International and Economist Intelligence Unit publications cover the work of colleagues.

2   Sarah Searight in Economist Intelligence Unit (EIU), Arabian Peninsula - Bahrain, Kuwait, Oman, Qatar, Saudi Arabia, United Arab Emirates, North and South Yemen: Economic Structure and Analysis, (London, Oct. 1988).

3   Quoted by Youssef Ibrahim, the reputed correspondent of the New York Times in the International Herald Tribune, 27 June 1990.

4   Ze'ev Schiff and Ehud Ya'ari, ed. and trans. Ina Friedman, Intifada: the Palestinian Uprising - Israel's Third Front (Simon and Schuster, New York, 1990).

GLOSSARY

Amir: emir, chief, prince.

bandar: a port.

bulaid: lit. a 'small town'.

fortaleza: fortress.

hajj: the 'greater' annual pilgrimage to Mecca, incumbent on all Moslems who are able to perform it.

Ibadi: the surviving branch of the early Islamic *Kharijite* movement. The Ibadis are found today in Oman, together with parts of east and north Africa.

Intifada: lit. a 'shaking': refers to the recent Palestinian uprising in the Occupied Territories.

Ka'ba: large cubic building at the centre of the Great Mosque in Mecca: Moslems face the Ka'ba when praying and it is circled during the rites of pilgrimage.

khanaqah: a Sufi convent.

laqab: an honorific or title.

madrasa: a school, Islamic college.

majlis: a meeting, social gathering or home reception; also used of the open court traditionally held by shaikhly rulers. The majlis is an important social institution in the Arab countries of the Gulf.

Malik: lit. 'king'.

Malik al-Islam: an honorific; (lit. 'King of Islam').

Masihi: Christian.

Mujahidin: lit. 'those waging *jihad*' or the so-called 'holy war'; used of the Afghan groups opposed to the regime in Kabul.

nisba: that part of the name which indicates the profession or origin of a person or their forebears.

qadi: a judge operating in the field of Islamic law.

qanat: man-made underground water-channel.

Qaulnama: agreement, treaty (here, Britain-Muscat).

Qizilbash: Turkish tribes who supported Isma^{c}il, the first Safavid Shah of Iran; the name derived from the red hat they wore.

ribat: lit. a 'fort' or 'hospice': originally military-cum-religious, with time some ribats became meeting-places for Sufis.

Shah: king.

shaikh: tribal leader; Sufi master; religious scholar; old man etc.

Shaikh al-Islam: honorific bestowed on religious leaders of high standing, first appearing in the later 4th century AH.

Shari^{c}a: Islamic law, derived in particular from the Koran and the Traditions of the Prophet. The four Sunni (q.v.) schools and others such as the Shi^{c}a (q.v.) approach the law according to different principles.

Shi^{c}a: originally referred to the Moslem faction which recognised Ali, son-in-law to the Prophet Muhammad, as his rightful successor. Thereafter it came to refer to that minority division of Islam which regards Ali and varying numbers of his descendants as *Imams*. It differs in theory and practice from Sunni (q.v.) Islam.

Shi^cite: belonging to the Shi^ca (q.v.).

Sultan: sultan, ruler.

Sunni: a follower of the *Sunna*, the customary words and actions of the Prophet, which are used as a fundamental religious guide and yardstick (beside the Koran); the majority division of Islam, as contrasted esp. with the Shi^ca (q.v.).

Suq al-Manakh: Gulf stock-exchange based in Kuwait (opened in 1977/8, collapsed in 1982).

tariqa: a Sufi order.

ulus: people, patrimony.

Wahhabi: adherent of *Wahhabism*, an Islamic sect founded in the eighteenth century, now especially prevalent in Saudi Arabia and Qatar. A steadfastly 'fundamentalist' interpretation of Islam in the tradition of Ibn Hanbal and Ibn Taimiya.

wali: a governor.

Wazir: vizier, minister.

ABBREVIATIONS

AA	anti-aircraft
ACDA	Arms Control and Disarmament Agency
ACM	airborne cruise missile
ADCO	Abu Dhabi Company for Onshore Oil Operations
ADMA	Abu Dhabi Marine Areas Operating Company
AH	Islamic calendar beginning with hegira in 622 AD
AHs	as preceding, reckoned in solar years
ALCM	air-launched cruise missile
AMCM	airborne mine-countermeasures
ARAMCO	Arabian American Oil Company
ARTEP	Asian Regional Team for Employment Promotion
ASW	anti-submarine warfare
ATBM	anti-tactical ballistic missile
AWACS	airborne warning and control system
/b	barrels
b.	bin/ibn - 'son of'
BCCI	Bank of Credit and Commerce International
BD	Bahraini Dinar
b/d	barrels per day
BM	battlefield management
BMET	Bureau of Manpower Employment and Training
BP	British Petroleum
C^3I	command, control, communications and intelligence
CBW	chemical-biological warfare
CENTO	Central Treaty Organisation
CFE	Conventional Forces in Europe
CFP	Compagnie Française des Pétroles

CIA	Central Intelligence Agency
CNA	Centre for Naval Analysis
CPE	centrally planned economy
CRAF	Civil Reserve Air Fleet
CSBM	Confidence- and Security-Building Measures
CSCE	Conference on Security and Co-operation in Europe
CW	chemical warfare
d.	died
DCS	defence communication system
DoD	Department of Defence
EC	European Community
EEC	European Economic Community
EIU	The Economist Intelligence Unit
ENI	Ente Nazionale Idrocarburi
EPLF	Eritrean People's Liberation Front
FRG	Federal Republic of Germany
FROG	free rocket over ground
FY	fiscal year
GATT	General Agreement on Tariffs and Trade
GCSS	Gulf Centre for Strategic Studies
GDP	gross domestic product
GNP	gross national product
HARM	high-speed anti-radiation missile
HOT	high-subsonic optically-guided tube-launched Franco-German anti-tank missile
ID	Iraqi Dinar
IISS	International Institute for Strategic Studies
ILO	International Labour Office
IMF	International Monetary Fund
INOC	Iraq National Oil Company
IPC	Iraq Petroleum Company
IR	Iranian Riyal
IRBM	intermediate-range ballistic missile
Kcal	kilocalorie
KD	Kuwaiti Dinar
Kl	kilolitre
km	kilometre
kt	kiloton
kwh	kilowatt-hour
LANTIRN	low-altitude navigation, targeting infra-red navigation system

LCC	amphibious command ship
LHA	amphibious assault ship (general purpose)
LKA	amphibious cargo ship
LNG	liquefied natural gas
LPD	amphibious transport dock
LPG	liquefied petroleum gas
LPH	amphibious assault ship
LSD	dock landing ship
MAP	Military Aid Programme
MEED	Middle East Economic Digest
MHC	coastal minehunter
MIT	Massachusetts Institute of Technology
MITI	Ministry for International Trade and Industry (Japan)
MLRS	multiple-launch rocket system
MPS	Maritime Prepositioning Force
MRBM	medium-range ballistic missile
mw(e)	megawatt of electricity
NADGE	NATO air-defence ground environment organisation
NASA	National Aeronautics and Space Administration
NATO	North Atlantic Treaty Organisation
NIC	newly industrialising country
NIOC	National Iranian Oil Company
NPR	New Persian Rupees
OAPEC	Organisation of Arab Petroleum-Exporting Countries
ODA	Official Development Assistance
OECD	Organisation for Economic Co-operation and Development
OPEC	Organisation of the Petroleum-Exporting Countries
OTRAG	Orbital Transport and Rocket AG
PAVETACK	radar
PDRY	People's Democratic Republic of Yemen
PLO	Palestine Liberation Organisation
PRC	People's Republic of China
QR	Qatari Riyal
R&D	research and development
RIIA	Royal Institute of International Affairs
rps	rupees

RPV	remotely piloted vehicle
SAM	surface-to-air missile
SIPRI	Stockholm International Peace Research Institute
SLCM	sea-launched cruise missile
SLV	single-launch vehicle
SOF	special operations forces
SR	Saudi Riyal
SSM	surface-to-surface missile
TOW	tube-launched optically-tracked wire-guided anti-tank missile
UNCTAD	United Nations Conference on Trade and Development
USAF	US Air Force
USCENTCOM	US Central Command
USGPO	US Government Printing Office
VSTOL	vertical and/or short take-off and landing
VTOL	vertical take-off and landing
WEV	The Western European Union
Y	Yen
YAR	Yemen Arab Republic

CONTRIBUTORS

Drs. J. Stace Birks and *Clive A. Sinclair* are Directors of Birks and Sinclair Ltd., a strategic planning and manpower development consultancy, with particular expertise in the Middle East and Arabian Gulf.

Professor Anthony H. Cordesman is currently Adjunct Professor of National Security Studies at Georgetown University, and United States Senate Adviser. He has held a number of senior positions in US government departments and has also served overseas in association with NATO. He has written extensively on the Middle East and the Gulf, the US and Soviet military balance, and the lessons of war.

Peter A. Davies is Chief Economist at British Petroleum.

Anoushiravan Ehteshami is a Research Fellow in Political Science and International Relations at the Centre for Arab Gulf Studies, as well as Lecturer in Middle East Politics in the Department of Politics, both at Exeter University. He is the author of works on political and strategic issues in the Gulf and the Middle East, and is currently Administrative Editor of the *BRISMES Newsletter*.

Dr Susumu Ishida is Professor at the Graduate School of International Relations, and Senior Research Fellow at the Institute of Middle Eastern Studies, both at the International University of Japan. He is the author of books on the economy of the Middle East.

Dr Rolf Müller-Syring is Research Fellow at the African and Middle East Studies Centre, Leipzig University. He has written a number of works on socio-economic, political and strategic issues in the Middle East, and has an especial interest in the question of militarisation in the Third World.

The Hon. Richard W. Murphy is Senior Fellow for the Middle East at the US Council on Foreign Relations. He was earlier Assistant Secretary of State for Middle East Affairs in the State Department during the Reagan Administration.

Professor Vitaly Naumkin, a renowned specialist and writer on the Middle East and south Arabia, is Deputy Director of the Institute of Oriental Studies, Moscow.

Professor Valeria Fiorani Piacentini holds the chair in the History and Institutions of Moslem Countries, and is Director of the Department of Political Sciences, both at the Università Cattolica del Sacro Cuore, Milan. She is a Middle East adviser to CeMISS and SIOI (Rome), as well as to the Italian Ministry of Foreign Affairs. She has conducted field-work in southern Iran and elsewhere, and has published extensively on historical subjects.

Clive A. Sinclair - vide Birks.

Dr Paul J. Stevens is Senior Lecturer in Economics at the University of Surrey, and in 1990 he was on sabbatical with the Economics Unit of British Petroleum.

Professor K. Subrahmanyam is Nehru Fellow at the Institute for Defence Studies and Analyses, New Delhi. He is well known for his writings on strategic issues in Asia.

John Townsend, who now works for *Business International*, was formerly economic adviser to the Sultan of Oman, and is the author of a standard work on the modern history of Oman.

HE Dr. Willem van Eekelen, formerly Netherlands Defence Minister and State Secretary for Foreign Affairs, is at present Secretary-General of the Western European Union.

Professor Alexei Vassiliev, a well-known expert and writer on the Middle East, and on African affairs, is Deputy Director of the Institute for African Studies in Moscow.

INDEX